International Conflicts and Collective Security, 1946-77

International Conflicts and Collective Security, 1946-77

The United Nations, Organization of American States, Organization of African Unity, and Arab League

Mark W. Zacher

PRAEGER PUBLISHERS
Praeger Special Studies

New York • London • Sydney • Toronto

Library of Congress Cataloging in Publication Data

Zacher, Marc W
   International conflicts and collective security,
1946-77.

   Includes bibliographical references and index.
   1. Security, International. 2. Regionalism
(International organization) I. Title.
JX1952.Z24   327'.116   78-19775
ISBN 0-03-044261-3

PRAEGER PUBLISHERS
PRAEGER SPECIAL STUDIES
383 Madison Avenue, New York, N.Y. 10017, U.S.A.

Published in the United States of America in 1979
by Praeger Publishers,
A Division of Holt, Rinehart and Winston, CBS, Inc.

9   038   987654321

Printed in the United States of America

TO

Jock, Mary, Rich, Ron,
Pam, and Jim

Acknowledgments

Many individuals have assisted me in the course of writing this study. I would, first of all, like to express my deepest gratitude to a number of former students who helped me with the research and suffered with me in analyzing the character of international alignment patterns and their relevance to collective security. Jock Finlayson and Mary Newbury made major contributions and to them I am most indebted. I also would like to express my deepest thanks to Rich Balfour, Ron Ewing, Pam Kirkpatrick, and Jim McConnell, who helped me with various aspects of the study. It is to these friends that I dedicate this study.

With respect to the general structure of the analysis I especially benefited from comments by, and discussions with, Lou Beres, Stan Michalak, and John Ruggie. Information and critiques—especially on the international politics of particular regions—were provided by Harriet Critchley, Eddie Dawisha, David Dewitt, Yale Ferguson, David Haglund, Robert Henderson, Roff Johannson, Malcolm Kerr, Frank Langdon, David Meyers, Tim Shaw, and Sheldon Simon. For the generosity of all these individuals I am most grateful.

To Maureen Gitta and Betty Greig I would like to express my thanks not only for their excellent secretarial assistance but also for their friendship during the trials of authorship. Bruce Warshavsky of Praeger Publishers was most helpful in suggesting revisions and facilitating the publication of the study. The Canada Council generously supported my research, and additional assistance also was provided by a grant for international security and strategic studies from Canada's Department of National Defence to the Institute of International Relations at the University of British Columbia.

Finally, to Carol, Nicole, and Glenn, who have tolerated my physical and mental absences from our local "collective" and have provided me with much more than "security," I would like to express my appreciation.

Contents

LIST OF TABLES AND FIGURE

International Conflicts and Collective Security, 1946-77

1

Collective Security: Background, Theory, and Research Design

The idea of collective security has excited the minds of both statesmen and scholars for most of this century. And the development of international organization has been preoccupied with the achievement of collective security to such an extent that one scholar was moved to describe the relationship between them in these words: "The twentieth century hope that international organizations might serve to prevent war, or, failing that, to defend states subjected to armed attack in defiance of organized efforts to maintain the peace, has been epitomized in the concept of collective security."[1] This antiwar orientation"[2] underlying the efforts to construct international organizations was especially apparent at the end of World War I, by which time most governments were appalled by the destructiveness of modern warfare and disillusioned with the apparent inability of military alliances and the entire "balance of power system" to protect their security and prevent war. Thus, the League of Nations was created in 1919 to institutionalize the ideals of peace and stability and to replace the discredited anarchic system that had hitherto existed.

Many proponents of the League clearly viewed it as the international community's salvation, as nothing less than the solution to the interminable problem of international violence. However, as Ernst B. Haas has noted, inherent in this conception was a fatal flaw: "Ever since its inception in 1919, international organization somehow has been expected to operate above and beyond politics."[3] It was assumed that the new system would automatically operate to prevent or terminate conflicts. By bringing the resources of all members of the international system to bear against an aggressor, it would assure that no aggression succeeded. In short, the belief was widely shared that the establishment of the League of Nations would "go down in history as the date of the birth of the new world."[4]

1

The exuberant expectations that accompanied the creation of the League were soon belied by its failure to terminate a number of aggressions and its complete emasculation in the face of the events leading to World War II. The League's failures did not, however, dampen the enthusiasm of many publicists and statesmen for a collective security system. A belief in the intrinsic value and necessity of collective security was a firmly held conviction among higher circles, in the American and British governments in particular. Prior to the end of World War II most of the world's states, excluding the Axis powers and their allies, entered into negotiations to create a new collective security body, and in June 1945 they met in San Francisco and formed the United Nations. Statesmen now recognized that without the inclusion of the Great Powers—whose partial exclusion had, of course, contributed to the League's demise—the new organization would likely share the fate of its predecessor. As Roland Stromberg has put it:

> Rising on the ashes of the League, the United Nations accepted more frankly the apparent truth that collective security is no good against the Great Powers. It strengthened the powers of the organization to intervene anywhere against a "breach of the peace" but at the same time it necessarily strengthened the veto power of the Great Powers. It relied on Great Power unanimity. [5]

While the greatest interest of most states at this time was in promoting security collaboration at the global level, there were also some movements in the direction of establishing regional collective security systems. Many states that belonged to particular regional groupings believed that a regional approach to interstate conflicts held more promise of eliciting collaboration. There was also concern among many states that global rivalries and divisions might inhibit the United Nations from dealing with some types of conflicts. Others were anxious to exclude some or all of the Great Powers from intervening in their regions; thus, they wanted to utilize regional organizations, rather than the Great Power-dominated United Nations, to manage conflicts. In March 1945 the Arab states formed the Arab League and bestowed upon it, inter alia, the function of resolving and terminating conflicts between them. In the previous month the Western Hemisphere states (20 Latin American countries and the United States) had met in Chapultepec, Mexico, and indicated their intention of forming a collective security organization. They also urged all states that were to participate in the upcoming San Francisco conference to include in the UN Charter provisions allowing regional bodies to manage conflicts among their own members. Their urgings were successful to the extent that Articles 51-54 were included in the Charter. In 1948 these Western Hemisphere states finally created their own regional organization, the Organization of American States (OAS). A third regional collective security body was created in 1963, when most of the independent African states agreed to form the Organization of African Unity (OAU).

The United Nations and the three regional organizations have witnessed a large number of crises and military encounters among their members, but in many cases the organizations have not acted to curtail the threats to, or breaches of, the peace. Moreover, there have been numerous occasions where they have, in fact, called for a termination of a threat or act of aggression, only to have these injunctions ignored by one or more of the conflicting parties. Thus, while these organizations may be, in the words of Arnold Wolfers, "the chief symbol of hope that someday international relations will be brought under the rule of law and that a community of nations will develop in which there will be no more war,"[6] it is obvious to all students of international politics that there has been a vast gulf between the ideals and goals that these bodies symbolize and their performances in interstate crises and wars.

Once it became apparent that the new United Nations could not institutionalize the ideal of collective security (namely, concerted diplomatic, economic, and military action to deter and terminate all armed attacks), many scholars and statesmen began to search for alternative ways of utilizing the United Nation's potential in conflict situations. Since collective security as it had hitherto been defined was no longer possible, "the political raison d'être of the United Nations changed." With collective security "having been proved Utopian, preventive diplomacy became the organization's approach to peace in our contemporary era."[7] The term collective security continued to be invoked by many commentators to describe a whole host of different measures and ideas such as pacific settlement, preventive diplomacy, and the general promotion of world peace. The term even came to be used in connection with the creation of such military alliances as NATO, despite the fact that, in its original definition, collective security connoted a new system designed to replace the world of alliances and balances of power. As Inis L. Claude has remarked: "In the half century that has elapsed since the concept of collective security gained prominence as the central feature of the Wilsonian scheme for reforming the international system, it has largely lost its clarity and specificity."[8]

Although neither the ideal of collective security nor the international organizations through which this ideal was to be implemented has borne out the expectations of the many commentators and statesmen who promoted both of them as the world's salvation, it is true

that the four postwar collective security bodies examined in this study
have sought to intervene in a significant number of international conflicts. Moreover, in a number of instances they have succeeded in
terminating conflicts and aggressions involving their members. Many
scholars have endeavored to explain both the failures and successes
of these organizations, not by studying their legal charters or principles but, rather, by analyzing the interests, policies, and resources
of their memberships and the nature of the overall global or regional
security systems. Relevant to these comments is one author's observation that "it has become banal to assert that the successes or failures of international organizations stem not so much from their for-
mal-legal covenant as from the changing configurations and distribu-
tions of power, systemic issues and forces, and the attitudes and resources of member states."[9] Kissinger has made a comparable point
specifically about the United Nations:

> The United Nations is not a world government; it is an
> organization of sovereign states. It is not an entity
> apart from its membership. It reflects the world con-
> text in which it operates: its diversity, its imper-
> fections, its many centers of power and initiative, its
> competing values, its worldly compound of nobility
> and tragedy. [10]

During the past two decades international relations scholars
have written many insightful studies about the influence of international
security relations on the conflict-management activities of these collective security organizations. Most of these studies, however, are
confined to particular historical eras, examine limited populations of
conflicts, or analyze particular patterns of organizational involvement
and success without integrating the findings into a general theoretical
explanation. [11] The lack of a general theory that relates the likelihood
of organizational intervention and success in conflicts to the character
of the international system, and thus permits both the explanation of
past behavior and the prediction of future behavior, has been noted by
several students of the subject. [12] But, to date, there have not been
any successful attempts to establish these linkages. A number of the
authors who have recognized these deficiencies have provided valuable
insights into the way in which the character of the international environment affects the behavior and success of collective security organizations, but they have been unable to trace satisfactorily how and
why particular environmental factors do or do not influence organizational intervention and success in conflicts. [13]

The central purposes of this study are: (1) to present a theory
of collective security that isolates some of the key factors that affect

the ability of collective security organizations to halt threats to, or breaches of, the peace involving their members and (2) to test this theory by examining the patterns of involvement and success of the United Nations, OAS, OAU, and Arab League in international conflicts during the period 1946-77. Subsequent sections of this chapter will present the theory of collective security and outline the research design employed in the study. Later chapters will analyze the patterns of action and success of the four organizations in light of this theory.

While this study hopefully will increase readers' understanding of the character of international conflicts in the postwar era, their international political milieus, the nature of collective security organizations' involvement in the conflicts, and the reasons for particular organizational interventions and their outcomes, it is hoped that it also will serve other purposes. The findings presented here should enhance the ability of students of international politics to predict which types of conflicts can be managed effectively by these organizations and which ones must be dealt with by other diplomatic means. It is not particularly fruitful to urge certain courses of action on an international organization or to condemn such a body for inaction or ineffectiveness if the bases of support necessary for its involvement and success do not exist. An intelligent approach to international conflict management must be predicated on an understanding of the constraints that are imposed on international organizations by the interests and policies of those groupings of states in whose hands the destinies of these bodies rest. To anthropomorphize the United Nations or any other collective security agency and to fail to realize that it is ultimately the creature of its member states will only blind individuals interested in eliminating international violence to the realities of international politics. And, in addition, it will likely lead to the enunciation of prescriptions for conflicts that are bereft of any chance of success. Collective security organizations are only one of a number of diplomatic instrumentalities that can be utilized to prevent and control international violence, and it is advisable to employ them only in circumstances in which they can perform effectively.

Another goal of this study is to offer insights into the particular conditions that must be met if collective security organizations are to assume a more prominent role in international conflict management. Although the analysis here does not focus on why the conditions supportive of these organizations' effectiveness develop, it does seek to identify what those conditions are. Any long-range strategy for institutionalizing conflict management within community organizations must ultimately come to grips with the promotion of certain underlying attitudes and policies among members of the international system. To improve our understanding of these conditions perceptibly assists the promotion of a more peaceful world order.

In linking the nature of international security politics to the activities and successes of collective security organizations, the following theory posits that it is the character of the security coalitions among their memberships and the allegiance of conflicting parties to these coalitions that largely govern not only an organization's response to a conflict but also the conflict outcome. Other factors such as the magnitude of a military encounter, the type of issue involved, and the use of particular diplomatic strategies in managing the conflict also, of course, have an impact. However, since the relationship between conflicts and international security politics is judged to be so central, our focus on this relationship seems justifiable. The application of the theory to the history of modern collective security systems can yield valuable insights but cannot, of course, account for the entire and very complex reality of international security politics.

The theory is presented in a detailed and logical fashion below. The hypotheses concerning organizational action and success are derived from a series of principles regarding the character of modern collective security bodies and the nature of state behavior. An understanding of these linkages and of the particular definitions of terms is important not only to evaluating the theory as a whole but also to following the discussions of the diplomacy surrounding various types of conflicts in later chapters. If the theory appears quite complex, this is because organizational intervention and success are affected by a host of different policies and goals on the part of states in the international system.

A THEORY OF COLLECTIVE SECURITY

Essentially two questions are involved: (1) why do collective security organizations intervene or fail to intervene in conflicts among their members to terminate a threat or act of aggression and (2) what accounts for the success or failure of such interventions? Organizational intervention is defined as the passage of a resolution calling on an aggressor to terminate its action and/or condemning its behavior. Such a directive may, but need not, be accompanied by the creation of mediatory, fact-finding, or peacekeeping missions that operate under organizational auspices. Organizational success is defined as the compliance of an aggressor with the directive soon after its passage. If a crisis or war continues for a considerable period of time after the passage of a resolution seeking to end it, or ends as a result of developments on the battlefield, then organizational success has not taken place. An aggressor is a state that threatens to employ or does employ military personnel against the citizens of another country. While an aggressing state will generally use its forces against the official military forces of another country, it may alternatively use its forces to fight on behalf of another official government against a rebel group seeking to overthrow or secede from it. Such participation in a civil war is often not viewed as aggression, but it is being included in this study's definition of the term.

The theory is structured along the following lines. Two initial sections outline (1) the prerequisites for organizational intervention and success and (2) some important features of the security policies of states. An understanding of the latter is crucial for determining whether members of collective security bodies will oppose particular aggressions and lend support to organizational action to terminate them. Some of the propositions put forward in these first two sections are quite uncontroversial, but are included in order to provide logical linkages within the theory. Others may be challenged by some students of international relations. The third and last section sets forth the various hypotheses regarding organizational intervention and success in particular types of international conflicts and indicates how these hypotheses are derived from the propositions presented in the first two sections.

The theory and the study that flows from it adopt a "rational actor approach" to the analysis of state behavior. They assume that states are centralized organizations that have certain policy goals and act to implement them in response to particular external conditions or events. [14] No attempt is made to investigate the bureaucratic or interest-group sources of policy. While the value of the approach taken here can be judged by the subsequent testing of the theory, it should be noted that it is extremely difficult to deviate from the rational actor paradigm when analyzing international security politics over a long period of time.

Principles Concerning Organizational
Intervention and Success

The prerequisite for organizational intervention is simply the support of that number or particular group of states that the charter of an organization requires for the passage of a resolution. * In most of the organizations studied here, two-thirds of the member states

---

*In writing about the United Nations, Inis L. Claude, Jr. has noted:

I offer the blunt assertion that the United Nations has no purposes—and can have none—of its own. It is, above all,

constitute the required number.* The prerequisites for organizational success are (1) that an aggression must be opposed by at least one of the major security groupings in the organization and (2) that it must not be supported by any major security grouping within the same organization. The likelihood of success is enhanced, of course, if all of the major military actors oppose an aggression. As long as states with significant military resources back an aggressor, there is little likelihood that quick compliance with a resolution will result. This assertion assumes that the resolutions of modern collective security organizations have little weight, in and of themselves, and that states' willingness to conform with organizational resolutions is dependent on the extent to which powerful groupings of member states are prepared to support and/or oppose directives passed by these international bodies. Relevant to this point, Ernst B. Haas, Robert L. Butterworth, and Joseph S. Nye have written: "These organizations are little more than governments linked in permanent conclave. They have no power and personality beyond the collective will of governments and no capacity to grow apart from the ability of governments to learn."[15] They have also commented, particularly with respect to the United Nations, that "success is assured only if the measures ordered by the UN happen to converge with what the governments in question already seem prepared to do."† It is contended here that

---

a tool, and, like other tools, it has possibilities and limitations, but not purposes. . . . The essential questions are: who has the handle in his grasp, and what are the purposes in his mind or will? . . . In large part the changingness of the United Nations is a reflection of the changes of purpose of states dominating the organization and of the changing fortunes of states and groups of states in the battle for control over it—that is, for the right to determine the uses to which it will be put. (Inis L. Claude, Jr., The Changing United Nations, [New York: Random House, 1967] pp. xvii–xviii)

*In all of the organizations under consideration in this study (except for the Arab League) it is two-thirds, although, in the case of the United Nations, conflicts are considered initially in the Security Council, where the five permanent members have a veto. In the Arab League all members except the aggressor have a veto.

†Ernst B. Haas, Robert L. Butterworth, and Joseph S. Nye, Conflict Management by International Organizations (Morristown, N.J.: General Learning Corp., 1972), p. 39. A comparable point has been

what aggressors are "prepared to do" is dependent on the patterns of support and opposition to their action exhibited by major security groupings.

Principles of State Behavior

There are two basic types of international security systems, consensual and competitive.* Both the general policies of states and their attitudes toward particular types of interstate conflicts differ in these two types of systems or coalition configurations. [16] In a consensual system, all or almost all members oppose the use of force for settling international differences. [17] In a competitive system or

---

made by Coral Bell except that she stresses the centrality of the Great Powers in the crisis-management activities of international organizations.

> The ability of the UN to provide inspection teams, peace-keeping forces, truce commissions, and the like has been an essential element in the success of what may be called the "tidying-up" phase of many a crisis. Yet when the UN role is examined more closely in particular crisis situations, it will be seen very often to consist of conferring legitimacy on crisis management by the Great Powers, and the same is true of the roles of other organizations such as NATO, or the OAS. (Coral Bell, The Conventions of Crisis: A Study in Diplomatic Management [London: Oxford University Press, 1971], p. 77)

*International security systems do not mirror those in other international-issue areas, and the system properties that determine their nature are generally quite different. (John C. Ruggie, "Contingencies, Constraints and Collective Security: Perspectives on UN Involvement in International Disputes," International Organization 28 [Summer 1974]: 506-7; J. David Singer, "The Global System and Its Sub-Systems: A Developmental View," in Linkage Politics, ed. James Rosenau [New York: Free Press, 1969], p. 31.)

International security systems at the global and different regional levels may be, but usually are not, structured along the same lines. (Michael Brecher, "International Relations and Asian Studies: The Subordinate System of Asia," World Politics 15 [January 1963]: 213-35; Oran Young, "Political Discontinuities in the International System," World Politics 20 [April 1968]: 369-92.)

configuration, on the other hand, all or at least some important members regard the use of force as legitimate or desirable under certain conditions. International security systems can, in fact, include both consensual and competitive elements simultaneously. On certain issues (for example, territorial revision) members may agree that the use of force is illegitimate; but with respect to other issues (for example, "national liberation"), they may accept the use of violence. While modern international security systems have been generally competitive, it is possible to identify certain regional political systems that have had strong consensual components.

In a consensual security system, each member will judge that a failure to oppose an aggression will increase the chances of repeated military transgressions. Also, each will fear that a failure to protect another state may lead that state and others to form limited-membership military defense groupings—thus undermining the foundations of the consensual system. Because of their general commitment to protect the security of all members, it is the mere threat or act of aggression, and not the particular policies of the states involved, that "triggers" their opposition to the aggressing state. As will be explained below, the situation is different in a competitive system, where certain characteristics of the aggressing and victim parties determine the policy responses of other member states.

In a competitive security system, at least some important members accept the legitimacy or desirability of using armed force against other states for certain purposes, and therefore many of them will tend to form security groupings or coalitions. The purposes of the groupings are to use force against other states that control values they covet and/or to protect themselves against attacks by certain other countries. In this study, these groupings are often called major groupings or coalitions in order to distinguish them from a nonaligned grouping. Very important, members of these competitive coalitions perceive that their success in realizing goals is dependent on their relative strength vis-à-vis each other,* and therefore they

---

*This is no more than a statement that states seek to increase the probability that they will be able to realize their policy goals as the result of a favorable (or at least not an unfavorable) ratio of resources between themselves and their supporters, on the one hand, and members of different groupings, on the other. Hans J. Morgenthau's proposition that states always seek to maintain or increase their power is basically addressed to this point. (See, in particular, Hans J. Morgenthau, Politics among Nations: The Struggle for Power and Peace, 4th ed. [New York: Alfred A. Knopf, 1967], pts I and II.)

will seek to (1) prevent their own members from leaving the coalition, (2) encourage members of rival coalitions to leave theirs, (3) prevent nonaligned states from joining a rival coalition, and (4) encourage nonaligned states to join theirs. While nonaligned states in a competitive system do not engage in formal military collaboration with each other, they are interested in preventing the major groupings from coercing other nonaligned countries into joining their coalitions, since the success of such endeavors could encourage comparable actions against other nonaligned states. Also, they oppose attempts by the major coalitions to prevent their members from adopting a policy of nonalignment.

What characteristic of a conflict determines the coalitions' responses to particular threats or acts of aggression—and, in particular, their opposition to an aggressing state? It is argued here that it is the alignments or affiliations of the aggressing and victim states with certain groupings, since these affiliations logically indicate how the success or failure of the use of force will influence the relative strength or distribution of resources among the groupings.* These alignment patterns can be classified as: (1) intercoalition, (2) intracoalition, (3) nonaligned-nonaligned, (4) aligned-nonaligned (where the aligned is the victim), and (5) aligned-nonaligned (where the nonaligned is the victim). †

----

*Pertinent to this point Richard Falk has noted, regarding the policies of states toward conflicts in the United Nations, "The nature of decisions and voting behavior is largely shaped by patterns of political affiliation that persist outside the halls of the United Nations; by hearing which state is making what sort of claim it is possible to predict who will vote how." (Robert Falk, "The United Nations: Various Systems of Operation," in The United Nations in International Politics, ed. Leon Gordenker [Princeton, N.J.: Princeton University Press, 1971], p. 222.)

†Other writers have commented on the salience of the alignments of conflicting parties, but they have not made the distinction between aligned-nonaligned conflicts according to which one was the aggressor. They have also not created subcategories of these categories according to the distribution of states in various groupings as is done later in this theory. (See, in particular, Ernst B. Haas, Robert L. Butterworth, and Joseph S. Nye, Conflict Management by International Organizations [Morristown, N.J.: General Learning Corp., 1972], pp. 25-26; and John C. Ruggie, "Contingencies, Constraints, and Collective Security: Perspectives on UN Involvement in International Disputes," International Organization 28 [Summer 1974]: 502-5.)

The policies of different groupings toward each type of conflict (that is, their support for, opposition to, or indifference toward, the aggression) will be presented in the following section. However, before these policies and their effects on patterns of organizational intervention and success can be analyzed, certain other general policies of security groupings that are relevant to these matters must be presented. Members of major security groupings will try to avoid wars with members of other major coalitions (especially their leaders) unless one or more of their own members is threatened or attacked. This proposition can certainly be challenged, since obviously the major wars (especially "world wars") of the past would not have taken place if this had always been the case. At the same time it is posited as generally valid, particularly at the global level, in the modern era of nuclear weaponry. [18]

Another policy of the members of major coalitions is to provide support and assistance to any member of their own coalition that is threatened or attacked. (One exception to this principle is mentioned below.) In cases of threats or attacks by members of other groupings, they will, of course, be concerned with protecting the relative strength of their grouping, but they also will defend an ally if it is attacked by another member of their own coalition. Since states join security groupings in order to obtain protection from armed aggressions, they will be predisposed to leave the grouping if their allies do not defend them. The one exception regarding the willingness of coalition members to defend an ally who is attacked by another coalition member is seen when the aggressor seeks to prevent the victim state from terminating its existing alignment with the coalition itself. *

In general, nonaligned states in a global or regional system will be reluctant to antagonize the members of major security groupings, since some cooperation with these coalitions and the latter's toleration of their own independent positions are necessary (or at least very important) for the maintenance of nonaligned positions. Hence, nonaligned states will be reluctant to take sides in security conflicts between members of rival major coalitions, and will not adopt partisan positions with respect to differences among members of a single major coalition. [19] At the same time they will seek assistance from, and cooperation with, the members of major coalitions when threatened or attacked by a member of another one.

There are also a number of general state policies concerning conflict management that are relevant to the politics of collective security organizations. First, states will not support the intervention

---

*An example of this type of conflict is the Soviet invasion of Hungary in 1956.

of any collective security organization in a conflict if they support the aggression or are indifferent regarding it, since obviously the purpose of such bodies is the curtailment of such aggressions. Second, states will tend not to back organizational involvement in those cases where they oppose an aggressor but are also concerned that public condemnation of its action might encourage its collaboration with a rival coalition. Third, when wars and crises occur between members of a single grouping (regardless of whether it is a major security coalition or a nonaligned grouping), other members of that grouping will want to exclude the participation of members of other coalitions from the conflict's management, since this would provide the latter with opportunities for encouraging one of the conflicting parties to reduce or terminate its alliance ties by offering it diplomatic support. Their preference will be to manage such conflicts within the framework of the coalition itself or in an organization in which their members predominate.

Hypotheses concerning Organizational
Intervention and Success

Before setting forth the hypotheses for both consensual and competitive systems and indicating how they are derived from the previous principles, certain additional characteristics of a competitive system must be described. Competitive systems or coalition configurations can be differentiated according to a variety of criteria, but for the purposes of this study the most important are two, namely, the number of coalitions in the system (its polarity) and the percentage of states in each coalition (its symmetry).* There is a marked

----

*In defining the international structure or the coalition configuration that influences the behavior and success of collective security organizations, Haas, Michalak, and Ruggie all include the polarity and distribution of resources within an international system, but Michalak and Haas also include several "policy variables." Ruggie implies that it is possible to deduce policies as a result of a knowledge of polarity and distribution of resources. This study basically adopts the same approach as Ruggie except that it explicitly sets forth a series of assumptions regarding state behavior, which are required for deducing states' policies from a knowledge of the polarity and distribution of resources in the system. (Ernst B. Haas, "Collective Security and the Future International System," in International Law and Organization, ed. Richard A. Falk and Wolfram Hanrieder [Philadelphia: J. B. Lippincott, 1968], pp. 299-355; Stanley J. Michalak, "The

tendency in competitive systems toward bipolarity, although there exist many historical cases of three or more major security actors or groupings (multipolarity). At the same time, it is usually possible in a multipolar system to identify a series of bipolar cleavages. Thus, if a significant conflict between two major coalitions occurs, the other major actors either side with one of the involved coalitions or assume a position of impartiality or nonalignment. This means that for any particular "intercoalition" security conflict it may well be possible to classify the states in the system into two antagonistic groupings and a number of nonaligned states, even if the system in question is generally multipolar. Systems that, in their structural characteristics, are clearly multipolar with respect to security politics have not been common among the global and regional systems analyzed in this study. Perhaps the best-known example of such a system has been Asia since the Sino-Soviet split in the early 1960s. However, as will be explained in the next chapter, the trend toward tripolarity in Asia was not significant enough to undermine the essentially bipolar international security system that prevailed at the global level. And since an Asian regional collective security organization has never existed, it is difficult to test the theory of collective security outlined here under conditions of multipolarity.

The percentage of states in both the major and nonaligned groupings is an important factor for analyzing competitive collective security systems because organizational intervention is dependent on support for a resolution by a large percentage of the membership, usually at least two-thirds. In the analysis of likely organizational intervention in various types of conflicts, the following terminology will be employed to describe groupings that constitute certain percentages of the membership. A dominant grouping constitutes a voting majority of at least two-thirds of the organization's membership, and a subordinate grouping consists of one-third or less. Also, a nondominant grouping constitutes less than two-thirds of the membership, and a nonsubordinate grouping more than one-third. Table 1 summarizes all of the hypotheses presented in the final section of the theory. Figure 1 portrays the entire structure of the theory.

League of Nations and the United Nations in World Politics: A Plea for Comparative Research on Universal International Organizations, International Studies Quarterly 15 [December 1971]: 387-441; John G. Ruggie, "Contingencies, Constraints, and Collective Security: Perspectives on UN Involvement in International Disputes," International Organization 28 [Summer 1974]: 493-520.)

TABLE 1

Hypotheses concerning Organizational Intervention and Success

Type of Conflict	Intervention	Success
Consensual system		
Threat or act of aggression	Yes	Yes
Competitive system		
Intercoalition conflicts		
Victim a member of dominant coalition (at least two-thirds)	Yes	No
Victim a member of nondominant coalition (less than two-thirds)	No	No
Intracoalition conflicts		
Between members of a nonsubordinate coalition (more than one-third)	No	No
Between members of a subordinate coalition (one-third or less)		
Attempt to prevent departure of victim to nonalignment grouping	Yes	No
Attempt to prevent departure of victim to nondominant rival coalition	No	No
Attempt to prevent departure of victim to dominant rival coalition	Yes	No
Victim not trying to leave coalition	No	No
Nonaligned-nonaligned	No	No
Aligned-nonaligned (victim aligned)	No	No
Aligned-nonaligned (victim nonaligned)	Yes	Yes

Threats or Acts of Aggression in a Consensual System

In the case of a conflict in a consensual system, almost all states will oppose the aggression and support organizational intervention to terminate it; and their backing of this course of action will assure compliance, that is, organizational success. They will oppose the aggressor because a failure to do so would lead the victim state and perhaps others to consider forming limited-membership alliances to protect their security, thus undermining the consensual system. In addition, a failure to oppose an aggression would increase the likelihood that all states in the system would judge that they could threaten

FIGURE 1

Model of a Theory of Collective Security

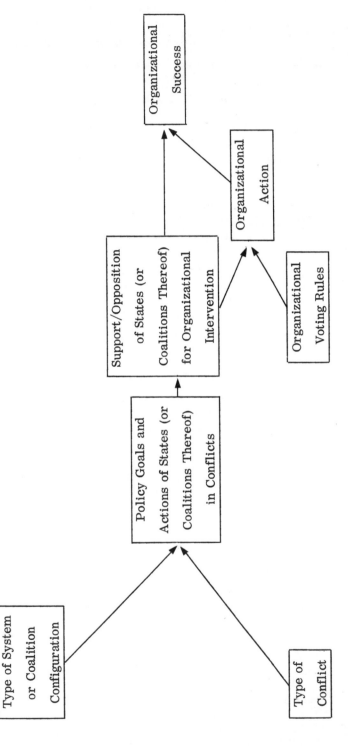

or attack other countries without evoking a collective security response
from the community.

Intercoalition Conflicts in a Competitive System

Conflicts between members of rival major coalitions will only
lead to organizational intervention if the allies of the victim state constitute a dominant grouping (at least two-thirds of the organization's
membership). Allies of the victim will, of course, oppose a threat
or act of aggression, since they will want both to prevent a decrease
in the relative strength of their own coalition and to assure each other
of their resolve to protect an ally when attacked. On the other hand,
the allies of the aggressing state will support its attempt to increase
the relative strength of their coalition and, hence, will oppose an organizational directive to halt the aggression. The nonaligned countries
will refuse to take a stand, since the outcome will redound neither to
their advantage nor to their benefit and will not affect their position
in the system. Thus, they will not support organizational intervention
in intercoalition conflicts.

Organizational success in the form of compliance with a resolution will not occur even if the organization does intervene, since the
aggressing state can count on the backing of a major security coalition.
Therefore, even if a victim of aggression belongs to a dominant grouping, attempts to implement collective security through the organization will be unsuccessful as long as the aggressing state is a member
of a major coalition and its allies continue to support it.

Intracoalition Conflicts

In all intracoalition conflicts between members of a nonsubordinate grouping (more than one-third of the organization's membership), organizational intervention will not occur. The allies of the
conflicting parties will prefer that the conflict be managed within their
own security grouping and will possess sufficient voting power to prevent the passage of an organizational resolution pertaining to the conflict.

Intracoalition conflicts between members of a subordinate grouping (one-third or less of the organization's membership) may be divided
into two subcategories, and the reader should be warned that the following discussion of such conflicts is quite complex. The first subcategory contains those conflicts that involve an attempt by a victim
state to leave its security coalition. If the victim state is seeking to
join the nonaligned grouping, organizational intervention will occur
because both the nonaligned states and those associated with the other
major coalition will favor it, the former because they can foresee an
increase in their number, and the latter because the departure of a

member of the rival coalition will have the effect of weakening its opponent group. Because the conflict involves members of a subordinate
grouping, the nonaligned states and those of the rival coalition will together constitute at least two-thirds of the organization's membership.

If the victim state is seeking to affiliate with the rival coalition,
organizational intervention will occur only if this rival grouping is
dominant (that is, constitutes at least two-thirds of the membership),
since then the rival coalition will itself possess the necessary voting
strength to secure passage of a resolution. If, however, the rival
coalition with which the victim state wishes to affiliate is nondominant,
then organizational intervention will not occur because only the members of this latter coalition, and not the nonaligned states, will support a call for a termination of the threat or act of aggression. The
nonaligned states, which have nothing to gain from the defection of a
state from one polar grouping to the other, will refuse to back organizational intervention in the conflict.

The second subcategory of intracoalition conflicts between members of a subordinate grouping are those that do not involve an attempt
by one or more coalition members to prevent the departure of another
of their number. In these conflicts, there will be no intervention by
the collective security organization because both the victim state and
the aggressor, as well as the other coalition members, will wish to
manage the conflict within the coalition rather than through the organization.

Finally, even if organizational intervention does occur in an
intracoalition conflict, compliance with a directive (that is, organizational success) will not ensue. Other coalitions will not provide
military support to the victim of an intracoalition conflict. Major
coalitions are not prepared to risk or become involved in a war with
members of the other major grouping unless one of their own allies
is threatened or attacked. While they may offer diplomatic backing
to a victim state in the other major security coalition, they will refuse to commit military resources to its defense since this would
likely precipitate an intercoalition war.

Nonaligned-Nonaligned Conflicts

Organizational intervention will not occur in conflicts between
nonaligned states because all groupings in the system will oppose it.
Other nonaligned countries will seek to discourage close diplomatic
and military collaboration between conflicting nonaligned states and
major coalitions, since they will fear that such collaboration may
lead the conflicting parties to join these coalitions. Accordingly, the
nonaligned states will support conflict management outside the organization, since the risk of major groupings supporting opposing sides

increases once it has been brought to the organization. The major coalitions themselves also will be reluctant to support either the victim or the aggressor state or, concomitantly, organizational intervention in a conflict between nonaligned states. If one of the major groupings backed one of the nonaligned parties with the hope that it would then join their coalition, this would almost inevitably lead to an alliance between the rival coalition and the other nonaligned state. Since the joining of rival major coalitions by the two nonaligned states would not improve these coalitions' positions vis-à-vis each other and would inevitably require financial assistance to the new allies, they will refrain from supporting either conflicting party and will oppose organizational involvement.

Conflicts between Aligned and Nonaligned (Where the Aligned Is the Victim)

Organizational intervention will not occur in such conflicts since the major coalition to which the victim does not belong, as well as the nonaligned group, will oppose it and the allies of the victim will be very reluctant to support it. The members of the major coalition to which the victim state does not belong will support the nonaligned aggressing state in order to encourage its collaboration with their grouping. Therefore, they will not, of course, back an organizational directive calling for a termination of its action. The nonaligned states will be cross-pressured in such a conflict because they will want to support a member of their grouping but will not want to offend the allies of the victim state. Hence, they are likely either to back the aggressor or to refrain from taking a stand. Neither of these positions would lead them to support an organizational directive calling on the aggressor to terminate its action.

The allies of the victim state will oppose the threat or act of aggression, since to do otherwise would encourage the victim and perhaps other coalition members to leave their grouping. At the same time, they will be concerned that their public condemnation of the aggressing nonaligned state could lead it to collaborate with and join the rival grouping, and, therefore, they will be reluctant to support an organizational debate where they would be pressured into such a condemnation.

Conflicts between Aligned and Nonaligned (Where the Nonaligned Is the Victim)

Both organizational intervention and success will occur in this type of conflict since all groupings will oppose the aggression. Both the nonaligned grouping and the grouping to which the aggressor does not belong will, of course, oppose the aggression and support an organizational directive calling for its termination. In the case of the nonaligned, they will perceive that the success of such an aggression would increase the likelihood of comparable actions against themselves and might reduce the membership of the nonaligned grouping. Members of the coalition to which the aggressor does not belong will oppose it, since its success would increase the relative strength of the rival coalition and since their backing of the nonaligned victim state would encourage that state and perhaps other nonaligned countries to collaborate with them.

The allies of the aggressor also will oppose it, since its action would encourage the victim state and other nonaligned countries to collaborate with, and perhaps formally join, the rival coalition. While they will be concerned about the possible alienation of their ally, which is the aggressor, there is little likelihood that it could be drawn into the other grouping, since the latter also opposes the aggression. Also, the allies of the aggressing state will be concerned that the rival coalition might offer the nonaligned victim state military assistance, and this could precipitate an intercoalition war. With all groupings opposing the aggression, organizational intervention and success will occur.

RESEARCH DESIGN

Prior to the analyses of the four collective security organizations, the last section of this chapter will examine how certain concepts have been operationalized, how the data have been acquired, and how the data have been analyzed. The first part of this section will outline operational definitions of the different types of conflicts to be examined in the study and how the information on them was compiled. The second part will discuss how the dependent variable in this study, organizational involvement, has been categorized for the different organizations. The third part will explain how the nature of the coalition configurations in the world and in the three regional systems examined here have been established and how states have been classified as members of the different groupings. The task of describing the coalition configurations and establishing states' memberships in them was the most difficult one in undertaking this study. And while the method of describing these deserves additional work by scholars in the future, it is hoped that the descriptions of the coalition configurations in the subsequent chapters have been sufficiently accurate so as to provide good foundations for the testing and development of the theory.* The

_____

*Michalak, in discussing past studies of collective security and prescribing standards for future ones, has remarked that the problem

fourth part of this section will discuss the analysis of the information gathered in this study.

The Population of Conflicts

Since this study is focusing on the collective security activities of international organizations, an initial decision was made to look solely at that population of conflicts in the world where large-scale military force had been employed by states against other states (wars) or where there had been an imminent possibility that force might be used (crises). The operational definitions of the above two types of conflicts are as follows. A war will be considered to have taken place where at least 500 armed individuals entered a state with the approval of their state of origin for the purpose of altering the government's policies and/or its character, or for the purpose of defending the government against attacks by internal opponents (provided it did engage in military operations). The figure of 500 was chosen since an examination of the number of troops involved in different conflicts indicated that it was a good dividing line between attacks meant to initiate large-scale combat and those meant solely to harass the opponent state. Operationally, a crisis will be judged to have existed when both of the immediate conflicting parties, or one of the conflicting parties and a permanent member of the UN Security Council, did one of the following things: (1) stated that a war was a significant possibility in the near future; (2) stated that if one party did not change a particular policy, it would use military force; or (3) mobilized some or all of their armed forces for either offensive or defensive purposes in such an anticipated war.

While the initial decision to concentrate solely on the above two types of conflicts seemed adequate when examining the role of the United Nations in international security conflicts (since the organization has, in fact, seldom dealt with small military encounters), to restrict the study to these two types of conflicts did not seem appropriate once the activities of the regional security organizations were closely examined. It was discovered that those organizations often dealt with small-scale military attacks, and this led to a decision to add a third category of conflict, military intervention, when analyzing

---

of achieving precision in the categorization of the international systemic variables is the most "confounding" one. (Stanley J. Michalak, "The League of Nations and the United Nations in World Politics: A Plea for Comparative Research on Universal International Organizations," International Studies Quarterly 15 [December 1971]: 418.)

these organizations. It is operationally defined as a situation in which between 25 and 500 armed individuals who were supported by their state of origin crossed from one country into another in order to alter the policies or character of the latter country's government. The bottom limit of 25 troops was employed so as to exclude minor border skirmishes or subversive interventions, and the stipulation that the attack had to have the support of the state from whence it originated was included so as to exclude those cases where groups of private citizens carried out attacks that were not associated with the foreign policies of their governments.

The strategy for determining the existence of all wars and crises in the world for the 1946-77 period, and also all military interventions involving members of the OAS, OAU and the Arab League, was initially to go through a large number of chronologies[20] and materials on the four collective security organizations. Then, further searches for information were made in secondary sources. It is quite possible that a small number of conflicts were missed that should have been included, but it is doubtful whether there were very many, or that their inclusion would challenge the findings of this study. One point that should be mentioned specifically with respect to the identification of conflicts for the chapter on the United Nations is that all wars and crises that took place in the world are included—regardless of whether the states were UN members. The reason for erring from a strict definition of the activities of a collective security organization (that is, intervention in conflicts between organizational members) is that the United Nations was conceived by most governments as a global collective security body. As will be noted later, there are strong indications that the absence of one or both of the conflicting parties from the United Nations was a real impediment to its intervention in such conflicts.

Organizational Involvement

In classifying types of organizational involvement in international conflicts, an initial decision was made to use three categories, although these were later slightly altered in the case of the OAS. The categories are No Action, Debate, and Recommendation/Judgment. In the case of the OAS there were some modifications in the last two categories because of that organization's unique pattern of behavior.

In collecting information on the nature of the organizations' involvements in different conflicts, both documents issued by the organizations and secondary sources were used. In the case of the United Nations, United Nations Yearbook and a large number of articles and books on that organization were the main sources.[21] With respect to the OAU it was possible to use the resolutions of meetings that are issued by that organization and a number of scholarly studies of the African body. [22] At the same time, the lack of any published debates or a record of defeated resolutions (other than some incomplete accounts of a few meetings) makes the analysis of the diplomacy of some of the inter-African conflicts very difficult. The problem of describing and classifying Arab League activities is even greater in that there are not even published resolutions. Fortunately, some fairly good accounts have come out in secondary sources. [23]

Coalition Configurations and States'
Affiliations with the Groupings

The largest and most difficult task in undertaking this study was the identification of the coalition configurations and the establishment of different states' affiliations with the groupings. It was a particularly awesome task in that it was necessary to do it for the global system and the three regional systems for each year that the organizations were in existence. This meant that by the mid-1970s it was necessary to classify approximately 150 states for the analysis of the United Nations, 25 for the OAS, 50 for the OAU, and 20 for the Arab League. The reason the alignment affiliations of all states in the international systems under study had to be classified for each year that the organizations were in existence is that it was necessary to have information on the distribution of states in various groupings, as well as on the alignments of the conflicting parties in each conflict.

In deciding what the central coalitions were in the world and three regional systems, the most important sources of information were the secondary analyses of the organizations in question, the foreign policies of their members, and the international political milieus in which they operated. These decisions—particularly as they applied to the regional systems—were discussed with a number of experts on the international politics of the different regions. While various sources of hard data were considered for establishing the existence of certain consensuses and axes of conflict, they were judged nonexistent, impossible to gather, or demanding much more work than was possible for this study. For example, an extensive textual analysis of the statements of government leaders of all states would have been very helpful, but such a task for all of the states in question for the time periods being dealt with would have been immense. Also, it is questionable whether the statements of some national leaders would have provided sufficient data on the most salient consensuses and axes of conflict and their governments' policies regarding them.

In establishing the most important coalition configurations for the international systems in question, the work was more difficult for the African and Arab regional systems than it was for the world (at least until the 1970s) and the Western Hemisphere systems. In the case of the world system, there was general agreement among observers that the cold war axis of conflict was the most central determinant of the policies of states toward international security conflicts when they were dealing with them in world forums; with respect to the Western Hemisphere or inter-American system, most observers pointed to the centrality of the communist-noncommunist axis of conflict and nonintervention consensus among the noncommunist states. When studying the international politics of Africa, there are often references to radical, moderate, and conservative groupings (or somewhat comparable terms), but there is only limited information on both the underlying issues and the affiliations of many states with these groupings. Since there are not extensive analyses on the foreign policies of many African states, and since records of OAU debates are not available, the task of defining the coalitions demanded the piecing together of information from primary and secondary sources and discussions with African specialists. In the case of the Arab world, there are few studies that focus on patterns of inter-Arab conflicts.* However, there are sufficient materials on particular countries and conflicts in the Middle East so that the major axes of conflict and groupings can be discerned.

Once the coalitions were identified, the basic criteria for determining states' affiliations with them were (1) the outward manifestations by a government in terms of statements and actions that it shared important security interests with one grouping and had significant conflicting interests with others and (2) some manifestations of consultation and foreign policy collaboration on international security matters with the members of a certain group.† In the cases of the African and Arab regional systems, it became difficult to apply this last criterion with respect to quite a few states, since there were no

_____

*One exception is Malcolm H. Kerr, The Arab Cold War: Gamal'Abd al-Nasir and His Rivals, 1958-1970 (London: Oxford University Press, 1971).

†On identifying states' alignments in the cold war system, Haas, Butterworth, and Nye wrote: "Evidence of alignment is membership in a treaty organization, regional collective self-defense arrangement, bilateral alliance of cold war origin, or very close diplomatic understanding on security issues." (Ernst B. Haas, Robert L. Butterworth, and Joseph S. Nye, Conflict Management by International Organizations [Morristown, N.J.: General Learning Corp., 1972], p. 8.) Our definition basically concurs with this, except that the existence of a "paper alliance" is not always viewed as establishing an alignment. See comments on Pakistan below.

formal organizations for most coalitions but, rather, patterns of informal consultation and association. In the case of the world system,
the series of cold war alliances and military aid programs made the
existence of collaboration easier to substantiate; and, in the case of
the inter-American system, the consultations and accords within the
OAS itself as well as the bilateral ties of the Latin American states
with the United States also afforded some easily observable indications
of consultation and collaboration.

While in the case of the world system the existence of multilateral and bilateral alliances did offer excellent indications of memberships in certain coalitions, they were not regarded as sufficient indicators of alignment for all states. In some cases where states did
not have formal alliances with the central members of the groupings
(for example, Israel with the United States), there were very strong
informal security ties; in other cases where there were formal alliances (for example, Pakistan in SEATO after 1961), there was not a
close affiliation with the grouping. The affiliations of most of the
African and Arab states with various groupings in their regional systems were generally easy to identify in that their statements, patterns
of consultation, and behavior—for or against different parties involved
in international conflicts—often clearly identified them as members of
certain groupings. At the same time, there were cases—especially
in Africa—where it was difficult to establish clearly such affiliations.
In the discussions of the alignments of different states in the subsequent chapters, the criteria for their classification as well as the
identity of those states that were difficult to categorize are noted.

One problem that arose in classifying the alignment affiliations
of parties to several disputes was that one "party" was, in fact, a
grouping of two or more states whose alignments differed. This problem occurred only with respect to six conflicts, all of which concerned
the United Nations but not the regional organizations. In the case of
the Arab-Israeli war of 1948, some Arab states were aligned with the
West (particularly Britain), and others were nonaligned. But, since
the two most prominent Arab participants were Western-aligned
(namely, Egypt and Jordan), the Arab "party" was assigned this affiliation. In the 1967 Arab-Israeli war, Egypt and Syria were aligned
with the Soviet coalition while Jordan was still pro-Western. The
decision, therefore, was to classify the Arab side as Soviet-aligned.
In the 1973 war Egypt was nonaligned while Syria remained Soviet-
aligned, but, since the former initiated the hostilities and was the
central Arab participant, the Arab side has been classified as nonaligned. Three other conflicts in which one "party" consisted of states
with different alignments were South Yemeni civil strife with North
Yemeni and Saudi Arabian intervention (1969-72), Portuguese Angolan
civil strife with Zairean and Zambian intervention (1968-74), and

Portuguese Guinean civil strife with Guinean and Senegalese intervention (1968-74).

Another problem with respect to the classification of conflicting parties occurred when these parties were not states but, rather, civil factions. While the government faction was usually easy to classify, it was sometimes more difficult for the rebel faction—especially if it was not receiving aid from outside states. Good examples of such parties include the group that overthrew the government in Gabon in 1964 and was expelled by the French one day later and the rebels that sought to overthrow the government in the Dominican Republic in 1965. In such cases as much information as possible was gathered in determining the foreign policy orientation of the rebel group, but, as in the two previously cited cases, it was sometimes difficult to find completely adequate information.

Some word is necessary on the extent to which the testing of the theory that was previously elucidated would be undermined by either a failure to identify accurately the most salient coalition configurations or an inaccurate classification of the alignments of states with the groupings. If the identification of the coalition configurations is inaccurate, then the whole subsequent exercise is undermined. On the other hand, if alignments of certain states in each organization are inaccurately classified, this need not seriously undermine the study. The categorization of states' alignments comes into the testing of the hypotheses in two ways: first, in that it shows the general distribution of states in various groupings during a particular period and, second, in that it indicates the alignment affiliation of the conflicting parties. If a few states are not classified correctly, it is unlikely that this will seriously distort the general distribution of states among the groupings. But, if the mistakes occur regularly with respect to countries that were parties to the conflicts under study, this could undermine the analysis. This basic distinction should be kept in mind in judging any differences that one might have with some of the alignment classifications.

The Analyses of the Four Organizations

Each of the following chapters on the four organizations is divided into three sections. The first provides a historical background to the formation of the organization and a description of those aspects of the organization that are pertinent to its collective security activities. The second section describes the coalition configurations among members of the organization. The third sets forth the hypotheses concerning organizational involvement and success that are applicable to the previously described coalition configurations and examines the

data on organizational involvement and success in international conflicts in light of these hypotheses. The data on organizational involvement are given in percentages in tables at the beginning of the section,
but it is often difficult to draw any firm conclusions on the basis of
the percentages because of the small number of conflicts falling into
individual cells. In order to obtain insights into the validity of the
entire theory and into why some of the conflicts were not managed as
hypothesized, certain aspects of the diplomacy surrounding the conflicts are discussed. (Short descriptions of all the conflicts as well
as citations on sources of information are presented in the Appendix.)
With respect to the examination of the conflicts in which the organizations did not intervene and succeed as predicted, particular attention
is given to determining if these occurrences were due to inaccuracies
or incompleteness within the theory or to inaccurate descriptions of
the coalition configurations. Any attempt to conceptualize the coalition configurations in a particular international system is bound to
leave out some elements that are relevant to particular conflicts, and
in such cases the character of organizational intervention and success
contrary to the hypotheses may be due to these factors rather than to
weaknesses in certain parts of the theory itself. This entire aspect
of the analysis is very important, since it provides insights into
whether and how the theory should be revised so as to enhance its explanatory and predictive ability.

In the sixth and final chapter of this study, the conclusions of
the four preceding chapters will be summarized. Apart from indicating the extent to which the analyses of the four organizations substantiated the hypotheses and the entire theory, there will be a discussion
of how the theory might be modified in the future—in particular, how
changing international conditions could require an alteration in some
of the basic assumptions of the theory. One of the central and most
powerful assumptions of the theory is that states perceive their security in terms of the strength of their coalition vis-à-vis that of
others—and hence oppose an increase in power by any other coalition.
This assumption may become increasingly inaccurate as modern
weapons technology and interdependencies make interstate warfare a
less probable means of conflict settlement and as security ties among
states become diversified and weaker. What this latter point indicates
is that any theory can only be as strong as the accuracy of its assumptions regarding state behavior and that the validity of such assumptions
can be altered by changes in world conditions. At the same time, it
is hoped that, while certain aspects of the theory may be time-bound,
the study will still be able to shed insights on the political dynamics
of past and future collective security organizations.

The theory of collective security outlined in this chapter and
tested in the next four is really a prism through which this study views

and analyzes conflict management by international organizations in the postwar era. It is not an all-encompassing paradigm that seeks to elucidate all of the factors that impinge on and shape the activities of these organizations in interstate conflicts. Rather, it serves to highlight one factor—the alignment patterns extant in particular international security systems—which was, a priori, judged to be a central determinant of how collective security bodies behave in the face of conflicts among their members.

NOTES

1. Inis L. Claude, Jr., Swords into Plowshares: The Problems of Progress of International Organization, 4th ed. (New York: Random House, 1971), p. 245.

2. Ibid., p. 216.

3. Ernst B. Haas, "Types of Collective Security: An Examination of Operational Concepts," American Political Science Review 49 (March 1955): 40.

4. M. Leon Bourgeois, first chairman of the League Council, in From Collective Security to Preventive Diplomacy, ed. Joel Larus (New York: John Wiley and Sons, 1965), p. 13.

5. Roland Stromberg, "The Idea of Collective Security," in From Collective Security to Preventive Diplomacy, ed. Joel Larus (New York: John Wiley and Sons, 1965), p. 276.

6. Discord and Collaboration (Baltimore: Johns Hopkins University Press, 1962), p. 176.

7. Larus, op. cit., p. 305.

8. Claude, Swords into Plowshares, p. 247.

9. Stanley J. Michalak, "The League of Nations and the United Nations in World Politics: A Plea for Comparative Research on Universal International Organizations," International Studies Quarterly 15 (December 1971): 387. See also Inis L. Claude, Jr., The Changing United Nations (New York: Random House, 1967), pp. xiii-xix; Ernst B. Haas, Robert L. Butterworth, and Joseph S. Nye, Conflict Management by International Organizations (Morristown, N.J.: General Learning Corp., 1972), pp. 1-4; and John G. Ruggie, "Contingencies, Constraints and Collective Security: Perspectives on UN Involvement in International Disputes," International Organization 28 (Summer 1974): 496-98.

10. "The Global Challenge and International Cooperation," speech delivered in Milwaukee, Wisconsin, July 14, 1975.

11. While it is impossible to mention all studies of collective security, it is possible to cite examples of several important types. Studies that focus on the conditions necessary for a perfect collective security system are Inis L. Claude, Jr., Power and International Relations (New York: Random House, 1962), pp. 190-204; Claude,

Swords into Plowshares, pp. 245-84; Stromberg, op. cit., pp. 273-84; Kenneth W. Thompson, "Collective Security Reexamined," Larus, op. cit., pp. 285-303; Wolfram F. Hanrieder, "International Organizations and International Systems," International Law and Organization, ed. Richard A. Falk and Wolfram F. Hanrieder (Philadelphia: J. B. Lippincott, 1968), pp. 278-98; Louis René Beres, "Bipolarity, Multipolarity and the Tragedy of the Commons," The Western Political Quarterly 26 (December 1973); 389-413. Studies that focus on why certain patterns of intervention and success have developed and that base their generalizations on a large and well-defined population of conflicts are Ernst B. Haas, "Collective Security and the Future International System," International Law and Organization, ed. Richard A. Falk and Wolfram F. Hanrieder (Philadelphia: J. B. Lippincott, 1968), pp. 299-344; Haas, Butterworth, and Nye, op. cit.,; Robert L. Butterworth, Moderation from Management: International Organizations and Peace (Pittsburgh: University Center for International Studies, University of Pittsburgh, 1978); Benjamin David Meyers, "The Organization of African Unity: Conflict Management by a Regional Organization" (Ph.D. diss., University of California, Los Angeles, 1973); Stanley J. Michalak, Jr., "The United Nations and the League of Nations," in The United Nations in International Politics, ed. Leon Gordenker (Princeton, N.J.: Princeton University Press, 1971), pp. 60-105; Ruggie, op. cit., pp. 493-520; Jerome Slater, A Reevaluation of Collective Security (Columbus, Ohio: Ohio State University Press, 1965); Joseph S. Nye, Peace in Parts: Integration and Conflict in Regional Organization (Boston: Little, Brown, 1971), pp. 129-72; William Coplin and J. Martin Rochester, "The Permanent Court of International Justice, International Court of Justice, League and United Nations," American Political Science Review 66 (June 1972): 529-50. Some examples of studies with a substantive focus like those above but whose analyses are not based on an examination of a large and defined set of conflicts are Claude, Swords into Plowshares, pp. 215-46, 312-34; idem., The Changing United Nations; idem, "The Management of Power in the Changing United Nations," in The United Nations System and Its Functions, ed. Robert W. Gregg and Michael Barkun (Princeton, N.J.: D. Van Nostrand, 1968), pp. 265-84; Stanley R. Hoffmann, "International Organization and the International System," International Organization 24 (Summer 1970): 389-413; Oran R. Young, "The United Nations and the International System," Gordenker, op. cit., pp. 10-59; and Mark W. Zacher, Dag Hammarskjold's United Nations (New York: Columbia University Press, 1970).

12. Michalak, "The League of Nations and the United Nations in World Politics," pp. 148-55; Michalak, "The United Nations and the League," pp. 66-67; Ruggie, op. cit., pp. 508-16; and Young, op. cit., p. 902.

13. Ibid. See in particular the studies by Michalak and Ruggie.

14. See Graham T. Allison, The Essence of Decision: Explaining the Cuban Missile Crisis (Boston: Little, Brown, 1971).

15. Haas, Butterworth, and Nye, op. cit., p. 46.

16. For another delineation of types of international systems and the policy orientations of states in these systems, see Morton A. Kaplan, System and Process in International Politics (New York: John Wiley, 1964), pp. 21-53.

17. For a very good discussion of a consensual security system and an ideal system of collective security, see Claude, Swords into Plowshares, pp. 245-83; and idem, Power and International Relations, pp. 94-115.

18. For an analysis of this development and its implications for conflict management, see Claude, The Changing United Nations, pp. 3-21.

19. On this tendency in the cold war international system, see Richard Rosecrance, International Relations: Peace or War? (New York: McGraq-Hill, 1973), pp. 275-76.

20. Deadline Data; Kessing's Contemporary Archives; Newsyear; Asian Recorder; Indian Recorder and Digest; Pakistan Horizon; Middle East Journal; African Research Bulletin; Africa Report; Africa Digest; African Diary; and Hispanic-American Report.

21. M. Margaret Ball, The O.A.S. in Transition (Durham, N.C.: Duke University Press, 1969); Gordon Connell-Smith, The Inter-American System (London: Oxford University Press, 1966); John C. Dreier, The Organization of American States and the Hemisphere (New York: Harper & Row, 1962); Lloyd Mecham, The United States and Inter-American Security, 1889-1960 (Austin, Tex.: University of Texas Press, 1967); Jerome Slater, The O.A.S. and United States Foreign Policy (Columbus: Ohio State University Press, 1967); Ann Van Wynen Thomas and A. J. Thomas, Jr., The Organization of American States (Dallas: Southern Methodist University Press, 1963); and David W. Wainhouse et al., International Peace Observation: A History and Forecast (Baltimore: Johns Hopkins University Press, 1966).

22. Books that include general accounts of the conflict-management activities of the OAU are Berhanykun Andemicael, Peaceful Settlement among African States: Roles of the United Nations and the Organization of African Unity (New York: UN Institute for Training and Research, 1972); Zdenek Cervenka, The Organization of African Unity and Its Charter (New York: Praeger, 1969); Meyers, op. cit.; Saadia Touval, The Boundary Politics of Independent Africa (Cambridge, Mass.: Harvard University Press, 1977); Jon Woronoff, Organizing African Unity (Metuchen, N.J.: Scarecrow Press, 1970).

23. See, especially, Hussein A. Hassouna, The League of Arab States and Regional Disputes (Dobbs Ferry, N.Y.: Oceana, 1975); Robert W. Macdonald, The League of Arab States (Princeton, N.J.: Princeton University Press, 1965), app. G.

2

The United Nations and
International Crises and Wars

THE BACKGROUND AND CHARACTER OF
THE UN COLLECTIVE SECURITY SYSTEM

Despite the tragic history of the interwar attempt at collective
security through the League of Nations, there still existed considerable enthusiasm within many governments and private groups during
World War II for the postwar creation of a global organization whose
purpose would be the prevention of aggressions. Interest in such a
project was perhaps greatest in the United States, where plans for the
establishment of the United Nations were closely tied to the general
planning of the postwar order carried out under President Franklin D.
Roosevelt and Secretary of State Cordell Hull. After 1941 Washington sought to convince its wartime allies of the merits of participating
in a postwar global security organization. From the very start of
these discussions, one central theme clearly emerged: whether oriented toward regionalism, as advocated by Moscow and London, or
toward universalism, as Washington favored, the new security system was to be premised on the hegemony and unity of the Great Powers. As Winston Churchill remarked to Joseph Stalin at Teheran:
"We are the trustees for the peace of the world."[1] The centrality of
the Great Powers was felt to represent a realistic recognition of the
fact that any new security organization could not possibly function
without the support, much less against the will, of any of them. Their
unity was thus to be the key to the postwar order, and their cooperation the basis of any collective action.
    Although concrete discussions concerning the proposed collective
security system were not initiated until the United States had entered
the war, the Atlantic Charter issued by Churchill and Roosevelt in
August 1941 contained many ideas that later were incorporated into

the UN Charter. [2] The 1943 Moscow Declaration on General Security committed the "Big Three" to press for the creation of "a general international organization, based upon the sovereign equality of all peace-loving states, and open to membership by all such states, large and small, for the maintenance of international peace and security." [3] The organizational framework that should be adopted as the basis of the new system was the subject of considerable discussion among the states concerned during the next year and a half. The Big Three, while in agreement on the dominant role they should play in the postwar order, differed markedly in specific approach. Stalin envisaged the creation of two "committees"—one concerned with European security and consisting of Britain, the Soviet Union, the United States, and possibly one additional European state; the other concerned with the Far East and made up of the Big Three and China. Churchill, too, favored regional committees for each of the European, Far Eastern, and Western Hemispheric regions, but united in a Supreme United Nations Council. [4] Roosevelt had also originally favored a regional approach, but by the time of the Teheran Conference in late 1943 the U.S. government began to support the concept of a universal organization. [5] In the U.S. scheme, this body would include a plenary body of all member states that would discuss and offer recommendations with respect to world problems, [6] although responsibility for directing the organization would remain in the hands of the "Four Policemen."

In the fall of 1944, following many months of extensive discussion, the four met at Dumbarton Oaks in Washington, D.C., and agreed to create a United Nations Organization whose main purpose would be the maintenance of international peace and security. All "peace-loving nations"* would be entitled to membership and would be equally represented in a General Assembly. This organ would be subordinate to a Security Council, composed of five permanent members—the four sponsoring powers and France—and six nonpermanent members elected for two-year terms by the Assembly. This executive organ would be empowered to investigate disputes between members and to determine the existence of threats to or breaches of the peace, and it would have at its disposal a whole panoply of measures, including the use of military force, to deal with aggressions. Security Council decisions would bind all UN members, who were to make arrangements to contribute forces and facilities to the organization to maintain peace and security. Also proposed was the establishment

---

*This phrase referred to all those states that had fought the Axis powers. (Leland M. Goodrich, Edward Hambro, and Anne Patricia Simons, Charter of the United Nations: Commentary and Documents [New York: Columbia University Press, 1969], pp. 89-90.)

of a Secretariat, an International Court of Justice, and various other agencies to promote the goals of the organization. [7]

Left unsettled, however, was the central question of what voting procedures should govern the decision-making process of the Security Council. While all the Great Powers agreed from the outset that the proposed security organization would be based on the principle of their unanimity, the extent to which this principle should operate in practice soon became a contentious issue. The Soviet Union insisted that the five permanent Council members must have an "absolute veto" on all questions, including procedural matters. Britain and the United States, on the other hand, argued for a "qualified veto" formula whereby a state would abstain from voting in the case of disputes in which it was itself involved, and then also advocated that the veto power should not be applicable to procedural questions. [8] Eventually, at the Yalta Conference of February 1945, the Soviets agreed to suspend the veto when a member of the Council was party to a dispute under consideration by that organ, but only if such a dispute did not amount to a threat to the peace and if no military or security action was undertaken by the Council in connection with the conflict, in which case each permanent member would retain full veto privileges. The Soviets also accepted a formula whereby substantive decisions would require the support of seven Council members (including the five permanent participants) while "procedural matters" would need the concurrence of any seven. *

Thus, the proposals drawn up at Dumbarton Oaks and Yalta clearly envisioned the institutionalization of the Great Power Concert in that the hegemony of the "Big Five" was to be guaranteed by both their permanent membership and special veto powers in the executive organ of the United Nations. It was hoped that the "imperative of unanimity" would secure their support for the new collective security system. [9] From this conception of the central role of the Great Powers it followed that, despite the assurances given by the permanent Council members that the veto would be used sparingly, no action

---

*At the San Francisco Conference in June it was decided that a decision to discuss a vote was a procedural matter but a decision to investigate it would be a substantive question. In case of a dispute as to whether an action was substantive or procedural, this was to be subject to the substantive voting procedure. (Ruth B. Russell and Jeanette E. Muther, A History of the United Nations Charter [Washington, D.C.: The Brookings Institution, 1958], pp. 731-35; Leland M. Goodrich, Edward Hambro, and Anne Patricia Simons, Charter of the United Nations: Commentary and Documents [New York: Columbia University Press, 1969], p. 220.)

would be undertaken against any of the five or their allies, or at the expense of any security interests deemed vital to them. It was clear, then, that the proposed United Nations would have utility mainly with respect to conflicts between states not closely associated with any of the Great Powers, or in the event of challenges to the status quo by the Axis enemies of the permanent Council members. On the latter point, one commentator has observed that the scheme for ensuring global security by means of the concert of the Big Five "represented the world's belated prescription for preventing the Second World War."[10]

In June 1945, 51 states attended the San Francisco Conference to consider the Great Powers' proposals for the creation of an international collective security organization. These proposals were for the most part approved by the states in attendance, but there were several minor changes in the draft of the charter submitted by the Great Powers at the opening of the conference that are relevant for our purposes. In particular, the changes made provided for a greater latitude of freedom for the General Assembly to involve itself in international security problems and also held out the prospect that regional organizations could attempt to manage conflicts between their members.

The signatories to the UN Charter, in expressing their desire to unite for the maintenance of international peace and security, agreed to "take effective collective measures for the prevention and removal of threats to the peace"; to bring about the settlement of international disputes by peaceful means; to refrain from both the threat and use of force against other states; and to lend every assistance to the United Nations in actions taken in accordance with the Charter.[11] It was also provided that the United Nations would "ensure" that nonmembers acted in accordance with these principles in order to avoid a repetition of the League's inability to respond to the aggressions of Germany and Japan that had led to the war that was still then raging.[12] To protect the national sovereignty of members, it was declared that, except in the cases of "enforcement measures" aimed at the alleviation of dangers to the international peace, the United Nations would not intervene in matters "essentially within the domestic jurisdiction of states."[13]

The Charter laid out an institutional framework for the organization that reflected the dominant role the Great Powers expected to play in the postwar order. With respect to the collective security functions of the United Nations, the Security Council was clearly superior to the General Assembly and was to have "primary responsibility" for the maintenance of peace and security. Composed of eleven states[14]—the five permanent members and six others elected by the Assembly for two-year terms[15]—the Council was granted wide powers to act in carrying out its security functions, with regard to both the pacific settlement of disputes (chapter 6 of the Charter) and the prevention and abatement of breaches of the peace and acts of aggression (chapter 7). The Council could investigate any situation that might "give rise to a dispute," either of its own volition or as a result of a request by a UN member. [16] After discussion of a problem or a conflict by the Council, in which a UN member whose interests were "specially affected" could be invited to participate, the organ could "recommend appropriate procedures or methods of adjustment" to the parties involved. [17] If the Council determined that the conflict was more serious and in fact constituted a threat to the peace, a breach of the peace, or an actual act of aggression, stronger measures could then be taken. The Council could call on the parties to carry out any measures it deemed necessary or desirable, or, if collective action was required, call on UN members to impose economic, diplomatic, or military sanctions against an aggressor. [18] The ability of the Council to implement such measures was ensured, in theory at least, by the general obligation of all UN members to "accept and carry out the decisions of the Council," and by a more specific undertaking to make available the facilities and armed forces agreed upon in negotiation with the executive organ. [19] A Military Staff Committee, composed of the chiefs of staff of the permanent Council members, was created to direct any military operations conducted under Council auspices. [20] Finally, while the Charter was not to impair states' "inherent right of individual or collective self-defense,"[21] the Council was to be informed of such actions and no "enforcement action" was to be taken under regional arrangements without the Council's authorization. [22] This attempt to harmonize the principle of UN primacy with the existence of regional security organizations only served to confuse the issue, and state practice soon established a norm that upheld the autonomy of regional collective security organizations. *

The voting regulations governing the Council's operations were those agreed to at Yalta, thus ensuring the existence of the ubiquitous Great Power veto and guaranteeing that the United Nations would function as the instrument of their concert or not at all.† If one of

---

*See Minerva Etzioni, The Majority of One: Towards a Theory of Regional Compatibility (Beverly Hills, Calif.: Sage, 1970), pp. 70-83; and Inis L. Claude, Jr., "The O.A.S., the U.N. and the United States," International Conciliation, no. 547 (March 1964), for a discussion of the ambiguity of the Charter and the evolution of practices in this area. Articles 51 through 54 opened the possibility for a major role in conflict management by regional organizations, and were included largely as a result of pressure from the Latin American states and the United States.

† Article 27. The 1965 amendments, which increased Council membership to fifteen, specified that the support of nine states—as opposed to seven—was required for the passage of a resolution.

them should become an aggressor, then the United Nations would be irrelevant and any collective action taken would not be under UN auspices. As Leo Pasvolsky, an official of the U.S. State Department, recounted:

> The underlying theory . . . was that if one of the major nations were to prove recalcitrant, or were to refuse to abide by the rules of international behavior that are being inscribed in the Charter, a situation would be created in which the recalcitrant nation might have to be coerced; and it was clear that no major nation could be coerced except by the combined forces of the other major nations. This would be the equivalent of a world war, and a decision to embark upon such a war would necessarily have to be made by each of the other major nations for itself and not by any international organization. [23]

As was mentioned earlier, the very restricted role granted to the General Assembly in international conflicts by the Dumbarton Oaks proposals was broadened at the San Francisco Conference. The Great Powers had sought to allow the Assembly only to discuss conflicts and to have no say in their management by the United Nations. [24] At San Francisco, however, the small and middle-sized states were able to secure the acceptance of Articles 10, 11, and 14, which permitted Assembly recommendations with respect to a conflict, provided that the Security Council was not dealing with it at the time. [25] The creation of an expanded Assembly role in conflict management, which reflected the concern of many states that disagreements between the permanent Security Council members might paralyze the United Nations in conflict situations, was originally envisioned as providing additional conflict management procedures to deal with exceptional cases. That such cases would, in fact, become common—not exceptional—occurrences was not anticipated by the delegates at San Francisco. Moreover, Article 18, which spelled out the voting rules for the Assembly, made it clear that the Assembly's ability to pass recommendations regarding international conflicts could not be stymied by the veto of any single power or small group of powers. Rather, all of its decisions on "important questions" were to be made with the approval of two-thirds of the states present and voting. Thus, although the Great Powers were able to retain the Security Council's sole right to initiate any enforcement actions, they were forced to allow the UN deliberative body, in which all members were represented, to pass collective judgments in the name of the organization once the Council had failed to take action.

Two other organs of the United Nations that are pertinent to its conflict-management activities are the secretary-general and the International Court of Justice, although this study will not focus on their activities. The secretary-general was provided with a greater political role than had been the case in the League of Nations system in that Articles 98 and 99 gave him the power to take on any functions delegated to him by the deliberative organs and also empowered him to "bring to the attention of the Security Council any matter which in his opinion may threaten the maintenance of international peace and security."[26] Moreover, probably as important as the formal powers delegated to the secretary-general was the general recognition that he would be an active diplomatic force in the management of conflicts between UN members. The International Court of Justice was a close replica of the Permanent Court of International Justice, which was the judicial organ within the League of Nations.[27] The court is generally unable to influence ongoing military conflicts, and it can only rule on the underlying issues in a conflict if the parties explicitly recognize its right to do so.

The key feature of the United Nation's collective security system for the purposes of this study is that, with the bestowal of broad powers on the General Assembly, two-thirds of the organization's membership can launch what has been defined as a formal UN "intervention" in a particular conflict. Unlike Security Council resolutions, those emanating from the Assembly are not binding, but the real weight of any international organizational intervention lies not so much in the legal status of its resolutions as in the pressure that the states supporting a resolution are able to exert in the international community. Also, as a result of the Uniting for Peace Resolution of 1950 the Assembly was granted the right to recommend collective action against an aggressor and to set up procedures for transferring an issue from the purview of the Council to the Assembly within a 24-hour period, thereby evading the restriction that the UN plenary body could not pass recommendations on a conflict while the Council was considering it.[28] In connection with this expanded Assembly power, Inis L. Claude has commented that the Assembly has "virtually replaced the Council as the agency bearing primary political responsibility within the United Nations," although, as the same author subsequently noted, this trend may be undergoing at least a partial reversal.[29] While the Soviet Union and, to a lesser extent, the other Great Powers were concerned to assert their primacy in international conflict management in 1945, they were forced to open the door to possible interventions by the entire UN membership, and this door has been thrown wide open almost from the beginning of the United Nations' history.

COALITION CONFIGURATIONS IN THE
INTERNATIONAL SYSTEM, 1946-77

The coalition configuration that dominated international security politics during the years 1946-77 was organized around the cold war axis of conflict and consisted of groupings led by the Western states and the Soviet Union as well as a nonaligned grouping. By this statement is meant that the policies of most states toward international conflicts were influenced largely by their expectations about how different outcomes would affect the relative strength and position of these groupings. In this section, a survey of some of the most influential literature on postwar international relations validates the coalition configuration sketched above and testifies to the centrality of the cold war for global security politics throughout the postwar era. (See Table 2, which outlines the membership of the three groupings.)

The crucial role of the major military powers in determining the character of international security relations is well known to most students of international politics. Their ability to both threaten the security of many states and protect that of allies means that most countries tend to view their own security interests as being strongly and inevitably affected by the policies of these major military powers. As George Modelski has remarked: "In times of crisis, the eyes of the world . . . turn upon the Great Powers: their reaction and response, or else their failure to act, serve as clues to countless others. The nation-state system accords them maximum attention and the widest visibility; their use or abuse of this privileged position invariably has profound consequences."[30] In the period since the end of World War II there have been only two truly "Great Powers," namely, the United States and the Soviet Union. Their military power has been so much greater than that of any other state that their relations have been the dominant motif in international security politics. The uniquely powerful position occupied by the two "superpowers" derives not only from their own military and political might but also from the fact that each leads an alliance consisting of other modern industrial states that possess significant, though in comparison vastly inferior, military power. According to one eminent international relations scholar, the superpowers, "through their own preponderant weight . . . determine the balance between them. That balance of power has been transformed from a multipolar into a bipolar one."[31] To assert that the dominant axis of conflict or coalition configuration that has influenced international politics since 1945 has been that involving the Western, Soviet, and nonaligned groupings does not imply that the primary causes of many international crises and wars did not originate in very local or idiosyncratic grievances and issues. Rather, it means that, when most states reacted to such conflicts in global diplomatic forums, uppermost in their calculations was the question of how different conflict outcomes would affect the relations among the three groups and their relative power positions.

That politico-military relations throughout the world have been decisively influenced by the cold war and the bipolar distribution of power that characterized it is attested to by the writings of many students of international relations. Henry Kissinger has noted that at times the bipolar global system has resembled a zero-sum game, where "a gain for one side appears as an absolute loss for the other."[32] Peter J. Fliess has observed that the bipolar contest tends to "overshadow the more diversified relations of the lesser powers, which find it difficult if not impossible, to resist sustained pressures of the superpowers. In particular, matters of prime importance such as the avoidance of war, are dealt with in terms of the exigencies of the bipolar balance.[33] Indeed, so pervasive has the theme of the cold war been in the study of international relations that, at least until recently, the field itself was dominated by "force- and security-oriented definitions" of its subject matter, which arose from the military and security concerns attending the cold war.[34] Donald J. Puchala and Stuart I. Fagan have also commented on the resilience of the "security politics paradigm," which became popular at the height of the cold war, in more recent international relations studies.[35] Scholars also have commented specifically on the impact of the cold war on the political processes of the United Nations. In connection with this, Claude has averred: "The fundamental feature of postwar international politics, the struggle between the Soviet Union and the United States—or, if we broaden our vision of it, between East and West—has had the general effect of making the United Nations a cockpit of rivalry, an arena for East-West competition, a battlefield rather than a peace conference."[36] Thus, the East-West conflict "has brought about the politicization of virtually every question that arises in the United Nations and in the specialized agencies where the leaders of the two blocs share membership, no matter how far removed from the political sphere the question may seem to be."[37]

While almost all students of international relations have seen the cold war axis of conflict as central to postwar security politics, differences exist both as to when it first became prominent and when, if at all, it ceased to be the most important factor affecting security issues. Haas has commented on the existence of Great Power unanimity, or unipolarity, in the international system until early 1948.[38] This view, however, is "a dissent from the orthodoxy of postwar bipolarity; among most analysts, "there is preponderant agreement on the bipolarity of the immediate postwar period."[39] Similarly, most scholars seem to have little difficulty supporting the proposition that the cold war contest was the dominant fact of international politics, especially with respect to security questions, until some time in the early 1960s. [40] As Hayward R. Alker and Bruce M. Russett showed in their statistical analyses of UN voting, the cold war was the most prominent "super-issue" that dominated the organization from 1947 to 1961. Indeed, its importance actually increased over time. *

A more serious challenge to the view that the cold war was central to international security politics arose with the claims of several authors that the international system entered an era of multipolarity in the early or mid-1960s. [41] The factors that these authors pointed to during the 1960s as marking the emergence of multipolarity are polycentrism, that is, the increasing influence of centrifugal tendencies within the two alliance systems; [42] detente, or the lessening of the threat of war and of general hostility between East and West; a decline in the ties of Third World countries to cold war blocs; and the emergence of other "poles" in the international system, such as China, Japan, and Western Europe. [43] It should be noted that while many writers contended that the bipolar international structure was being undermined, most were ambiguous as to the impact of this new multipolarity on global security politics. Several attempts were made to fuse the concepts of bipolarity and multipolarity into one model. Brzezinski has spoken of a gradual move toward mixed conflict-cooperation between the major powers beginning in the early 1960s; [44] Kissinger has posited the notions of military bipolarity and political multipolarity; [45] Spanier has argued that there occurred a transition from intense bipolarity to bipolycentrism around 1963; [46] Spiegel has offered the concept of a "bimodality" model that leaves the superpowers at the top but removes some of the restrictions on lesser powers inherent in the strict bipolar model; [47] and Hoffmann has put forth the idea of different "layers" constituting the international system's structure— "the fundamental, latent bipolar stratum; the manifest layer of polycentrism; and an emergent layer of multipolarity." [48] A well-known effort is that of Morton Kaplan whose "loose bipolar" and "very loose bipolar" models seek to reconcile the palpable military preeminence of the superpowers with the existence of widely diffused economic and political power in the system. [49]

The key question to pose in connection with this study is, With respect to what matters of international politics did the cold war configuration tend to dominate in the 1946-77 period? It is contended

---

*If Alker and Russett had concentrated solely on UN voting with respect to international crises and wars and had excluded voting on other matters, the significance of the cold war axis of conflict probably would have been even more marked. (Hayward R. Alker and Bruce M. Russett, World Politics in the General Assembly [New Haven, Conn. : Yale University Press, 1965], pp. 56, 68-69, 89-94, 113, 126, 135.)

here that global security politics remained strongly influenced throughout the postwar period by the cold war. During the late 1960s and the 1970s many scholars found that in regard to security issues the "old" coalition configuration tended to predominate. Oran R. Young, after reviewing a number of the developments in international politics that worked to undermine the cold war system, wrote: "While it is quite true that recent years have witnessed a marked decline in bipolar relationships in the international system, there is little evidence to suggest a sharp movement in the direction of clear-cut multipolarity."[50] A recent study echoed Young's conclusion: "While several international actors are beginning to form blocs of reliable behavior and while these blocs have considerable command over events in either regional or subject areas, they have not yet achieved the status of third powers in the sense of having global influence to determine the outcomes of events."[51] Thus, "the global balance of power," this study concludes, "is in a transitional phase of incipient multipolarity, in which the secondary power centers are still more attached to the primary than the independent poles."[52] Yale H. Ferguson and Walther F. Weiker also have asserted that the cold war continues to be central to world security politics and that multipolarity, regional integration, and polycentrism have not "had much effect on, for example, current superpower rivalry in the Middle East, Washington's warning to Moscow about the possible establishment of a Soviet submarine base in Cuba or the essentially bilateral nature of the SALT talks."[53] Z. Brzezinski observed in 1972 that of all the states in the international system, "only two are truly powers in the sense that they wield effective military, political and economic leverage. Indeed, their power is so highly disproportional to all the others that on the power plane the world is, and is likely to remain, a bipolar one."[54] There also have been many other scholars who have argued in a similar vein in support of the centrality of East-West issues to general international security politics.[55]

One of the major premises of those analysts who view the international system as developing toward polycentrism and multipolarity since the mid-1960s is that the strongly competitive and hostile relationship between NATO and the Warsaw Pact states was significantly altered and tempered. There is, however, from the perspective of the late 1970s, little indication that the pervasive sense of competition and mistrust ever disappeared or subsided greatly in intensity, or that the states involved ceased to view these alliances as crucial to their security. Serious strains did at times plague both alliances, but did not lead to a fundamental weakening of them, let alone their demise. One event that saw the members of both groupings (or most of them) come to a new appreciation of the salience of their respective alliance systems was the Czech crisis of 1968.

Thomas W. Wolfe has offered this succinct comment concerning the effect of the 1968 events on the Western alliance:

> In the process of stamping out the Czech reform ex-
> periment, the Soviet Union, unwittingly perhaps, made
> clear that it was premature to think of a Europe inde-
> pendent of Soviet—and American—power let alone a
> reconciled Europe knit together by a unifying "Euro-
> pean idea." At best what the Soviet action seemed to
> promise was that they might again look forward to an
> indefinite period of bipolar alliance arrangements
> aimed at maintaining an uneasy status quo.[56]

As this and many other of the above citations indicate, there was indeed some serious questioning of the importance of and need for the
cold war groupings beginning in the early 1960s, but these groupings
have in fact remained the central actors and determined the context
of international security politics. And, as will be shown later, when
international conflicts were brought to the United Nations they were
often dealt with and perceived according to cold war loyalties and expectations, often in the process emasculating the organization's collective security potentialities.[57]

Some international relations scholars reacted to the deepening
Sino-Soviet rift in the 1960s by positing a tripolar model of the international system, particularly with respect to Asia.[58] While a case
can be made that in the Asian theater China possessed sufficient military and political power to constitute a "pole," it was not the case
that Peking could assume such a role in other areas of the world. As
Richard Rosecrance has commented: "In years past, and particularly
when she was convulsed by the Cultural Revolution, China played a
minor role in world affairs. She either had not developed a worldwide
pattern of interests, or that pattern was not a stable one."[59] The
markedly inferior military position of China relative to the superpowers, and her aloofness from any major alliance system after the split
with Moscow, further inhibited Peking from emerging as a major
actor in international security politics. And, although this has begun
to change in the 1970s, recent estimates indicate that China still
spends less than a quarter of what the United States spends on defense[60]—Chinese military power has never been brought into action
outside of Asia. Those analysts who predicted a marked reduction in
the gap between Chinese military power and that of either of the superpowers appear, on balance, to have greatly exaggerated the pace
of Peking's military development.[61] Moreover, even in Asia, China
cannot be considered an independent "pole" in such conflicts as the
Vietnam War, since in that case it sided with the Soviet Union against

the United States and other Western states, despite the existence of a serious rift with the Soviets. Nonetheless, several of the conflicts that occurred in Asia, such as those between India and Pakistan in 1965 and 1971, need to be viewed from a perspective that recognizes the independent position of China in the continent.[62] China's impact in these Asian conflicts will be discussed in the next section.

It should be recalled that in the theory of collective security set forth in Chapter 1 certain assumptions are made concerning the policies of the members of international coalitions. The central assumption is that states seek to increase the relative strength of their grouping vis-à-vis others by preventing the departure of their own members, by preventing the alignment of uncommitted states with rival coalitions, and by encouraging the movement of rival coalition members toward a nonaligned stance if they cannot be attracted into their own grouping. Except for the case of the Soviet bloc during the latter part of Stalin's rule when, as will be noted below, the Kremlin failed to some extent to actively solicit uncommitted states, the above assumption is viewed as reflective of the behavior of the cold war coalitions throughout the entire 1946-77 period.

The general policies of the superpower-led coalitions have been well summarized by one scholar who wrote: "The attempts of the superpowers at political consolidation mainly follow three lines: first, to draw their allies together into a working unit; second, to win new allies; and third, to encourage and strengthen the resistance of the uncommitted to the influence of the opposing bloc."* For most of the postwar period, both Washington and Moscow have exhibited a "fascination with the Third World, seen as a potentially decisive stake in the superpowers' contest."[63] For the Western states, these policies were associated with the general strategy of containment, which was formally articulated in 1947.[64] This doctrine was based on the simple

---

*Peter J. Fliess, International Relations in the Bipolar World (New York: Random House, 1968), p. 75. For an excellent discussion of why the major military powers view allies as important, even in the age of nuclear deterrence, see ibid., pp. 101-3. On the question of the policies of the blocs to prevent the disaffection of alliance members, see ibid., p. 123; and Morton A. Kaplan, "Bipolarity in a Revolutionary Age," in The Revolution in World Politics, ed. Morton A. Kaplan (New York: John Wiley & Sons, 1962), p. 252. On their attempts to attract the uncommitted states into their alliance systems and to prevent the integration of these states into the rival one, see Richard N. Rosecrance, Action and Reaction in World Politics (Boston: Little, Brown, 1963), pp. 209-12.

hypothesis that the larger the number of Western allies, the less likely the possibility of Soviet aggression. According to Kissinger: "For a decade and a half after the second world war, the United States identified security with alliances. A global network of relationships grew up based on the proposition that deterrence of aggression required the largest possible grouping of powers. "[65]

While the United States in particular sought to incorporate almost all states outside the communist grouping into its extensive alliance system, it usually displayed tolerance and even a friendly disposition toward nonaligned states for fear that failure to do so would run the risk of forcing these states to seek closer relations with the Soviet grouping. [66] The same was also generally true for Soviet policy, although during the late 1940s and early 1950s there was a tendency for Moscow to regard Third World nations, even those states not explicitly linked to the West, as de facto members of the Western grouping. To be sure, there were occasions when the Soviets did seek to promote ties with nonaligned states, such as the early support they rendered to the nascent state of Israel after its establishment in 1948. For the most part, however, Soviet leaders adhered to the "two camp doctrine" articulated by Andrei Zhdanov, at least until Stalin's passing in 1953. [67] After that time the Soviet Union began to encourage the Afro-Asian states to adopt nonaligned and anti-Western foreign policies. In a sense, then, early postwar Soviet policy was not completely "rational" in terms of what the previous chapter set forth as a "rational policy" for international coalitions in competition with each other.

Since 1954, Soviet goals in the Third World have been to try to bring these states into an alliance with the Soviet Union, but, where this was not possible, it was content to encourage their nonalignment and ensure that they did not become attached to the Western bloc.

> The essential purpose of Soviet efforts in this period was
> not to strive for immediate control over these areas,
> but in the first instance to deny them to the West, by
> drawing nationalist leaders of the underdeveloped world
> into a loose coalition of anti-Western states. The
> trend of Soviet policy was therefore identified as "work-
> ing with the national bourgeoisie, " and it was more
> concerned with influencing the orientation of these
> nationalist leaders in world politics than in overthrow-
> ing them by revolutionary action on the part of local
> communist parties. [68]

With the advent of this policy, which came to be associated with the general doctrine of "peaceful coexistence, " the Soviet grouping began to operate in a more traditional diplomatic fashion, and this basic orientation has continued to the present. [69]

Another point that should be made in connection with the policies of the coalitions is that, while they were desirous of detaching allies from their opponent's grouping, they did not attempt to implement this policy by promoting or initiating military intervention such that an intercoalition war would become likely. Their language at times indicated a commitment to "liberate" states associated with their major rival, but, generally, they confined their activity to diplomatic and economic assistance. Only when an ally was directly felt to be threatened (for example, the United States and China in the Korean War, the United States in the Vietnam War) did central alliance members show a willingness to resort to force.

Prior to discussing the memberships of the three groupings set out in Table 2, several points should be made concerning the identification of states' alignments. A decision was made not to choose any particular indicator, such as the existence of an alliance, despite the fact that a formal alliance appears to be the best indicator of alignment. [70] This is because no single indicator was felt to reflect adequately the alignment between states outside of NATO and the Warsaw Pact with the members of those alliances. Pertinent to this matter is Robert Osgood's comment that "America's alliances in Asia, the Middle East, and Africa indicate far less about the real nature and extent of American military commitments than NATO indicated in Europe. They are much less significant than the network of commitments other than alliances in the area." [71] Other indicators that a state was aligned with a particular grouping are that it viewed one of the polar groupings, or key members thereof, as a protector of its security; that it shared common definitions of "enemies" (especially in its own region); that it had important economic and military aid ties with this major grouping; and that it was openly antagonistic toward the policies and interests of the other grouping (especially in its own region). [72] John Herz, in commenting on the desire of the Great Powers to secure allies in the Third World, has provided a useful summary of some of the indicators of alignment.

> Defense agreements, military aid, training of troops, establishment of bases, economic-financial ties through investments, aid, exclusive or predominant trade relations, currency arrangements, all of these are common means to establish or maintain influence which, especially in the case of the newly independent . . . and weak units, frequently amounts to dependency. [73]

The president of Tanzania, Julius Nyerere, noted in 1970 that, given the decline in the blocs' monolithic character and the greater inter-

TABLE 2

Global Coalition Configurations, 1946-77

Western Grouping
Belgium (1945)
Canada (1945)
Cyprus (1960)
Denmark (1945)
France (1945)
Greece (1945)
Iceland (1946)
Ireland (1955)
Italy (1955)
Luxembourg (1945)
Malta (1964), 1964-mid-1971,
  early 1972-77
Netherlands (1945)
Norway (1945)
Portugal (1955)
Spain (1955)
Turkey (1945)
United Kingdom (1945)
United States (1945)
West Germany (1973)

Australia (1945)
China (1945), 1946-late
  1971
Fiji (1970)
Iran (1945), 1946-50, mid-
  1953-77
Japan (1956)
Kampuchea (1955), early 1970-
  early 1975
Laos (1955), 1959-mid-1960,
  1964-early 1974
Malaysia (1957)
New Zealand (1945)
Pakistan (1947), 1947-49,
  1953-late 1962
Papua New Guinea (1975)
Philippines (1945)
Samoa (1976)
Singapore (1965)
Thailand (1946)

Bahrain (1971)
Egypt (1945), 1946-52, 1976-
  77
Iraq (1945), 1946-mid-1958
Israel (1949), 1950-77
Jordan (1955)
Kuwait (1963)
Lebanon (1945), 1957-mid-
  1958
Libya (1955), 1955-late
  1969
Morocco (1956), 1956-59,
  1975-77
Oman (1971)
Qatar (1971)
Saudi Arabia (1945)
Sudan (1956), 1976-77
Tunisia (1956)
United Arab Emirates
  (1971)

Benin (1960), 1960-74
Botswana (1966)
Cameroun (1960)
Central African Empire
  (1960)
Chad (1960)
Congo (1960), 1960-mid-1963
Ethiopia (1945), 1945-57
Gambia (1965)
Gabon (1960)
Ghana (1957), early 1966-77
Ivory Coast (1960)
Lesotho (1966)
Liberia (1945)
Madagascar (1960), 1960-mid-
  1972
Malawi (1964)
Mauritania (1961), 1961-mid-
  1964, 1975-77
Niger (1960)
Rwanda (1962)
Senegal (1960)

Seychelles (1976), 1976-mid-
  1977
Sierra Leone (1961)
South Africa (1945)
Swaziland (1968)
Togo (1960)
Uganda (1962), 1971-72
Upper Volta (1960)
Zaire (1960), late 1960-
  77

Argentina (1945)
Bahamas (1973)
Barbados (1966)
Bolivia (1945), 1946-mid-
  1969, mid-1971-77
Brazil (1945), 1946-late
  1960, mid-1964-77
Chile (1945), 1946-late 1970,
  late 1973-77
Colombia (1945)
Costa Rica (1945)
Cuba (1945), 1946-58
Dominican Republic (1945)
Ecuador (1945)
El Salvador (1945)
Grenada (1974)
Guatemala (1945), 1946-50,
  mid-1954-77
Haiti (1945)
Honduras (1945)
Jamaica (1962), 1962-early
  1972
Mexico (1945)
Nicaragua (1945)
Panama (1945)
Paraguay (1945)
Peru (1945), 1946-late 1968,
  late 1975-77
Surinam (1975)
Trinidad and Tobago (1962)
Uruguay (1945)
Venezuela (1945)

Soviet Grouping

Albania (1955), 1955-60
Bulgaria (1955)
Byelorussian SSR (1945)
Czechoslovakia (1945), early
1948-77
East Germany (1973)
Hungary (1955)
Poland (1945)
Romania (1955)
Ukrainian SSR (1945)
USSR (1945)
Yugoslavia (1945), 1946-early
1948

Laos (1955), 1976-77
Mongolia (1961)
Vietnam (1977)

Algeria (1962), 1964-mid-
1965
Egypt (1945), 1964-mid-1972
Iraq (1945), 1959-60, 1966-
77
Libya (1955), 1974-77
South Yemen (1967)
Syria (1945), early 1966-
early 1974

Angola (1976)
Congo (1960), 1965-77
Ethiopia (1945), 1975-77
Ghana (1957), 1963-early 1966
Guinea (1958), 1959-61
Mali (1960), 1962-65
Somalia (1960), late 1969-mid-
1977

Cuba (1945), mid-1960-77
Guatemala (1945), early to
mid-1954

Nonaligned Grouping

Albania (1955), 1961-77
Austria (1955)
Czechoslovakia (1945), 1946-
early 1948
Finland (1955)
Malta (1964), mid-1971-early
1972
Sweden (1946)
Yugoslavia (1945), early 1948-77

Afghanistan (1946)
Bangladesh (1974)
Burma (1948)
Bhutan (1971)
China (1945), late 1971-77
Kampuchea (1955), 1955-early
1970, early 1975-77
India (1945)
Indonesia (1950)
Iran (1945), 1951-mid-1953
Laos (1955), 1955-58, mid-
1960-63, early 1974-mid-1975
Maldives (1965)
Nepal (1955)
Pakistan (1947), 1950-52, late
1962-77
Sri Lanka (1955)

Algeria (1962), 1962-63, mid-
1965-77

Egypt (1945), 1953-February
1958, September 1961-63,
mid-1972-75
Iraq (1945), mid- to end
1958, 1961-65
Israel (1949), 1949
Libya (1955), late 1969-73
Morocco (1956), 1960-74
Lebanon (1945), 1946-56, mid-
1958-77
Sudan (1956), 1956-75
Syria (1945), 1946-February
1958, September 1961-65,
early 1974-77
UAR (Egypt and Syria), Febru-
ary 1958-September 1961
Yemen (1947)

Benin (1960), 1975-77
Burundi (1962)
Cape Verde Islands (1975)
Comoros (1975)
Congo (1960), mid-1963-64
Djibouti (1977)
Equatorial Guinea (1968)
Ethiopia (1945), 1958-74
Ghana (1957), 1957-62
Guinea (1958), 1958, 1962-77
Guinea-Bissau (1974)
Kenya (1963)

Madagascar (1960), mid-1972-77
Mali (1960), 1960-61, 1966-77
Mauritania (1961), mid-1964-74
Mauritius (1968)
Mozambique (1975)
Nigeria (1960)
São Tomé and Principe (1975)
Seychelles (1976), mid- to end
1977
Somalia (1960), 1960-late 1969,
mid- to end 1977
Tanzania (1961)
Uganda (1962), 1962-70, 1973-
77
Zaire (1960), July-September
1960
Zambia (1964)
Zanzibar (1963-64), late 1963-
early 1964

Bolivia (1945), late 1969-mid-
1971
Brazil (1945), late 1960-early
1964
Chile (1945), late 1970-late 1973
Cuba (1945), 1959-mid-1960
Guatemala (1945), 1951-53
Guyana (1966)
Jamaica (1962), early 1972-77
Peru (1945), late 1968-late 1975

Note: The date in parentheses after each UN member indicates the date it joined the organization. If there are no dates following the date of joining, this indicates that it was a member of
that particular grouping for the entire period it belonged to the United Nations. On the other hand,
if there are dates, this indicates that it was only a member of that grouping for a particular period
of time. Under each grouping states are divided into subgroups by region: Europe, the United
States, and Canada; Asia and Australasia; Middle East, sub-Saharan Africa; and the Western Hemisphere (excluding the United States and Canada). The names of states in 1977 are used in this table.
Sri Lanka was Ceylon before 1972; Zaire—the Congo (Kinshasa) before 1971; Benin—Dahomey before 1974; and Kampuchea—Cambodia before 1975. The union of Egypt and Syria between February
1958 and September 1961 was called the United Arab Republic (UAR). Egypt retained the name UAR
until 1971. However, we have used the name Egypt after the dissolution of the union.

action between them, it is particularly inappropriate to view the existence or absence of a military treaty as the definitive indicator of alignment. According to Nyerere, the key determinant of nonalignment is "a refusal to be party to any permanent military or diplomatic identification with the great powers."[74] In other words, a state's attitude is as important as the existence of formal military ties.

A cardinal principle of nonaligned states is "noncommitment in the cold war between the United States and the Soviet Union."[75] While almost all Third World states have at times claimed to be nonaligned, many of them have, in fact, been members of the competitive polar coalitions. It is true that most of the states classified below as nonaligned are part of the Third World, but the two are not at all synonymous. In fact, a minority of Third World states have legitimate claim on the nonaligned label in the global security system. Only states that have built up relationships with both groupings, and which have refused to side with one coalition in international security politics, are labeled as nonaligned. Some states have important ties with both coalitions but nonetheless support only one on security issues. Iran, which has important trade links with the Soviet Union but is associated with the Western coalition in politico-security affairs, is a good example of such a state.

There have been some significant changes in the size and voting power of the different coalitions during the period 1946-77 when the United Nations' membership grew from 55 to 149,* although the alterations in voting power have not been as large as some might think. The Soviet grouping remained relatively stable in the range of 9 to 12 percent. The Western coalition at first constituted almost

---

*Some states are not members of the United Nations. The most important of these are Switzerland, Rhodesia, Taiwan, North Korea, and South Korea. On October 21, 1971, the General Assembly decided that the People's Republic of China was the legitimate representative of the Chinese poeple, displacing Taiwan from the General Assembly and the Security Council. Prior to the Communist victories in Indochina in 1975, what is now the single state of Vietnam was divided into the two states of North and South Vietnam, neither of which was in the United Nations. The new state of Vietnam was admitted in 1977. Indonesia withdrew from the United Nations in January 1965 but returned in September 1966. Syria and Egypt formed the United Arab Republic in February 1958, but in October 1961 Syria resumed its membership in the United Nations as a separate state. Egypt continued to be known as the UAR until September 1971. The Soviet Union effectively has three votes at the United Nations, since the Ukrainian SSR and Byelorussian SSR are members of the organization but, in fact, are subordinate republics within the USSR.

80 percent of the United Nations' membership but then declined, so that during the late 1960s and the 1970s this grouping fluctuated in the range of 55 to 60 percent. And the nonaligned grew from around 11 percent in 1946 to between 25 and 30 percent of the United Nations' membership in the last decade. An important change occurred in 1961 in that after that time the Western coalition ceased to be a "dominant" grouping (that is, it comprised less than two-thirds of the UN membership). According to the former Irish diplomat and UN official, Conor Cruise O'Brien, prior to the 1958 Lebanese conflict the United States almost always had its policies approved in the United Nations, whereas afterward the Western bloc became increasingly reliant upon the support of the Afro-Asian states in order to secure passage of a resolution. [76] O'Brien's observation confirms that there occurred a crucial decrease in Western voting power in the United Nations between the late 1950s and early 1960s.

The strength of the Western grouping has always rested on the inclusion in it of most of the states of both Western Europe and the Western Hemisphere. Of the West European states belonging to the United Nations, only Austria, Finland, Sweden, and Malta (June 1971 to March 1972)* were not members of the Western coalition for the entire period under examination. In the Western Hemisphere the only states outside the Western grouping were Cuba (since Fidel Castro's assumption of power in 1959), Brazil (during its phase of nonalignment from October 1960 until the military coup in March 1964), Chile (under the regime of Salvador Allende, November 1970 to September 1973), Jamaica (since the accession to power of the Manley regime in March 1972), Guatemala (under the regime of Jacobo Arbenz, 1951 to 1954), Peru (from the 1968 revolution until the replacement of the president in early 1975), and Bolivia (under the leftist regimes of Alfredo Ovando and Juan José Torres in 1969 to the military coup in August 1971). [77] Other states in Latin America, such as Mexico (especially under President Luis Echeverría, 1970 to 1976), Argentina (under the regime of Juan Perón, 1945 to 1955), and Panama (during its recent attempts to wrest control of the Panama Canal

---

*From June 1971 to March 1972 Malta followed a more nonaligned foreign policy than hitherto, increasing contacts with the Soviet Union, China, and such radical Arab states as Libya. The British governor-general and NATO's naval commander were dismissed by the Maltese government. Following British agreement to pay considerably more "rent" for the use of military facilities on the island, Malta once again permitted NATO to use these facilities. (See W. Howard Wriggins, "To the Highest Bidder," The Round Table 258 [April 1975]: 167-85.)

from the United States) have at times exhibited nonaligned behavior, but any claims to a nonaligned status that these or other Latin American states might have made have been belied by their mistrust of, and limited ties with, the communist states and their extremely intimate links with the United States in the security and economic spheres.[78] Despite numerous instances of strongly nationalist policies opposed by Washington, most Latin American states have remained under United States influence. Manifestations of nationalism have rarely challenged security interests regarded as vital by the United States, and when a Latin American state did implement policies regarded as intolerable by Washington—as did the Arbenz regime in Guatemala and that of Allende in Chile—the United States did not hesitate to promote, or even to engineer, its demise.

Numerous African states also have been members of the Western coalition. In many cases these states retained close ties with their former colonial metropoles. For example, Sierra Leone and Gambia remained dependent on Britain; Ivory Coast, Senegal, and most other former French territories were heavily influenced by France; and Belgium continued to play a crucial postindependence role in Zaire (formerly Congo-Kinshasa) and Rwanda. These and other African states, which had very close relations with their former colonial rulers, and hence were part of the Western grouping, were often criticized for their "neo-colonial" behavior by the nonaligned and pro-Soviet states. The Republic of South Africa, as well as Britain, exercised considerable leverage over Malawi, Botswana, Lesotho, and Swaziland after these states achieved their independence. The United States was also an influential power in the continent, particularly in connection with the policies of such states as Liberia and Zaire. The large number of African states included in the Western grouping reflects the continuing salience of the colonial tie in Africa.

Middle Eastern states that have supported the West in international security affairs include, in addition to Israel, Tunisia, Saudi Arabia, Qatar, Oman, Jordan, Bahrain, Kuwait, and the United Arab Emirates. It should be noted, however, that while these states have had very close ties to the West, and particularly to the United States and Britain, they nonetheless have strongly opposed Western support of Israel.

The 1973 oil embargo revealed that these "pro-Western" Arab countries were prepared to punish the West for its support of Israel and that they wished to precipitate "a major re-thinking of American interests and long-range policies by American decision makers toward all Arab national interests."[79] In general, however, these Arab states have evidenced a pro-Western foreign policy orientation, have opposed the Soviet Union's efforts to expand its influence in the area, and have grown increasingly dependent on the Western economies as markets for their oil and as sources of supply.[80] Four other Arab states that became more pro-Western in the 1970s were Morocco, Mauritania, Egypt, and the Sudan, the most remarkable change being in the case of Egypt, which was in the pro-Soviet grouping until mid-1972.[81]

With respect to Asia and Australasia, the UN member states that affiliated with the Western coalition included Thailand, the Philippines, Australia, New Zealand, Japan, Singapore, Malaysia, Laos (1958-59, 1964-74), Iran (except for a brief period in the early 1950s), and Pakistan (except during 1950 and 1951 and since the Friendship Treaty was signed with China in late 1962). Taiwan was also a member of the Western grouping, although it was expelled from the United Nations in 1971, and several Micronesian states are also classified as pro-Western. In general, the United States enjoyed more success in incorporating many Asian countries into its network of anticommunist alliances than was often the case elsewhere in the Third World. It should be noted that, while Pakistan remained in SEATO until November 1972, it is classified as nonaligned from the date of the treaty with China, since it became significantly dependent on Peking rather than Washington for military and political support and generally felt betrayed by its alliance partners in its conflicts with India. The U.S. arms embargo on Pakistan and India from 1965 to 1970 was not a policy designed to placate its "ally," and Pakistan moved closer to China to secure the support it needed.[82]

The Soviet grouping has consisted of the East European states with which Moscow is formally allied through the Warsaw Pact and a number of Third World states that have closely identified with the Soviet bloc's international security and political interests. In the Afro-Arab world, Egypt (1964 to July 1972), Syria (1966 to early 1974),* Iraq (1966 to 1977),[83] Libya (1974 to 1977),[84] Ethiopia (since 1975), South Yemen (1968 to 1977),[85] Somalia (1970 to June 1977),†

---

*According to one analyst, "Syrian actions in the Lebanese conflicts appear to have caught Moscow badly off guard and severely strained relations between the two countries." (Morris Rothenberg, "Recent Soviet Relations with Syria," Middle East Review 10 [Summer 1978]: 5.) In fact, Soviet-Syrian relations suffered initial deterioration in the aftermath of the 1973 war, when Syria accepted the U.S.-sponsored disengagement agreement. Although ties with Moscow remain extensive, this study regards Syria as outside the Soviet coalition as of 1974. (See also R. D. McLaurin, Mohammed Mughisuddin, and Abraham R. Wagner, Foreign Policy Decision Making in the Middle East [New York: Praeger, 1977], pp. 247, 264-65.)

†Somalia's relations with the Soviet Union deteriorated markedly in 1977 as a result of the latter's support for Marxist Ethiopia in its

Angola (since it achieved independence in late 1975), and Congo-Brazzaville (mid-1963 to 1977) have been recent members of the Soviet grouping.* Associated with the Soviet coalition for brief periods in the past were Algeria (during the latter years of Mohammed Ben Bella's rule, 1964 to July 1965), Ghana (during Kwame Nkrumah's last years of power, 1963 to February 1966), Guinea (1959 to 1961), and Mali (1962 to 1965).† In Asia, China (until 1961), Mongolia, Vietnam (which entered the United Nations in September 1977), and Laos (since mid-1975) were members of the Soviet grouping.[86] It should be noted that North Korea and North Vietnam were generally pro-Soviet but were never in the United Nations. Finally, Cuba (since 1960) and Guatemala (for a brief time in early 1954) are also included in the Soviet grouping.

Although the nonaligned grouping has grown considerably since the founding of the United Nations, it does not comprise as many states as might be expected, since many countries' assertions of nonalignment are belied by their behavior and relationships with foreign powers. Cuba and Iran may claim to be nonaligned, but most observers have no difficulty classifying them as members of the Soviet and Western groupings, respectively. Of the European states, Austria, Finland, Sweden, Malta (June 1971 to March 1972), and Yugoslavia (since 1948) have been nonaligned. Czechoslovakia was nonaligned until the Soviets moved to exert control in 1948; Albania has been, since 1961, a committed foe of the Soviet Union and was a close ally of Peking until 1977. Among the Asian states there have been a large number nonaligned, including Afghanistan, Burma, Bhutan, China (since 1961), Sri Lanka (since 1954), India, Indonesia,‡ Nepal, and

---

conflicts in the Horn of Africa. Soviet advisers and personnel were expelled and use of base facilities was denied. (J. Bowyer Bell, "Strategic Implications of the Soviet Presence in Somalia," Orbis 19 [Summer 1975]: 402-411.)

*The attachment of Angola, Congo-Brazzaville, and Ethiopia to the Soviet coalition is more fully explained in Chapter 4.

†In 1963 and 1964 Ghana became especially close to the Soviets and anti-Western in orientation; this ended with Nkrumah's ouster in February 1966. Guinea expressed strong affinities for the Soviet bloc's international policies from 1959 to 1961, after which time Guinea complained of Soviet interference in its affairs and, in fact, expelled the Soviet ambassador. From 1962 to 1965 the Keita government in Mali was very hostile to the West and sympathetic to the Soviet coalition; but this orientation was altered somewhat in 1966, and Mali reentered the franc zone in early 1967.

‡While Indonesia is classified as nonaligned for the entire period since its independence in 1949, it did have close ties to both China

the Maldives. Iran was nonaligned from 1951 until August 1953, when the government of Premier Mohammed Mossadegh, which had sought to exert control over American and British oil interests, was overthrown. Laos was nonaligned from 1954 until the rightist coup in 1958, and then again from mid-1960 until the entente between the neutralist and rightist forces in 1963. Pakistan sought to pursue a nonaligned foreign policy for a brief period in the early 1950s, and it has been nonaligned since it moved closer to China in late 1962. Kampuchea (formerly Cambodia) was nonaligned from 1954 until the rightist takeover in March 1970; since the Communist victory in April 1975, it has maintained very close relations with Peking and evinced hostility for almost every other country.

Of the Afro-Arab states the nonaligned grouping has had as members, some of the best known are Nigeria, Zambia, Tanzania, and the Sudan (until its move toward the West in late 1975). Algeria's inclusion in the nonaligned group since the overthrow of Mohammed Ben Bella could be challenged on the basis of its palpably radical foreign policy and its pro-Soviet positions on many issues. However, it remains closely tied to the West economically, and most observers report that it is not so much pro-Soviet as committed to its own ideological policies. [87] Among the Afro-Arab states that have been nonaligned are Egypt (1953 to 1963, July 1972 to December 1975), Iraq (July 1958 to December 1958, 1961 to 1965), Libya (September 1969 to early 1974), Lebanon (1946 to 1956, mid-1958 to 1977), Morocco (1960 to 1974), Mauritania (mid-1964 to 1974), Syria (1946 to 1957, October 1961 to February 1966, and since early 1974), Yemen, Burundi, Ethiopia (until early 1975), Equatorial Guinea, Kenya, Malagasy Republic (since the ouster of President Philibert Tsiranana in June 1972), Mauritius, Somalia (before the coup that brought Muhammad Siad Barre to power in October 1969, and then since the deterioration in relations with Moscow in mid-1977), and Uganda (except for a brief time in the early years of Idi Amin's rule). Many other Afro-Arab states, including some of those that have only recently attained independence, also have been nonaligned for part of the postwar

---

and the USSR in the early and mid-1960s. Following the creation of Malaysia in the fall of 1963 and its decision to withdraw from the United Nations, its strongest affiliation was with China, which was itself now nonaligned in the competitive struggle between the Soviet and Western groupings. For this reason it cannot be classified as pro-Soviet. With the ouster of Sukarno in October 1965, relations with the West improved considerably but its nonaligned status remained intact. (See Franklin Weinstein, Indonesian Foreign Policy and the Dilemma of Dependence [Ithaca, N.Y.: Cornell University Press, 1976].)

era; these are listed in Table 2. Examples are Benin (formerly Dahomey, since the October 1974 coup), Ghana (in the 1958 to 1962 period of Nkrumah's rule), Guinea (for a short time in 1958 just after independence and then since the deterioration in relations with Moscow in late 1961), Mali (1960 to 1961, 1966 to 1977), and Mozambique (since independence in June 1975).* Several new states are classified as nonaligned, although in some cases the paucity of information on their politics makes classification a hazardous process. Comoros, Cape Verde, São Tomé and Principe, Guinea-Bissau, Djibouti, and Seychelles (since the ouster of James Mancham in June 1977) have been placed in the nonaligned grouping for the brief period since their independence in the mid-1970s. Finally, Israel is classified as nonaligned from 1948 to 1950, since it was receiving aid from the Soviets and was not yet perceived as a Western ally, and Congo-Kinshasa (renamed Zaire in 1971) is also placed in the nonaligned grouping for the early months of its independence in 1960 when Patrice Lumumba was president.

Few Latin American or Caribbean states have adopted nonaligned foreign policies or sought to move outside the Western security system. Only Cuba (during Castro's early rule from 1959 to mid-1960), Brazil (1961 to the military coup of 1964), Chile (under President Salvador Allende), Guyana (since independence in 1966), Peru (1968 to early 1975), Bolivia (September 1969 to the military coup in August 1971), Guatemala (1951 to 1953), and Jamaica (since the accession to power of Manley in February 1972) have pursued foreign policies of nonalignment. [88] The policies of many of the states mentioned in this survey of the three groupings are described in the chapters on the regional organizations. The memberships of the three groupings for the period 1946 to 1977 can be found in Table 2.

THE UN PATTERNS OF
INTERVENTION AND SUCCESS

During the years 1946-77 there were 93 crises and wars, and they fall into eight of the categories of conflicts that were described

---

*FRELIMO, the governing party of independent Mozambique, has more extensive ties with Peking than Moscow during the independence struggle; in general, Mozambique has not followed the pro-Soviet course of states as have Angola and Ethiopia. It has much more extensive ties with Portugal than does Angola, and it collaborates closely with Tanzania on foreign policy issues. The author is grateful to Robert Henderson for information on Mozambique's foreign policy.

in the theory. These general categories of conflicts and the specific types of conflicts that are encompassed by them are outlined below. Also, the projections for organizational involvement and success in them are listed in the columns on the right-hand side of the page. In reviewing the hypotheses, it should be recalled that a dominant coalition is one constituting over two-thirds of organizational membership, and a subordinate one, less than one-third.

Type of Conflict	Intervention	Success
Intercoalition (victim a member of a dominant coalition)	Yes	No
Soviet versus Western, where the latter was the victim, 1946-60		
Intercoalition (victim a member of a nondominant coalition)	No	No
Soviet versus Western, where the former was the victim, 1946-77		
Soviet versus Western, where the latter was the victim, 1961-77		
Intracoalition (nonsubordinate)	No	No
Between members of Western grouping, 1946-77		
Intracoalition (subordinate, victim not trying to leave coalition)	No	No
Between members of Soviet grouping—did not involve attempt to prevent victim state from leaving coalition, 1946-70		
Intracoalition (subordinate, victim trying to join nonaligned)	Yes	No
Between members of Soviet grouping—involved attempt to prevent victim state from joining nonaligned grouping, 1946-77		
Aligned-nonaligned (victim nonaligned)	Yes	Yes
Western or Soviet versus nonaligned, where the latter was the victim, 1946-77		
Nonaligned-aligned (victim aligned)	No	No
Western or Soviet versus nonaligned, where the former was the victim, 1946-77		
Nonaligned-nonaligned	No	No
Between nonaligned, 1946-77		

Table 3 categorizes all the international crises and wars that occurred during the years 1946-77 according to type of conflict and

TABLE 3

UN Involvement in Crises and Wars, 1946–77

	No UN Debate	UN Debate	UN Recommendation/Judgment	Number of Conflicts
Hypothesis: No UN Intervention				
Intracoalition (subordinate—no attempt by victim to leave coalition)		Czechoslovakia–USSR et al., 1968 (W)(#80)		1
Number	0	1	0	1
Percent	0	100	0	—
Aligned-nonaligned (victim aligned)	Pakistan–Afghanistan, 1955 (C)(#15) Pakistan–Afghanistan, 1961 (W)(#43) Netherlands–Indonesia, 1962 (C)(#46) Ivory Coast and Ghana–Guinea, 1966 (C)(#75) Portuguese Guinean civil strife (with Guinean and Senegalese intervention), 1968–74 (W)(#83) Angolan (Portugal) civil strife (with Zambian and Zairean intervention), 1968–74 (W)(#83) Mozambique (Portugal) civil strife (with Tanzanian and Zambian intervention), 1968–74 (W)(#84) Uganda–Tanzania, 1972 (W)(#96) South Vietnam–China, 1974 (W)(#103) Moroccan civil strife (with Algerian intervention), 1976–77 (W)(#110) Mauritanian civil strife (with Algerian and Moroccan intervention), 1976–77 (W)(#111) Ethiopian civil strife (with Somalian and Cuban intervention), 1976–77 (W)(#113) Vietnam–Cambodia, 1977 (W)(#116)	Lebanese civil strife (with threat of UAR and U.S. intervention), 1958 (C)(#28) Kuwait–Iraq, 1961 (C)(#40) Portugal–India, 1961 (W)(#45) Malaysia–Indonesia, 1963–65 (W)(#59)	North Yemeni civil strife (with UAR and Saudi intervention), 1962–67 (W)(#49) Israel–Egypt and Syria, 1973 (W)*(#101)	
Number	13	4	2	19
Percent	68	21	11	—
Intercoalition (victim a member of a nondominant coalition)	Laotian civil strife (with North Vietnamese intervention), 1960–61 (W)(#37) West Germany–East Germany (Berlin), 1961 (C)(#41) Upper Volta–Ghana, 1963 (W)(#50)	Guatemala–Nicaragua and Honduras, 1954 (W)(#11) South Vietnamese civil strife (with North Vietnamese, U.S. et al. intervention),	Egypt, Syria, and Jordan–Israel, 1967 (W)*(#78) Angolan civil strife (with Cuban, Zairean, and South African intervention),	

56

Intracoalition (nonsubordinate)	Laotian civil strife (with North Vietnamese and Thai intervention), 1964–75 (W)(#66) South Yemeni civil strife (with Saudi and North Yemeni intervention), 1969–72 (W)(#89) Jordanian civil strife (with threat of Iraqi and actual Syrian intervention), 1970 (W)(#90) Cambodian civil strife (with North Vietnamese, South Vietnamese and U.S. intervention), 1970–75 (W)(#92) Omani civil strife (with Iranian, Jordanian, and British intervention), 1970–76 (W)(#93) Kuwait–Iraq, 1973 (W)(#99) Zaire–Angola, 1977 (W)(#114) Libya–Egypt, 1977 (W)(#115)	vention), 1960–75 (W)(#38) Cuba–United States, 1961 (W)(#39) Cuba–United States, 1962 (C)(#47) Iraq–Iran, 1972–75 (W)(#98)	1975–77 (W)(#108)	
Number	11	5	2	18
Percent	61	28	11	—
Nonaligned-nonaligned	Costa Rica–Nicaragua, 1948 (W)(#5) Haiti–Dominican Republic, 1949 (C)(#7) United Kingdom–Saudi Arabia, 1952 (C)(#9) Costa Rica–Nicaragua, 1954 (C)(#12) Costa Rica–Nicaragua, 1955 (W)(#14) Saudi Arabia–United Kingdom, 1955 (W)(#16) Algerian (France) civil strife (with Moroccan and Tunisian intervention), 1956–62 (W)(#20) Spain–Morocco, 1957 (W)(#24) Honduras–Nicaragua, 1957 (W)(#21) Dahomey–Niger, 1963–64 (C)(#56) Gabon–France, 1964 (W)(#62) Honduras–El Salvador, 1969 (W)(#86) United Kingdom–Guatemala, 1975 (C)(#106)	Tunisia–France, February 1958 (C)(#26) Tunisia–France, May 1958 (C)(#27) Dominican Republic–United States, 1961 (C)(#44) Haiti–Dominican Republic, 1963 (C)(#51) Dominican civil strife (with U.S. intervention), 1965 (W)(#67) Cypriot civil strife (with threat of Turkish intervention), 1967 (C)(#79)	Tunisia–France, 1961 (W)(#42) Cypriot civil strife (threat of Turkish and Greek intervention), 1963–64 (C)*(#57) Cypriot civil strife (Turkish intervention), 1974 (W)(#104) Spain–Morocco, 1975 (W)(#105)	
Number	13	6	4	23
Percent	57	26	17	—
	India–China, 1962 (W)(#48) Algeria–Morocco, 1963 (W)(#54) Ethiopia–Somalia, 1964 (W)(#60) India–Pakistan, April–May 1965 (W)(#69) Rhodesian civil strife (Zambian and Mozambican intervention), 1973–77 (W)(#102)	Sudan–Egypt, 1958 (W)(#25)	India–Pakistan, August–September, 1965 (W)*(#70) Pakistani civil strife (Indian intervention), 1971 (W)(#94) East Timor civil strife (Indonesian intervention), 1975–76 (W)(#107)	

(continued)

TABLE 3 (continued)

	No UN Debate	UN Debate	UN Recommendation/Judgment	Number of Conflicts
	Lebanese civil strife (with Syrian intervention), 1975–76 (W)(#109)		Mozambique–Rhodesia, 1976–77 (W)(#112)	
Number	6	1	4	11
Percent	55	9	36	—
Hypothesis: UN Intervention, but Not Success				
Intracoalition (subordinate—attempt by victim to become nonaligned)			Hungary–USSR, 1956 (W)(#19)	
Number	0	0	1	1
Percent	0	0	100	—
Intercoalition (victim a member of a dominant coalition)	United States et al.–USSR (Berlin), 1948 (C)(#4) Nationalist China–Communist China, 1954–55 (W)(#13) Nationalist China–Communist China, 1958 (C)(#29)	Laotian civil strife (North Vietnamese intervention), 1959 (W)(#33)	Greek civil strife (Albanian, Bulgarian, and Yugoslav intervention, 1946–49 (W)(#1) South Korea–North Korea, 1950–53 (W)(#8)	
Number	3	1	2	6
Percent	50	17	33	—
Hypothesis: UN Intervention and Success				
Aligned-nonaligned (victim nonaligned)	Syria–Iraq, 1949 (C)(#6) Burma–Communist China, 1956 (W)(#17) India–Communist China, 1958 (W)(#30) Laotian civil strife (North Vietnamese intervention), 1963 (W)(#53) Chadian civil strife (French intervention), 1968–77 (W)(#81) China–USSR, 1969 (W)(#85) North Yemen–South Yemen, 1972 (W)(#97)	Syria–Turkey, 1957 (C)(#23)	Israel–Arab States, 1948 (W)(#3) India–Pakistan, 1947–48 (W)(#2) Egypt–Israel, United Kingdom, France, 1956 (W)*(#18) Congo–Belgium, 1960 (W)*(#35) Congo civil strife (threat of Western and/or communist intervention, 1960–62 (C)*(#36) Guinea–Portugal, 1970 (W)*(#91)	
Number	7	1	6	14
Percent	50	7	43	—

Note: C = crisis; W = war; * = success. The number after each conflict identifies the location of the conflict description in the Appendix.

extent of UN involvement. The classification of the conflicts in Table 3 reveals that the United Nations has intervened most frequently in those types of disputes that the theory posited would be most amenable to organizational involvement. However, the relationships are certainly not as strong as anticipated. As will be analyzed below, a number of the conflicts—which, contrary to expectations, elicited UN intervention—could possibly be recategorized under those types of conflicts in which intervention was hypothesized. And this would make the figures accord more closely with the theory's projections.

Of the five types of conflicts in which UN intervention was not posited, the prediction of no intervention held true for only one, namely, intracoalition conflicts within a subordinate grouping that did not involve an attempt by the victim state to leave the coalition. There was, however, only one conflict of this type. In aligned–nonaligned conflicts where the victim was aligned, the United Nations intervened in 11 percent of the cases (2 out of 19); in intercoalition conflicts where the victim was affiliated with a nondominant grouping, intervention was recorded in 11 percent (2 out of 18); in conflicts between members of a nonsubordinate coalition, intervention occurred in 17 percent of the cases (4 out of 23); and of nonaligned–nonaligned conflicts, the United Nations became substantively involved in 36 percent (4 out of 11). Clearly, it is the last category of these five that is most strongly at variance with the theory's predictions, and several arguments will be adduced below to explain this result. In the other four types of conflicts in which it was expected the United Nations would not intervene, the data provide significant support for the hypotheses.

With respect to two types of conflicts it was hypothesized that the United Nations would intervene but not be successful. This prediction did hold for all intracoalition conflicts within a subordinate grouping where the victim state was attempting to achieve a position of nonalignment, but there was only a single conflict of this type. In intercoalition conflicts where the victim state was a member of a dominant coalition, the organization intervened in 33 percent (2 out of 6)—considerably below what was expected. But, as anticipated, it was not successful in bringing about a short-term cessation of violence in these two conflicts. The only type of conflict in which both intervention and success were expected was that between aligned and nonaligned parties where the victim was nonaligned. Of the 14 conflicts falling into this category, 43 percent (6 out of 13) elicited UN intervention, and the United Nations was successful in 4 of these 6. As will be noted later, several wars and crises placed in other categories in which the United Nations did intervene and was successful could very easily be placed in this category, and this fact does strengthen the hypothesis.

The only conflict between members of a subordinate grouping where the victim state was not trying to leave the coalition was the invasion of Czechoslovakia by the Soviet Union and other Warsaw Pact states in 1968. As is well known, the invading states feared that the long-term effect of Czechoslovakia's internal policy of liberalization and its foreign policy of normalizing relations with Western states would be its departure from the alliance. The Czech government did, in fact, seek a UN intervention against the invasion of the Warsaw Pact states, but the involvement of the United Nations never went beyond a Security Council debate where a resolution calling for the withdrawal of the invading states was vetoed by the Soviet Union. The issue was never referred to the General Assembly, since the Western grouping did not have the voting power to secure passage of a resolution and did not perceive that anything could be gained from a resolution in any case. There was a very strong tendency on the part of the Third World nonaligned countries to view such a conflict as irrelevant to their own independence and security.

In only 2 of the 19 conflicts between aligned and nonaligned parties where the aligned was the victim did the United Nations intervene, although it did debate an additional 4. For the most part the reasoning behind the expectation of no organizational intervention was substantiated by the diplomacy surrounding the conflicts. The allies of the victim state often sought to mediate the conflicts and were generally very reluctant to criticize the aggressing nonaligned parties. Also, the members of the coalition to which the victim did not belong almost invariably backed the aggressor.

There were 13 such crises and wars which were never even discussed by the United Nations. During the two 1955 and 1961 conflicts between Pakistan and Afghanistan, the United Kingdom and the United States sought to promote peaceful settlements of the disputes so as to discourage increasing reliance by Afghanistan on the Soviet Union. During the Dutch-Indonesian crisis of 1962 over the Indonesian claim to West Irian, the U.S. diplomat, Ambassador Ellsworth Bunker, negotiated a settlement, and only after this accord and the termination of the crisis did the parties bring the issue to the United Nations for its approval of a temporary UN political-military authority to rule the territory between the time of the Dutch departure and the Indonesians' assumption of control. In this case the United States was particularly concerned that continued Dutch control over West Irian could cause the increasing alienation of Indonesia from the Western grouping, and hence it urged the Dutch to hand over the territory.* In the Guinean

---

*The allies of the Netherlands, contrary to the theory's projections, failed to support it. This was because Dutch control of West

threat to Ghana and the Ivory Coast in 1966, none of the Western powers explicitly condemned Guinea, although France made it clear that an invasion would provoke its intervention.

Three other conflicts that were never brought to the United Nations involved the provision by several African states of base camps to opponents of Portuguese rule in Angola, Mozambique, and Portuguese Guinea. The Western powers obviously had no interest in being seen as defenders of Portuguese colonialism and, in fact, exerted diplomatic pressure on Lisbon to give up its colonial legacy since it was sullying the Western image in Africa. The backing by the radical Tanzanian regime of an attempt by Ugandan exiles in 1972 to overthrow the "reactionary" Amin regime occurred at a time when doubts about Amin were already beginning to arise in the West. This reinforced the predilection of the Western powers not to criticize and alienate the nonaligned Tanzanian government of President Nyerere. The Western nations also shied away from condemnations of the post-1975 Algerian-backed interventions in Morocco and Mauritania on behalf of Western Saharan nationalists, despite the fact that they had diplomatically backed the Madrid Accord of November 1975—and that France was providing material assistance and piloted aircraft to the besieged countries. The Western states wished to refrain from pushing Algeria into stronger ties with the Soviets. In the case of Somalia's attempt to wrest control of the Ogaden region of Ethiopia from the Marxist regime in Addis Ababa in 1977, the Soviets and Cubans certainly provided extensive assistance to their beleaguered new ally, but they did not seek to secure an international condemnation of Somalia. The Soviet coalition consciously sought to maintain amicable relations with Somalia and to prevent greater collaboration between the latter and the West.

Two recent conflicts of this type in Southeast Asia were the Chinese expulsion of the South Vietnamese from the Paracel Islands in 1974 and the Cambodian-provoked war between Kampuchea (Cambodia) and Vietnam in 1977. In the former case, both the United States and the USSR refrained from condemning the Chinese takeover of the disputed islands. Moreover, they opposed a South Vietnamese request for a Security Council debate of the issue. In the case of the Kampuchean provocations the Soviets sought to keep the door open to a rapprochement with the pro-Peking government in Phnom Penh, although the latter's antipathy for Soviet-allied Vietnam made this unlikely.

Irian was viewed as an instance of "standing aggression" by most Third World countries. The Western states generally pursued similar policies in other cases of attacks against colonial regimes by neighboring states—some of which are analyzed below.

In all four conflicts that elicited solely UN debate (the Lebanese crisis of 1958, the Iraqi threat to Kuwait in 1961, the Indian takeover of the Portuguese enclaves in the subcontinent in 1961, and the Indonesian military action against Malaysia between 1963 and 1975), the Soviet Union vetoed Western-supported resolutions calling for a cessation of the threats of acts of aggression by the nonaligned states. In the case of the Lebanese crisis, a resolution was passed in June 1958 creating an observer force that would report on any infiltration from the United Arab Republic (UAR) into Lebanon and deter such infiltration; but the resolution, which was supported by the UAR, did not judge that such infiltration had actually taken place nor recommend that the UAR cease such a policy. In a situation where the leaders of the two major world coalitions were supporting different parties, the Security Council could only pass such a neutral resolution.

The two cases of aggression by nonaligned states against aligned ones in which, contrary to our expectations, the United Nations intervened, were the Yemeni war of 1962-67 and the Egyptian-Syrian attack against Israel in October 1973. When examined in detail, the management of neither dispute undermines the reasoning in the theory regarding this type of conflict. Following the outbreak of the Yemeni civil war in 1962 and the dispatch of large-scale Egyptian and then small-scale Saudi Arabian assistance to the republicans and royalists, the United States feared that the conflict's continuation would drive the Yemeni republican government and its Egyptian ally into seeking greater assistance from, and closer ties with, the Soviet Union. Therefore, it dispatched Ambassador Ellsworth Bunker to the Middle East in the spring of 1963 to try to bring about a peaceful settlement. He was able to secure a disengagement agreement that included a stipulation that a UN observer force be created to oversee the carrying-out of the accord. The only time that the conflict reached the United Nations was in June 1963, when the observer force was set up and withdrawal was requested. However, the disengagement agreement did not end the fighting or lead to the withdrawal of the large UAR and small Saudi contingents. In 1964 the observer force was finally withdrawn, and the issue was never debated in the United Nations again. In the case of the 1973 Middle East war, the Soviets vetoed cease-fire resolutions during the first week while the Egyptians and Syrians were scoring gains on the battlefield. Only when the tide of battle changed and Israel began to achieve gains at the expense of its Arab opponents did the Security Council call for a cease-fire. By then the conflict had taken on the character of an aggression by a Western-aligned state against nonaligned ones. The Soviets were then, of course, anxious to protect the Arabs; and the Western countries, particularly the United States, wanted to prevent the alienation of (and, in fact, to befriend) the Arab powers—especially the Anwar Sadat regime. [89]

A third group of conflicts in which UN intervention was not hypothesized were <u>intercoalition disputes in which the victim did not belong to a dominant grouping.</u> [90] The Soviet grouping never came close to constituting a voting majority in the United Nations, and the Western coalition fell below the two-thirds mark after 1960. Hence, all conflicts between members of these groupings in which a Soviet member was the victim, or during the years 1961-77 in which a Western member was the victim, were not expected to evoke UN demands for a cessation of hostilities. In fact, 11 of the 18 such crises and wars were never brought to the United Nations; 5 elicited solely a debate; and only 2 led to calls for cease-fires.

Of the 16 conflicts in this category that did not lead to organizational intervention, 4 concerned the Indochina imbroglio from the early 1960s through 1975; 6 were between Western and Soviet allies in the Middle East after 1968—with Iraq involved in 4 of them and South Yemen and Jordan in 2 each; 3 involved U.S. or U.S.-backed threats or interventions against Soviet allies in the Western Hemisphere—namely, Guatemala in 1954 and Cuba in both 1961 and 1962; only 1 occurred in sub-Saharan Africa—Zaire-Angola in 1977; and 1 in Europe—the Berlin crisis of 1961. Regarding the largest and most drawn-out of these intercoalition conflicts—the war in South Vietnam —Bloomfield has identified the major factors that impeded the involvement of the United Nations. These were the inability of either the Western of Communist states to secure the support of two-thirds of the UN membership, the lack of membership of key participants or interested parties in the United Nations (Communist China and North and South Vietnam), and a desire on the part of the United States for "unhampered unilateral policy freedom" with respect to Communist threats. [91] Haas has underlined the importance of this last reason for the impotence of the United Nations in the Vietnam War and in other interbloc conflicts: "An America determined to realize its vision abroad, in a Cold War setting, will not be enmeshed [in the United Nations], as proved by Vietnam above all else. Direct confrontations between the big powers will be solved directly by them, not by the UN."[92] During the 1940s and 1950s, when the Western grouping constituted a dominant coalition within the United Nations, the United States and other Western powers showed some willingness, as will be indicated below, to seek UN legitimization of their policies, although even then it was not as great as anticipated.

The two intercoalition conflicts in the 1960s and 1970s that did evoke resolutions requesting an end to hostilities were the Middle East war of 1967 and the Angolan civil war. A number of factors peculiar to these conflicts explain the UN involvement in each of them. In the case of the Israeli invasion of Egypt, Syria, and Jordan, the Arab side has been classified as Soviet-aligned since both Egypt and Syria are viewed as Soviet allies at this time. However, this categorization is certainly open to question given the fact that Jordan was pro-Western and many of the other Arab states that identified with the three "front-line" states had varied cold war orientations. Also, the Egyptian and Syrian ties to the Soviets were not as strong as those of, for example, North Vietnam, Cuba, or Angola. Western, and more particularly U.S., concern about how the Israeli action would affect Arab relations with the West unquestionably influenced its decision to back a cease-fire and curtail the Israeli advance. At the same time, the fact that the United States did not force a complete withdrawal on the Israelis—as had occurred in 1956—probably resulted in part from the pro-Soviet orientation of the major protagonists as well as their provocative behavior prior to the outbreak of the war.

The Angolan civil war, in which Cuban, Zairean, and South African troops became involved, only evoked UN action in connection with the specific issue of South African assistance to the anti-MPLA forces. In the spring of 1976 Kenya, on behalf of a number of African states, successfully sought a Security Council request for a South African withdrawal. And, in fact, South Africa did withdraw its troops after it had secured certain assurances pertaining to border security and protection of a hydroelectric project in Angola from the Luanda government. The Cuban and Zairean activities were completely ignored since it was quite obvious that a consensus could not be achieved on the cold war dimension of the conflict. Only insofar as the dispute involved the "racial" issue of South Africa's attempts to control its surrounding environment could consensus and accord be attained.

Of the 23 intracoalition conflicts between members of a nonsubordinate grouping, 19 of them, as hypothesized, did not elicit substantive UN intervention. These were all between members of the Western grouping, and most of them were settled either within formal organizations of the alliance system or by informal diplomatic negotiations. In most instances there were very deliberate attempts by the allies of the conflicting parties to keep the conflicts out of the United Nations.

Of the 19 intracoalition conflicts in which the United Nations did not act to prevent or terminate an aggression, 9 were between OAS members,* all except two of these were largely managed within the

---

*On the more frequent use of the OAS, Inis Claude has written: "In the case of the OAS, its use has been motivated in some instances less by the ideal of preventing the overburdening of the United Nations, or capitalizing upon the effectiveness of regional machinery, than by the insistence of the United States upon handling disputes in a forum which it dominates with less difficulty than the world organization."

OAS.* The United Nations did discuss the Dominican crisis of 1965 and the U.S. dispatch of 20,000 troops to that country, and it also passed several resolutions calling for a cease-fire between the conflicting Dominican Republic factions. At the same time, the United Nations never called for a withdrawal of the U.S. troops. It definitely played a secondary role to the OAS in the management of the conflict; although the UN observer, José Mayobre, did have some influence in the negotiations leading to its resolution. With respect to the other 10 intracoalition conflicts in which the United Nations did not intervene, the reluctance of the members of the Western grouping to have differences between them aired in the global forum was clearly manifested and explains the lack of a UN role in these cases. In the crises between Dahomey and Niger in 1963, Dahomey voiced an interest in taking the conflict to the United Nations, but was urged not to follow this course and to settle it within the French West African grouping by both France and other French West African states. [93] In the two Tunisian-French crises of February and May 1958, Tunisia initially secured Security Council debates of the conflicts, but was later persuaded by the United States and the United Kingdom to withdraw its complaints from the United Nations so that they could assist the parties in achieving a peaceful settlement of their differences. [94] During the Cypriot crisis of 1967, when there was a threat of Turkish and Greek intervention, Cyprus secured a Security Council debate of the conflict; and, following the inability of the council members to achieve a consensus, its members informally agreed to urge Secretary-General U Thant to mediate the dispute. However, the major mediator in the conflict was not U Thant but a U.S. official, Cyrus Vance, and his efforts were supplemented by those of two other Western statesmen, Manlio Brasio, secretary-general of NATO, and Lester Pearson, prime minister of Canada. Throughout such conflicts the Western states were obviously anxious not only that the differences between coalition members be resolved but also that they be kept out of the United Nations, where Soviet backing of one of the parties might encourage it to leave the Western coalition.

(Swords into Plowshares, 3d ed., [New York: Random House, 1964], p. 114. See also, Claude: "The O.A.S., the U.N. and the United States," International Conciliation, vol. 547 [March 1964].) On the general preference of alliance members for managing their conflicts within an alliance organization rather than the United Nations, see Yashpal Tandon ("The Peaceful Settlement of International Disputes," International Relations 2 [April 1964]: 555-76).

*These were the crises between Nicaragua and Costa Rica in 1954 and the American threat to intervene in the Dominican Republic in 1961.

The four intracoalition conflicts in which the United Nations did intervene were the Tunisian-French war of 1961, the Cypriot crisis of 1963-64, the Turkish invasion of Cyprus in 1974, and the very unusual Spanish-Moroccan war of 1975. To a significant extent the United Nations interventions in the two former conflicts can be explained by the fact that they resembled conflicts between nonaligned and aligned states where the victim was nonaligned. In fact, Tunisia and Cyprus accepted invitations to the Belgrade Nonaligned Conference of 1961 and the Cairo Conference of Nonaligned States (1964), in part because of their positions in these conflicts; undoubtedly our judgment that Tunisia and Cyprus were members of the Western grouping could be challenged. In the Tunisian-French conflict, which concerned the French use of military force to prevent its expulsion from the naval base at Bizerte, most of France's Western allies supported the UN resolutions calling for its withdrawal since they were concerned about alienating Tunisia and other Third World states from the Western coalition. While France did at first refuse to accede to UN demands while the organization was seized with issue, it did agree to leave the base several months thereafter.

The Cypriot crisis posed a very serious threat of Turkish and Greek intervention on behalf of the Turkish and Greek Cypriot communities during the last two weeks of December 1963, and the crisis continued at a lower level during the first several months of 1964. When fighting broke out between the Turkish and Greek Cypriot communities in December 1963, the British were able to negotiate a cessation of hostilities, and their troops, which were stationed at bases in Cyprus, policed the cease-fire. After the accord there was still a possibility of renewed fighting, and the Greek Cypriot government called upon the United Nations to consider the conflict. While the Security Council was unable to pass a resolution on the substantive merits of the conflicting positions, there soon developed demands, particularly from the Greek Cypriots, for UN involvement in the policing and settlement of the conflict. During January and February 1964, while fears of renewed fighting persisted, there were continual negotiations both within and outside of the United Nations concerning methods of preventing a war and achieving a long-term settlement. The NATO states wanted the cease-fire to be policed by a NATO force. The Greek Cypriot government, however, realizing that the Western powers would not support its position and perceiving support for its views from the nonaligned states and the Soviet Union, called for the creation of a UN force to police the cease-fire and for the settlement of the substantive issues within a UN context. After lengthy negotiations the Western states acquiesced to the Greek Cypriot demands since they did not want to alienate a large body of the UN membership. On this point Alastair Buchan has written that the management of the

Cypriot conflict "proved beyond doubt that a nonaligned country such as Cyprus, still less an Afro-Asian one, would never accept action by the NATO alliance when it has the whole political resources of the nonaligned world at its disposal in the General Assembly. Some political leaders in NATO despise the UN, but few are prepared to contemplate Western action that risks an adverse resolution in the Assembly. "[95]

The 1974 Turkish invasion of Cyprus was provoked by a military coup in the latter state that saw the overthrow of President Makarios by a faction committed to union ("enosis") of Cyprus with Greece under the leadership of Nicos Sampson, who became the new president. Makarios had been, at least outwardly, committed to an independent and militarily nonaligned Cyprus and had thus succeeded in garnering considerable diplomatic support from the Soviet bloc and the nonaligned countries. His policy of tolerating the separation of the Greek and Turkish communities by the UN force had led the NATO countries to discourage a Turkish intervention. Once a new government came to power committed to union with Greece, both the diplomatic support for the Cypriot government and the external restraints on Turkey began to crumble. The result was Turkey's invasion and occupation of approximately 40 percent of the island. The NATO states felt compelled to back Security Council resolutions calling for a cease-fire and withdrawal, out of deference to Greece; but, given preinvasion events on Cyprus and the critical international reaction to the Cypriot coup and the military Greek government's support of it, they did not feel a need or justification to force a Turkish withdrawal. Likewise, the Soviets and nonaligned supported the resolution in the hope of possibly restoring the status quo ante, but they had reservations about the Sampson government (which fell soon after the invasion) and also lacked leverage over Turkey. Turkey's ability to expand its control even after the initial cease-fire and its refusal to comply with Security Council requests for a withdrawal were due to the unique background of this intracoalition conflict.

The last of the four intracoalition conflicts in which the United Nations called for a withdrawal of forces was the 1975 Moroccan "invasion" of the Spanish Sahara, launched in order to encourage Spain's dividing the territory between it and Mauritania. The Security Council resolution was specifically aimed at the march of several hundred thousand Moroccan civilians into the territory, and in this it was successful. However, unpublicized at the time was the entry of regular Moroccan forces into other areas of the territory in order to fight the forces of the leftist Spanish Saharan independence movement. The Western powers agreed to support the demand of their Spanish ally (as well as the Communist states and most nonaligned countries) that the Spanish government not be militarily forced to cede the territory.

While they felt compelled to do so because Spain was a Western ally, it seems that they concurrently encouraged Spanish acceptance of the demands of the moderate pro-Western regimes in Morocco and Mauritania. And in less than two weeks after the Moroccan withdrawal, Spain did cede the territory to the two African countries. It was definitely unusual for an intracoalition military encounter to be brought to the United Nations, but the fact that the substantive issues were resolved with considerable behind-the-scenes influence of the coalition leaders is congruent with the patterns of settlement evidenced in most intracoalition disputes.

Of all the hypotheses positing that there would be no UN intervention in particular types of conflicts, that pertaining to conflicts between nonaligned states appears most susceptible to challenge after an examination of the data concerning the frequency of organizational intervention. Of the 11 crises and wars in which both parties were nonaligned, the United Nations, contrary to the theory's projections, intervened in 4 (36 percent) of them. That this type of conflict has often been managed in a manner inconsistent with the theory can largely be attributed to the fact that many of these cases either occurred in the complex quasi-tripolar Asian setting after 1962 or involved the very peculiar "nonaligned" state of Rhodesia.

Of the seven conflicts in which the United Nations did not call for cessations of the use of force, four—the Sudanese-Egyptian war of 1958, the Algerian-Moroccan war of 1963, the Somali-Ethiopian war of 1964, and, to a lesser extent, Syrian intervention in Lebanon in 1975-76—reflected the predictions of the theory. The Sudanese did succeed in securing a UN debate before the Egyptian decision to withdraw from the former's territory, but during the debate it was clear that the United States and USSR would not adopt partisan positions. Both major groupings wished to avoid alienating the disputants and encouraging them to seek greater collaboration with the opposing grouping. In the Moroccan-Algerian war of 1963 Morocco sought the support of France and the United States and asked them to back UN involvement in the conflict, but both Western states refused these requests in order not to alienate Algeria.[96] The Soviet Union and China also followed comparable courses in this conflict in that they never condemned Morocco for its attack.[97] All of these powers urged that the parties try to settle the conflict within an African context. In the case of the 1964 war between Somalia and Ethiopia, Somalia called on the Soviet Union to support its position in a UN Security Council debate on the issue, but the Soviet Union rejected its request and urged that Somalia settle its differences with its neighbor in collaboration with other African states. In fact, the Soviet Union sent a high-ranking diplomat, Yakov Malik, to both countries during the war to persuade them to end their conflict.[98]

The politics surrounding the Syrian intervention in Lebanon in 1975-76 were extremely complex. The fighting in Lebanon was between rightist Christians and an alliance of leftist Moslems and Palestinians, and throughout the dispute the Lebanese government engaged in periodic but unsuccessful attempts to promote a national reconciliation. Syria initially became involved in late 1975 and January 1976, when it allowed Palestinian forces under its control to assist the leftist side. However, its large-scale intervention did not begin until March, when first the Palestinians under its control and then its own forces intervened to prevent a leftist victory and to promote the formation of a broad-based government. During this struggle the United States certainly did not want to alienate Syria by harsh criticism, but, more important, in the latter phase of Syrian involvement Washington favored its aims and provided "more than tacit support for Syria."[99] The Soviets, on the other hand, were opposed to later Syrian policy and finally in the fall of 1976, did criticize it, although not in very strong terms.[100] In many ways, the Syrian intervention was treated and evolved more as an aggression by a nonaligned party against an aligned one rather than one between nonaligned states.

The conflicts between "nonaligned" states in Asia in which the United Nations did not become involved were the Sino-Indian war of 1962 and the Indo-Pakistani war of April-May 1965. In the former case, which occurred in the incipient period of tripolarity in Asia, the United States provided diplomatic support and military aid to India while the USSR and most nonaligned countries did not diplomatically commit themselves. Given this situation and the fact that Peking was not represented in the organization, India judged it wiser not to take the issue to the United Nations. In a sense, this was an intercoalition conflict in which China was one pole and India was aligned with another —namely, the United States. In the other conflict, Pakistan conducted a limited military action into India's Rann of Kutch in April-May 1965. Pakistan at this time was pursuing a nonaligned course in the tripolar Asian theater. Both the Soviet Union and the Western powers were very concerned that Pakistan's conflict with India would drive it into closer collaboration with China (which was backing Pakistan), and they sought to promote a settlement of the conflict rather than adopt partisan positions. The United Kingdom was most active as a mediator and it secured acceptance of a cease-fire and withdrawal of forces. Within the tripolar Asian setting other states tended to view the conflict as an aggression by a nonaligned state against an aligned one rather than a war between nonaligned parties.

The last conflict between nonaligned states in which the United Nations never became involved was the entry of black Rhodesian nationalists from Zambian and Mozambican base camps into Rhodesia between 1973 and 1977. In this case almost all UN members supported the assistance provided by Rhodesia's neighbors to the rebels—or at least were not prepared to oppose it for fear of alienating the African states. There was a general consensus on the desirability of promoting the downfall of white-dominated regimes in southern Africa; therefore very few UN members favored organizational action to impede such armed interventions.

Of the four conflicts between nonaligned states in the bipolar cold war system in which the United Nations did intervene, two involved India and Pakistan; one, Rhodesia's armed attack into Mozambique; and a final one, Indonesia's absorption of East Timor. In the large-scale Indo-Pakistani War of August-September 1965, which began with raids by Pakistani tribesmen into Kashmir, the Security Council called for a cease-fire and withdrawal on several occasions, and diplomatic and economic pressure by the Western powers and the Soviet Union did have some influence in bringing about compliance. Both cold war blocs were supporting India as a counterweight to China in Asia—in a sense, India could be conceived as bialigned in the Asian setting—but they were also very concerned that "nonaligned" Pakistan might become more closely tied to China because of its dispute with India. The superpowers gave de facto backing to India by supporting the territorial status quo, but they did try to behave outwardly as impartial mediators concerned with the preservation of peace. An important reason for their pursuing an end to the war through the United Nations was that Peking was not then represented and had very few allies in the organization.

In late 1971 another major war occurred between India and Pakistan. It began with India's provision of base camps and weapons to Bengali separatists, and this was followed, first, by Pakistani attacks against these bases and then by a large-scale military intervention by the Indian army. By this time the international environment had undergone some significant changes from what it had been in the mid-1960s. The USSR was strongly backing India as a counterweight to China, and its ties to Pakistan had seriously deteriorated. China had emerged as the major ally of Pakistan against India. However, the West, and the United States in particular, was adopting a somewhat impartial and aloof stance toward this competition in South Asia between the two Communist powers and their local allies. With the escalation of the war in early December, the Security Countil met and the Soviets vetoed a resolution calling for a cease-fire and withdrawal of troops. A comparable resolution backed by China and the United States (with France and the United Kingdom abstaining) was then passed by the General Assembly. The United States decided to "tilt" toward Pakistan and China in the conflict because of its emerging rapprochement with Peking. However, as long as the USSR was backing the militarily superior Indians and the United States was unwilling to commit its military resources, there was no compliance with the resolution—at least until an independent Bangladesh had emerged.

The conflict between nonaligned states involving Rhodesia arose from the latter's reprisal raids into Mozambique in 1977. The Security Council condemned Rhodesia and called for the end to the attacks since the great majority of UN members backed Mozambique's assistance to the rebels trying to topple the white-dominated regime. As a conflict between nonaligned parties, it was unique because of the widespread disapproval of the Smith regime by all groupings.

Another was between nonaligned parties in which the United Nations intervened (and which somewhat approximates a traditional conflict between nonaligned countries) was the Indonesian invasion of East Timor in December 1975. Indonesia supported East Timorese groups favoring integration of the territory with Indonesia and invaded immediately following a declaration of independence by the largest party favoring the creation of an independent state. Both the Security Council (in December and early 1976) and the General Assembly called for Indonesian withdrawal. All of the permanent council members voted for the December resolutions, although their opposition was not particularly strong,[101] and the United States as well as Japan abstained on the second Security Council resolution. The United States and Japan actually preferred that the territory not come under the control of the leftist proindependence party, Fretilin, but felt some obligation to assuage the pique of Portugal (whose control had been forcibly terminated) and to oppose what was a case of open aggression. The Soviets and Chinese would probably have preferred a Fretilin-controlled state but were wary about alienating Indonesia, which was obviously not going to be persuaded to withdraw. In the end they all bowed to the fait accompli of the large regional nonaligned power, with which they all hoped to have good, cooperative relations in the future.

As was mentioned at the beginning of the discussion of conflicts between nonaligned parties, the divergences from the hypothesis resulted largely from the impact of China's ability to act as an independent pole in some Asian conflicts and the conflictual behavior of that unique "nonaligned" state, Rhodesia. If, in the case of the Asian conflicts discussed above, one recategorizes the parties in terms of their links with the three major power centers, they can be understood in terms of the logic of theory. The theory may require some development to account for various contingencies in a tripolar setting—an issue that is discussed in further detail in the conclusion of this book.

The first of the two categories of conflicts in which UN intervention but not success was hypothesized was <u>intracoalition conflicts</u> <u>within a subordinate grouping where the aggressing state was trying</u> <u>to prevent the victim from becoming nonaligned</u>. The only conflict of this type was the Soviet invasion of Hungary in 1956. As hypothesized, the United Nations did call for a cease-fire and withdrawal of Soviet forces, but the Soviets did not comply with the directive. Immediately following the Hungarian announcement of its withdrawal from the Warsaw Pact and its declaration of neutrality on November 1, 1956, there were fears of a possible Soviet military attack against the new Hungarian government, and the UN Security Council met to consider the crisis. At the same time the Western powers, particularly the United States, sought to avoid any impression that they would militarily challenge the Soviet sphere of influence in Eastern Europe. Following the Soviet military attack on November 3, the Security Council and then the General Assembly met to consider the war, and the assembly passed a resolution calling for an end to the Soviet aggression. Since the Western powers were not willing to use military force to prevent the Soviet Union's maintenance of the cohesion of its military alliance, the assembly's resolutions had no impact on military developments in Hungary.

The second type of conflict in which UN intervention but not success was hypothesized was <u>intercoalition conflicts where the victim state was a member of a dominant coalition</u>—namely, the Western coalition between 1946 and 1960. Of the six conflicts in this category only two (33 percent) were managed as predicted. They were the Greek civil war (with Albanian, Bulgarian, and Yugoslav support for the Greek Communists) between 1946 and 1949 and the Korean War of 1950-53. As is evident by the duration of the wars, the UN resolutions in support of the Western parties were not complied with by the Communist states. Instead, both wars were terminated as a result of events on the battlefield rather than by external pressure on the aggressing parties to cease their actions against the non-Communist victim states.

The Nationalist Chinese-Communist Chinese conflicts of 1954-55 and 1958 were never brought to the United Nations, and the Berlin crisis of 1948 was only brought to the Security Council after the perceptions of a possible military conflict had effectively disappeared. In the case of the Laotian civil strife with North Vietnamese intervention in 1959, there was a Security Council debate and the council did dispatch an investigatory group (as a result of the Western position that the dispatch of such a group constituted a "procedural" as opposed to "substantive" matter); but when the investigatory body was unable to substantiate the Laotian government's claims, there was no further attempt to involve the United Nations in the dispute. In the case of the Nationalist Chinese-Communist Chinese conflicts and the Laotian crisis, the absence of two of the states from the United Nations (Communist China and North Vietnam) certainly had some influence on the United Nations' role; but there were other relevant factors as well. In seeking to identify these factors it is instructive to look at the Berlin crisis of 1948, which began in June and which was not brought to the UN Security Council until October—a month or two after the serious possibility of an armed conflict had disappeared. According to Philip Jessup, the U.S. ambassador to the United Nations in 1948, the Western powers were hesitant to bring the issue to the United Nations since they thought that solutions to major issues of war and peace between the Great Powers should be sought privately before resort to a multilateral body; they were not completely set on what the Western policy should be; and they did not want to be pushed into compromises on such a critical issue by smaller and nonaligned states in the organization. [102] Along with these points Bloomfield's remark about the U.S. desire for "unhampered unilateral policy freedom," made in connection with U.S. policy toward the use of the United Nations in the Vietnam War, should be recalled. [103] From the above comments it is clear that the leaders of major coalitions, even when they can secure support for their position in a conflict with the members of another major coalition, may, in fact, not seek such support if they are unsure as to the precise policies that they themselves wish to pursue. Also, on matters that are crucial to their own security, the Great Powers are very reluctant to allow for even the possibility that they might in the future be pressured to accept a particular policy that they would not otherwise adopt.

The one type of conflict in which both UN intervention and success were hypothesized was conflicts between aligned and nonaligned parties where the nonaligned one was the victim. [104] Of the fourteen conflicts that fall into this category, six (43 percent) elicited UN intervention; and in four of these the organization did achieve significant success. Also, there were several conflicts in other categories that had important similarities with this type, and in which the United Nations did pass substantive resolutions with which the parties complied. These will be discussed at the end of this section.

The four conflicts in which the United Nations both intervened and was successful were the Suez crisis of 1956, the Belgian intervention in the Congo in 1960, the Congo crisis of 1960-62, and the Portuguese intervention in Guinea in 1970. In the Suez crisis the United States and most of the Western allies of Israel, France, and the United Kingdom opposed their military interventions in Egypt in both Security Council and General Assembly debates, and they forced them to terminate the aggressions and withdraw. The Western states' opposition to the military policies of their French, British, and Israeli allies was significantly influenced by a fear that Egypt and other nonaligned countries would be pressured into greater collaboration with the Communist states and that Egypt might call for and obtain Soviet military support—thus provoking an interbloc military conflict.

What is often known as "the Congo crisis" was in fact two separate, although very related, conflicts. On the one hand, there was

the Belgian intervention in the Congo in the second week of July 1960
to protect its own citizens after the breakdown of law and order in the
newly independent Congolese state; and, on the other hand, there was
also a threat of intervention by external parties on behalf of the secessionist province of Katanga, the central government, and possibly
other groups. When Belgium intervened in the Congo and was condemned by the nonaligned Congolese government of Premier Lumumba,
the United States and other Western states were very concerned that
a continued Belgian military presence in the Congo could lead the central government to turn to the Communist states for military support
to expel the Belgians, thus fostering very close ties between the Congo
and the Soviet Union and possibly leading to a military conflict between Communist and Western troops in that African state. They thus
supported the withdrawal of Belgian forces and the creation of a UN
peacekeeping force to maintain law and order in the Congo. On the
policies of the Western states at this time, Alastair Buchan has commented that "it became clear even to those countries who were distrustful of getting too deeply involved in the affairs of their colonial
allies, that the latter's decision might affect the standing and policy
of them all."[105]

While the UN force in the Congo was created to supervise the
withdrawal of Belgian forces, its major purpose was to maintain law
and order in the country so as not to create opportunities for external
intervention on behalf of Congolese political factions. In particular,
there was a fear in July 1960 that Belgium, the United Kingdom, or
France, or some combination of these, might seek to assist the secessionist regime in Katanga, which would lead the central government of Prime Minister Lumumba to call for assistance from the
Communist states. The following two and a half years were excep-
tionally turbulent ones in the Congo, although no outside states sent
their own forces to fight on behalf of particular Congolese factions.
In the end the crisis was resolved when a government under Premier
Cyrille Adoula, which had good relations with both the nonaligned and
Western countries, came to power and when the United States put
strong pressure on the Belgians and the British to support a UN military action against Katanga for the good of general Western interests
in Africa. In particular, the United States feared that, if the central
Congolese government was unable to secure control over Katanga, it
would seek outside assistance from the Communist and radical nonaligned states.[106]

In the Guinean-Portuguese conflict of 1970 Portugal sent approximately 500 Guinean and Portuguese nationals into Guinea to overthrow the government of President Sékou Touré. This action was
motivated by Lisbon's opposition to Guinea's provision of base camps
and assistance to Portuguese Guinean nationals trying to expel the

Portuguese colonial regime. The United Nations sent an investigatory committee to Guinea, which documented Portuguese complicity in the attack; the Security Council then condemned the attack and called for an end to such military actions. Although Portugal denied involvement in the incident, it did not launch or back further actions of this type.

The two conflicts of this type in which the United Nations intervened but was not successful were the Arab-Israeli war of 1948 and the Indo-Pakistani war or 1947-48. In both cases UN resolutions calling for a termination of the fighting went unheeded (although there were intermittent cease-fires during 1948) and the conflict outcomes were determined by the military strength of the conflicting parties. UN mediators in both wars were instrumental in arranging the final cease-fires, but these cease-fire agreements were basically recognitions of Israeli and Indian military victories. The reason for the lack of UN success in these conflicts was the adoption of policies by particular outside powers that were contrary to the "rational" policies set forth in the theory (and which were generally altered in later years). In the Indo-Pakistani war the Soviet Union failed to support the nonaligned victim state (India) since, "viewing the non-communist world from the rigid 'two camps' theory, it appeared that India's profession of nonalignment was meaningless."[107] In this situation the Western powers did not feel pressured to exert influence on Pakistan to halt the military action for fear of Indian reliance on the Soviet Union. Rather, they could urge the parties to settle their conflicts and allow the military strength of the respective parties to determine the outcome. In the Arab-Israeli war of 1948 the Arab states were generally closely tied to, and received assistance from, the United Kingdom, whereas Israel was supported by both the USSR and the United States. While the Soviet Union was pursuing a "rational" policy of supporting a nonaligned state that was being attacked by states closely associated with a Western power, the two major Western powers, the United States and the United Kingdom, were de facto supporting opposite sides in the conflict; even then, each was cross-pressured. Since Israel had the Soviet Union and the most influential of the two Western powers (the United States) on its side, it was able to expand its territorial sphere of control during each round of fighting with the Arabs. Both the external ties of the Arabs and Israelis in this conflict and the military superiority of the nonaligned state to the aligned aggressing state are anomalies in postwar international politics, and these factors explain the unique developments of this conflict.

Of the eight conflicts between aligned and nonaligned parties where the nonaligned was the victim, and in which the United Nations did not become substantively involved, one—the Syrian-Turkish crisis of 1957—did elicit a debate. In mid-September 1957 a large Turkish force was mobilized on the border with Syria in order to pressure the latter state to alter its increasingly anti-Western policy. In October Syria called on the United Nations to debate the threat of Turkish military intervention, and the conflict was discussed intermittently by the General Assembly during the last ten days of October. Following (and perhaps, significantly, because of) Syrian and other nonaligned states' criticisms of the threat to Syria, the Turkish force was withdrawn at the end of the month. Therefore, the basic dynamics of this conflict were not very different from those in which the United Nations did become substantively involved.

Of the seven conflicts of this type that were never brought to the United Nations, the lack of UN involvement in one of them, the Syrian-Iraqi crisis of 1949, can be attributed to the Soviet view during the late 1940s and early 1950s that almost all postcolonial states were allies of the Western imperialist powers. Despite Syrian protestations of nonalignment and its refusal to establish close military and political ties with the Western powers, the Soviet Union nonetheless viewed it as a tool of U.S. and French imperialism.[108] Given this Soviet hostility, the Syrian government probably did not view the United Nations as a forum in which it could mobilize important groups of states against the threat of pro-British Iraq. Two of the other conflicts in this category, the Communist Chinese conflicts with Burma and India in 1956 and 1958, concerned the Chinese seizures of small and remote pieces of territory, which the Burmese and Indian governments did not discover until some time after they had occurred. The absence of UN involvement in them can be explained by the facts that Communist China was not a member of the United Nations and that they concerned small remote areas rather than an issue such as the character of the governments of the victim states. The fourth of these seven conflicts concerned the Pathet Lao and North Vietnamese military operation against the Laotian government of Prince Souvanna Phouma in 1963. The lack of UN intervention here was due both to the non-membership of North Vietnam in the United Nations and the linkages between this conflict and the Communist-non-Communist struggle in Indochina. Many states probably viewed this conflict more as an interbloc one than as an attack by an aligned party against a nonaligned state.

The next of these conflicts was the French dispatch of several thousand troops in 1968 to fight on behalf of the Chadian government against rebels who had close religious (Islamic) and political ties with Sudan, Libya, and Algeria. While the lack of UN involvement can be attributed to both the relatively small size of the French military assistance and the fact that its troops were invited by the government of the country, it also can be partly explained by French political and economic leverage with the Soviet Union and the North African states—

factors that are not included in this study's conceptualization of the cold war international system. The Soviet support for the Chadian government and its labeling of the Moslem rebels as "feudal reaction-aries"[109] may have been due to French-Soviet understandings regarding their respective European and African policies. In the case of Libya and Algeria the French government probably was able to exert some influence as a result of its economic ties with these states.*

The last two aggressions by aligned against nonaligned parties were the small and short-lived Soviet attack against Chinese troops along the Ussuri River in 1969 and the South Yemeni incursion into North Yemen in 1972. In the former case, the armed encounter was quite minor in size and Peking was not then in the United Nations. Also, in the tripolar Asian system it was viewed as an intercoalition conflict. The incursion of Soviet-aligned South Yemeni forces into North Yemen occurred while these troops were chasing rebels, opposed to the radical Aden regime, across the border. Although North Yemen is classified as nonaligned, it had, in fact, developed an increasingly pro-Western orientation by this time, largely as a result of its close relations with Saudi Arabia. Thus, this conflict was viewed by many states in the region as an intercoalition one.

In reviewing the seven conflicts in this category in which, contrary to our predictions, the United Nations did not become involved, several factors appear to have had an important influence on the diplomacy surrounding the disputes. First, several of these disputes were very small-scale or involved minor pieces of territory that were not deemed significant by the victim states. Another point to note is the absence of China and North Vietnam from the United Nations, an absence that had an impact in four of the seven conflicts. Finally, as was mentioned earlier, some of the disputes in this category could alternatively be classified as interbloc conflicts, in which case the lack of a UN response would not be unexpected.

Apart from the 14 conflicts that were classified as acts or threats of aggression by aligned against nonaligned states, 4 other conflicts placed in different categories exhibited characteristics very similar to the nonaligned-aligned category. And the fact that the United Nations intervened in these latter 4 conflicts does lend additional credence to the hypothesis of organizational intervention that was postulated for such conflicts. The intracoalition conflicts involving French action against Tunisia in 1961 and the Turkish threat to invade Cyprus in 1963-64 could be recategorized if Tunisia and

---

*Interestingly, Libya expelled the headquarters of the Chadian rebel organization, FROLINAT, following the French sale of Mirage jets to Libya in 1970.

Cyprus were reclassified as nonaligned rather than pro-Western, a change that could be supported since both states did at least claim to be nonaligned. Moreover, Tunisia and Cyprus were invited to the 1961 and 1964 conferences of nonaligned countries, in large part because of the outwardly nonaligned positions that they adopted in these two conflicts. The intercoalition Arab-Israeli war of 1967 could also be categorized differently. Two of the major Arab participants attacked by Israel (Egypt and Syria) were Soviet allies at the time, but Jordan and most of the other Arab states certainly were not. Western sensitivity to these latter Arab countries was revealed in the extensive diplomatic pressure put on Israel to curtail its military advances and accept a cease-fire. The Arab-Israeli war of 1973 is classified as an aggression by a nonaligned state against an aligned one. However, it was in the latter stage of this conflict, when "aligned" Israel was making gains at the expense of "nonaligned" Egypt, that the Security Council reached a consensus on the question of a cease-fire and the Western states once again applied pressure on Israel to accept it. Thus, the nature of these four conflicts and the diplomacy surrounding international efforts to terminate them tends to provide support to the hypothesis concerning aggressions by aligned states against nonaligned.

On the basis of the preceding analysis of the patterns of UN intervention and success in international crises and wars, it is possible to state a number of conclusions—including suggestions for modification of the theory. First, there is a strong tendency, in conflicts between states belonging to the same coalition, regardless of whether they are both members of a major coalition or a nonaligned grouping, for the United Nations to refrain from intervention except when one state is trying to leave a very small grouping and its rival grouping constitutes over two-thirds of the UN membership (for example, the Soviet intervention in Hungary). The allies of conflicting parties in such conflicts see UN involvement as offering an opportunity to other groupings to attract one of the conflicting parties from its existing alignment affiliation by offering it political support in the conflict, and they are understandably interested in preventing such an occurrence. Also, in the case of conflicts between nonaligned parties, the major coalitions generally see little advantage in attracting one conflicting party to their grouping when it means the likely affiliation of the other disputant with a rival coalition. As previously noted, two of those conflicts between nonaligned parties in the cold war system that did elicit UN intervention could be reclassified in the tripolar Asian system; in another, the aggressing state was that unique nonaligned (or isolated) country of Rhodesia.

Second, there is a strong tendency for the United Nations not to become involved in intercoalition conflicts—even when the victim state is a member of a grouping constituting over two-thirds of the organization's membership. Even in this latter type of conflict, there seems to have been considerable reluctance to encourage UN involvement when the dominant Western coalition's policy had not been clearly agreed upon or when there might have been some interference by other UN members in their policy-formulation process. Even in those few cases where the United Nations did intervene, its recommendations were certainly not complied with, since the aggressor was part of a major, if subordinate, security coalition.

Third, in conflicts between aligned and nonaligned states where the aligned was the victim, there was little indication of a proclivity for the United Nations to intervene. In general, the allies of the victim states were reluctant to support UN action against aggressing nonaligned states since to have done so may have encouraged their cooperation with the rival grouping.

Fourth, the previous analysis indicates that in a competitive system the type of conflict in which UN intervention and success are most likely is that between aligned and nonaligned parties where the nonaligned is the victim state. The percentage of the conflicts in this category that elicited UN intervention (43 percent) is considerably higher than the comparable percentages for other types of conflicts, and, as noted previously, four other conflicts in which the United Nations intervened could very well be classified in this category. Also, of the eight conflicts in which the UN interventions met with success, four fell into this category, and three others might be reclassified as such. It is only in this type of conflict that all groupings are likely to support the victim state, since the allies of the aggressing state usually see its actions as undermining their coalition's general strategic position in world politics.

Fifth, the failure of the United Nations to intervene and succeed in particular conflicts as hypothesized is attributable to three major factors—the adoption of policies by particular groupings contrary to the theory's assumptions, certain inaccuracies in the portrayal of the world security system, and the relevance of particular variables not included in the theory. An example of a situation where a coalition's policies did not coincide with the assumptions in the theory was the Soviet Union's adoption of the "two camp doctrine" in the late 1940s and early 1950s, which led to its general refusal to court the nonaligned states. This policy undoubtedly influenced the management of the Indo-Pakistani war of 1947-48 and the Syrian-Iraqi crisis of 1949. Another possible example was the Soviet policy of not challenging the French sphere of influence in Africa, as revealed by its stance toward French involvement in the Chadian civil war. The most important aspect of world security politics not covered in the description of the coalition configuration was the tripolar competition in Asia, which had an important effect on a number of conflicts. At the same time, one can certainly analyze these conflicts from the perspective of the theory.

An analysis of the patterns of UN behavior and success indicates that the theory probably excluded certain relevant variables. One factor undoubtedly is the nonmembership in the United Nations of one or both conflicting parties (particularly Communist China), although the mere inclusion of conflicts involving such states meant that the study erred from focusing on a strict definition of collective security.[110] Another factor is the level of escalation or the magnitude of violence of conflicts, in most of the 19 conflicts in which the United Nations became substantively involved, there was large-scale international or civil violence. The organization intervened in only two crises or threats to international peace, and in both (the Congo and Cypriot crises) there was significant civil violence. It seldom became substantively involved in wars in which the aggressors (including states invited to send forces by "legitimate" governments) dispatched fewer than several thousand troops.

Last, the data on the conflicts indicate that the United Nations has been substantively involved in a relatively small percentage of the total number of international crises and wars in the period 1946-77, although it is true that some of the most important international conflicts have been managed through diplomatic collaboration within the organization. While the United Nations intervened in 19 (20 percent) of the 93 conflicts, it only met with success in 8 of these. At the same time, in at least 5 others (the Indo-Pakistani war of 1947-48, the Arab-Israeli war of 1948, the Tunisian-French war of 1961, the Moroccan-Spanish conflict of 1975, and the South African involvement in the Angolan civil war in 1975-76) its interventions did have some influence on the nature of the outcomes. Unless there are some important changes in the structure of the international security system, particularly a move in the direction of a consensual system, the theory would indicate that the future role of the United Nations in world security politics is unlikely to increase a great deal. Indeed, if the limited role of the United Nations in Asian conflicts since the early 1960s—in which the tripolarity occasioned by China's break from the Soviet Union has had an important effect—is any indication of what might occur in a multipolar global security system, one cannot be too sanguine about the relevance and impact of the organization in future international conflicts.

NOTES

1. Winston S. Churchill, Closing the Ring (Boston: Houghton Mifflin, 1951), p. 361.

2. See Ruth B. Russell and Jeanette E. Muther, A History of the United Nations Charter (Washington, D. C. : The Brookings Insti- tuition, 1958), app. B, p. 975.

3. Ibid. , app. D, p. 977.

4. Churchill, op. cit. , p. 363.

5. Cordell Hull, The Memoirs of Cordell Hull, vol. 2 (New York: Macmillan, 1948), pp. 1643-46.

6. Russell and Muther, op. cit. , pp. 154-55.

7. Russell and Muther, op. cit. , app. I, pp. 1019-28.

8. Ibid. , p. 447.

9. U.S. , Department of State, United Nations Conference on International Organization (Washington, D. C. : Department of State, 1946), p. 813.

10. Inis L. Claude, Jr. , Swords into Plowshares, 3d ed. (New York: Random House, 1964), p. 70. This precise quote does not ap- pear in the fourth edition (1971) but the general point is made on pp. 76-78.

11. Article 1.

12. Goodrich, Hambro and Simons [cited on p. 33], p. 59.

13. Article 2.

14. In 1965 this article was amended to enlarge the council to 15 members.

15. Article 23.

16. Articles 33, 34, and 35.

17. Articles 31 and 36.

18. Articles 40, 41, and 42.

19. Articles 25 and 43.

20. Article 47.

21. Article 51.

22. Article 53.

23. Claude, Swords into Plowshares, p. 140.

24. Ibid. , pp. 175-76.

25. Debates on these issues are summarized in Goodrich, Ham- bro and Simons, op. cit. , pp. 111-44; and Russell and Muther, op. cit. , pp. 750-76.

26. For discussion of these powers and some of their implica- tions, see Goodrich, Hambro and Simons, op. cit. , pp. 584-92; and Russell and Muther, op. cit. , pp. 854-60. Analyses of the secre- tary-general's diplomatic activities are contained in Mark W. Zacher, "The Secretary-General and the United Nations' Function of Peaceful Settlement, " International Organization 20 (Autumn 1966): 724-49; and Leon Gordenker, The UN Secretary-General and the Maintenance of Peace (New York: Columbia University Press, 1967).

27. For discussions of the creation of the court, see Goodrich, Hambro and Simons, op. cit. , pp. 544-71; and Russell and Muther, op. cit. , pp. 864-96.

28. Goodrich, Hambro and Simons, op. cit., pp. 122-23, 130.

29. Claude, Swords into Plowshares, pp. 177, 179.

30. George Modelski, Principles of World Politics (New York: The Free Press, 1972), p. 159.

31. Hans J. Morgenthau, Politics among Nations, 4th ed. (New York: Random House, 1968), p. 3.

32. Henry Kissinger, American Foreign Policy (New York: W. W. Norton, 1969), p. 56.

33. Peter J. Fliess, International Relations in the Bipolar World (New York: Random House, 1968), pp. 7-8. See, also, Paul Seabury, The Rise and Decline of the Cold War (New York: Basic Books, 1967), p. 137.

34. Robert O. Keohane and Joseph S. Nye, Jr., "International Interdependence and Integration," in Handbook of Political Science, vol. 8, ed. Fred I. Greenstein and Nelson W. Polsby (Reading, Mass.: Addison-Wesley, 1975), p. 363.

35. Donald J. Puchala and Stuart I. Fagan, "International Politics in the 1970s: The Search for a Perspective," International Organization 28 (Spring 1974): 248.

36. Inis L. Claude, Jr., The Changing United Nations (New York: Random House, 1967), pp. 32-33.

37. Ibid., p. 35.

38. Ernst B. Haas, "Collective Security and the Future International System," in International Law and Organization, ed. Richard A. Falk and Wolfram F. Hanrieder (Philadelphia: J. B. Lippincott, 1968), p. 312.

39. Joseph L. Nogee, "Polarity: An Ambiguous Concept," Orbis 17 (Winter 1975): 1194, 1197.

40. See, for example, Z. Brzezinski, "How the Cold War Was Played," Foreign Affairs 51 (October 1972): 207; John W. Spanier, Games Nations Play: Analyzing International Politics (New York: Praeger, 1972), p. 82; and Raymond F. Hopkins and Richard W. Mansbach, Structure and Process in International Politics (New York: Harper & Row, 1973), p. 125.

41. See, for example, Cecil Crabb, Jr., Nations in a Multipolar World (New York: Harper & Row, 1968); Alastair Buchan, "The End of Bipolarity," Adelphi Paper, no. 91 (London: IISS, November 1972); and Ronald J. Yalem, "Tripolarity and the International System," Orbis 15 (Winter 1972): 1051-63.

42. Leo Mates, Nonalignment: Theory in Current Policy (Dobbs Ferry, N. Y.: Oceana, 1972), p. 299; Roy Jenkins, Afternoon on the Potomac: A British View of America's Changing Position in the World (New Haven, Conn.: Yale University Press, 1972), p. 57.

43. Nogee, op. cit., pp. 1199-1200. Rosencrance has referred to the nonaligned grouping as a third "pole," but this conceptualization

appears to be an exception. See Richard Rosecrance, Action and Reaction in World Politics (Boston: Little, Brown, 1963), pp. 210-16.

44. Brzezinski, "How the Cold War Was Played," p. 207.

45. Kissinger, op. cit., p. 65.

46. Spanier, op. cit., p. 82.

47. Steven Spiegel, "Bimodality and the International Order: The Paradox of Parity," Public Policy 18 (Spring 1970): 383-412.

48. Stanley Hoffmann, "International Organization and the International System," World Politics 24 (Summer 1970): 393.

49. Morton Kaplan, "Variants on Six Models of the International System," in International Politics and Foreign Policy: A Reader in Research and Theory, ed. James N. Rosenau (New York: The Free Press, 1969), pp. 300-1.

50. Oran R. Young, "The United Nations and the International System," International Organization 22 (Autumn 1968): 912.

51. Steven J. Rosen and Walter S. Jones, The Logic of International Relations (Cambridge, Mass.: Winthrop, 1977), p. 227.

52. Ibid., p. 231.

53. Yale H. Ferguson and Walther F. Weiker, eds., Continuing Issues in International Politics (Pacific Palisades, Calif.: Goodyear, 1973), p. x.

54. Z. Brzezinski, "The Balance of Power Delusion," Foreign Policy 7 (Summer 1972): 55-56.

55. Hans J. Morgenthau, Politics among Nations, 5th ed. (New York: Knopf, 1973), pp. 338-45; Stanley Hoffmann, Gulliver's Troubles or the Setting of the American Foreign Policy (New York: McGraw-Hill, 1968), p. 21; Kenneth Waltz, "International Structure, National Force and the Balance of World Power," Journal of International Affairs 21 (Summer 1967): 231; Richard Rosecrance, ed., The Future of the International Strategic System (San Francisco: Chandler, 1973), p. 6; Humphrey Trevelyan, "Reflections on Soviet and Western Policy," International Affairs 52 (October 1976): 527; Kaplan, "Variants on Six Models of the International System," p. 300; Donald J. Puchala, International Politics Today (New York: Dodd, Mead, 1971), p. 254; and Kurt London, The Permanent Crisis: Communism in World Politics (Waltham, Mass.: Blaisdell, 1968), pp. 4-5.

56. Thomas W. Wolfe, Soviet Power and Europe, 1945-1970 (Baltimore: Johns Hopkins University Press, 1970), pp. 4-5, 386-426.

57. Hoffmann, "International Organization and the International System," pp. 390, 393-4.

58. See Yalem, op. cit.; and Hedley Bull, "The New Balance of Power in Asia and the Pacific," Foreign Affairs 49 (July 1971): 660-81.

59. Richard Rosecrance, International Relations: Peace or War (New York: McGraw-Hill, 1973), p. 277.

60. The Military Balance, 1977-78 (London: IISS, 1977), p. 54.

61. Two commentators who made such predictions are Yalem, op. cit.; and Arthur Burns, "Military-Technological Models and World Order," International Journal 24 (Autumn 1969): 797, 799.

62. Seabury, op. cit., p. 121.

63. Stanley Hoffmann, "Choices," Foreign Policy 12 (Fall 1973): 4

64. Brzezinski, "How the Cold War War Played," p. 148.

65. Kissinger, op. cit., p. 65.

66. Fliess, op. cit., pp. 136-39; Kaplan, "Bipolarity in a Revolutionary Age," p. 252.

67. The birth and demise of this doctrine are outlined in Alvin Z. Rubinstein, ed., The Foreign Policy of the Soviet Union (New York: Random House, 1972), pp. 407-11.

68. Marshall D. Shulman, Beyond the Cold War (New Haven, Conn.: Yale University Press, 1966), p. 65. Also see Rubinstein, op. cit., pp. 410-11; Kaplan, "Bipolarity in a Revolutionary Age," p. 260; and David T. Cattell, "The Soviet Union Seeks a Policy for Afro-Asia," in New Nations in a Divided World: The International Relations of the Afro-Asian States, ed. Kurt London (New York: Praeger, 1963), pp. 167-69.

69. Fliess, op. cit., pp. 123-24; Shulman, op. cit., pp. 56-57.

70. Henry Teune and Sig Synnestvedt, "Measuring International Alignment," Orbis 9 (Spring 1965): 80.

71. Robert Osgood, Alliances and American Foreign Policy (Baltimore: Johns Hopkins University Press, 1968), p. 92.

72. Three recent articles that consider the role and importance of nonmilitary forms of assistance to developing countries are David E. Albright, "The Soviet Union and Africa: Soviet Policy," Problems of Communism 27 (January-February 1978): 20-39; George T. Yu, "The Soviet Union and Africa: China's Impact," in ibid., pp. 40-50; Donald F. McHenry and Kai Bird, "Food Bungle in Bangladesh," Foreign Policy 27 (Summer 1977): 72-88.

73. John Herz, "The Territorial State Revisited: Reflections on the Future of the Nation-State," in International Politics and Foreign Policy: A Reader in Research and Theory, ed. James N. Rosenau (New York: The Free Press, 1969), p. 85.

74. H. Hveem and T. Willets, "The Practice of Nonalignment," p. 3, unpublished manuscript (quotation taken from The Nationalist, April 14, 1970).

75. G. Pope Atkins, Latin America in the International Political System (New York: The Free Press, 1977), p. 378.

76. "Conflicting Concepts of the United Nations," in International Law and Organization, ed. Richard A. Falk and Wolfram F. Hanrieder (Philadelphia: J. B. Lippincott, 1968), pp. 187-88.

77. On Peru's foreign policy since the 1968 revolution, see Robert H. Swanbrough, "Peru's Offensive: Solidarity for Latin American Independence," in Latin America: The Search For a New

International Role, ed. Ronald G. Hellman and H. Jon Rosenbaum, (New York: Halsted, 1975), pp. 115-30. G. Pope Atkins describes Peru's foreign policy since 1968 as "essentially neutralist." See his Latin America in the International Political System (New York: The Free Press, 1977), p. 260. On Jamaica, see Wendell Bell, "Independent Jamaica Enters World Politics: Foreign Policy in a New State," Political Science Quarterly 92 (Winter 1977): 687-703. On Bolivia, see F. Parkinson, Latin America, The Cold War and the World Powers, 1945-1973 (Beverly Hills, Calif.: Sage, 1974), pp. 235-37.

78. On Mexico, see Edith B. Couturier, "Mexico," in Latin American Foreign Policies: An Analysis, ed. Harold E. David and Larman C. Wilson (Baltimore: Johns Hopkins University Press, 1975), pp. 117-35. On Panama, see Thomas L. Karnes, "The Central American Republics," in ibid., p. 148. In general, see Martin C. Needler, An Introduction to Latin American Politics: The Structure of Conflict (Englewood Cliffs, N.J.: Prentice-Hall, 1977); Graham H. Stuart and James L. Tigner, Latin America and the United States, 6th ed. (Englewood Cliffs: Prentice-Hall, 1975); and Atkins, op. cit., pp. 258-61.

79. Emile A. Nakhleh, Arab-American Relations in the Persian Gulf (Washington, D.C.: The American Enterprise Institute for Public Policy Research, 1975), p. 2.

80. Ibid. See also William R. Polk, The United States and the Arab World, 3d ed. (Cambridge, Mass.: Harvard University Press, 1975), pp. 211-445; Mordechai Abir, Oil, Power and Politics (London: Frank Cass, 1974); John B. Kelley, "Saudi Arabia and the Gulf States," in Critical Choices for Americans, Vol. X: The Middle East: Oil, Conflict and Hope, ed. A. L. Udovitch (Lexington, Mass.: D. C. Heath, 1976), pp. 427-62.

81. See Chapters 4 and 5 for discussion of these states' foreign policies.

82. Richard C. Thornton, "South Asia: Imbalance on the Subcontinent," Orbis 19 (Fall 1975): 866-69. On the global security orientations of the non-Communist Southeast Asian states, see Sheldon W. Simon, "The ASEAN States: Obstacles to Security Cooperation," Orbis 22 (Summer 1978): 415-39.

83. On Iraq, see Robert O. Freedman, Soviet Policy toward the Middle East since 1970 (New York: Praeger, 1975), pp. 23, 28-29, 68-73.

84. Ibid., pp. 142-44, 176-77.

85. Ibid., pp. 104-5, 135. See also, Robert W. Stookey, "Red Sea Gate-Keepers: The Yemen Arab Republic and the People's Democratic Republic of Yemen," Middle East Review 10 (Summer 1978): 39-47.

86. Dick Wilson, "Sino-Soviet Rivalry in Southeast Asia," Problems of Communism 23 (September-October 1974): 39-51.

87. See Sam Younger, "Ideology and Pragmatism in Algerian Foreign Policy," The World Today 34 (March 1978): 107-14; John Mercer, "Confrontation in the Western Sahara," The World Today 32 (June 1976): 230-39.

88. F. Atkins, op. cit., pp. 258-61.

89. For an account of U.S. efforts to secure a halt to the Israeli military advance, see Gil Carl Alroy, The Kissinger Experience: American Policy in the Middle East (New York: Horizon Press, 1975), p. 83.

90. The inability of the United Nations to deal constructively with interbloc conflicts has been noted by many students of the United Nations. Stanley Hoffmann, "International Organization and the International System," International Organization 14 (Summer 1970): 293-94; Ernst B. Haas, Robert L. Butterworth, and Joseph S. Nye, Conflict Management by International Organizations (Morristown N.J.: General Learning Corp., 1972), p. 47; Claude, The Changing United Nations, pp. 23-43; Mark W. Zacher, Dag Hammarskjold's United Nations (New York: Columbia University Press, 1970), pp. 54-62, 133-39; Yashpal Tandon, "The Peaceful Settlement of International Disputes," International Relations 2 (April 1964): 569-70; Evan Luard, Conflict and Peace in the Modern International System (Boston: Little, Brown, 1968), pp. 81-82.

91. Lincoln P. Bloomfield, The U.N. and Vietnam (New York: Carnegie Endowment for International Peace, 1968), pp. 10-13.

92. Ernst B. Haas, Tangle of Hopes: American Commitments and World Order (Englewood Cliffs, N.J.: Prentice-Hall, 1969), p. 75.

93. Saadia Touval, The Boundary Politics of Independent Africa (Cambridge, Mass.: Harvard University Press, 1972), p. 121; West Africa, January 11, 1964, p. 39.

94. G. Barraclough, Survey of International Affairs·1956-58 (London: Oxford University Press, 1962), pp. 432-34, 440-42; Keesing's Contemporary Archives 11 (May 31-June 17, 1958): 16203-8.

95. Crisis Management: The New Diplomacy (Boulogne-sur-Seine, France: The Atlantic Institute, 1966), p. 28.

96. Touval, op. cit., pp. 132-33; B. Andemicael, Peaceful Settlement among African States: Roles of the United Nations and Organization of African Unity (New York: United Nations Institute for Training and Research, 1972), p. 71; J. Woronoff, Organizing African Unity (Metuchen, N.J.: Scarecrow Press, 1970), p. 453.

97. Touval, op. cit., pp. 132-33.

98. Ibid., pp. 149-50; Woronoff, op. cit., p. 459; Andemicael, op. cit., p. 9; Catharine Hoskyns, Case Studies in African Diplomacy:

II—The Ethiopia-Somalia-Kenya Dispute, 1961-67 (Dar es Salaam, Tanzania: Oxford University Press, 1969), p. 23.

99. Leila Meo, "The War in Lebanon," in Ethnic Conflict in International Relations, ed. Astri Suhrke and Lela Garner Noble (New York: Praeger, 1977), p. 118.

100. Morris Rothenberg, "Recent Soviet Relations with Syria," Middle East Review 10 (Summer 1978): 5-9.

101. Robert Lawless, "The Indonesian Takeover of East Timor," Asian Survey 16 (October 1976): 962-63.

102. "The Berlin Blockade and the Use of the U. N.," Foreign Affairs 50 (October 1971): 167.

103. Bloomfield, op. cit., p. 10.

104. The literature on the United Nations and collective security has not addressed itself to this particular type of conflict, although Haas, Butterworth, and Nye have focused on conflicts between aligned and nonaligned states without differentiating between those in which the aligned and nonaligned parties were the victim states, op. cit., pp. 25-26.

105. Crisis Management: The New Diplomacy (Boulogne-sur-Seine, France: The Atlantic Institute, 1966), p. 24.

106. On the importance of the emergence of common interests between the moderate Afro-Asian states and the United States and the importance of this consensus for the UN operation, see Yashpal Tandon, "The Internationalization of the Civil War: Lessons from the Congo, Nigeria and Vietnam," in Africa in World Affairs: The Next Thirty Years, ed. Ali A. Mazrui and Hasuh Patel (New York: Third Press, 1973), p. 66.

107. Arthur Stein, India and the Soviet Union: The Nehru Era (Chicago: University of Chicago Press, 1969), pp. 26-27.

108. Walter Z. Laqueur, The Soviet Union and the Middle East (New York: Praeger, 1959), p. 152.

109. Africa Confidential 2 (April 3, 1970): 5.

110. The influence that the absence of conflicting parties or important external states from the United Nations has in impeding UN intervention is discussed in Claude, Swords into Plowshares, p. 218; Bloomfield, op. cit., p. 13.

3

The Organization of
American States and
Inter-American Conflicts

THE BACKGROUND AND CHARACTER
OF THE OAS COLLECTIVE SECURITY SYSTEM

The establishment of the OAS in 1948 was a culmination of efforts extending back to the early nineteenth century to establish the regional security system in the Western Hemisphere. As early as 1826, Simon Bolivar had organized the first Hispanic-American Conference, with the goal of creating a League of American States that would provide the new Latin American nations with protection from both the European colonial powers (particularly Spain) and the growing ambitions of the United States. While this conference and successive ones in 1847 and 1856 agreed on general treaties in which each state undertook to guarantee and defend the sovereignty of the others, the treaties went unratified when taken back to the Latin American capitals. Also, the movement failed to attract support from the one country conspicuously absent from the conferences, namely, the United States. It was reluctant to engage in foreign commitments and had no desire to restrict its freedom of action in the Western Hemisphere, especially after the enunciation of the Monroe Doctrine in 1823. [1] Nevertheless, the unsuccessful conferences did lay the foundation for future inter-American collaboration, and the treaties incorporated for the first time "fundamental rules of national behavior destined later to become basic features of inter-American cooperation: non-intervention, territorial integrity, arbitration, and the renunciation of war."[2]

By 1889, Washington's growing interest in extending its commercial interests in Latin America and in forestalling the growth of European influence in the hemisphere led it to take up the cause of inter-American cooperation, inaugurating what has been called the "new Pan-Americanism."[3] In 1890, the U.S. government hosted the First International Conference of American States. The outcomes of this conference and of subsequent ones reflected the domination of the United States in economic matters and a clear divergence of U.S. and Latin American interests in the politico-security field.[4] For example, the International Union of American Republics, which was established at the 1890 meeting for the promotion of economic cooperation, was to have its headquarters in Washington, D.C. and function under the supervision of the U.S. secretary of state. Also, on the contentious questions of the civil rights of foreigners in American states and the "right of conquest," the conference failed to reach any accord since the United States refused to agree with the vast majority of Latin American governments that its citizens in other American states should always come under the laws of those states and that all states in the hemisphere should renounce all claims to territories acquired by military force.

Some progress was made in the commercial sphere at the second Conference in 1901,[5] but efforts to secure an inter-American treaty providing for the pacific settlement of disputes were largely unsuccessful. While most delegates signed a protocol of adherence to The Hague Convention (which included a provision for voluntary arbitration), only six, excluding the United States, ratified a compulsory arbitration convention that was so weak that, in the words of one scholar, it amounted to "little more than an undertaking to agree to arbitrate."[6]

Meanwhile, U.S. involvements in Panama and Cuba widened the gulf between itself and the Latin American republics. Symbolizing this great divergence of views was the "Roosevelt Corollary" to the Monroe Doctrine. Enunciated in 1904, it set forth the "right" of the United States to exercise an "international police power" in the hemisphere. This U.S. policy effectively stalled further efforts to create a viable security system, for just as the Latin Americans were determined to prevent the establishment of any mechanism that might legitimize Washington's interventionism, the United States would not allow its de facto hegemony to be fettered by legal commitments.[7] From this time until World War I the inter-American conferences steered clear of politico-security issues. U.S. involvement in the Mexican revolution and its interventions in the Dominican Republic, Haiti, and Nicaragua during this period served to reinforce the impression that Pan-Americanism was indistinguishable from Washington's domination of the hemisphere.

The outbreak of World War I did not change this basic division and illustrated as well the lack of solidarity among the Latin American states themselves. Nor did the arrival of Woodrow Wilson to office dampen the hostility felt by the Latin Americans for U.S. policies and attitudes. In particular, the Wilson administration's rejection of an inter-American defensive alliance, proposed by Uruguay as part of the "Pan American Pact" which Wilson himself had advocated, was a blow to Latin American hopes for a change in U.S. policies.[8] The new League of Nations was first seen by the southern states as a possible counterpoise to U.S. influence, but that organization's quickly revealed weaknesses dashed this hope. Washington made it clear that the Monroe Doctrine was in no way vitiated by the new League system, and U.S. refusal to join the organization reinforced this argument. Nevertheless, the membership of the Latin American states in the League enhanced their sense of independence and provided a useful experience with international organization.[9]

During the 1920s only limited progress toward the development of regional machinery for conflict settlement was recorded. Most notable was the approval in 1923 of the Gondra Treaty, which provided that if disputes could not be settled by normal diplomatic means they would be submitted to a commission of inquiry (to be appointed by the parties themselves). The Commission of Jurists, charged with codifying American international law, was also reorganized, and in 1927 produced a draft code of the "rights and duties of states," which condemned intervention by governments in the internal affairs of others. However, at the Sixth Inter-American Conference, held in Havana in 1928, the United States announced that, while it was not an interventionist power, it might feel compelled to engage in temporary "interpositions."[10] Not surprisingly, this stance became an issue of conflict between the Latin Americans and the United States. Nor was the Special Conference on Conciliation and Arbitration in 1929 successful in supplanting the mistrust with which the United States was still regarded by the Latin Americans. By this time, "the gap between ideals and actuality had grown too wide . . . to be hidden by platitudes about inter-American solidarity. . . . Only a change in U.S. policy could make inter-Americanism meaningful for the other twenty members of the inter-American system."[11]

Such a change soon took place. Beginning with Hoover's measures to restore Latin American confidence—the repudiation of the Roosevelt Corollary, the withdrawal of troops from Haiti and Nicaragua, and the modification of Washington's diplomatic recognition policy*—it culminated in the "Good Neighbor Policy" of President Frank-

---

*Washington abandoned its recent de jure recognition policy, which had been regarded as a form of interventionism by Latin American governments, in favor of a de facto policy. (J. Lloyd Mecham, The United States and Inter-American Security, 1889-1960 [Austin: University of Texas Press, 1967], p. 113.)

lin D. Roosevelt.[12] Enunciated in 1933 at the Seventh Inter-American Conference, this policy accepted nonintervention as the basic principle of inter-American relations. While the term "nonintervention" was difficult to define in a regional system characterized by the predominance of one member, and while it was apparently interpreted by Washington as referring only to armed intervention,[13] relations with the southern states did improve markedly. Many Latin American governments became much more receptive to proposals for inter-American arrangements for collective security and collective defense since they were now somewhat less fearful that such arrangements would become instruments for U.S. intervention. At the 1936 Conference for the Maintenance of Peace, for example, two important new instruments were agreed on—a Convention for the Maintenance, Preservation, and Reestablishment of Peace and a Convention to Coordinate, Extend, and Secure the fulfillment of Existing Treaties between the American States. The former recommended that all signatories consult in the event of a threat to or attack against any of them and the latter envisioned a six-month cooling-off period in the event of a possible armed conflict.[14] However, neither these conventions nor the 1938 Declaration of Lima, which reaffirmed the "continental solidarity" of the American states, merited the highly enthusiastic praise they elicited. The Good Neighbor Policy, while ushering in a period of improved north-south relations, neither eliminated all inter-American dissension nor led to any substantive growth of regional security institutions. Continuing Latin American suspicions of U.S. motives, conflicts of interest between various American regimes, and Axis jibes at Washington's hemispheric economic policies effectively blocked such a development.

World War II, however, served to put the principles of solidarity and consultation into actual operation. Three Meetings of Consultation of Foreign Ministers held in 1939, 1940, and 1942 concerning hemispheric neutrality and security brought the American states closer to a working security system. In 1940 they agreed that a violation of the sovereignty of an American state by a non-American one would be regarded as an act of aggression against them all. A five-nation Inter-American Peace Committee was also established to help solve disputes between American states by suggesting "measures and steps conducive to settlement."* When the United States declared war on the Axis powers, all of the Latin American states, except Chile and

---

*Gordon Connell-Smith, The Inter-American System (London: Oxford University Press, 1966), p. 115. This committee never functioned during the war, but was to be revived in the OAS framework.

Argentina, at least severed their relations with them and participated in an Inter-American Defense Board, sponsored by Washington to encourage participation in regional security plans.

As the Allied victory drew nearer, there were signs of a revival of the old tensions between Washington and the Latin Americans, who were uneasy about the emergence of the United States as a "superpower," preoccupied with global commitments and involved in plans for a world security organization dominated by the Great Powers. Even more unsettling, especially for the conservative regimes, was the prospect of Soviet influence in the region. Consequently, they began to proclaim their support for inter-American principles and collaboration. [15] And, at a meeting in Mexico City in February 1945, they persuaded the United States to accept a "Resolution Concerning Reciprocal Assistance and American Solidarity," which became known as the Treaty of Chapultepec. Since the treaty transformed the inter-American system from an alliance into a collective security system, the United States, caught between the conflicting forces of regionalism and universalism, was obliged to make a proviso that regional arrangements were to be consistent with the principles of the United Nations and that the American states should seek a "harmonizing formula" that would not bring the inter-American organization into conflict with the United Nations. Such a formula was found in the "Vandenberg Resolution" (Article 51 of the UN Charter), which recognized the "inherent right of individual or collective self-defence if an armed attack occurs." It removed the possibility that a permanent member of the UN Security Council could, as a result of the use of the veto, prevent regional action against aggression.* This resolution of Washington's dilemma between regionalism and universalism set the stage for the creation of a security organization in the Western Hemisphere.

Within three years of their agreement at Chapultepec, the 21 Western Hemisphere states had institutionalized an inter-American security system. The two major steps in this process were the signing of the Inter-American Treaty of Reciprocal Assistance at Rio de Janeiro in 1947 and the formulation of the Charter of the Organization of American States at the Ninth Inter-American Conference held at Bogotá in 1948.† The Charter contained the basic inter-American

---

*J. Lloyd Mecham, The United States and Inter-American Security, 1889-1960 (Austin: University of Texas Press, 1967), p. 273. As a result of pressure from the Latin American states and certain forces within the U.S. government, Articles 53-54 were included in the UN Charter, which encouraged resort to regional collective security organizations.

†The Charter was signed by 21 states—Argentina, Bolivia, Brazil, Chile, Colombia, Costa Rica, Cuba, Dominican Republic, Ecua-

norms that had developed over the years: recognition of the sovereignty and independence of states, opposition to aggression, the peaceful settlement of disputes, the principles of collective security and
continental solidarity, social justice, and economic cooperation.[16]
It also created a number of organs whose functions included preventing and terminating armed conflicts between the member states.
These were the Inter-American Conference (superseded by the General Assembly since the formulation of the Revised Charter in 1967),
the OAS Council (now the Permanent Council), and the Meeting of
Consultation of Ministers of Foreign Affairs. A fourth body that had
been created in 1940, the Inter-American Peace Committee (superseded in 1967 by the Inter-American Committee on Peaceful Settlement), was soon added to the above three, although the OAS Charter
was not formally altered to include it.

The Inter-American Conference (General Assembly) and the
Council (Permanent Council) are of only marginal importance to the
actual collective security operations of the OAS. The effectiveness
of the former—which was a continuation of the inter-American conferences that preceded the OAS—was curtailed by the infrequency of
its meetings (every five years), despite its designation as the "supreme organ" of the OAS. The Assembly, established in Article 52
of the Revised Charter, has the same functions as did the Conference
(in addition to new ones in the economic and technical fields), and
meets annually. But to date it has not enlarged its activities in the
security field. The security capabilities of the Council were also
quite limited. Unless it met as the Organ of Consultation, it could
only "take cognizance, within the limits of the present Charter, and
of inter-American treaties and agreements, of any matter referred
to it by the Inter-American Conference or the Meeting of Consultation
of Ministers of Foreign Affairs."[17] Both this restriction and that
specifying that the Organ could only make recommendations to individual states in such matters were left basically unchanged in the new
Charter,[18] although the potential for a greater role in peaceful settlement does exist as a result of its ability to refer disputes to the Inter-American Committee on Peaceful Settlement.[19]

More salient to the OAS security system is the Meeting of Consultation of Foreign Ministers, which has become the "principal pol-
icy-determining organ of the OAS."[20] It may meet at the request of

---

dor, Guatemala, Haiti, Honduras, Mexico, Nicaragua, Panama, Paraguay, Peru, El Salvador, the United States, Uruguay, and Venezuela.
It entered into force in 1951 after 14 states had ratified it. Barbados
and Trinidad and Tobago were admitted in 1967, Jamaica in 1969,
Grenada in 1975, and Surinam in 1977.

one member state and with the approval of a majority of the members to deal with "questions of an urgent nature and common interest that require prompt and immediate action."[21] In the case of an armed attack on an American state or within the security zone designated by Article 4 of the Rio Treaty,* a meeting is to be convoked "without delay" by the chairman of the Council, who convokes simultaneously a meeting of the Council itself.[22]

Either the Meeting of Consultation of Foreign Ministers or the Council may meet as the Organ of Consultation,[23] which is the key component in the inter-American security system. This body was originally institutionalized under the Rio Treaty, in which the substantive commitments of the OAS states to collective action are contained. In keeping with the distinction made in the UN Charter between armed attacks and other acts of aggression, the treaty states that when an armed attack takes place within the security zone, each signatory may "determine the immediate measures which it may individually take to meet the attack." Meanwhile, the Organ of Consultation is to meet immediately to examine such measures and secure agreement on collective action.[24] In situations where an American state is threatened by an act of aggression other than an armed attack, an outside conflict, or "any other act or situation" endangering the peace of the hemisphere,† the Organ is also to meet without delay to agree on measures to assist the victim of aggression or maintain the security of the continent.[25]

The options open to the Organization in both types of situations cover a wide range. Members may call for a suspension of hostilities, the withdrawal of diplomatic representatives, the breaking of diplomatic relations, the partial or total rupture of economic relations, and, if necessary, the use of armed force.[26] Of central importance to the efficacy of these provisions are the voting regulations governing the Organ. The Rio Treaty provides that all decisions require the approval of two-thirds of the members—except that in an inter-American conflict the parties are not included in the vote.[27] When the specified majority decides on any of the measures listed above, all

---

*Slight modifications in the wording of Articles 3 and 4 were made in the Protocol of Amendments to the Rio Treaty of 1975. (Alfred Pick, "Protocol Signed at San José Provides Reform of Rio Treaty," International Perspectives, September/October 1975, pp. 25-30.

†In the San José Protocol of 1975 the concept of indirect aggression is retained, but it is made clear that there is no commitment to come to the aid of a nonmember state. Also, whereas in the original treaty no attempt is made to define aggression, in the protocol Article 9 has been redrafted to define aggression at considerable length.

signatories are bound to act in concurrence, with the exception that no state is required to use armed force without its consent.* The acceptance of this limitation on national sovereignty represents a "historic modification" of the policies of most American states.[28]

While not explicitly recognizing the very important Rio Treaty, the OAS Charter did adopt it in implicit terms, declaring that the "principles of continental solidarity and collective self-defense should be fulfilled by the application of measures and procedures established in the special treaties on the subject."[29] The Charter also authorized the Council to act provisionally as the Organ of Consultation when an armed attack took place within the security region, and it established an Advisory Defense Committee to advise the Organ with regard to military cooperation "arising in connection with the application of existing special treaties on collective security."[30] Taken as a whole, these security provisions give the OAS a potential for strong and immediate collective action. †

At the same time, the Charter was notably deficient in providing for means of peaceful settlement of conflicts between its members. The Charter declared that all disputes should be submitted to "peaceful procedures"—direct negotiation, good offices, mediation, investigation, conciliation, judicial settlement, arbitration, or other means agreed on by the parties.[31] But no obligation was imposed in this respect. A special treaty, the Treaty on Pacific Settlement (known as the Pact of Bogotá) was devised at the 1948 Conference "to establish adequate procedures for the pacific settlement of disputes" and to "determine the appropriate means for their application, so that no dispute between American states shall fail of definitive settlement within a

---

*Article 20, Rio Treaty OAS Charter. In the San José Protocol of 1975 a provision is added to the voting requirements of Article 17, stating that to revoke the measures taken under Article 8, which deals with mandatory sanctions, a vote of a simple majority will be required. This change was prompted by some states' attitudes toward the 1964 sanctions against Cuba, which were already being ignored by several parties to the Rio Treaty, such as Peru, Argentina, Panama, Venezuela, and Colombia, as well as those states that became members of the OAS after 1964 and therefore were not bound by the decision. (Alfred Pick, "Protocol Signed at San José Provides Reform of Rio Treaty," International Perspectives, September/October 1975, pp. 25-30.)

†The new members of the OAS (Barbados, Jamaica, and Grenada) have not, however, joined the Rio Treaty and some of the older members are unhappy with this situation. (Alfred Pick, "Protocol Signed at San José Provides Reform of Rio Treaty," International Perspectives, September/October 1975, p. 25.)

reasonable period."[32] The treaty represented a significant departure from earlier pacts in that it bound all American states to settle their differences by peaceful procedures—including compulsory arbitration if all other means failed. And in the event that this obligation was not fulfilled, it envisioned collective measures taken by the Meeting of Consultation.[33] However, since the majority of states have not been willing to give the Pact full ratification, it has become an operative part of the inter-American security system.*

To make up for the resulting weakness of the OAS in the conflict settlement area, the American states in 1948 reactivated the Inter-American Peace Committee (IAPC), which had been created in 1940 and was composed of five states. The committee was given the authority to study and give its opinion on any inter-American dispute brought to its attention by any American state. While its decisions were only recommendatory, it was able during the late 1940s and early 1950s to capitalize on its flexible and informal nature to promote the settlement of several conflicts.[34] In 1956, however, the IAPC was effectively immobilized when the Council approved statutes for the committee that required the consent of both conflicting parties before it could act.[35] Such was the burden of the new statutes that in 1959, when faced with the task of resolving serious tensions in the Caribbean, the Meeting of Consultation was obliged to give the IAPC temporary authority to investigate a dispute on the request of a single state. Under the Revised Charter of 1967, a successor to the IAPC was created, the Committee on Peaceful Settlement. It is a "subsidiary organ of the Council," and can take up disputes only at the request of the parties or the Council chairman.[36] If requested by one party, the Committee can also be asked by the Council to offer its "good offices" to conduct an investigation and to seek a settlement—but only with the other party's consent.[37] If such an offer is refused, its only recourse is to the Permanent Council thereof, and if the refusal continues, it can then submit a report to the General Assembly.[38] Nevertheless, the Committee remains a useful tool at the Council's disposal, and has played a significant role in inter-American conflict settlement.

The key aspect of the Charter for this study is that any substantive action by the OAS in any conflict has generally required the con-

---

*Brazil, Costa Rica, Dominican Republic, El Salvador, Haiti, Honduras, Mexico, Panama, and Uruguay ratified the treaty. Substantial (in many cases, nullifying) reservations have been made by Argentina, Bolivia, Ecuador, the United States, Nicaragua, Paraguay, and Peru. The five remaining states—Chile, Colombia, Cuba, Guatemala, and Venezuela—have signed but failed to ratify. (M. Margaret Ball, The O.A.S. in Transition [Durham, N.C.: Duke University Press, 1969], p. 429.)

sent of two-thirds of the membership (excluding warring parties). The only exception to this rule related to the ability of the Inter-American Peace Committee or its successor to investigate and mediate a conflict between any two members—at times with the approval of one conflicting party and at other times with that of both. However, one can assume that in such cases two-thirds of the membership would have given their approval if consulted.

COALITION CONFIGURATIONS IN INTER-AMERICAN RELATIONS, 1948-77

The two dominant themes which emerge from the literature of postwar inter-American security relations and the OAS are the overriding opposition of most Western Hemisphere states toward communist governments and movements and an adherence to the nonintervention norm by the non-Communist states with respect to their own relations. Since the only communist or pro-communist governments in the hemisphere were Guatemala from late 1953 to June 1954 and Cuba since mid-1960, the inter-American system can be described as a consensual one for the years 1948-53 and mid-1954 to mid-1960, and a very asymmetric bipolar one (with a nonintervention consensus within the dominant grouping) for the first half of 1954 and the years since mid-1960.

Two other themes concerning inter-American security relations that are often mentioned in writings on the subject relate to the particular types of conflicts within the dominant non-Communist grouping. First, it is put forward that interventions by the United States in Latin American countries are not treated like the aggressions of other hemispheric states and instead are supported or at least tolerated by the weaker states in the hemisphere. And second, it is stated that for a particular period of time (1959 to 1962 or 1963) a majority of states did not oppose interventions by democratic states against authoritarian ones—and, in fact, supported them. While there is some evidence that U.S. interventions during the entire postwar period and democratic states' aggressions against authoritarian ones during the years 1959-63 were treated differently by the OAS members, the evidence on these matters is not at all clearcut. Despite the fact that there is some doubt regarding the importance of these two factors and that they relate to a small number of conflicts within the inter-American system, they will be examined in subsequent parts of this chapter, since they certainly had some influence and have been discussed a great deal in the literature on inter-American relations.

The Noncommunist-Communist Axis of Conflict

At the time of the founding of the OAS in 1948, the cold war between the Soviet and Western groupings was already the most important factor in world security relations. There was little doubt on which side the American states fell at that time. And except for Guatemala between 1950 and 1954 (nonaligned but with a definite procommunist orientation in late 1953 and early 1954), Cuba since 1959 (nonaligned in 1959 and early 1960 and procommunist afterward), Brazil from 1960 to 1963 (nonaligned), Peru from 1968 to 1975 (nonaligned), Bolivia from 1969 to 1971 (nonaligned), Chile from 1970 to 1973 (nonaligned), and Jamaica since 1972 (nonaligned), that orientation has remained basically unchanged.[39] One author noted in 1969 that the foreign policies of the Latin American states were noteworthy for the fact that they did not follow the "desatellization" process going on elsewhere in the world and have remained instead "within the anachronistic framework of the Cold War."[40] During the late 1960s and early 1970s it appeared that this pattern might change as openly leftist or at least left-leaning regimes came to power in countries such as Peru, Ecuador, Bolivia, Chile, Jamaica, and Argentina. However, with the exception of Jamaica, most of these regimes have since been replaced by right-wing regimes or have moderated their leftist policies. Even with the upsurge of economic nationalism and the new pragmatism that has characterized the trade relations of many American countries in the 1970s, the majority have remained strongly opposed to communism. The result of this anticommunist orientation among most Latin American states has been a highly asymmetric bipolar configuration when conflicts have taken place between the Communist and non-Communist states. Indeed, in such situations in the past this axis has clearly dominated other considerations, including the nonintervention norm, often leading observers to view the OAS as an "anti-communist alliance" rather than a collective security body.[41]

The basic anticommunist orientation of the Latin American states was reflected in several OAS declarations very early in the Organization's history. At the founding conference at Bogotá in 1948, for example, members of the Organization passed a Resolution on the Preservation and Defense of Democracy in the Americas, which declared that "by its anti-Democratic nature and interventionist tendency, the political activity of international communism or any other totalitarian doctrine is incompatible with the concept of American freedom."[42] A similar resolution, stressing the importance of suppressing communist subversion, was also passed at the Fourth Meeting of the Foreign Ministers in 1951.[43] When, by 1954, Guatemala became the first American state to break the anticommunist consensus, Washington responded by proposing to the Tenth Inter-American Conference in 1954 a Declaration of Solidarity for the Preservation of the Political Integrity of the American States against the Intervention of International Communism. While the declaration did not envision that OAS sanctions would be imposed against such "threats," and while Latin American approval was eventually secured on the understanding that the resolution was merely "preventative,"[44] one could deduce from it that the Organization would not act with complete impartiality in conflicts between Communist and non-Communist states.

Fidel Castro's ascendancy in Cuba aroused the anticommunist bias of the OAS. While there were a number of indications of the Castro government's sympathy for socialism and the Soviet grouping in 1959 and early 1960, it was not until July 1960 that Khrushchev's offer of protection to Cuba and Castro's statements in return revealed a formal association between Cuba and the Soviet camp. Prodded by the United States, the OAS met at San José, Costa Rica in August 1960 to discuss the question of Sino-Soviet intervention in the hemisphere and Cuba's encouragement of it. The Declaration of San José fell short of what the United States had wanted in that it made no mention of Cuba and the USSR. At the time some Latin American states were still very reluctant to criticize Cuba directly since they still sympathized with some of the goals and policies of the Castro government. However, there was no doubt about the general orientation of the Latin American countries, given their unanimous backing for the declaration's condemnation of extrahemispheric intervention, the acceptance of it by an American state, and Sino-Soviet exploitation of the economic and social situation in the hemisphere.[45]

By the time that the OAS members next met to discuss the issue of Cuba and its foreign policy in January 1962, many of the Latin American states had become much more critical of the Cuban government as a result of its promotion of subversion in democratic as well as authoritarian countries and its increasing ties with the Soviet Union and its allies. Consequently, at the all-important conference in Punta del Este the Castro regime was excluded from further participation in the OAS, although two states (Cuba and Mexico) opposed the resolution and five abstained.[46] Members were unanimous, however, in their condemnation of Cuba during the 1962 missile crisis, when they were confronted with the reality of substantial military ties between China and the USSR.* And, when Cuban subversion in Venezuela was

---

*On October 23, 1962, the Council as Organ of Consultation condemned "Sino-Soviet aggression through Cuba" and urged individual states to take appropriate steps to remove the threat—thereby legitimizing U.S. actions in the crisis. (Gordon Connell-Smith, The Inter-American System [London: Oxford University Press, 1966], p. 257.)

sufficiently documented in 1964, the OAS agreed (with four abstaining) on binding economic sanctions against the recalcitrant state.[47] It was clear that, while they might vary in their willingness to take specific steps against communist governments, the American states were strongly opposed to their existence (especially when they had extra-hemispheric ties) in the Western Hemisphere and were not averse to registering that opposition through the OAS.

Since the OAS deliberations on the Cuban problem between 1960 and 1967, the antipathy of the Latin American system toward anticommunism has not been as highly visible. No large Cuban interventions have occurred and no communist regimes have come to power in the hemisphere since then, so the Latin Americans have not had to make a demonstrable response. As noted previously, openly leftist or left-leaning regimes have appeared at various times in Peru, Ecuador, Bolivia, and Chile, but all have taken extreme care not to follow in Castro's footsteps, knowing full well what the response of the United States and the majority of American states would be.* Several states also resumed direct relations with Cuba during the late 1960s and early 1970s, and in July 1975 it was finally resolved at the San José Conference to give OAS members freedom to lift the sanctions against Cuba (the vote was 16 in favor, 3 against, with 2 abstentions).[48] However, these developments were only a result of the fact that Cuba was then inactive—or impotent—as a subversive force in Latin America and that the Latin Americans, as always, wished to assert their independence of the United States. With the fall of the Torres regime in Bolivia, the Allende regime in Chile, and the Perón regime in Argentina, the general shift to the right by the governments of Peru, Ecuador, and Panama, and the increasing influence of the extremely conservative regime in Brazil in the years immediately prior to the end of this study, anticommunism was still a very powerful force in Latin America.

The Nonintervention Consensus

While the anticommunist predispositions of most of the Western Hemisphere states have led them to act in a prejudicial manner in

---

*The Allende regime in Chile (1970-73) is a good case in point. Though a self-proclaimed Marxist, Allende did not denounce the Rio Treaty or the Mutual Assistance Agreement with the United States, and showed no intention of switching his sources of procurement of military supplies from the United States. (F. Parkinson, Latin America, The Cold War, and the World Powers 1945-1973 [Beverly Hills, Calif.: Sage, 1974], p. 239.)

conflicts between communist and noncommunist parties, the great majority of noncommunist states have generally opposed military interventions by one of their own number against another. As was previously described, the doctrine of nonintervention became an integral part of the inter-American systems following the acceptance of the doctrine (at least as far as armed intervention was concerned) by the United States in 1933. When the OAS itself was formed, the doctrine was given a central normative position in the inter-American security system, as the members agreed in Article 15 of the Charter that: "No state or group of states has the right to intervene, directly or indirectly, for any reason whatever, in the internal or external affairs of any other state." This provision was meant to apply not only to armed intervention but also to "any other form of interference," and to that end it was further agreed in Articles 16 and 17 that political and economic coercion by one state against another was prohibited. *

A number of reasons have been advanced for what Ferguson has termed the "ritualistic veneration" given by Western Hemisphere states to the principle of nonintervention. [49] These include: the strong fear by Latin American states that the United States might use its vast economic and military superiority to intervene in their countries—and a concomitant desire to bind the United States to the doctrine of nonintervention; the desire of the Latin Americans to discourage intervention by their neighbors; the desire of both the Latin Americans and the United States to deter the military intrusion of extracontinental powers; the American desire to promote stability among Latin American states so that their economic and military interests will not be disrupted; the Western orientation of most of the Western Hemisphere states on cold war issues (which negates one possible source or justification for intervention); and a considerable heterogeneity among OAS members with respect to their domestic political systems (which means that there is no effective consensus to support intervention aimed at the promotion of a particular kind of political system). On the last point, then, Slater has accurately noted that support for nonintervention became "the lowest common denominator of mutual interest—the maintenance of the existing system." [50] When conflicts have arisen between noncommunist states, then, the principle of nonintervention has been salient in determining policies of individual states

---

*The San José Protocol to the Rio Treaty contains a new article that supports collective economic security (that is, opposes "economic aggression"). The article was adopted by a vote of 20-1, with the single negative vote by the United States. (Alfred Pick, "Protocol Signed at San José Provides Reform of Rio Treaty," International Perspectives, September/October 1975, p. 29.)

and the collective behavior of the OAS. Indeed, when the principle has been challenged within the system, the strong consensus against such challenges has made possible a high degree of effective activity.

An Acceptance of the U.S. Interventions

The policies and influence of the United States have been posited as being very influential in the development of the communist-noncommunist axis of conflict and the nonintervention doctrine, but it has also been suggested that the Western Hemisphere superpower has been able to prevent OAS action with respect to its interventions against other states in the region. While the United States has been less susceptible to action by the OAS than other members when it has intervened in another American state, it is still questionable whether "the Colossus of the North" has been and is as free to act in the Western Hemisphere as a number of writers think. The reasons for holding this position will be presented in some detail in the last section of this chapter. But it should be noted here that the involvement of the communist issue in postwar American interventions in the Western Hemisphere and the small number of such interventions make such conclusions open to question.

Many contend that the United States can always bring sufficient economic and military power to bear on the Latin American states to force them to accept American policy. One author, Minerva Etzioni, has commented that "in cases of United States-Latin American controversy . . . the disproportionate distribution of power among the parties has made the OAS incapable of using the same flexible diplomatic techniques it has developed in dealing with strictly Latin American disputes."[51] However, another writer, Jerome Slater, has taken a more moderate position. In his view: "While the United States obviously exercises great influence in the OAS and occupies a central role in the collective decision-making process, it does not dictate policy. Rather it bargains, negotiates, and compromises, and although it can usually in effect veto action it strongly opposes, it by no means invariably gets its own way."[52] George Meek's quantitative study of U.S. influence in the OAS appears to confirm Slater's view. Between 1948 and 1974, of 124 proposals introduced or cosponsored by the United States in the OAS, its overall "batting average" was only 0.604 (and between 1961 and 1974 it was only 0.536).[53] Thus, it appears, particularly in the last decade, that while the superpower can probably prevent any particular action from being taken against it, it is not free to exclude the OAS, and in fact often has to accept some kind of OAS involvement that alters its own interventionist policies.

An Acceptance of Democratic States'
Interventions in Authoritarian States, 1959-63

A number of authors have posited that from 1959 to 1962 or 1963
the forces of democracy gained the upper hand (in both a numerical
and psychological sense) in the Western Hemisphere and that most
OAS members no longer sought to prevent and terminate aggressions
by democratic states against authoritarian ones.[54] What changed the
traditional support of many of the Latin American states for the nonintervention norm was the coming to power in the late 1950s of several
"democratic" governments—most notably those in Cuba and Venezuela.
The victory of Fidel Castro's forces in Cuba was particularly influential in creating a kind of "democratic euphoria" that gave the impression that the forces of social democracy were on the ascendancy
in the hemisphere. And it led many of the democratic or quasi-demo-
cratic states to give the promotion of democracy a high priority among
their goals in inter-American relations.[55] According to students of
the OAS, by 1962 or 1963 this period had ended for several reasons.
First, most Latin Americans became disenchanted when the government in Cuba became staunchly communist;[56] second, there were successful coups by authoritarian forces in a number of Latin American
countries;* and third, by late 1963 or certainly by early 1964, the
U.S. policy of actively promoting democratic regimes in the hemisphere was suddenly abandoned.[57]
While many of the "democratic" states were predisposed to support or tolerate aggressions against authoritarian regimes for three
or four years, this predisposition did not dominate their policy making
and hence that of the OAS, in all such conflicts. As will be indicated
in the last section of this chapter, many of the Latin American states,
including the democratic ones, were seriously cross-pressured by
their desire to both maintain the doctrine of nonintervention and yet
be responsive to the popular democratic currents of the times.

THE OAS'S PATTERNS OF
INTERVENTION AND SUCCESS

Between 1948 and 1977 there were 19 wars, crises, and military interventions involving OAS members. They fall into three of

---

*Robert Burr has remarked: "Following the 1962 military coup
in Peru, most Latin American nations indicated little taste for cooperative political action against anti-democratic political forces." (Our
Troubled Hemisphere [Washington: Brookings Institution, 1967], p. 70.)

the categories of conflicts outlined in the theory, and both these categories and the specific types of inter-American conflicts that are encompassed by them are set forth below.

Type of Conflict	Intervention	Success
Intercoalition (victim a member of a subordinate coalition)—conflicts between noncommunist and communist states where the latter was the victim, 1954, 1960-77	No	No
Intercoalition (victim a member of a dominant coalition)—conflicts between communist and noncommunist states where the latter was the victim, 1960-77	Yes	No
Threats or acts of aggression in a consensual system—conflicts between noncommunist states, 1948-77	Yes	Yes

The last type of conflict—conflicts between noncommunist states—requires some explanation since all such conflicts are viewed as violations of the nonintervention norm in a consensual international system. Such a system definitely existed for the years 1948 to 1953 and mid-1954 to mid-1960. However, during the first half of 1954 (when there was a procommunist regime in Guatemala) and in the years since mid-1960 (when a communist government existed in Cuba) there was strictly speaking a very asymmetric bipolar configuration and not a consensual one. In the theory it was hypothesized that in such a system members of a coalition would seek to resolve conflicts between themselves outside the collective security body. This did not take account of the fact that when one "pole" is a single state, the large majority of states can effectively exclude it from the decision-making process. In fact, the OAS formally excluded the Castro government from participating in its deliberations in January 1962. Because of this fact one can say that there was a consensual system among the participating member states.

In the previous section it was noted that a number of students of inter-American relations have argued that the nonintervention consensus was undermined by a democratic-authoritarian axis of conflict between 1959 and 1963 and an acceptance by Latin American states of U.S. interventions. These two theses would lead one to hypothesize that the OAS would not have sought to prevent or terminate the aggressions of democratic states against authoritarian ones during the years 1959-63 or those of the United States against Latin American states throughout the history of the Organization. There is undoubtedly some

TABLE 4

OAS Involvement in Inter-American Conflicts, 1948-77

	Hypothesis: No Intervention, Intercoalition (victim a member of a nondominant coalition)	Hypothesis: Intervention but Not success, Intercoalition (victim a member of a dominant coalition)	Hypothesis: Intervention and Success, Violations of Nonintervention Norm
No OAS action	Cuba-United States, 1961 (W) (#39)		Peru-Ecuador, 1953-55 (MI) (#10) Costa Rica-Nicaragua, 1954 (C)(#12) Paraguay-Argentina, 1959-60 (MI)(#34)
Number	1	0	3
Percent	33 1/3	0	21
OAS debate	United States-Cuba, 1962 (C) (#47)		Dominican Republic-Venezuela and Cuba, 1959 (MI)(#31) Dominican civil conflict (with threat of U.S. intervention), 1961 (C)(#44)
Number	1	0	2
Percent	33 1/3	0	14
OAS investigatory/mediatory committee	Guatemala-Nicaragua and Honduras, 1954 (W)(#11)		Costa Rica-Nicaragua, 1955 (W)*(#14) Honduras-Nicaragua, 1955 (W) *(#21) Haiti-Cuba, 1959 (MI)(#32) Haiti-Dominican Republic, April-May 1963 (C)*(#51) Haiti-Dominican Republic, August 1963 (MI)*(#52) Dominican civil conflict (with U.S. intervention), 1965 (W) (#67)
Number	1	0	6
Percent	33 1/3	0	43
OAS investigatory/mediatory committee and judgment		Venezuela-Cuba, 1963 (MI)(#55) Venezuela-Cuba, 1967 (MI)(#77)	Costa Rica-Nicaragua, 1948 (W)*(#5) Haiti-Dominican Republic, 1949-50 (C)*(#7) Honduras-El Salvador, 1969 (W)*(#86)
Number	0	2	3
Percent	0	100	21
Number of conflicts	3	2	14

Note: W = war; C = crisis; MI = military intervention; * = success. The number after each conflict identifies the location of the conflict description in the Appendix.

validity to these theses, although the evidence relating to them is some-what limited and/or contradictory; and they will be discussed in the latter parts of this section.

In Table 4 the patterns of OAS involvement in inter-American conflicts are presented, but before analyzing these, certain unique aspects of the table and the classifications of the inter-American conflicts will be noted. First, the types of organizational involvement set forth in the table are slightly different from those employed for other organizations. Instead of the last category being "recommen-dation/judgment," the following two types of involvement have been substituted—"investigatory/mediatory committee" and "investigatory/mediatory committee and judgment." The reason for this alteration is that the OAS seldom passed resolutions directed against a particular state during the course of a conflict since the members were reluctant to alienate a state and inhibit its cooperation with the Organization.[58] Rather, it generally created an investigatory/mediatory committee whose purposes were informing the members about the facts of the conflict, conveying the views of the members to the conflicting parties, and promoting the termination of the threat or act of aggression. In a few cases, it made rather oblique judgments of wrongdoing after the conflicts had terminated, but in only one case, the Honduran-El Sal-vadorian war of 1969, did it specifically call for a cease-fire and with-drawal during the course of the conflict. Second, given the above mod-ification of the definition of "organizational intervention," there has also been a change in the definition of "organizational success." Rather than defining success as compliance with an organizational di-rective, it will be defined as the termination of the threat or existence of military activities during the course of an OAS committee's involve-ment in it.

From an examination of the table it is clear that the OAS's pat-terns of involvement and success conform very closely to the hypo-theses. Of the three conflicts between communist and noncommunist states where the communist one was the victim, the OAS intervened in only one, and in that case (the invasion of Guatemalan exiles from Honduras and Nicaragua into Guatemala in 1954) the IAPC did not reach Guatemala prior to the overthrow of the government and did not carry on its investigation thereafter. With respect to the two conflicts between communist and noncommunist states where the noncommunist one was the victim, the OAS set up investigatory committees, con-demned the activities of the communist state and approved diplomatic and economic sanctions against it. Of the fourteen conflicts between noncommunist states the OAS intervened in nine (64 percent), and achieved success in seven of the nine. Also, in one of the two in which it did not achieve success (the invasion of Haiti by exiles from Cuba in 1959), the invasion had failed prior to the dispatch of the IAPC; and

in the other (the Dominican conflict of 1965) it certainly influenced the
character of the U.S. military action.

Of the three conflicts between communist and noncommunist
states in which the communist country was the victim, the one conflict that was never even debated by the OAS was the U.S.-sponsored
invasion of Cuba by Cuban exiles in 1961. Cuba, probably recognizing
that most OAS members were strongly prejudiced against it, did not
even call for an OAS debate but rather called on the United Nations to
condemn the U.S. action.* In the case of the American threat to invade Cuba in 1962 during the Cuban missile crisis, not only did the
Latin American states fail to support Cuba, but they supported a U.S.-
backed resolution calling on all OAS members to take action to prevent Cuba from receiving missiles to ensure that the weapons did
not become a threat to the hemisphere. Three Latin American countries (Bolivia, Brazil, and Mexico) stated that their backing of this
resolution did not include approval of the use of force against Cuba,
but there was little doubt that all of the OAS members were strongly
opposed to an increase in the power of that Communist state. It is,
of course, possible to interpret Cuba rather than the United States as
being the state threatening the peace in this particular conflict, but
the Cuban threat was solely a long-range potential one, whereas the
American threat was a very immediate one.

The only conflict of this type in which the OAS did "intervene"
was the invasion of Guatemala by exiles from Honduras and Nicaragua
in June 1954. Following the invasion on June 18, Guatemala called on
the Inter-American Peace Committee to send an investigatory body to
verify the aggressive activities of its neighboring states, but several
days later it rescinded its request since it perceived that it was more
likely to receive assistance from the United Nations than from the
OAS, whose members were anticommunist. Only after a second meeting of the UN Security Council on June 25 failed to provide it with any
assistance because of the Western states' support for OAS management of the conflict did Guatemala renew its request for an IAPC investigation. Prior to the committee's arrival in Guatemala, the government was overthrown, and there was never again an attempt by the
IAPC or the OAS Council to investigate the conflict, if the committee

---

*In a committee of the UN General Assembly, five Latin Amer-
ican states supported a resolution that could be considered a vague
criticism of the United States, but the remaining Latin American
countries backed a resolution, supported by the United States, that
called on all parties in the area to settle their differences peacefully.
(Minerva M. Etzioni, The Majority of One: Towards a Theory of Regional Compatibility [Beverly Hills, Calif.: Sage, 1970], pp. 156-58.)

had arrived in Guatemala during the fighting, it is highly unlikely that it would have provided a great deal of assistance to the Guatemalan government, as a result of the anticommunist sentiments of most of the OAS members. The United States in particular was strongly opposed to any action that would impede the success of the invasion, and as Slater has written: "The strategy of the United States in the period immediately following the invasion was to give the attacking forces sufficient time to overthrow the Arbenz government, while preventing that regime from obtaining assistance from either the UN or the OAS. To this end it was necessary for the OAS to take just enough action to justify the exclusion of the UN, but not so much as to endanger the success of the Castillo Armas coup."[59] In such cases of aggression against a communist state, most of the OAS members wanted the collective security system to fail, and, as is indicated by the previous three conflicts, they were eminently successful in this policy.

There were only two conflicts between communist and noncommunist states in which the latter was the victim which clearly fall within our definition of military intervention. These concern the Cuban dispatch of guerrilla forces and weapons to Benezuela in late 1963 and 1967.* In each of these conflicts Venezuela submitted complaints to the OAS regarding the Cuban interventions, and in both cases the Council set up investigatory committees to verify the charges. In the case of the first conflict there was a hiatus between the issuance of the report in February 1964 with its formal condemnation of Cuba and the establishment of sanctions against it in July 1964, since a number of states were reluctant to approve the diplomatic and economic sanctions against Cuba that the majority advocated. It was only after the military coup in Brazil in April 1964, which brought a very anticommunist government to power, that a voting majority in favor of the sanctions came into existence. At the July 1964 meeting the OAS

---

*In 1959 there were accusations by a number of countries, particularly the Dominican Republic and Haiti, of Cuban support for invasions of their countries, but these conflicts do not fall within this particular category since during 1959 Cuba was not a self-proclaimed Communist state and was not viewed as such by other Latin American countries. In November 1960, there were allegations by Nicaragua of Cuban assistance to an exile invasion force of 200-300, but despite the fact that Cuba was a Communist state at that time, this conflict is not included since there were no more than a handful of Cubans in the force and since it had been organized in Costa Rica (without any assistance from the government of the latter state). The small amount of Cuban assistance, thus, does not qualify it for inclusion in the population of conflicts being analyzed in this study.

called for a mandatory break in diplomatic and consular relations, a suspension of trade except in foodstuffs and medicine, and a suspension of all sea transport except that necessary for humanitarian purposes.* The OAS's consideration of the Cuban sponsorship of the landing of guerrillas and weapons in Venezuela in May 1967 was considered in conjunction with lesser forms of Cuban subversion in other Latin American countries following the All-Peoples Solidarity Conference in Havana in October 1966.[60] Following an OAS committee's verification of Cuban subversive activities in Venezuela and other Latin American countries during the summer of 1967, the Council condemned the Cuban actions and reiterated its support for the sanctions against Cuba that had been adopted in 1964. As will be clearer following the analysis of conflicts between noncommunist states, the OAS's willingness to condemn an aggressor and initiate sanctions against it were much greater when the aggressing state was communist than when it was noncommunist.

Drier has written that "the outright failures of the regional collective security system . . . have been those concerned not with truly inter-American disputes but with broader power conflicts, essentially those of the Cold War, which lie outside of the competence of a regional system as such. Such was the case of Guatemala in 1954 and of Cuba since 1960."[61] This statement by Drier is only partially correct. Where conflicts within the Western Hemisphere took on a distinctly cold war character and where a communist state was the victim, the collective security system certainly failed to function; but where the victim was a noncommunist state, it operated with remarkable vigor. While the policies of most OAS members in both types of conflicts were governed by their opposition to communism, in one group of disputes there was a dovetailing of the purposes of a collective security system and their anticommunism, and in the other category of disputes there was a head-on conflict between these imperatives.

As was previously noted, there were fourteen conflicts between noncommunist states in the hemisphere, and the OAS became substantively involved in nine of these. Of the other five, there were three that were never even debated by the Organization. In the first of the three conflicts, Ecuador initiated a number of border clashes with Peru between 1953 and 1955, but Peru did not bring the issue to the OAS, probably because it was only a harassing action on the part

---

*Mexico, Chile, Bolivia, and Uruguay opposed the resolution, and Argentina abstained; but all except Mexico complied with its strictures. (Jerome Slater, The O.A.S. and United States Foreign Policy, [Columbus: Ohio State University Press, 1967], pp. 169-71.)

of Ecuador. Also, Peru could always appeal to the "guarantor" powers (one of which was the United States) of the settlement of the 1942 dispute between it and Ecuador. The second conflict was the Nicaraguan threat to Costa Rica during the summer of 1954, and on that occasion the U.S. dispatch of five planes to Costa Rica was sufficient to persuade Nicaragua to end its threat of military intervention. Since the Nicaraguan troops never crossed the border and the crisis was relatively short-lived, Costa Rica apparently felt that there was no need to take the issue to the OAS. The third conflict involved armed forays by Paraguayan exiles from Argentina into Paraguay in 1959-60. The authoritarian Paraguayan regime claimed that Argentina was assisting the exiles but did not appeal to the OAS, perhaps because it feared a rebuff.

The two conflicts between non-Communist states that the OAS only debated were the Venezuelan and Cuban sponsorship of an exile invasion of the Dominican Republic in 1959 and the U.S. threat to intervene in the Dominican Republic in 1961. In both cases the failure of the OAS to act was due to the antiauthoritarian sentiments of many OAS members. In the case of the intervention in the Dominican Republic in 1959, the Dominican Republic government withdrew its complaint from the OAS when its representatives perceived that many Latin American states would refuse to offer protection or support to the autocratic Trujillo regime. In the case of the U.S. threat to intervene in the Dominican Republic in 1961, the United States was seeking to deter the overthrow of the Joaquim Balaguer government by forces who had been associated with the former Dominican Republic dictator, General Rafael Trujillo, who had been assassinated the previous spring. The Balaguer government was cooperating with the OAS in organizing democratic elections at this time, and therefore the U.S. threat to defend it militarily went unopposed by the great majority of OAS states. The only country that publicly opposed the U.S. action was Cuba, which called for an OAS debate of the American threat, since it feared that acceptance of American intervention in the domestic politics of OAS members would establish a precedent for future actions against itself.

Of the nine conflicts involving noncommunist states in which the OAS did intervene, it achieved success in seven of them in that during the course of its intervention the threats or acts of military aggression were terminated. In one of the cases in which it did not succeed, the Cuban sponsorship of an exile invasion of Haiti in 1959, the intervention had been defeated prior to the IAPC investigation. In the other conflict, the American intervention in the Dominican Republic civil war of 1965, the OAS certainly influenced the character of the American intervention as well as the outcome of the civil conflict, but it certainly did not terminate the American military presence in the Dominican Republic. As will be noted later, the OAS responses to this latter conflict were significantly due to a fear that a communist or procommunist government could emerge from the domestic turmoil.

The first two conflicts out of the seven in which the OAS did intervene (the Nicaraguan support for an exile invasion of Costa Rica in 1948 and the Dominican Republic threat to Haiti in December 1949-January 1950) were the only two cases in which the OAS explicitly criticized the behavior of the aggressing or threatening states after the termination of the conflicts. But even in these two cases it balanced its criticisms of these states with observations that other states were engaged in plotting aggressive interventions against them. In the case of the sponsorship of an exile invasion of the democratic state of Costa Rica by the authoritarian Nicaraguan regime, the OAS committee judged that the attack on Costa Rica had originated in Nicaragua, and it helped to supervise a cessation of hostilities and a withdrawal of forces. Several months later the OAS Council did implicitly criticize Nicaragua by stating that it should have taken measures to prevent the entry of the exile force into Costa Rica, but it also called on Costa Rica to withdraw its support from the Caribbean Legion, which was preparing military actions against authoritarian regimes in the Caribbean region. In the Dominican Republic-Haitian conflict, the committee reported that the Dominican Republic regime was supporting antigovernment groups in Haiti and had mobilized forces on its border with Haiti, and it assisted in normalizing relations between the two states. The Council criticized the Dominican Republic afterward for acting contrary to the principles of the inter-American system, but it also noted that the Dominican Republic was the object of subversive plots in Guatemala and Cuba. In both cases the primary objectives of the OAS were the termination of the conflicts and the promotion of agreements or understandings aimed at preventing future support for the political opponents of the other state. There was also a clear policy of not singling out one state for condemnation so as to inhibit its cooperation with the Organization.

When there was another invasion of Costa Rica by exiles from Nicaragua in early 1955, an OAS committee verified the attack and afterward helped the two states to establish a demilitarized zone along their common border. During the course of the fighting the OAS Council passed a vague resolution that sanctioned the U.S. dispatch of several planes to Costa Rica, but neither during nor after the fighting did it condemn the Nicaraguan government. Again, in 1957 Nicaragua was involved in a conflict with one of its neighbors, but this time it was an attempt by Nicaragua to seize a piece of territory that had been awarded to Honduras by international arbitration in 1905. In this case the committee was given a mandate not only to report on the facts of the conflict and to assist the parties in terminating their hostilities but also to assist them in reaching a settlement of substantive issues. The committee was instrumental in promoting a cease-fire and a withdrawal of forces, and it later obtained agreement from the two governments to submit their dispute to the International Court of Justice (which in 1960 awarded the territory to Honduras).

Between 1959 and 1963 there were a number of conflicts (including the two discussed above that only elicited debate) that involved attempts by "democratic" states in the hemisphere to overthrow authoritarian regimes.* While the OAS did show some partiality in favor of the "democratic" aggressors in these conflicts, it certainly did act to uphold the nonintervention norm (at least to a significant extent) in three of them. In 1959 Haiti complained that it had been invaded by an exile force from Cuba, and it asked the Inter-American Peace Committee to investigate the intervention. The IAPC did establish that the force had come from Cuba, and it tried to enter Cuba in order to investigate whether the Cuban government had supported it. But it was denied entry to the latter country. While the IAPC did not call for further OAS action in the conflict, its report can be taken as an implicit indictment of Cuban complicity.

In 1963 there were two conflicts between Haiti and the Dominican Republic, which were due largely to attempts by the Dominican Republic regime to overthrow the autocratic dictatorship of President François Duvalier in Haiti. During the crisis in late April and early May there was a great deal of friction between the two governments as a result of the Haitian government's attempt to arrest its political opponents who had sought asylum in the Dominican Republic embassy, the refusal of Haiti to permit the departure of the asylees, and Dominican Republic support for Haitian groups opposed to the government. When Haiti complained that the Dominican Republic was planning to invade it and was supporting antigovernment forces, and when the Dominican Republic regime countered with condemnations of Haitian policy toward the asylees, the OAS dispatched a committee to assist the parties in securing a settlement and preventing an outbreak of war. The Haitian government thought that both this committee and a subsequent one were partial in favor of the Dominican Republic gov-

---

*There was only one attempt by an authoritarian government to overthrow a democratic one during this period, and it was the dispatch of a small group of men by the Dominican Republic regime to assassinate President Betancourt of Venezuela in 1960. Because it did not involve an intervention of more than 25 men, it is not included in this analysis. The OAS did condemn the Dominican Republic regime for this action, and it also initiated diplomatic and trade sanctions against it.

ernment. However, the committees were very instrumental in securing agreements on some of the issues that had exacerbated relations
between the countries and in obtaining a demobilization of the Dominican Republic forces on the border. The Council also rejected a Dominican Republic and U.S. request that the OAS create a force to overthrow the Haitian government and promote the formation of a democratic government in that country. Thus, while the Haitian government may have felt that the OAS and its committee were prejudiced in
favor of the Dominican Republic in that they failed to condemn the latter state, the Organization definitely acted to prevent either a unilateral or multilateral military action against the Duvalier regime.
There was a recurrence of the conflict between these two states several months later, in August 1963, when Haiti complained that several
groups of Haitian exiles had entered its territory from the Dominican
Republic and that they had been supported by the government of the
latter state. Again, while the OAS committee that was dispatched to
investigate and mediate the conflict did not condemn the Dominican
Republic regime as Haiti wished, it was effective in securing informal
agreements from the two governments not to support military interventions by each other's exiles. In both stages of this conflict in 1963,
the OAS members, or at least a significant number of them, may have
shown a reluctance to condemn a democratic government that was seeking to promote the overthrow of an authoritarian one, but at the same
time they felt pressured to uphold the principle of nonintervention and
discourage military attacks against the authoritarian regime.

Probably the most complex of all the conflicts in which the OAS
has been involved was the Dominican Republic civil war of 1965, in
which the United States intervened militarily. The Dominican Republic regime had come to power in September 1963, when the country's
army overthrew the democratic government of Juan Bosch. Then,
during the last week of April 1965, Dominican Republic groups that
generally recognized Bosch as their leader sought to overthrow the
authoritarian government, which was backed by the army leaders.
Within four days of the outbreak of fighting the United States intervened militarily because it feared that there was a strong communist
element in the rebel force that might gain control of the Dominican
Republic government if the rebellion succeeded. During early May
the OAS both established a committee to promote a cease-fire between the warring factions and set up an Inter-American Peace Force
to prevent a renewal of fighting between the groups. Later OAS mediators and the Peace Force were very influential in securing a cease-
fire, obtaining the two factions' acceptance of a provisional government, and promoting free elections in the country. During the early
weeks of the conflict many of the Latin American states voiced disapproval of the unilateral character of the U.S. intervention, but the

great majority voiced implicit support for the basic purpose of the U.S. action. Their implicit approval of the U.S. intervention and their support for the OAS's involvement in the resolution of the domestic conflict were undoubtedly due in part to pressures exerted by the U.S. government. But much more fundamental were the interrelated goals of both the authoritarian and many democratic (for example, Costa Rica and Venezuela) governments that a communist regime should not be allowed to emerge from the domestic chaos in the Dominican Republic and that non-Western Hemispheric states should be excluded from the management of the conflict.* It is also noteworthy, however, that once the fears of the emergence of a communist regime began to fade as the true character of the rebels was understood by outside observers, most OAS members tried to make sure that the Inter-American Peace Force (including the U.S. contingent) acted in an impartial and nonprejudicial manner toward both parties.[62]

The last conflict to be discussed is the Honduran-El Salvadorian war of 1969, and it is the one conflict in which the OAS called for a cease-fire and withdrawal during the course of a conflict and also threatened to impose sanctions if the aggressor did not withdraw. The Council also created a committee to investigate the facts of the conflict and to promote its directives and backed the successful attempt of the OAS secretary-general to mediate a final settlement. The reason for El Salvador's attack on Honduras was its government's resentment of the treatment of Salvadorians living in Honduras; and as part of the final settlement the OAS was able to achieve an agreement between the two countries concerning treatment of each other's nationals. The reasons that the OAS responded more strongly to this aggression than to others were that the conflict involved clashes between the regular armed forces of two states and that it did not involve an ideological issue that caused other Latin American states to side with one of the parties.

---

*Jerome Slater, Intervention and Negotiation: The United States and the Dominican Revolution (New York: Harper & Row, 1970), pp. 79-80; "The Limits of Legitimization in International Organizations: The Organization of American States and the Dominican Crisis," International Organization 23 (Winter 1969): 54-55; Yale H. Ferguson, "The Dominican Intervention of 1965: Recent Interpretations," International Organization 27 (Autumn 1973): 534. There were five states that did oppose the creation of the Inter-American Peace Force (IAPF) since it would represent a legitimization of U.S. intervention; they were Chile, Mexico, Peru, Ecuador, and Uruguay. The resolution creating the IAPF was only passed by a bare two-thirds majority—with one vote coming from the representation of the besieged regime in the Dominican Republic.

The preceding analysis of the OAS's patterns of intervention and success in inter-American conflicts is generally supportive of both the previously articulated hypotheses and the description of the coalition configuration in inter-American relations. First, in a very asymmetric configuration, as existed between communist and noncommunist states in the hemisphere, a collective security organization will not act to protect a member of a small subordinate grouping, but will act forcefully when a member of the dominant grouping is threatened or attacked by a member of the subordinate one. During the 29 years of the OAS's history that have been analyzed in this study, the Organization did little to defend communist states when they were attacked, whereas it acted forcefully when the communist country was the aggressor. Second, the Organization acted quickly and effectively in the great majority of those conflicts between the noncommunist members who supported the nonintervention norm. At the same time, in so doing, the OAS generally refrained from any condemnations of the aggressing states so as not to inhibit their collaboration with the Organization. As Slater has commented:

> The majority of the OAS have felt that in the interest of
> hemispheric solidarity the primary goal of collective
> action in intra-hemispheric conflicts should be the quick
> restoration of the status quo ante and the resumption of
> amicable or at least acceptable relations between the
> disputants. The naming and condemning of an aggres-
> sor would have exacerbated tensions and perhaps pre-
> cipitated a walkout. [63]

In those few conflicts of this type where the Organization failed to intervene, the lack of response was due in most cases to the strongly antiauthoritarian sentiments of many states in the 1959-63 period.

Third, while the antiauthoritarian predispositions of a significant number of OAS members did have some effect on the OAS collective security system during the years 1959-63, they did not have the overriding influence that is often attributed to them. They were responsible for the failure of the Organization to respond to the Cuban and Venezuelan intervention in the Dominican Republic in 1959, the U.S. threat to intervene in that same country in 1961, and probably the Paraguayan-Argentine conflict of 1959-60. However, they did not prevent the Inter-American Peace Committee from carrying out an investigation of the Cuban intervention in Haiti in 1959, and mediating the two conflicts between Haiti and the Dominican Republic in 1963. Also, the majority of OAS members refused to go along with the Dominican Republic and U.S. request for a collective OAS intervention in Haiti at the time of the first Haitian-Dominican Republic conflict in May 1963. In these latter conflicts a number of OAS members showed a reluctance to identify the democratic state as an aggressor but did support OAS activities that would prevent and deter military actions against the autocratic regimes. Many of the members were cross-pressured by their support for democracy and their adherence to the nonintervention norm, but most of them (at least after 1961) gave priority to the principle of nonintervention.

Finally, it is difficult to accept the viewpoint of some students of inter-American relations that the Latin American countries automatically accepted interventions by the United States since all of the threats or acts of U.S. military intervention concerned either attempts to undermine communism in the hemisphere or to promote democratic governments during the 1955-63 period. With respect to the Bay of Pigs invasion in 1961 the absence of OAS action was undoubtedly due to the anticommunist sentiments of most members,* and in the case of the Cuban missile crisis, not only did the Latin American states not criticize the U.S. policy but they actually supported it. As was previously noted concerning the Dominican Republic crisis of 1965, the acceptance of the U.S. intervention by most Latin American states and their creation of an OAS force (which included the U.S. troops) were due significantly to the fact that they shared with the United States a concern that the civil war could lead to "another Cuba" in the Caribbean. Also, when their fears regarding the emergence of a communist regime (which were admittedly influenced by the U.S. government) began to disappear, they put strong and effective pressure on the U.S. government not to use its troops in a manner prejudicial to either of the domestic factions. The only other case of a threat or act of U.S. intervention was the threat to intervene in the Dominican Republic in 1961 if forces loyal to the Trujillo family tried to overthrow the Balaguer government that was cooperating with an OAS committee in organizing democratic elections. In all of the four conflicts cited above, it is thus possible to posit that the failure of the Latin Americans to condemn the threats or acts of U.S. intervention were due more to their anticommunism or their antiauthoritarianism than to their fear of opposing the United States. The United States undoubtedly has had, and still does have, a great deal of influence in shaping

----

*During the debate of the conflict in the UN General Assembly's First Committee, Mexico did strongly oppose the U.S. action, and Bolivia, Brazil, Chile, and Ecuador offered much milder criticisms of the U.S. action. The other OAS members did not offer any critical comments. (Minerva M. Etzioni, The Majority of One: Towards a Theory of Regional Compatibility [Beverly Hills, Calif.: Sage, 1970], pp. 156-57.)

political developments in the Western Hemisphere. However, it is probably incorrect to judge that the Latin American states would have accepted, or would accept, U.S. military interventions in a subservient fashion. It should be recalled that the major precondition for their joining an inter-American collective security system was the U.S. acceptance of the doctrine of nonintervention, and most of them would not set aside their adherence to this doctrine unless they perceived that a U.S. intervention was directly or indirectly aimed at an extrahemispheric threat to themselves. *

In conclusion, it is important to note that the OAS has been remarkably active and successful in bringing about the termination or at least the de-escalation of most security conflicts in the Western Hemisphere—particularly when compared to the frequency of intervention and success of other collective security bodies. In fact, the OAS has had such a stabilizing effect on the hemisphere that there has not been a single military conflict between member states since 1969; and though future conflicts cannot be ruled out, † the continued existence of the OAS is bound to inhibit the outbreak of such disputes. The general adherence of most states at most times to the principle of nonintervention and the pressure which the United States has been able to exert behind OAS decisions[64] have been largely responsible for these developments. While the Latin American states in recent years have pursued policies at variance with those of the United States in many international-issue areas (particularly economic ones), there is little indication of fundamental or even important change in their policies toward military conflicts in the hemisphere. Ideological and economic differences have not led to hostile security relations between them, and the Latin American states and the United States both seem to view adherence to the nonintervention norm as furthering their long-term interests. ‡

---

*During the 1970s the Latin Americans have been particularly sensitive on the issue of U.S. domination of the OAS. They have sought additional reassurances from the United States of its continued support for the doctrine of nonintervention (particularly in the economic sphere) at conferences such as the Tlatelolco Conference in 1972, and they have sought substantive changes in the OAS system to make it more relevant to their, rather than U.S., interests. (G. Pope Atkins, Latin America in the International Political System [New York: Free Press, 1977], chap. 10.)

† As of the end of 1977 there were still territorial disputes brewing between Argentina-Chile, Chile-Bolivia-Peru, Peru-Ecuador, and Colombia-Venezuela.

‡ While, on the whole, in recent years Latin Americans have sought to downplay the collective security aspects of the OAS and em-

NOTES

1. Arthur P. Whitaker, The Western Hemisphere Idea: Its Rise and Decline (Ithaca, N. Y.: Cornell University Press, 1965), pp. 34-38.

2. J. Lloyd Mecham, The United States and Inter-American Security, 1889-1960 (Austin: University of Texas Press, 1967), p. 46.

3. Ibid., p. 48.

4. Thomas F. McGann, Argentina, The United States and the Inter-American System, 1880-1914 (Cambridge, Mass.: Harvard University Press, 1957), pp. 130-48.

5. Ibid., pp. 188-217.

6. Gordon Connell-Smith, The Inter-American System (London: Oxford University Press, 1966), p. 46.

7. On the reservations of the United States and the Latin Americans toward a stronger inter-American system, see ibid., pp. 49, 53-54; Jerome Slater, The O.A.S. and United States Foreign Policy (Columbus: Ohio State University Press, 1967), p. 20.

8. Whitaker, op. cit., p. 123; Connell-Smith, op. cit., p. 55.

9. Connell-Smith, op. cit., p. 57.

10. Ibid., pp. 61-63. Albert K. Weinberg, Manifest Destiny: A Study of Nationalist Expansionism in American History (Baltimore: Johns Hopkins University Press, 1935; reprint ed., Chicago: Quadrangle Books, 1963), pp. 442-43.

11. Ibid., p. 73.

12. An excellent account of the formulation and character of this policy is Bryce Wood, The Making of the Good Neighbor Policy (New York: Columbia University Press, 1961), pp. 118-67 and passim.

13. Connell-Smith, op. cit., p. 90.

14. Mecham, op. cit., pp. 131-32.

15. Minerva M. Etzioni, The Majority of One: Towards a Theory of Regional Compatibility (Beverly Hills, Calif.: Sage, 1970), pp. 52-53.

16. Article 5, OAS Charter.

17. Article 50.

18. Article 80, rev. OAS Charter.

19. Articles 83-88.

---

phasize the economic and social aspects, even the most "progressive" regimes, such as those in Peru and Mexico, have made no effort to withdraw entirely from the collective security system. (G. Pope Atkins, Latin America in the International Political System [New York: Free Press, 1977], pp. 347, 379-80.)

20. M. Margaret Ball, The O.A.S. in Transition (Durham, N.C.: Duke University Press, 1969), p. 163.

21. Articles 39 and 40, OAS Charter.

22. Article 43.

23. Article 52.

24. Article 3(3), Rio Treaty.

25. Article 6.

26. Articles 7 and 8.

27. Articles 17 and 18.

28. Mecham, op. cit., p. 284.

29. Article 25, OAS Charter.

30. Articles 43 and 44.

31. Article 21.

32. Article 23.

33. Article 50, Pact of Bogotá.

34. John C. Dreier, The Organization of American States and the Hemisphere Crisis (New York: Harper & Row, 1962), p. 38.

35. Mecham, op. cit., p. 328.

36. Articles 83 and 84, rev. OAS Charter.

37. Article 86.

38. Articles 87 and 88.

39. On the strong military, political and economic ties of the Latin American states with the Western countries (especially the United States), see Herbert Goldhammer, The Foreign Powers in Latin America (Princeton, N.J.: Princeton University Press, 1972), pp. 18-78.

40. Espartaco, "The 'Latin American Crisis' and its External Framework," in Latin American International Politics, ed. Carlos Alberto Astiz (Notre Dame: University of Notre Dame Press, 1969), p. 20.

41. Slater, The O.A.S. and United States Foreign Policy, p. 110; idem, A Reevaluation of Collective Security: The O.A.S. in Action (Columbus: Ohio State University Press, 1965), p. 25; and Gordon Connell-Smith, "The Inter-American System: Problems of Peace and Security in the Western Hemisphere," in International Organization in the Western Hemisphere, ed. Robert W. Gregg (Syracuse: Syracuse University Press, 1968), p. 90.

42. Slater, The O.A.S. and United States Foreign Policy, p. 110.

43. Mecham, op. cit., pp. 431-33.

44. Slater, The O.A.S. and United States Foreign Policy, p. 120.

45. Mecham, op. cit., pp. 458-61; Slater, The O.A.S. and United States Foreign Policy, pp. 142-48.

46. Ibid., p. 156.

47. Slater, The O.A.S. and United States Foreign Policy, p. 171.

48. Alfred Pick, "Protocol Signed at San José Provides Reform of Rio Treaty," International Perspectives, September/October, 1975, p. 29.

49. Yale Ferguson, "Reflections on the Inter-American Principle of Non-Intervention: A Search for Meaning in Ambiguity," Journal of Politics 32 (August 1970): 629.

50. Slater, The O.A.S. and United States Foreign Policy, p. 38.

51. Etzioni, op. cit., p. 135. See, also, Connell-Smith, "The Inter-American System," p. 340.

52. Slater, The O.A.S. and United States Foreign Policy, pp. 174-75.

53. George Meek, "U.S. Influence in the Organization of American States," Journal of Inter-American Studies and World Affairs 17 (August 1975): 319.

54. John C. Drier, "The Organization of American States and United States Foreign Policy," International Organization 17 (Winter 1963): 45-47; idem, "The Special Nature of Western Hemispheric Experience with International Organization," in Gregg, ed., op. cit., p. 35; Etzioni, op. cit., p. 172; Slater, The O.A.S. and United States Foreign Policy, p. 189; idem, A Reevaluation of Collective Security, p. 30; Yale F. Ferguson, "The United States and Political Development in Latin America: A Retrospect and a Prescription," in Contemporary Inter-American Relations: A Reader in Theory and Issues, ed. Yale F. Ferguson (Englewood Cliffs, N.J.: Prentice-Hall, 1972), pp. 348-71.

55. Dreier, "The Organization of American States and United States Foreign Policy," p. 35.

56. Slater, The O.A.S. and United States Foreign Policy, p. 184.

57. Ibid., pp. 245-50.; Ferguson, "The United States and Political Development in Latin America: A Retrospect and A Prospect," pp. 71-75 and passim.

58. Slater, A Reevaluation of Collective Security, p. 41.

59. Slater, The O.A.S. and United States Foreign Policy, pp. 122-23.

60. Cuban policy of assisting Venezuelan and other Latin American revolutionaries, as well as its differences with the USSR on this matter, are described in D. Bruce Jackson, Castro, the Kremlin and Communism in Latin America (Baltimore: Johns Hopkins University Press, 1969), pp. 68-119.

61. Dreier, "The Special Nature", p. 34.

62. Jerome Slater, Intervention and Negotiation: The United States and the Dominican Revolution (New York: Harper & Row, 1970), pp. 73-74 and passim.

63. Slater, A Reevaluation of Collective Security, p. 41.

64. Ibid., p. 37.

4

The Organization of African Unity and Inter-African Conflicts

THE BACKGROUND AND CHARACTER
OF THE OAU COLLECTIVE SECURITY SYSTEM

The formation of the Organization of African Unity in May 1963 is generally regarded as the most important milestone in the development of Pan-Africanism. The political genesis of this movement can be traced back at least to 1900, when the first Pan-African Congress was held in London, its two central concerns at the time being the eradication of the "derogatory image of Africans and Negroes prevalent in Europe" and the combating of "racial discrimination everywhere." To accomplish these tasks the participants advocated publicizing existing injustices and exerting pressure for both liberal reforms and eventual majority rule in Africa. [1] Since most of the delegates to the early Congress meetings were American and West Indian in origin, the movement tended to be preoccupied with achieving equality for blacks in these societies, and at first devoted little attention to the political future of Africans.

This situation began to change by the interwar period. American and West Indian participation in the congresses declined and that of Africans increased. As a result, the movement became more concerned with African problems and priorities. By the 1930s Britain had become the center for Pan-African thought and agitation, and the growth of black students' and friends' associations supplemented the activity of the congresses. Under the leadership of such future luminaries of African politics as T. R. Makonnen and Jomo Kenyatta, these associations adhered to the dictum of George Padmore that the achievement of national independence by the African colonies had to precede attempts to promote continental unity. They agitated against continued colonial rule and forged strong links with and between political parties, labor unions, and other interest groups in Africa.[2] By 1945 the movement had become almost solely concerned with the issue of independence for the African colonies. The fifth Congress, held at Manchester in that year, marked the beginning of a phase of intense anticolonial struggle. The Pan-Africanists' determination not to "starve any longer while doing the world's drudgery in order to support a false aristocracy and a faded imperialism" ushered in the postwar era of African decolonization that culminated in the independence of most African colonies in the late 1950s and early 1960s.[3]

By the early 1960s there had developed among the newly independent African states some serious divisions over such questions as the nature and extent of Pan-African cooperation and the character of their foreign and domestic policies. The most important initial division was between those who sought to uphold and legitimize the principle of national sovereignty and those who, like President Nkrumah of Ghana, saw the political unification of Africa as the most pressing priority. In 1958 Nkrumah called a Conference of Independent African States at Accra to which representatives were sent from Egypt, Ethiopia, Liberia, Libya, Tunisia, Morocco, Sudan, and Ghana. While the governments of all these states agreed that the colonial powers should proceed speedily toward the setting of independence dates for all remaining colonial territories of Africa (including Algeria), the issue of African unity proved more contentious, as most delegates exhibited hostility to Nkrumah's continentalist proposals. The Final Declaration emphasized the necessity of safeguarding the "hard-won independence, sovereignty and territorial integrity" of African states.[4] A second Conference was held in 1960, and once again there was widespread opposition to Nkrumah's Pan-Africanist conceptions, with Nigeria arguing that political unification was premature and warning against any leader purporting to act as a "Messiah of Pan-Africanism."[5]

Faced with this solid opposition from almost all African governments, Nkrumah resorted to alternative strategies to promote his Pan-African ideas. In particular he tried to foster support among African publics and nongovernmental groups such as trade unions and student groups by organizing the All-African Peoples Congress. This body endorsed Nkrumah's views at its 1958 and 1960 conferences and called for the establishment of a "Commonwealth of African States." Since this body and those who composed it in fact commanded no significant political influence in Africa, Nkrumah concurrently tried another approach. In 1958, at his instigation, the Union of African States was created. At first composed of only Ghana and Guinea, this organization was open to all African states that shared the goal of African unity as defined in the Nkrumahist philosophy. The fact that Mali was the only other state to add its weight to the union (in 1960) testifies to the lack of support among African leaders for Nkrumah's brand of Pan-Africanism. Lacking significant African support, the union was dissolved in 1963.

By 1960 the issue of a Pan-African political federation had receded in importance, despite Nkrumah's attempts to keep it alive, and instead the independent African states began to quarrel over ideological and foreign policy issues. The event that most clearly served to crystallize these differences among African states was the Congo crisis that began in July 1960, but the issue of Algerian independence and the claims of Morocco on Mauritanian territory also tended to sharply divide African opinion. In the drawn-out Congo crisis, the split between those Congolese elements who were radical and preached nonalignment and those favoring pro-Western and conservative policies was really a microcosm of the division then existing among the new African states as a whole. [6]

The various political divisions characterizing inter-African relations at this time led to the formation of rival groups of states in 1960 and 1961. [7] The Brazzaville Group, formed in December 1960, was composed of 12 newly independent Francophone states, all of which wished to maintain close ties with France and friendly relations with the West in general. The Brazzaville Group—formally known as the Union of African States and Malagasy—voiced support for the then conservative Congolese regime of President Joseph Kasavubu and affirmed their continued friendship for France (although they appealed to Paris to allow Algeria to determine the character of its own government.)[8] The radical African states—Ghana, Guinea, Mali, the UAR, and Morocco—then formed their own association, known as the Casablanca Group, in January 1961.* These states backed former Congolese Prime Minister Patrice Lumumba and his leftist allies in the struggle for power in the Congo and declared that the UN role in the civil war was prejudicing the struggle against neo-colonialism in Africa. Their "African Charter" emphasized the centrality of decolonization and nonalignment in African international relations. However, the Casablanca states did not heed Nkrumah's call for African unification, and most of them would only agree to an intensification of "efforts for the creation of an effective form of cooperation among the African states in the economic, social and cultural domains."[9]

---

*The reason for Morocco's attendance at (and sponsorship of) the conference was that it hoped to garner support for its claim to Mauritania. Its own political system and ties with the West made it an anomaly in the radical camp. Libya and Ceylon attended the founding conference but failed to attend later meetings or to sign the Protocol to the Charter. The provisional government of Algeria was also represented, and signed the Charter and Protocol.

The Monrovia Group, made up of both the members of the Brazzaville Group and most of those states that had hitherto remained aloof from the rival blocs— Liberia, Nigeria, Somalia, Sierra Leone, Togo, Ethiopia, Libya, and Tunisia—was formed in May 1961. While the non-Brazzaville states that joined the Monrovia Group were often labeled as "moderates" by observers, [10] they in fact held political views closely resembling those of the conservative Francophone states. Like the Brazzaville Group, the new participants opposed political or military intervention by African states in each other's affairs and eschewed any idea of African political unification. Although they basically favored some form of nonalignment, these states actually supported cooperative ties with the West. At its founding conference the Monrovia Group states supported the central government of the Congo and the UN role in the country, took a moderate stand on the contentious issue of Algerian independence, and stated that African unity would be achieved not through political integration but rather through "social solidarity and political identity." [11] The Monrovia Group noted with regret the absence of members of the Casablanca Group but decided that another conference of African states should soon be held, at which a formal charter for an organization of African states would be drawn up. Accordingly, a meeting was held in January 1962 at Lagos, Nigeria, and the Organization of African and Malagasy States was established.* The charter of the organization again emphasized territorial integrity and political sovereignty and condemned the practice of subversion or interventionism by any African state in the affairs of another.

Thus by 1962 two distinct coalitions (the Casablanca and Monrovia Groups) had crystallized in Africa. These two groups of states took issue with one another over the question of the type of political, military, and economic ties that should be maintained with former colonial metropoles. And they also quarreled over the legitimacy of subversion to eradicate African regimes that the Casablanca states regarded as "neo-colonial," and, to a lesser extent, over the desirability of fostering socialism in Africa. It should be noted that within the Monrovia Group all members were agreed in opposing subversion (especially that emanating from radicals), but there were differences with respect to the proper type of relationship to be sought with the West. A number of Monrovia states, such as Ethiopia and Somalia, which had attended the 1961 Belgrade Conference of Nonaligned States, were proponents of African nonalignment, but as a whole their nonalignment was not markedly anti-Western as was that of the radical Casablanca states.

---

*The Monrovia states were joined in this by Tanganyika and Congo—Leopoldville.

The antagonism between rival African blocs did not seem to augur well for the future of Pan-African cooperation, but by 1963 a number of changes on the African political landscape had altered this situation somewhat. First, several of the specific sources of dispute which had contributed to the intergroup hostility, such as the Congolese crisis, the Moroccan-Mauritanian conflict, and the Algerian war of independence, had by 1963 either disappeared or subsided in intensity. Second, the Casablanca states had come to feel somewhat isolated from the prevailing trends of African politics, and hence they were willing to compromise their radical positions to some extent—particularly regarding the issue of Africans' intervening in the affairs of another African state to promote "progressive" regimes. The conservative states too were prepared to compromise in some areas if as a result they could elicit a commitment from the radical states to preserve the status quo. With each bloc now willing to alter earlier positions, the way was clear for the formation of an organization of which all independent African states would be members.

It was Emperor Haile Selassie of Ethiopia who initiated the events that led directly to the creation of the OAU when he invited all independent African states except South Africa and Togo* to attend a meeting at Addis Ababa in May 1963. All those invited agreed to attend with the single exception of Morocco, which objected to the presence of Mauritania. After much debate—notably on the subject of African political unification, a proposition that once again failed to capture the imaginations of most of the assembled African leaders—the delegates agreed on the Charter of the Organization of African Unity.† The Charter was signed on May 25, 1963, by the 30 independent states attending the meeting—Algeria, Burundi, Cameroun, the Central African Republic (which became the Central African Empire in 1977), Chad, Congo, Congo-Leopoldville (which became Zaire in 1971), Dahomey (which became Benin in 1975), Ethiopia, Gabon, Ghana, Guinea, Ivory Coast, Liberia, Libya, Malagasy Republic, Mali, Mauritania, Niger, Nigeria, Rwanda, Senegal, Sierra Leone, Somali Republic, Sudan, Tanganyika (which became Tanzania in 1965), Tunisia, Uganda, the UAR, and Upper Volta; and the OAU came into formal existence in December of the same year. The continuing process of decolonization in Africa expanded the OAU membership by 19 to include 49 states

---

*The Togolese government had just come to power as a result of a coup d'etat and many African governments wanted to discredit such political violence.

†For a description of the conference, see, Vincent Bakpetu Thompson, Africa and Unity: The Evolution of Pan-Africanism (New York: Humanities Press, 1969), pp. 181-99.

by December 1977: Morocco, Togo, Kenya (1963), Malawi, Zambia (1964), Gambia (1965), Botswana, Lesotho (1966), Equatorial Guinea, Mauritius, Swaziland (1968), Guinea Bissau (1974), Angola, Mozambique (1975), Cape Verde Islands, Comoros, São Tomé and Principe, Seychelles (1976), and Djibouti (1977).

The governing principles on which the African states agreed for their new organization were in large part borrowed from the Lagos Charter of the Monrovia Group. Thus, they reflected a very conservative conception of international organization, in that the inviolable integrity of the nation-state and its right to choose whether it would be bound by organizational decisions were recognized as the key features of the relationship between member states and the OAU itself. This conservative organizational orientation is expressed most clearly in Article III of the Charter, where "the sovereign equality of all member states," "non-interference in the internal affairs of states," and "respect for the sovereignty and territorial integrity of each member state and for its unalienable right to independent existence" are listed as the first three principles governing the functioning of the OAU. Two other principles spelled out in Article III—those calling for the decolonization of all African territories and the adoption of foreign policies of nonalignment by African states— were viewed as concessions to the more radical states, but these were in fact rather hollow victories, given that they were not accompanied by any precise statements concerning appropriate government actions or foreign policies.

Described in the Charter as the "supreme organ" of the OAU, the Assembly of Heads of State and Government has as its central task the promotion of the purposes of the Organization, the coordination of all its activities, and the reviewing of the "structures, functions and acts" of all organs and specialized agencies created in accordance with the Charter.[12] Composed of all the heads of state (or their delegated representatives), the Assembly meets annually in ordinary session and, if requested by a member and concurred in by a majority of member states, may be called into extraordinary session.[13] All Assembly resolutions, aside from procedural questions, require a two-thirds majority vote;[14] even then such resolutions are of a nonobligatory nature, as is true of the resolutions of all OAU organs. N. J. Padelford has noted, in connection with the nonobligatory character of OAU resolutions, that "the only power implicit in the system is that of the opinion of the other states."[15] A second organ, the Council of Ministers, is subordinate to the Assembly and is composed of the foreign ministers (or their designates) of all member states and meets twice annually.[16] Its resolutions—which are of course nonbinding—require only a simple majority vote,[17] but may be reviewed and nullified by the Assembly.[18]

Less salient to the security activities of the OAU are the Secretariat and the Commission on Conciliation, Mediation, and Arbitration. According to Article XVI, the administration of the OAU is to be carried out by a Secretariat headed by an administrative secretary-general—a phrasing which indicates the preference of Africans for a neutral, civil-servant type of head rather than for one who will seek to initiate or guide OAU operations.[19] The Commission was created as a result of a separate protocol formulated in July 1965.[20] It provided for the election of 21 Assembly members to serve on the Commission,[21] which was empowered to assist in settling disputes among members, either by acting as a group or through the mediation of individual members chosen by the parties to a dispute.[22] The Commission can act, however, only when requested by one of the involved parties, the Assembly, or the Council, and only when both disputants approve its intervention—limitations that again reflect the marked reluctance of African states to permit any incursion on their sovereignty. It is instructive to note that even with these strong safeguards, the OAU has never employed the Commission in any inter-African dispute, preferring instead to create ad hoc commissions or mediators in response to specific conflict situations.

While the OAU lacks strong normative and institutional bases for influencing inter-African conflicts, its basic voting rule (a two-thirds majority) allows it to intervene in a conflict as readily as any other organization. And although it is true that all of its resolutions only have the force that "the object states" attach to the opinions of the supporters of a given resolution, this is, in fact, a characteristic of all the collective security organizations examined in this study. With respect to the security functions of the OAU one scholar has observed that "the Organization is there and may be used if the disputing members so desire, but they are not committed to its utilization, nor to accepting any conflict settling advice that may be forthcoming."[23] If the OAU has weaknesses as compared to other collective security bodies, they derive not so much from its Charter as from the patterns and intensity of policy differences among members and the lack of material resources at the disposal of the Organization.[24]

COALITION CONFIGURATIONS IN
INTER-AFRICAN RELATIONS, 1963-77

During the period of the OAU's existence, African interstate-relations—including the wars, crises, and military interventions that occurred in the African system—have been influenced by both two basic consensuses and at least one strong axis of conflict. Thus, the coalition configuration in the African international system has been a mixed consensual-competitive one. The two consensuses were the support of member states for the territorial boundaries inherited from the colonial era, and their opposition to secessionist movements and to external assistance to such movements. The axis of conflict arose as a result of differences between rival African coalitions concerning their external alignments and the legitimacy of interventions against governing regimes. This is an important area of conflict in Africa despite the fact that the African states formally expressed their opposition to interventionism and subversion in both Article III of the OAU Charter and a special resolution passed in 1965.[25] Thus, although scholars have identified the prohibition of intervention in internal affairs as a "norm" of the African international system,[26] many African states have, in fact, not adhered to this norm, at least with respect to disputes that did not have territorial revisionist or secessionist overtones. In particular, inter-African conflicts originating in divergent foreign policy and/or ideological orientations have often been fertile soil for interventionist practices.

Although the strength of these two consensuses has varied in different periods, they have continued to exercise an important impact on the norms and practice of inter-African conflict management right up to the present. And while in recent years another axis of conflict rooted in religious differences (Moslem-non-Moslem) has become more prominent in African affairs, the ideological/foreign policy axis of conflict identified above has clearly been the most prominent mode of competitive behavior among OAU members.

The Consensus on Territorial Boundaries

It has become commonplace to criticize the "artificial" boundaries that the independent African countries had the misfortune to inherit from their former colonial masters. As early as the Pan-African Congress of 1945 the colonial powers were accused of using boundaries to thwart African independence and the natural unity of the African people.[27] The case against existing territorial boundaries in Africa was taken up in the postindependence era most forcefully by President Nkrumah of Ghana, who argued that political federation of the continent was the course that Africans should follow. Nkrumah, however, was able to gain support for his proposals from just two other states, Guinea and Mali,[28] who joined his ill-fated project for political union. As was noted above, the other independent African states eschewed any notion of political union and preferred to concentrate on the consolidation of their own governing systems, many of which were extremely fragile. Nkrumah failed even to secure the support of Ghana's fellow Casablanca states for his proposals, although they did consent to the creation of several Pan-African committees.[29] Most African states agreed with the consensus that had been reached at the initial meeting of the Monrovia Group in May 1961, namely, support for the equality and territorial integrity of all African states, and for their "cooperation throughout Africa based on tolerance, solidarity, and good-neighbor relations."[30] Overwhelming African support for the principle of "territorial integrity"* was evidenced by the inclusion of Article III into the OAU Charter and by the passage of a special resolution in July 1964 by the OAU Assembly. In the latter case all OAU members—except Morocco and Somalia, both of which had territorial claims against their neighbors—pledged themselves "to respect the borders existing on the achievement of national independence."[31] The following statement by Mali's President Modibo Keita at the 1963 Addis Ababa meeting is indicative of general African sentiment on this issue:

> If all of us here are truly animated by the ardent wish to achieve African unity, we must take Africa as it is, and we must renounce any territorial claims if we do not wish what we might call "black imperialism" in Africa. . . .
> African unity demands of each one of us complete respect for the legacy that we have received from the colonial system, that is to say: maintenance of the present frontiers of our respective states.[32]

The more conservative states exhibited even more hostility to the political unification proposals, as can be seen in the remarks of President Tsiranana of Malagasy:

> Should we take race, religion, or language as criteria for settling our boundaries a few states in Africa would be blotted out from the map. Leaving demagoguery aside, it is not conceivable that one of our individual states would consent to be among the victims for the sake of unity.[33]

---

*The only reason that the majority of states of the Addis Ababa conference did not go beyond their inclusion of a principle favoring the "territorial integrity" of all states and set forth a principle advocating respect for preindependence borders was a fear that Morocco and Somalia might refuse to join the Organization. (Saadia Touval, The Boundary Politics of Independent Africa [Cambridge, Mass.: Harvard University Press, 1972], pp. 83-86.)

Many scholars of inter-African politics have endeavored to explain the strong attachment of African states to the existing territorial boundaries of the continent. Zdenek Cervenka has offered four reasons for the African states' predisposition to favor the territorial status quo (and hence to oppose territorial revisionism and secessionism): the absence of stability and cohesion in many African states, a condition that would be exacerbated by territorial conflicts; the association, in the eyes of most African states, of the notion of the self-preservation of the state as a political unit with the maintenance of the status quo; the vulnerability of most states to territorial claims and secessionist pressures supported by neighboring states; and the fragile "tribal balance" on which many regimes depend for their survival.[34] Woronoff argues that a fifth factor, namely, the possibility that Africa could break up into a larger number of smaller, weaker, and hence more dependent units, also supports and legitimizes the principle of territorial integrity. In his view, the African states "dread a 'Balkanization' that might conceivably turn Africa into a mass of small and unviable states highly dependent upon foreign powers."[35] J. S. Nye, with some originality, has subsumed all of these factors under what he terms a "glass house" theory, the central postulate of which is that "people who live in poorly integrated states do not throw tribes."[36] In sum, it is clear that regardless of the particular explanation one attaches to the popularity of the principle of territorial integrity among OAU states, its existence is indisputable. And this fact has served to stabilize inter-African relations and to promote the involvement of the OAU in territorial conflicts among African states.

The Consensus against Secession

A second consensus characterizing inter-African relations has been the strong opposition of African states to secessionist movements and to external support for such movements. Their views on this matter were clearly set forth in 1967 when the Assembly passed a resolution condemning any form of secession in independent Africa.[37] The consensus on secession is closely linked to that on territorial integrity, and, as noted above, African support for the two principles derives from essentially the same concerns.* Most African states

---

*Jonah has noted the consensuses on both territorial revisionism and secession, but has remarked that "the evidence on the issue of secession is not as strong as that on boundary questions." (James O. C. Jonah, "The U.N. and the O.A.U.: Roles in Maintenance of International Peace and Security in Africa," in Africa and International

are susceptible to secessionist pressures and, as A. S. Kamunu has
written, African leaders have therefore viewed the problem through
a "domino theory" frame of reference:

> There has come into existence in post-colonial Africa
> what amounts to a "domino theory" of secessions . . .
> [which] postulates that a secession anywhere in Africa
> would create a demonstration effect that would bring
> with it the disintegration of existing states and the
> complete balkanization of the continent. [38]

The reactions of African states to specific instances of attempted
secession illustrate the deep fear that the prospect of secession en-
genders among them. The two most important cases have been the
attempts by animists and Christians of the southern Sudan to achieve
autonomy from the Moslem north and by the Ibo population of eastern
Nigeria to form the independent state of Biafra.* The French scholar
Philippe Decraene wrote in 1968, as these conflicts were raging, that
"in both cases there exists a tacit accord among African leaders both
not to encourage the initiatives of the separatists and to avoid public
discussion of any aspects of the conflicts."[39] In the case of the Sudanese civil war, the southern rebels received very little support
from other African states, despite their racial and religious affinity
with much of black Africa[40] and the unpopularity of the leftist Sudanese
regime in many quarters. No African state ever publicly supported
the secessionists' cause or sought to impede the Sudanese government's
efforts to suppress the rebellion by asking for the intervention of either
the OAU or any other organization.

The response of African states and the OAU to the Nigerian civil
war provides a further example of African leaders' antipathy for secession.[41] In September 1967, over three months after the Biafrans
had declared their independence, the OAU considered the conflict, and

---

Organization, ed. Yassin El-Ayouty and Hugh C. Brooks [The Hague:
Martinus Nijhoff, 1974], p. 144.)

*Another good example of the African states' opposition to se-
cession and external assistance to such movements occurred prior to
the formation of the OAU, and that was their reaction to the attempt
on the part of Katanga to secede from the Congo between 1960 and
1962. (Ernest W. Lefever, Uncertain Mandate: Politics of the U. N.
Congo Operation [Baltimore: John Hopkins University Press, 1967],
p. 159.) An exception is the case of the Eritrean secessionist movement, which was backed by some Arab states and is discussed in the
final section of this chapter.

the African states came down firmly on the side of the central government when they condemned secession in any member state and stated that the situation under consideration was purely an internal Nigerian affair. A six-nation OAU commission was created to consider the matter but, not insignificantly, its mandate was to assure Nigeria of "the Assembly's desire for the territorial integrity, unity, and peace of Nigeria."[42] While there appeared a slight crack in the unity of African states behind the central government when Tanzania, Gabon, the Ivory Coast and Zambia extended recognition to Biafra in April and May 1968, the overwhelming majority of OAU members sided unreservedly with the Nigerian central government throughout the course of the civil war. Later in 1968, the OAU Assembly again backed the federal government (except for the four states which now recognized Biafra), and called on the Biafran leaders to cooperate with the central government "in order to restore peace and unity to Nigeria."[43] The strong disposition of African states to oppose secession in the Nigerian case unquestionably influenced the attitudes of external powers and discouraged extracontinental support for the Biafrans.

The Axis of Conflict over Alignment,
Ideology, and Subversion

Many students of African international relations have commented on the division of African states into various conflictual groupings during the period under examination. The issues over which they have divided include the nature and extent of their politico-security ties to the West and their general attitude toward Western interests in the international community; the legitimacy of attempting to install governments with which they share common views by a variety of means, including subversion; and, to a lesser extent, their ideological orientation, especially an advocacy of socialism. While the titles that observers have assigned to these groupings have differed, they have nonetheless conveyed essentially the same message. In the 1960s these competing camps were labeled by different scholars as the "revolutionaries" and the "moderates;"[44] "radicals" and "moderates;"[45] advocates of "unity as movement" and "unity as alliance;"[46] "radicals," "moderates," and "conservatives;"[47] and "aligned with NATO," "nonaligned pro-West," "nonaligned," and "nonaligned pro-East."[48] While most writers during the last 15 years have identified two key groupings, it is posited here that there have, in fact, been three informal coalitions in African international politics, which have developed as a result of different predispositions with respect to the issues mentioned above. One group of states has consistently argued for, although not always exhibited, a definite nonaligned foreign policy orientation, and has made hostility toward both close ties to the West and identification with Western interests the key principles animating this conception of Africa's nonalignment. These states have strongly supported and sought to encourage the formation of other African governments with similar views. This support has been rendered by a variety of means, including the use of subversive practices such as assisting groups seeking the overthrow of a particular regime. Finally, most states in this grouping have subscribed to some form of socialist ideology, although rarely have their societies been organized according to the precepts of socialistic egalitarianism. A second group of states has also favored nonalignment, but has not defined it in such an explicitly anti-Western sense as the first grouping. These states have found it much easier to maintain good relations with both the West and with those African states closely tied or sympathetic to the West than has the first grouping. Also, their foreign policies have not been so suffused with socialist principles and verbiage. A final group of African states has been inclined to align, or at least seek, very close relations with the West while vigorously opposing the efforts of the first group to promote the spread of socialism and anti-Western regimes throughout the continent. These three coalitions will be called radical nonaligned, moderate nonaligned, and moderate pro-Western, respectively. It should be noted that the middle group of moderate nonaligned states is, in an inter-African context, a "nonaligned" grouping, situated as it is between the two polar coalitions in the African system.

Before proceeding to describe the membership and characteristics of these coalitions in more detail, the views of a number of scholars on the salience of this particular axis of conflict to inter-African politics should be mentioned. It is instructive to recall that at the time of the OAU's formation in 1963 many Africans expected that the various blocs that had hitherto dominated African foreign relations would disappear.* Clearly, however, this expectation has been belied by the record of African international politics since 1963. McGowan notes that while the African blocs that antedated the OAU "had ceased to exist" as formal organizations soon after 1963, the existence of the OAU "did not appreciably change African foreign policy behavior toward the Cold War" in the 1960s and the African states were far from united with respect to East-West issues.[49] Mortimer has averred

---

*This was the expectation or at the least the aspiration of most African politicians, and it was shared by at least one student of African international relations. (Robert Good, "Changing Patterns of African International Relations," American Political Science Review 18 [September 1964]: 632-64.)

that "throughout the 1960s, inter-African politics revolved around a
few central debates, which divided the continent into two relatively
stable groupings commonly identified as 'revolutionary' and 'moderate' Africa."[50] McKeon, in analyzing the first several years of the
OAU's existence, commented on the relevance of this division for
OAU politics: "The OAU's difficulties are thus due in large measure
to the division of its members into two camps, and their inability or
unwillingness to resolve their differences within the framework of
the Organization."[51]

Other writers have commented on the continuation of these competitive groupings into the 1970s. Claude Welch has noted that African reaction to the accession to power of General Idi Amin in Uganda
in 1971 "replayed the divisions between 'radicals' and 'moderates'
that had marked an earlier period of the OAU's history."[52] Scholar-
ship on several recent inter-African disputes in the Western Sahara,
Angola, and the Horn of Africa also testifies to the persistence of the
foreign policy/ideological axis of conflict among African states.[53]
Particularly striking is Cervenka's observation that "[T]he deep differences revealed by the Angolan crisis which originate primarily in
the different countries' . . . ideological orientation and their choice
of non-African partners have not subsided over the years but become
even sharper."[54] Even Timothy Shaw, who discussed the passing of
rival African "blocs," noted the differences between the less cohesive
"'moderate' and 'radical' factions,"[55] and the series of ideological
crises in Africa since Shaw's analysis in 1975 serves to reinforce the
impression of major political cleavages between African states. Thus
it is clear that there have existed marked divergences in foreign policy and ideological orientation among the African states throughout the
period under examination. And, although these differences seldom
had a dominant influence on territorial or secessionist conflicts, they
often exercised a strong and palpable impact in inter-African conflicts concerning other issues.

It is important to note some of the problems that arise when one
attempts to place the independent African states into the three categories mentioned above. First, the number and rapidity of regime
changes in Africa lead to many shifts of foreign policy and ideological
preference. Libya, Ghana, and Ethiopia are only three examples of
regime changes resulting in major shifts in foreign policy and alignment. Second, some states' changes in orientation are gradual, and
it is difficult to identify the date of transition from one grouping to another. This is certainly the case with several North African states
in the 1970s. Another problem derives from the fact that certain
states placed in one category may have marked political differences
vis-à-vis other states in the same category. For example, in the
radical nonaligned grouping there are some states that have had strong

TABLE 5

Inter-African Coalition Configurations, 1963-77

Moderate Pro-Western

Benin (1963), 1963-late 1974	Lesotho (1966)	Seychelles (1976
Botswana (1966)	Liberia (1963)	Sierra Leone (1963)
Cameroun (1963)	Libya (1963), 1963-mid-1969	Sudan (1963), 1976-77
Central African Empire (1963)	Malagasy Republic (1963), 1963-mid-1972	Swaziland (1968)
Chad (1963)	Malawi (1963)	Togo (1963)
Egypt (1963), 1976-77	Mauritania (1963), 1963-64, 1975-77	Tunisia (1963)
Gabon (1963)	Morocco (1963), 1975-77	Uganda (1963), 1971-72
Gambia (1965)	Niger (1963)	Upper Volta (1963)
Ghana (1963), early 1966-77	Rwanda (1963)	Zaire (1963)
Ivory Coast (1963)	Senegal (1963)	

Moderate Nonaligned

Burundi (1963), early 1965-77	Kenya (1963)	Nigeria (1963)
Comoros (1976)	Malagasy Republic (1963), mid-1972-77	Sudan (1963), 1972-75
Djibouti (1977)	Mauritania (1963), 1965-74	Uganda (1963), 1963-70, 1973-77
Egypt (1963), 1972-75	Mauritius (1968)	Zambia (1964)
Ethiopia (1963), 1963-74	Morocco (1963), 1963-74	

Radical Nonaligned

Algeria (1963)	Egypt (1963), 1963-mid-1972	Mali (1963)
Angola (1975)	Equatorial Guinea (1968)	Mozambique (1975)
Benin (1963), late 1974-77	Ethiopia (1963), 1975-77	São Tomé and Principe (1976)
Burundi (1963), 1963-early 1965	Ghana (1963), 1963-early 1966	Somalia (1963)
Cape Verde Islands (1976)	Guinea (1963)	Sudan (1963), 1963-71
Congo (1963)	Guinea-Bissau (1974)	Tanzania (1963)
	Libya (1963), mid-1969-77	

Note: The date in parentheses after each OAU member indicates the date it joined the Organization. If there are no dates following the date of joining, this indicates that it was a member of that particular grouping for the entire period it belonged to the Organization. On the other hand, if there are dates, this indicates that it was only a member of that grouping for a particular period of time. The names of states in 1977 are used in the chart. Zaire was Congo-Kinshasa before 1971 and Benin was Dahomey before 1974. Egypt was the United Arab Republic (UAR) until 1971.

135

links with Communist China (Tanzania, Burundi, 1963–January 1965), while others have enjoyed very close relations with the Soviet Union (Angola, Libya, and Somalia in the 1970s). Finally, the paucity of information on many African countries, not to mention the complex and idiosyncratic character of their policy-making processes, further complicates the attempt to group the African states according to the typology presented above. In Table 5 all OAU members are listed under one of three groupings for the period 1963–77. (Some states, of course, have been members of more than one grouping during this period.) Before proceeding to elucidate the reasons for classifying the African states in particular coalitions, it should be noted that no grouping has even been "dominant" in the sense that it has constituted two-thirds or more of the OAU's membership. The moderate pro-Western states generally constituted a simple majority, but this always fell well below the two-thirds mark.

With respect to the moderate pro-Western grouping, there have always been a large number of French-speaking African states that have maintained close economic, political, and often military ties with France.[56] These states have mistrusted both Communist countries and those African regimes that exhibit radical and anti-Western political orientations. They have established close relations with one another within several associations of French-speaking African states.[57] Cameroun, Central African Republic (Central African Empire after December 1976), Chad, Dahomey (before 1975), Gabon, Malagasy Republic (before June 1972, when President Tsiranana was ousted), Niger, Senegal, Togo, and Upper Volta have been placed in the moderate pro-Western grouping. Two former Belgian colonies— Zaire (the Congo before 1971) and Rwanda—have also retained strong ties with their former metropole, and in the case of Zaire with the United States, as well. In a unique position is Liberia, which of the African states, has the closest historical affiliation with the United States, and which maintains economic and military agreements with Washington.[58] Four southern African states—Botswana, Lesotho, Malawi, and Swaziland—have tended to promote close ties and a friendly attitude to the West, and have, in addition, been susceptible to South African influence. Gambia, Sierra Leone, and Ghana (after February 1966) can also be classified as moderate pro-Western, since they have not adopted radical ideologies and have fostered co-operative relations with Western states. The North African states of Libya (before the 1969 revolution) and Tunisia have also been included in this grouping. Libya was generally conservative and Western oriented in its foreign policy under King Idris, and even permitted an American air base on its territory. The inclusion of Tunisia in this category could be challenged on the basis of that state's efforts in the 1960s to terminate its military relationship with France. However, in terms of fundamental foreign policy orientations Tunisia must be viewed as conservative in that it not only opposed the radical Africans' attempts to force their particular conception of nonalignment onto the continent but also exhibited noticeable sympathy with the West in its disputes with the communist world. [59]

Morocco and Mauritania are assigned to this grouping for the years 1975-77. During the 1960s Morocco sought to offset French influence by cultivating fruitful relations with both Washington and Moscow. Moreover, it was allied with the radical Casablanca states in the early 1960s as part of its policy of securing African diplomatic support for its claims on Mauritania. But the credible nonaligned position it had established in the 1960s was undermined in the next decade, as the inherent distrust felt by the regime of King Hassan II for the radical states of the Afro-Arab world found expression in a more conservative and pro-Western foreign policy. [60] Similarly, Mauritania's move toward nonalignment in late 1964 was reversed in the 1970s, as military ties to France were strengthened and joint efforts with Morocco to annex the Western Sahara placed it in the moderate pro-Western camp once again. [61]

This coalition grouping gained two more members in the mid-1970s as the vicissitudes of politics in the Middle East and the Horn of Africa caused the once radical nonaligned states of Egypt and the Sudan to drastically revise their foreign policies and external alignments. In the case of Egypt, the accession to power of Anwar Sadat following the death of Nasser in 1970 soon brought to an end the central role the country had played among the African radicals. In 1972 Sadat expelled thousands of Soviet military and technical personnel, [62] and the defeat of the Arab states in the 1973 Yom Kippur War led to a further reduction of ties with Moscow and rapidly increasing cooperation with the United States. Indeed, in 1978 the Sadat regime is in the vanguard of those African states who denounce in no uncertain terms the role of the Soviet Union in the continent and the developing world as a whole. [63] As one analyst has noted, in the 1970s Egypt has come to be regarded as "a pillar of moderation" by the West, and "her influence and prestige are frequently exploited to counter the influence of 'progressive' and subversive elements" in the Afro-Arab world. [64] In the case of the Sudan, the communist-instigated coup attempt against President Ghaffar Numeiry in 1971 led that country "to move away from the Soviet Union" and to seek "political, economic and military alliances with the West and with the moderate Arab countries, particularly Saudi Arabia and Egypt." [65] Another aborted coup attempt in 1976, allegedly inspired by Libya with Soviet encouragement, prompted the Sudanese to adopt a strongly anti-Soviet and pro-Western line. [66] Although classification necessarily involves a certain degree of arbitrariness, both the Sudan and Egypt have been placed in the moderate pro-Western grouping for the years 1976 and 1977, since it appears that Soviet activities in the region and Ethiopia's turn to

Moscow in 1976 served to crystallize the conservative tendencies in both states' foreign policies.[67]

The last two African states included in this grouping are the Seychelles (from the time of its independence in June 1976 until the ouster of President Mancham in June 1977) and Uganda (during the first two years of General Amin's rule). In the case of the Seychelles, close ties to Britain and strong economic links, through tourism, with South Africa, determined to a large degree the attitude of this poor microstate toward international and regional affairs, although the new regime that came to power in June 1977 has sought to pursue a more nonaligned external policy.[68] The overthrow of Uganda's President Milton Obote by General Amin in January 1971 was greeted favorably by the British and Israelis, with whom the new president had long been associated, and was condemned by the radical nonaligned states, who regarded Amin as reactionary and neocolonial and who tried to block OAU recognition of the new regime.[69] Throughout 1971 Amin's policies tended to support Western interests and while this began to change in 1972, it was not clear until the following year that the country had adopted a more nonaligned foreign policy,[70] although erratic and idiosyncratic might be a more accurate description.

On the other extreme are the radical nonaligned states, of which the central members since 1963 have been Algeria, Congo-Brazzaville, Guinea, Mali, Tanzania, UAR (until July 1972), Ghana (until the overthrow of Nkrumah in February 1966), and Libya (since the accession to power of Colonel Muammar al-Qaddafi in September 1969).* Somalia and Sudan (until the abortive communist-inspired coup in 1971) are also placed in this group on the basis of their radical postures, ties to the Communist states, and anti-Western orientations.† Burundi is classified as a radical nonaligned state from 1963 until the change in government in January 1965. This is a rather anomalous case in that while Burundi's foreign policy in this brief period resembled that of an archetypal radical state, its internal monarchical

---

*These states are consistently identified as "radical" or "revolutionary" states in Robert Mortimer, "The Algerian Revolution in Search of the African Revolution," Journal of Modern African Studies 8 (September 1970); Immanuel Wallerstein, Africa: The Politics of Unity (New York: Random House, 1967); Nora McKeon, "The African States and the O. A. U." International Affairs 42 (July 1966); Robert Good, "Changing Patterns of African International Relations," American Political Science Review 18 (September 1964); and Patrick McGowan, "Africa and Nonalignment: A Comparative Study of Foreign Policy," International Studies Quarterly 12 (September 1968).

†Military aid agreements between the Sudan and the USSR existed prior to 1972, and Soviet pilots flew missions on behalf of the Sudanese government against southern rebels.

structure tended to separate it from this grouping.* Zanzibar, during its brief independence from December 1963 to April 1964, is another state that clearly falls into the radical camp. Ethiopia is also included in this grouping for the years 1975-77, since the military regime that came to power in September 1974 had by early 1975 acquired a distinctly Marxist political coloration and later became, along with Angola, the Soviet Union's staunchest ally in Africa.[71] Equatorial Guinea, which gained independence in October 1968, has also developed a generally radical and anti-Western foreign policy and has been a recipient of Cuban and North Korean military aid and personnel.[†] The regime of Major Mathieu Kerekou, which overthrew the civilian president of Dahomey in October 1974, shortly thereafter renamed the country Benin and adopted a strongly Marxist ideology. Thus, Benin is classified as radical nonaligned for the period November 1974-77. Lastly, the five states that became independent as a result of Portugal's hasty withdrawal from its African territories have all been assigned to the radical nonaligned category. Liberation struggles in Angola and Mozambique culminated in victories by two revolutionary movements—MPLA and FRELIMO, respectively—and then in the establishment of the first "authentic Marxist-Leninist regimes" in Africa's history.[72] Earlier, in 1974, the revolutionary Partido da Independencia da Guine e Cabo Verde had taken control of what became Guinea-Bissau (formerly Portuguese Guinea), and the new state added its weight to the radical camp.[73] Cape Verde and São Tomé and Principe, two small former Portuguese colonies, also achieved independence in the wake of the Portuguese revolution and joined the coalition of radical African states.

The intermediate group of moderate nonaligned states contains the remainder of those African states that have participated in the OAU regional system during the 1963-77 period but that have not been classified in either of the other two categories. States placed in this grouping have established credible nonaligned positions in that they have eschewed alliances and military accords with the Great Powers and generally sought to promote cordial relations with both Western and communist states. Unlike the radicals, however, these states

---

*The explanation of this anomalous situation is complicated and can be found in René Lemarchand, Rwanda and Burundi (London: Pall Mall Press, 1970), pp. 383-401. (See, also, Bruce D. Larkin, China and Africa, 1949-1970 [Berkeley: University of California Press, 1971], pp. 87, 127-28.)

†Colin Legum, ed., African Contemporary Record, 1976-77, p. B503. The United States broke diplomatic relations with Equatorial Guinea in March 1976 following alleged maltreatment of its diplomats.

have not conceived of nonalignment as entailing a commitment to challenge and oppose Western interests and attack at every opportunity the vestiges of Western influence in the continent. Nor have the moderate nonaligned always viewed the Soviet Union or China as "allies" in the fight against Western "imperialism," a proposition to which many of the radical states have subscribed. Finally, these states have not usually supported the attempts by many radical states to promote the spread of "socialist" regimes that, once in power, would adhere to the radicals' own conception of nonalignment. The moderate nonaligned have tended to oppose attempts to subvert pro-Western African regimes and have been able to maintain good relations with such regimes despite the political differences between them.

The states placed in this grouping are Ethiopia (before 1975), Kenya, Morocco (before 1975), Mauritania (from mid-1964 until about the end of 1974), Burundi (after January 1965), Mauritius, Uganda (until January 1971 and then once again beginning in 1973), Zambia, Madagascar (after June 1972), and Nigeria. The Sudan and Egypt are classified as moderate nonaligned for the years 1972-75, as this period was a transition phase between their memberships in the radical and moderate pro-Western groupings. Also placed in this category are the Comoros, a former French colony that achieved independence in July 1975,[74] and the Republic of Djibouti, the former French Territory of the Afars and Issas, which was granted independence in June 1977. Although several thousand French troops remain in Djibouti, the new state seems likely to evolve a cautious, nonaligned foreign policy as a result of its delicate position in the strife-torn Horn of Africa.[75]

Several of these states deserve special comment. Under the regime of Haile Selassie, Ethiopia certainly had closer ties to the West, and particularly to the United States, than it had to the Soviet bloc, but in general it sought to promote friendly relations with communist states and to avoid any impression of being a defender of Western policies and interests. Moreover, Ethiopia was recognized by the other African states as a state that often attempted to bridge the divisions among them. Burundi, after the ouster of the pro-Chinese faction in early 1965, also maintained a fairly equidistant stance with respect to the major blocs, although there have been occasions when it has tended toward the Western states.[76] Mauritania's move toward a nonaligned position in the mid-1960s can be attributed to the affinities of its Moorish majority for the country's North African neighbors and to its desire to prevent these Arab states from ever again supporting Morocco's claims to Mauritania.[77] Morocco, until the mid-1970s, endeavored to foster friendly relations with Moscow and the radical African states, and in general Rabat adhered to nonaligned positions in world forums.[78] Only in the mid-1970s did it evolve a more conservative foreign policy as a result of its campaign to annex the Western Sahara, its concern over Algerian and Libyan policies, and its uneasiness regarding Soviet and Cuban influence in the continent. Kenya's nonalignment in the 1970s may be questioned on the basis of its military agreements with the United Kingdom, but its general foreign policy orientation was toward nonalignment. Perhaps Kenya should be seen as occupying the pro-Western extremity of the moderate nonaligned group, while Zambia and Uganda under Obote (until January 1970)[79] can be viewed as occupying a position within this grouping closer to the radical states. The record of Ugandan foreign policy since the overthrow of Obote (even since 1973) does not indicate that the Amin regime has been consistently radical in orientation. [80]

There are a variety of ways of ascertaining the political and foreign policy orientations of the African states. One is to examine the pattern of their establishment of diplomatic relations with the communist states. While the relationships are not precise, in general the radical nonaligned before 1970 established diplomatic relations with both the Soviet Union and the People's Republic of China immediately upon independence (for example, Guinea, Mali, Somalia, Burundi). The moderate nonaligned states tended, before 1970, to initiate relations soon after independence with Moscow but to delay doing so with China (for example, Ethiopia, Morocco, Nigeria, Mauritania). Finally, the moderate pro-Western states were inclined to delay establishing relations with the USSR and often to eschew relations with China before 1970 (for example, Botswana, Gabon, Ivory Coast, Niger).[81] In the 1970s the situation has changed as Moscow and Peking have competed for influence in Africa in the same way as the Soviets once did (and continue to do) with the United States. Moreover, Peking has recently allied itself with the Western efforts to check Soviet advances in the continent.*

Additional information concerning external ties and policy preferences can be adduced by studying voting behavior. For example, one study of voting at the United Nations for the years 1960-68 found that on the "East-West" issues the ex-French African states voted most often with the West whereas the "radicals" sided overwhelmingly with the Soviet bloc. [82] Also, data concerning military and economic aid patterns help to reveal which states were supported by East and West. Christopher Stevens found that there was a link between the foreign policies of the African states and their receipt of economic aid from the USSR. In particular, "progressive" states such as

---

*China's nonmilitary aid has actually outstripped that of the USSR. (George T. Yu, "The USSR and Africa: China's Impact," Problems of Communism 27 [January-February 1978]: 42.)

Guinea, Mali, Algeria, Egypt, and Somalia were major beneficiaries of Soviet aid policies. [83] Since for the Kremlin "one of the criteria for assessing whether a country is 'progressive' or not is its determination to break away from 'imperialist economic domination,'" a decision by Moscow to aid an African state may indicate that that state practices an anti-Western and radical foreign policy. [84] Finally, how the African states have voted in the OAU on various questions is another important indicator. [85]

THE OAU'S PATTERNS OF INTERVENTION AND SUCCESS

During the years 1963-77, there were 26 conflicts between OAU members and these fall within four of the categories of conflicts that were outlined in the theory. These categories as well as the specific types of inter-African conflicts occurring during the 14 years under study are listed below. To the right of each category are the projections concerning organizational intervention and success.

Type of Conflict	Intervention	Success
Threats or acts of aggression that violate a consensual norm		
Attempts to alter boundaries	Yes	Yes
Aid to secessionist movements	Yes	Yes
Intercoalition conflicts (victim a member of a nondominant grouping)—radical nonaligned versus moderate pro-Western	No	No
Intracoalition (nonsubordinate grouping)—between members of moderate pro-Western grouping	No	No
Aligned-nonaligned (where victim is aligned)—aggressions by a moderate nonaligned state against either a radical nonaligned or a moderate pro-Western state	No	No

Table 6 outlines the patterns of OAU involvement in the 26 wars, crises, and military interventions that have occurred between OAU members since 1963. It was predicted, on the basis of the theory, that only in those conflicts concerning issues on which a broad consensus existed among African states—namely, territorial revisionism and aid to secessionist movements—would the preconditions for OAU intervention and success be present. In four (57 percent) of the seven

TABLE 6

OAU Involvement in Inter-African Conflicts, 1963–77

	Hypothesis: Intervention and Success		Hypothesis: No Intervention		
	Territorial Revisionism	Aid to Secessionist Movements	Intercoalition (victim a member of a nondominant coalition)	Intracoalition (nonsubordinate)	Aligned-Nonaligned (victim aligned)
No OAU action	Ethiopia–Somalia, 1965–67 (MI)(#71) Kenya–Somalia, 1965–67 (MI)(#72) Ethiopian civil strife (with Somalian intervention), 1977 (W)(#113)	Ethiopian civil strife (with Sudanese intervention), 1964–65 (MI)(#63) Ethiopian civil strife (with Sudanese intervention), 1969–71 (MI)(#88)	Rwanda–Burundi, 1963–64 (MI)(#58) Chadian civil strife (with Sudanese intervention), 1965 (MI)(#68); 1966 (MI)(#73) Ghana and Ivory Coast–Guinea, 1966 (C)(#75) Congo (B)–Congo (K), 1969 (MI)(#87) Equatorial Guinea–Gabon, 1972 (MI)(#95) Uganda–Tanzania, 1972 (W)(#96) Zaire–Angola, 1977 (W)(#114) Libya–Egypt, 1977 (W)(#115)	Dahomey–Niger, 1963–64 (C)(#56)	Tanzania–Burundi, 1973 (MI)(#100)
Number	3	2	9	1	1
Percent	43	100	64	100	50
OAU debate			Angolan civil strife (with Zairean intervention), 1975–77 (W)(#108) Moroccan civil strife (with Algerian intervention), 1976–77 (W)(#110) Mauritanian civil strife (with Algerian and Moroccan intervention), 1976–77 (W)(#111)		Rwanda–Burundi, 1966 (MI)(#76)
Number	0	0	3	0	1
Percent	0	0	22	0	50
OAU recommendation/judgment	Algeria–Morocco, 1963 (W)*(#54) Ethiopia–Somalia, 1964 (W)*(#60) Kenya–Somalia, 1964 (MI)*(#61) Upper Volta–Ghana, 1963–65 (W)*(#50)		Congolese civil strife (with intervention by Congo [B] and Burundi), 1964–65 (MI)(#64) Niger–Ghana, 1964–65 (MI)*(#65)		
Number	4	0	2	0	0
Percent	57	0	14	0	0
Number of conflicts	7	2	14	1	2

Note: W = war; C = crisis; MI = military intervention; * = success. The number after each conflict identifies the location of the conflict in the Appendix.

143

conflicts involving territorial revisionism, the OAU intervened and succeeded in effecting their termination. In two of the remaining territorial revisionist conflicts (Ethiopia-Somalia, 1965-67; Kenya-Somalia, 1965-67) the previously enunciated OAU position was an important factor affecting the conflict outcomes. In the final conflict, falling into this category (Ethiopia-Somalia, 1977), while the OAU as a whole refused to debate the issues involved, the committee the Organization had created in 1973 to mediate the dispute did meet and issue a statement confirming the inviolability of territorial boundaries —an implicit criticism of the Somali position in the conflict.[86] Contrary to the theory's projections, neither of the two conflicts involving aid to secessionist movements (both between Ethiopia and the Sudan) elicited OAU intervention.

In the other three types of conflicts neither OAU intervention nor success were hypothesized. As predicted, the single intracoalition conflict was not dealt with by the African organization. Also, in both of the two aligned-nonaligned disputes where the victim was aligned, the OAU failed to "intervene" according to the definition employed in this study. However, in one of them the OAU did appoint a mediator to assist the parties in reaching an accord. Nine (64 percent) of the fourteen intercoalition conflicts witnessed no OAU involvement, while the OAU debated (but did not intervene) in three intercoalition conflicts. Of the two intercoalition conflicts in which the OAU did intervene, it achieved success in one of them. In conclusion, it is clear that the hypotheses on conflicts in which OAU intervention was not predicted have been supported by the data. However, the hypotheses predicting organizational intervention and success were not substantiated as strongly as anticipated. In particular, the OAU's behavior with respect to conflicts involving external assistance to secessionist movements diverges significantly from the hypothesis put forth earlier. The reason for this divergence, as will be analyzed below, probably lies in an inadequate portrayal of a certain aspect of the coalition configuration and the relatively small assistance provided to the secessionist group.

During the first 14 months of its existence, the OAU was confronted with four territorial conflicts between its members, and its consideration of these disputes culminated in the already mentioned resolution of July 1964, which supported the existing territorial delimitations among African states. In all of these conflicts the Organization achieved a significant measure of success. In retrospect, this early period in the OAU's history, when the "spirit of Addis Ababa" was prominent among African states and "the enthusiasm with which the African leaders viewed the OAU's prospects"[87] was infectious, may have marked the zenith of the Organization's effectiveness with inter-African conflict resolution. The first conflict to attract the

attention of the young organization was the Moroccan invasion of Algeria in October 1963. The termination of this war was mediated
jointly by President Modibo Keita of Mali and Emperor Haile Selassie
of Ethiopia, the latter being able to offer his good offices not only in
his own capacity but also on behalf of the OAU since he was then president of the OAU Assembly and since the provisional secretariat of the
Organization was at that time entrusted to Ethiopia.[88] At a special
meeting in Bamako of the Algerian, Moroccan, Ethiopian, and Malian
heads of state an accord was drafted declaring a cease-fire, creating
a military commission constituted by the four states to establish a demilitarized zone, and calling for an extraordinary meeting of the OAU
Council to set up a commission to ascertain responsibility for the war
and offer proposals for the settlement of the dispute. In mid-November, while Morocco was continuing to occupy certain areas of Algeria,
the Council met and approved the agreement between the four states
and, accordingly, set up a seven-nation committee to mediate the conflict. More importantly, the Council also requested that all OAU members "scrupulously respect all the principles" of the OAU Charter, and
this meant de facto that the Council upheld the principle of the integrity of existing boundaries, which is contained in Article 3(3) of the
Charter. Following this meeting, a major diplomatic effort to secure
compliance with the accord was launched by the cease-fire committee
created at the earlier Bamako conference but now "under the aegis of
the OAU."[89] Faced with almost universal opposition to its claims,
Morocco reluctantly agreed to withdraw behind the former border in
February 1964, although it did not renounce its claims against its
neighbor until the early 1970s.

The Ethiopian-Somali and Kenyan-Somali conflicts occurred
simultaneously and were considered by the OAU at the same meetings.
In January 1964 large numbers of Somali tribesmen crossed from
Somalia into both Ethiopia and Kenya as part of the Somali government's plan to pressure these two states to cede certain parts of their
territories populated by ethnic Somalis to Mogadishu. In early February Somalia launched a large-scale military attack against Ethiopia. Ethiopia and Kenya then called on the OAU to intervene against
these Somali aggressions, and on February 14 the Council of Ministers
met and called for a cessation of fighting and requested all OAU members to assist the disputants in effecting a cease-fire. On February
24 the Council reiterated these requests and also asked Ethiopia and
Somalia to settle their conflict in accordance with Article 3(3) of the
OAU Charter. This latter request was tantamount to opposing Somali
claims. In March President Ibrahim Abboud of the Sudan offered his
services as a mediator and was able to secure the two disputants' adherence to a cease-fire along the original territorial boundary. These
OAU interventions, as well as the July 1964 resolution declaring all

existing borders inviolable, soon led to a cessation of the incursions by Somali tribesmen into the two neighboring countries until mid-1965, when they began once again.

The last of the four territorial conflicts in which the OAU intervened was that between Upper Volta and Ghana. This conflict in fact antedated the formation of the OAU in that in early 1963 Ghana occupied a strip of territory along its border with Upper Volta. Upper Volta chose not to bring the issue to the attention of the OAU until after the Organization had passed the special resolution concerning territorial boundaries. In July 1964, after most OAU members had made plain their antipathy to territorial revisionism, the Ghanaian representative to the OAU announced that his government was prepared both to withdraw from the disputed area and to enter into negotiations with Upper Volta in order to demarcate the border between them. While at first Ghana refused to honor these promises, it finally did comply in mid-1965, following the threat by Upper Volta and its French-speaking West African allies to boycott the OAU Assembly meeting scheduled to be held in Ghana in the fall of 1965.

The three territorial conflicts in which the OAU did not formally intervene were recrudescences of the Ethiopian-Somali and Kenyan-Somali conflicts discussed above. Between 1965 and 1967 raiding parties regularly crossed from Somalia into the two neighboring states to harass government officials. Attempts by various African leaders to mediate the conflicts were of no avail until the change of government in Somalia in 1967. In September 1967 President Kenneth Kaunda of Zambia initiated a mediation attempt and achieved some success in that the parties agreed to cease provocative actions and to restore normal relations. This phase of the agreement was given the formal blessing of the OAU Assembly in September 1967. At this same Assembly meeting, the emperor of Ethiopia and the prime minister of Somalia agreed that their governments should enter into negotiations to settle the dispute and normalize diplomatic relations, and while the issues underlying the conflict were not resolved, an end to the border incursions was brought about. The OAU did not formally involve itself in the recrudescences of these two conflicts between 1965 and 1967 because the members felt they had clearly enunciated their views on these conflicts in particular and on territorial revisionism in general back in 1964. Moreover, the OAU was reluctant to antagonize the aggressor—in these cases Somalia—by explicit criticism. Most African states prefer to set forth the general principles applicable to the settlement of a conflict (provided such principles are extant) rather than use the OAU for explicit action against a member whose policies contravene these principles. The reason for this caution is easily adduced: the desire to assure the continued survival of the OAU. Thus, the OAU "has never considered expelling a member," even when behavior in open contravention of the Organization's principles and decisions takes place. [90] Also, as Berhanykun Andemicael has noted: "There seems to have developed a belief among the majority of OAU member states that African solidarity may be threatened more by active involvement of the OAU in intermember disputes than by a modest role."[91]

The final recurrence of the Ethiopian-Somali conflict was in 1977, when Somalia took advantage of the chaotic state of Ethiopian politics under the shaky military regime that came to power in 1974 to assist the Western Somali Liberation Front in its efforts to detach the Ogaden region from Ethiopia. While the Ethiopian government failed to secure an emergency session of the OAU in August 1977, an eight-nation mediation committee created in 1973 to arbitrate the recurring border dispute between the two states did convene and issue a statement confirming the integrity of boundaries inherited from the colonial era—implicit criticism of the Somali position in the dispute. However, two cleavages among OAU members impeded Council or Assembly support for Ethiopia and the consensual norm concerning territorial boundaries in this conflict. On the one hand, the tension between the radical and conservative states made many of the latter reluctant to support the Marxist Ethiopian government that was being supported by Soviet economic and military assistance and Cuban troops. On the other, some Moslem countries shied away from backing the Ethiopian regime, dominated by the Coptic Christian community, against the Moslem Somalis. [92]

Contrary to the hypothesis on conflicts concerning external aid to secessionist movements, the OAU did not become involved in the two inter-African conflicts of this type. Both conflicts arose from the Sudan's provision of arms and base camps to members of the Eritrean Liberation Front (ELF) who were fighting for the independence of Eritrea from Ethiopia. During both phases of this conflict, in 1965 and 1969-71, small groups of Ethiopian troops crossed into Sudanese territory to attack ELF rebels. That the OAU did not intervene in these conflicts is probably attributable to their relatively small scale and to the fact that they were viewed in terms of the Moslem-non-Moslem axis of conflict mentioned earlier. There appears to be a great reluctance on the part of many African governments to openly discuss this cleavage among them. Not only would open discussion of such conflicts seriously divide the predominantly Moslem and non-Moslem states, but it could also sow seeds of dissension within many African states that contain both religious groupings. Ali Mazrui had this prescient comment to make in 1975 with respect to the possible effects of a drawn-out war between the predominantly Christian Ethiopian government and the overwhelmingly Moslem Eritrean separatists: "A protracted war could result in tensions between blacks and

Arabs, Muslims, and non-Muslims, all over Africa. While it seems likely that the religious factor will be played down by the propaganda machines of both sides, the danger of large-scale continental cleavages is certainly there."* If the Ethiopian-Sudanese conflict had escalated into a war in the mid-1960s, it might have proved possible to determine the priority that the African states (particularly those whose populations are largely Moslem) attached to opposition to external aid to secessionist movements, on the one hand, and support for their religious brethren, on the other. But since this did not occur, it is difficult to speculate regarding these priorities. †

In the other three types of inter-African conflicts OAU intervention was not expected. The single intracoalition conflict was between Dahomey and Niger in late 1963 and early 1964 and, as hypothesized, it was not settled within the framework of the OAU but rather by negotiations with the grouping of French West African states of which both disputants were members. The first of the two aligned-nonaligned conflicts with the aligned as the victim involved the military intervention of Tutsi tribesmen from Burundi into Rwanda in 1966. The OAU did briefly discuss the issue in September 1966, and while it did not pass a recommendation, it did request President Joseph Mobutu of the Congo-Kinshasa to act as a mediator. The Congolese government enjoyed good relations with Rwanda and had been improving relations with Burundi throughout 1966. President Mobutu was able to mediate an accord in early 1967. The 1973 conflict between Tanzania and Bu-

---

*"Black Africa and the Arabs," Foreign Affairs 53 (July 1975): 737. The issue is also touched on in: I. William Zartman, "The Sahara: Bridge or Barrier?", International Conciliation (January 1963); and Keith Irvine, "The Sahael—Africa's 'Great Divide", Current History 64 (March 1973): 18-20. The populations of seven African states are more than 90 percent Moslem—namely, Somalia, UAR, Libya, Tunisia, Algeria, Morocco, and Mauritania. The populations of another six are between 60 percent and 90 percent Moslem—namely, Sudan, Niger, Mali, Senegal, Gambia, and Guinea. Three—Ethiopia, Chad, and Nigeria—are between 30 percent and 50 percent and another seven are between 15 percent and 25 percent. (Vernon McKay, "The Impact of Islam on Relations Among the New African States," in Islam and International Relations, ed. J. Harris Proctor [New York: Praeger, 1965], p. 163.)

†Again in 1977 the Sudanese began to aid the Eritreans, but only with material assistance—not with base camps and personnel. By this time the Eritreans enjoyed almost total control over their own province. (Peter Schwab, "Cold War on the Horn of Africa," African Affairs 77 [January 1978].)

rundi resulted from ethnic strife in Burundi in 1972 and 1973, which caused hundreds of thousands of deaths and led many Hutu to flee into Rwanda and Tanzania. These refugees initiated several small incursions into Burundi but their actions were not prompted or supported by the Rwandan and Tanzanian governments. On several occasions in 1973 Burundian forces crossed into Tanzania and killed both Hutu refugees and Tanzanian villagers. Tanzania responded by closing the border. President Mobutu of Zaire mediated the dispute and it was never considered by the OAU. These two conflicts are rather anomalous and the policies and disinterest of many African states toward them were probably not influenced by a concern that their outcomes could affect the future alignment orientations of the two parties. The unique ethnic source of the conflicts and the lack of a real ideological hostility between the states concerned were largely responsible for these attitudes by most African states.

The largest number of inter-African disputes have been inter-coalition conflicts between moderate pro-Western and radical non-aligned states. In all there were 14 in the period 1963-77. As discussed earlier, no OAU intervention was expected in this type of conflict since neither grouping constituted a two-thirds voting majority. The antagonism between these two groups of states has been a constant source of tension in African foreign relations, and in fact antedates the formation of the OAU itself.

Nine intercoalition conflicts did not elicit any OAU involvement. In the first of these conflicts, Tutsi tribesmen originally from Rwanda, but living at the time in Burundi, sought to overthrow the government of Rwanda in late 1963 and early 1964. These refugees were supported by the government of Burundi since it was controlled by members of the Tutsi tribe. During the course of this dispute the Burundi government was dominated by a faction with strong diplomatic links and aid ties with Communist China, whereas Rwanda enjoyed close relations with Belgium and the West. Had the OAU debated the conflict, the two polar groupings of African states would undoubtedly have stood firm behind their respective members, and such a confrontation would have exacerbated the hostility between the groupings and made cooperation within other areas of OAU activity more difficult. This reasoning is borne out by Meyers, who noted: "To have energetically pursued their charges and their implications might have permanently split the Organization on lines similar to the pre-1963 division as the more radical African states would have supported the host to the refugees while the conservative Africans supported the country of origin."[93] Two other intercoalition conflicts that did not evoke an OAU response occurred in 1965 and 1966 and both involved Chad and the Sudan. In both cases the Sudanese government's provision of base camps and assistance to Chadian rebels was the cause of the dispute, as the rebels carried out raids into Chad from Sudanese territory. Moreover, the Sudanese permitted the rebels to set up an "Islamic Government of Chad in Exile" in the Sudan. Both the ideological and religious differences between the antagonists—which reflected the radical/conservative and Moslem/non-Moslem cleavages among African states as a whole—impeded OAU consideration of the two conflicts. Significantly, the 1966 conflict was mediated by President Hamani Diori of Niger, whose country, like Chad, had strong political links with France, but who was himself a Moslem, as were the Sudanese. Two other intercoalition conflicts resolved outside the OAU framework were Guinea's threat to reinstate the recently deposed President Nkrumah of Ghana in 1966 and the backing of Congo-Kinshasa for an attempt to overthrow the government of Congo (Brazzaville) in 1969.

Four more recent intercoalition conflicts between members of the moderate pro-Western and radical nonaligned groupings also failed to involve the OAU. In August 1972 a dispute over ownership of two uninhabited islands arose between Equatorial Guinea and Gabon, and several minor clashes along the border took place. The dispute was resolved within the context of the Conference of East and Central African States, with the presidents of Zaire and Congo-Brazzaville— moderate pro-Western and radical nonaligned states, respectively— mediating. Although a commission created to examine the competing claims eventually came under OAU auspices, the Organization never formally considered the conflict. Like many intercoalition African conflicts, this dispute threatened to involve outside powers and to undermine the position of the OAU. As one analyst has written: "There was some possibility that Gabon's close ties to France and good relations with Rhodesia and South Africa—in sharp contrast with Equatorial Guinea's relations with the Soviet Union, China, and North Korea—might make extra-regional intervention a possibility."[94]

In September 1972 a conflict broke out between Tanzania and Uganda as a result of Tanzania's backing of an invasion by some 1,000 Ugandan exiles who sought to reinstate Milton Obote, the former president of Uganda, who had been overthrown in January 1971 by General Amin. At this time the Amin regime was regarded by many African radicals such as President Nyerere of Tanzania as neocolonialist and pro-Western because of Amin's historical links with Britain and Israel and because he ousted the increasingly radical Obote. It was not until after this conflict that Amin's anti-Western and anti-Israeli policies developed.[95] Had this Ugandan-Tanzanian conflict been brought to the OAU, it would unquestionably have evoked the division between the moderate pro-Western and radical nonaligned groupings. The dispute was eventually mediated by the president of Somalia with the assistance of the OAU secretary-general.

The last two intercoalition conflicts in which there was no OAU intervention or debate occurred in 1977. In the first of these conflicts, some 2,000 armed rebels claiming to be Congolese refugees crossed into Zaire's Shaba province from Angola in early March.* Eventually Moroccan troops (airlifted by France) became involved in the fighting and were instrumental in the defeat of the rebels. Members of the moderate pro-Western grouping voiced support for the central government of Zaire, while radical nonaligned states such as Libya, Algeria, and Angola condemned both the Moroccan intervention and the Mobutu regime. The conflict "resolved" itself on the battlefield and never elicited an OAU response. The brief war between Egypt and Libya in July 1977 was the culmination of a long deterioration in their relations and was preceded by numerous instances of subversion by each state into the other's affairs. Libya did complain to the OAU about Egyptian "aggression" but no organizational response was forthcoming. The two states were among the most outspoken members of their respective blocs and harbored deep animosities for each other. Hostilities were brought to an end as a result of the mediation efforts of various African and Arab heads of state and officials, including Presidents Etienne Eyadema of Togo and Houari Boumédienne of Algeria; but the underlying tensions in Egyptian-Libyan relations continued.

Examination of the role of the OAU in the three intercoalition conflicts that elicited an organizational debate (but not an intervention) reveals the inherent difficulties that this type of conflict has posed for the Organization. The Angolan civil war (1975-77), which involved three rival Angolan factions as well as Cuban, Zairean and South African forces, was debated by the African states at a January 1976 emergency OAU summit. The provision by Zaire of base camps and some personnel to the pro-Western FNLA was brought up in the course of the debate but was not the major focus. Rather, the OAU members were concerned with the formation of a reconciliation government versus immediate recognition of the Marxist MPLA as well as with the Cuban and South African interventions. Twenty-two states backed a resolution recognizing the MPLA as the legitimate government of Angola, while an equal number of states opposed this and instead supported a resolution calling for a government of national reconciliation and an end to foreign intervention (the latter point reflecting the unease felt by many conservative and moderate African states over the massive Cuban involvement).[96] South African intervention on the

---

*In May 1978 there was a repetition of the 1977 incident. French, Belgian, and Moroccan forces intervened in support of the Zairean government.

side of the anti-MPLA factions (FNLA and UNITA) may have caused some moderate states such as Ghana, Niger, Mauritius, and Nigeria to side with the more radical states. Had Pretoria not become embroiled in the Angolan civil war, a majority of OAU members (but not two-thirds) would likely have supported the second resolution. In any case, the strength of the ideological division paralyzed the OAU and prevented it from assuming any role in the settlement of the conflict.

The two conflicts involving Algerian intervention in Morocco and Mauritania in 1976 and 1977 occurred following the Spanish decision in November 1975 to divide the Western Sahara between the latter two states. Spain ceded de facto control over most of the territory to the two states in November, although it did not formally transfer sovereignty until the end of February 1976. In January Algeria began to aid the local Saharan independence movement, Polisario, in its attempt to gain control of the territory and establish an independent state. In January and February large contingents of Algerian troops fought Moroccan forces in the Moroccan zone of the Western Sahara. Later, Algeria provided military aid and base camps to Polisario forces. The initial OAU debate in February focused on the issue of who should control the territory, but the Algerian intervention was brought up by Morocco and Mauritania. The OAU states divided over the first question and did not vote on the question of Algerian intervention. [97] While the moderate pro-Western states for the most part opposed recognition of Polisario as the legitimate government of the disputed territory, the radical and moderate nonaligned groups tended to back Polisario. In June 1976 Mauritania explicitly asked for OAU action against Algeria but almost all OAU members were reluctant to deal with this question. The deep divisions among the African states, as well as a fear that Morocco, Mauritania, and their allies might leave the Organization, convinced OAU members to shy away from discussion of these disputes, although by the middle of 1976 even some of the pro-Western grouping were refusing to back Moroccan and Mauritanian expansion into the Western Sahara.

Two intercoalition conflicts did prove amenable to an OAU intervention, although in only one of these was the Organization able to successfully defuse the situation. The conflict concerning support by Burundi and Congo-Brazzaville for the rebels agitating against the conservative, pro-Western government in the Congo-Kinshasa in 1964-65 provides a further illustration of how resistant intercoalition disputes have been to OAU involvement. In September 1964 the OAU Council of Ministers met to consider the provision of material aid and base camps to the rebels, as well as the problems associated with the Kinshasa government's use of mercenaries and U.S. and Belgian aid. The Council passed a resolution that called on the Congolese government to cease recruiting mercenaries and to expel those already present. The resolution also requested that both Congolese factions cease hostilities and seek a national reconciliation; that all outside parties refrain from actions that might aggravate tensions; and that President Kenyatta of Kenya head a ten-nation commission whose purpose was to be the creation of a national reconciliation Kinshasa government and normalization of the latter's relations with its neighbors. OAU intervention in this conflict can be explained by the fact that the various African groupings were able to interpret the rather vaguely worded Council resolution according to their own preferences. The radical nonaligned states felt that the resolution called for an end to U.S. and Belgian assistance to the government of Moise Tshombe, whereas the moderate pro-Western states interpreted the resolution as ordering a cessation of external assistance to the anti-Tshombe rebels. [98] The next two months revealed the impotence of the OAU injunctions. As the fighting continued, the external parties continued their involvement and the OAU commission secured little success in endeavoring to carry out its mandate. At the end of November the situation deteriorated when the United States airlifted Belgian paratroopers into the Congo to rescue Western hostages held captive by the rebels—an action that in fact seriously weakened the rebels' position.

At an emergency session of the OAU Council in December 1964 the divisions among the African states were all too clear and no consensus was possible. Further attempts by both the Council and the OAU commission in early 1965 to deal with the conflict were also unsuccessful because of the divergent positions of the African groupings. The commission, which was "composed mostly of states with strong partisan views on the question," was unable to articulate a common stand with respect to the conflict, and the Council was similarly divided. [99] The OAU was unable either to influence the policies of the Congolese factions or to dissuade external actors from involving themselves in the dispute. In connection with this Woronoff has remarked: "Since Africa in general was . . . polarized, some states backing the 'legitimate' government and some the 'nationalist', it was in no position to give a lesson to outside powers or discourage their interference." [100]

The single conflict between members of these two groupings in which the OAU both intervened and succeeded was that arising from Ghanaian support for subversive interventions into Niger in 1964 and 1965. A number of West African countries complained about the subversive practices of the Nkrumah regime during this period, but only in the case of Niger is there evidence of large-scale intervention. Several exile groups desirous of ousting Niger's government entered the country in late 1964, and in April 1965 an attempt was made on the life of President Diori by a person who had been trained in Ghana.

In May, eight Francophone West African states announced they would boycott the OAU Assembly meeting scheduled to be held in Accra in September unless Ghana expelled all political exiles. Many African states were fearful that a boycott by these states would presage the disintegration of the OAU; so a special meeting of the OAU was held in June to discuss the issue. Ghana agreed to cease its interventionist activities and to expel the exiles, and the Council then noted this agreement and passed a resolution urging all members to attend the fall meeting of the Assembly. While Ghana did not expel the exiles (prompting eight states in the end to boycott the Assembly), it did cease supporting subversive interventions. In retrospect, one can conclude that it was only the possession of a unique form of leverage by the victim state and its allies (namely, a threat not to attend the OAU meeting) that permitted OAU intervention and success in this intercoalition conflict.

Examination of the patterns of OAU intervention and success in inter-African conflicts indicates that the major inadequacy in the hypotheses concerning organizational involvement was with respect to conflicts in which external assistance was rendered to secessionist groups. That the theory failed to predict OAU behavior in such cases is probably attributable to an inaccurate portrayal of the coalition configurations rather than to any inherent flaw in the theory itself. In particular, the religious tension (Moslem-non-Moslem) characterizing inter-African politics was not taken into account when the coalitions were defined. The strength of this division among African states was such as to overpower the consensus on secession. It should be noted, however, that this consensus has been adhered to by African states in several other instances of attempted secession. In the cases of Biafran and southern Sudanese secessionist pressures, for example, no inter-African conflicts arose because OAU members were careful not to provide significant assistance to those seeking secession. Where there have been either religious or ideological divisions underlying a conflict that reflect those existing among the African states as a whole, governments have recognized that consensuses are unobtainable and that even debate of such conflicts would only serve to weaken the OAU and perhaps threaten its very existence. As Nye has observed: "Where consensus and impartiality broke down, the OAU was unable to play any role."*

---

*J. S. Nye, Peace in Parts (Boston: Little, Brown, 1970), p. 159. Nye based his conclusion on an analysis of a smaller population of inter-African conflicts. Another comparable conclusion regarding the conflict management role of the OAU can be found in B. D. Meyers, "The Organization of African Unity: Conflict Management by a Regional Organization" (Ph. D. diss., University of California, Los Angeles, 1973), p. 239.

In surveying the OAU's activities as a collective security body during the years 1963-77, it is obvious that its effectiveness peaked during the first three years. Since 1965 it has not intervened (that is, passed a resolution calling for a cessation of a military action) in a single conflict. Its early successes were due almost entirely to the occurrence of four territorial conflicts in the years 1963-64. Since then the only important attempts at territorial aggrandizement have arisen from Somali irredentism, a fact that attests to the influence of the early OAU stands. These Somali actions did not elicit OAU involvement in 1965-67 because the violence was at a low level and because OAU members felt they had clearly expressed their views in 1964. However, the Somali aggression of 1977 did not evoke a clear OAU response because of some African states' affinity or antagonism for the conflicting parties. This conflict was like almost all of the conflicts in the post-1965 era in that it tended to split the OAU membership on ideological and/or religious lines. For the most part it was conflicts between radical nonaligned and moderate pro-Western states that dominated this era, but those between Moslem and non-Moslem states also caused serious cleavages among the Africans in several cases. There is also little prospect of such cleavages dissipating so as to support an expanded role for the OAU as an African collective security agency in coming years.

If the OAU's role in conflict management has declined with the ending of the optimistic "spirit of Addis Ababa" around 1966,[101] its activities in this area have nonetheless had some modest positive effects. It has provided a forum in which differences that have led or might have led to violence have been reduced through negotiations. Its meetings have often informally or formally produced mediatory initiatives that have had some fruitful effects. Such accords have then sometimes received an OAU imprimatur of support, increasing the likelihood that they will be respected. Also, it is important to note that the OAU has played a more active role on issues pertaining to conflicts between African and non-African states. Many OAU members now view the Organization's major function as creating "a consensual 'African foreign policy' towards extra-African issues" rather than as acting as "an effective agent of mediation" for collective security.[102]

NOTES

1. Clarence Contee, "The Emergence of Du Bois As An African Nationalist," Journal of Negro History 54 (January 1969): 55-56.
2. See George Padmore, Pan-Africanism or Communism? (London: Dennis Dobson, 1956), pp. 144-51.

3. Colin Legum, Pan-Africanism: A Short Political Guide (New York: Praeger, 1962), p. 32. For a good review of 1900-45 period, see Vincent Bakpetu Thompson, Africa and Unity: The Evolution of Pan-Africanism (New York: Humanities Press, 1969), pp. 3-63.

4. Legum, op. cit., app. 4, p. 157.

5. Ibid., p. 47. For an account of these conferences, see Thompson, op. cit., pp. 126-34.

6. Thompson, op. cit., pp. 141-58.

7. Thompson, op. cit., pp. 150-75.

8. Legum, op. cit., app. 13, pp. 197-200.

9. Legum, op. cit., pp. 205-10.

10. Robert Good, "Changing Patterns of African International Relations," American Political Science Review 18 (September 1964): 633-34.

11. Legum, op. cit., app. 17, pp. 216-19.

12. Articles VII and VIII.

13. Article IX.

14. Article X.

15. N. J. Padelford, "The Organization of African Unity," International Organization 18 (Summer 1964): 525.

16. Article XIII.

17. Article XIV(2).

18. Article VIII.

19. Padelford, op. cit., p. 534.

20. Article XIX.

21. Article II(2) of Protocol. For text and commentary, see T. O. Elias, "The Commission of Mediation, Conciliation and Arbitration of the Organization of African Unity," British Journal of International Law 40 (1964): 336-55.

22. Article XX of Protocol.

23. Benjamin David Meyers, "The Organization of African Unity: Conflict Management by a Regional Organization" (Ph.D. diss., University of California, Los Angeles, 1973), p. 77. See, also, Richard E. Bissell, "African Unity Twelve Years Later," Current History 68 (May 1975): 193.

24. Meyers, op. cit., p. 94.

25. OAU Doc. AHG/Res. 27 (II), October 21-25, 1965.

26. W. Scott Thompson and I. William Zartman, "The Development of Norms in the African System," in The Organization of African Unity After Ten Years, ed. Yassin El-Ayouty (New York: Praeger, 1975), p. 5.

27. Legum, op. cit., p. 136.

28. Ibid., pp. 160-61, 175.

29. Ibid., pp. 187-97.

30. Ibid., p. 198.

31. OAU Doc. AHG/Res. 16 (I), July 17-21, 1964; Saadia Touval, The Boundary Politics of Independent Africa (Cambridge, Mass.: Harvard University Press, 1972), pp. 86-90.

32. Jon Woronoff, Organizing African Unity (Metuchen, N.J.: Scarecrow Press, 1970), pp. 139-40.

33. Ibid., p. 140.

34. Zdenek Cervenka, The Organization of African Unity and Its Charter (New York: Frederick A. Praeger, 1969), p. 93.

35. Woronoff, op. cit., p. 625.

36. J. S. Nye, Peace in Parts (Boston: Little, Brown, 1971), p. 165. Additional comments on the strength and significance of the principle of territorial integrity can be found in Immanuel Wallerstein, Africa: The Politics of Unity (New York: Random House, 1967), pp. 76-77; Berhanykun Andemicael, Peaceful Settlement among African States: Roles of the United Nations and the Organization of African Unity (New York: United Nations Institute for Training and Research, 1972), pp. 5, 20.

37. Anylonoro S. Kamunu, "Secession and the Right of Self-Determination: An OAU Dilemma," Journal of Modern African Studies 12 (October 1974): 370.

38. Ibid., p. 366.

39. Philippe Decraene, "L'Afrique noire est le cadre de nombreux conflits armes," Le monde diplomatique (April 1968), p. 9.

40. Touval, op. cit., pp. 118, 154. Uganda and Congo (Leopoldville) did allow some minor material assistance to be sent to the rebels through their territory.

41. For discussions of OAU actions in the Nigerian civil war as well as the opposition of the great majority of the states to secessionist movements, see, Kaye Whiteman, "The OAU and the Nigerian Issue," The World Today 24 (November 1968): 449-53; Touval, op. cit., pp. 96-98; Meyers, op. cit., pp. 182-88.

42. OAU Doc. AHG/Res. 51 (IV), September 11-14, 1967.

43. OAU Doc. AHG/Res. 54 (V), September 13-16, 1968; Andemicael, op. cit., pp. 33-34.

44. Robert Mortimer, "The Algerian Revolution in Search of the African Revolution," Journal of Modern African Studies 8 (September 1970): 363.

45. Nora McKeon, "The African States and the O.A.U.," International Affairs 42 (July 1966): 406.

46. Immanuel Wallerstein, Africa: The Politics of Unity (New York: Random House, 1967), pp. 18-24.

47. Robert Good, "Changing Patterns of African International Relations," American Political Science Review 18 (September 1964): 633.

48. Patrick McGowan, "Africa and Nonalignment: A Comparative Study of Foreign Policy," International Studies Quarterly 12 (September 1968): 278.

49. McGowan, op. cit., p. 280.

50. Mortimer, op. cit., p. 363.

51. McKeon, op. cit., p. 406.

52. Claude Welch, "The OAU and International Recognition: Lessons from Uganda," El-Ayouty, ed., op. cit., p. 103.

53. John Mercer, "Confrontation in the Western Sahara," World Today 32 (June 1976): 230-39; Peter Schwab, "Cold War in the Horn of Africa," African Affairs 77 (January 1978): 17-20; Thomas Henriksen, "Angola and Mozambique: Intervention and Revolution," Current History (November 1976): 153-57.

54. Zdenek Cervenka, "The OAU in 1976," in African Contemporary Record, 1976-77, ed. Colim Legum (New York: Africana, 1977), p. A75.

55. Timothy Shaw, "Discontinuities and Inequalities in African International Politics," International Journal 30 (Summer 1975): 371.

56. For a discussion of the nature of the French military commitment and aid programs, see Chester Crocker, "France's Changing Military Interests," Africa Report 13 (June 1968): 20-22. For a discussion of Togo's security ties with France, see Touval, op. cit., p. 157.

57. Lynn Mytelka, "Genealogy of Francophone West and Equatorial African Regional Organizations," Journal of Modern African Studies 12 (June 1974): 297-320.

58. Waldemar A. Nielsen, The Great Powers in Africa (New York: Praeger, 1969), p. 367.

59. Bruce D. Larkin, China and Africa, 1949-1970 (Berkeley: University of California Press, 1971), pp. 134-35, 173; Charles Gallagher, "The Maghrib and the Middle East," in Political Dynamics in the Middle East, ed. Paul Y. Hammond and Sidney S. Alexander (New York: Elsevier, 1972), pp. 409-10.

60. Gallagher, op. cit., pp. 400, 410; William H. Lewis, "North Africa: The Eye of the Storm," Current History 73 (December 1977): 224.

61. Lewis, op. cit., p. 198.

62. Chester A. Crocker, "The African Dimension of Indian Ocean Policy," Orbis 20 (Fall 1976): 653.

63. Lewis, op. cit., p. 197.

64. Mordechai Abir, Oil, Power and Politics (London: Frank Cass, 1974), p. 37.

65. Feraidoon Shams B, "Conflict in the African Horn," Current History 73 (December 1977): 200.

66. Peter Schwab, "Cold War on the Horn of Africa," African Affairs 77 (January 1978): 18-19.

67. Ethiopawi, "The Eritrean-Ethiopian Conflict," in Ethnic Conflict in International Relations, ed. Astri Suhrke and Lela G. Noble (New York: Praeger, 1977), pp. 138-40.

68. Kessing's Contemporary Archives (August 5, 1977), pp. 28485-86.

69. Welch, op. cit., pp. 363-68.

70. Susan Aurelia Gitelson, "Major Shifts in Recent Ugandan Foreign Policy," African Affairs 76 (July 1977): 359-80.

71. Schwab, op. cit., pp. 15-19.

72. Ibid., p. xxxi. See, also, John Marcum, "Southern Africa after the Collapse of Portuguese Rule," in Africa: From Mystery to Maze, ed. Helen Kitchen (Lexington, Mass.: D. C. Heath, 1976): pp. 77-134.

73. Fenner Brockway, The Colonial Revolution (London: Hart-David, MacGibbon, 1973), pp. 412-14.

74. Colin Legum, ed., African Contemporary Record, 1976-77, pp. B169-70.

75. Kessing's Contemporary Archives (June 24, 1977), p. 28416.

76. Lemarchand [cited on p. 139], pp. 383-401.

77. Touval, op. cit., pp. 130-31.

78. Gallagher, op. cit., pp. 406-10.

79. Gitolson, op. cit., pp. 302-04.

80. Ibid., pp. 355-80.

81. Charles B. McLane, Soviet-Middle East Relations (London: Central Asian Research Centre), pp. 118-19; and Soviet-African Relations (London: Central Asian Research Centre, 1974), pp. 180-82.

82. David A. Kay, New Nations in the United Nations, 1960-68 (New York: Columbia University Press, 1970), pp. 226, 230, 234, 238-39.

83. Christopher Stevens, The Soviet Union and Black Africa (London: Macmillan, 1976), p. 193. See, also, Yu [cited on p. 141].

84. Stevens, op. cit., p. 195.

85. For the Congo crisis of 1964-65 see Wallerstein, op. cit., p. 90, and Andemicael, op. cit., p. 23; the 1971 crisis over the recognition of Uganda, Welch, op. cit.; the recognition of Polisario during the Western Saharan crisis, Kessing's Contemporary Archives (May 28, 1976), pp. 27747-48; and the MPLA versus coalition government issue during the Angolan crisis, Africa Research Bulletin 13 (1976): 3883, 3926.

86. Kessing's Contemporary Archives (October 28, 1977), p. 28634.

87. Zdenek Cervenka, "Major Policy Shifts in the OAU, 1963-73," in Foreign Relations of African States, ed. Kenneth Ingham (London: Butterworths, 1974), p. 327.

88. Andemicael, op. cit., pp. 6-7.

89. Patricia Burko Wild, "The Organization of African Unity and the Algerian-Moroccan Border Conflict," International Organization 20 (Winter 1966): 34.

90. Colin Legum, "The Organization of African Unity—Success or Failure?," International Affairs 51 (April 1975): 212.

91. Andemicael, op. cit., p. 13.

92. Schwab, op. cit., pp. 17-20; Feraidoon Shams B, op. cit., pp. 195-204.

93. Meyers, op. cit., p. 138.

94. B. D. Meyers, "Intraregional Conflict Management by the OAU," International Organization 28 (Summer 1974): 356.

95. Welch, op. cit., pp. 103-9; Gitelson, op. cit., pp. 364-66.

96. Africa Research Bulletin 13 (1976): 3883, 3926.

97. The division is described in Keesing's Contemporary Archives (May 28, 1976), p. 27747.

98. Wallerstein, op. cit., pp. 97-98.

99. Andemicael, op. cit., p. 26; Wallerstein, op. cit., p. 91.

100. Woronoff, op. cit., p. 498. See, also, Linda B. Miller, "Regional Organizations and the Regulation of Internal Conflict," World Politics 19 (July 1967): 590-91; I. William Zartman, International Relations in the New Africa (Englewood Cliffs, N.J.: Prentice-Hall, 1966), pp. 39-40.

101. Cervenka, "Major Policy Shifts in the OAU, 1963-73," pp. 327, 332.

102. Timothy Shaw, "Regional Cooperation and Conflict in Africa," International Journal 30 (Autumn 1975): 684. See, also, R. A. Akindele, "Reflections on the Preoccupation and Conduct of African Diplomacy," Journal of Modern African Studies 14 (1976): 560.

5

The Arab League and
Inter-Arab Conflicts

THE BACKGROUND AND CHARACTER OF THE
ARAB LEAGUE COLLECTIVE SECURITY SYSTEM

The League of Arab States, which was established in 1945, was
in a sense the product of two conflicting movements in the Arab world
—the quest for Arab unity and the centrifugal forces favoring Arab
separatism. The former originated as a cultural theme with the
"Arabization" of the "Fertile Crescent," the Arabian peninsula, and
Egypt by Arab conquerors in the seventh century A. D. , and continued
to thrive even during 300 years of Ottoman rule from the sixteenth
through the nineteenth centuries. The genesis of modern Arab separatism, on the other hand, dates from the gradual decline of Ottoman
suzerainty in the nineteenth century, which witnessed the establishment of autonomous provinces by insurgent vassals of the sultan and
the advent of European colonizers in the area.

Arab hopes for the unification of the few areas remaining under
Turkish control in 1914 were temporarily encouraged by Britain during World War I, but were frustrated by the Treaty of Sèvres in 1920
that divided the Arab lands into 25 separate entities, mostly under
British and French control. This fragmentation, combined with the
aloofness of Egypt from general Arab concerns and the bitter rivalry
between the Hashemite dynasties of Iraq and Transjordan and the
Sauds of Saudi Arabia, posed insuperable impediments to Arab unity
in the interwar years. Moreover, the manner in which the various
anticolonial movements achieved success tended to entrench the forces
of national separatism. As J. S. Raleigh observes: "The consum-
mation of national liberation within the restricted area of a separate
national state created vested interests and transformed independence
from a vague goal into a definite asset that could no longer be endan-

gered, sacrificed or even restricted for the sale of supranational aspirations and ideas."[1] As a result, while Arab unity remained an effective and popular rallying point for those areas still under colonial
control, its appeal to the governments of the independent Arab states
became limited to one basic issue—the widely shared desire to free
the Arab world of non-Arab influence, particularly in the form of the
proposed Jewish state in Palestine.

The idea of Arab unity, however, was given new impetus by
Britain during World War II. The defeat of French forces in Syria
and Lebanon and the growing power and prestige of the Axis states in
the Middle East led Britain, as the only Allied power remaining in
the area, to increasingly regard Pan-Arabism as a means of securing
Arab cooperation in the Allied war effort.[2] On May 29, 1941, the day
after an attempted anti-British coup in Iraq, Anthony Eden signaled
London's new attitude toward Arab unity:

> The Arab world has made great strides since the settle-
> ment reached at the end of the last war, and many Arab
> thinkers desire for the Arab peoples a greater degree of
> unity than they now enjoy. In reaching out towards this
> unity they hope for our support. No such appeal from
> our friends should go unanswered. It seems to me both
> natural and right that the cultural and economic ties be-
> tween the Arab countries, and the political ties too,
> should be strengthened. His Majesty's Government,
> for their part, will give their full support to any scheme
> that commands general approval.[3]

Shortly thereafter, Britain began to support the claims of Syria and
Lebanon against the French and to persuade Egypt to assume a greater
role in Arab affairs. London's support for Arab unity was again expressed by Eden in 1943 with the reminder that "the initiative would
have to come from the Arabs themselves."[4]

The "Blue Book" proposals submitted by General Nuri al-Sa'id
of Iraq to the British in early 1943 constituted the first concrete plan
for Arab unity. Motivated partially, if not primarily, by the realization that an Arab solution was necessary to the emerging "Palestine
Question," Iraq proposed the Federation of the Fertile Crescent
States—Syria, Lebanon, Palestine, and Transjordan, which were in
turn to be federated with Iraq in an "Arab League" that would be open
to other Arab states. Special arrangements were spelled out for the
protection of the Jewish inhabitants of Palestine, the religious plu-
ralism of Jerusalem and the Christian Maronites of Lebanon.[5] The
most populous Arab state, Egypt, viewed the Iraqi plan as an attempt
to bring a large part of the Arab world under the domination of the

Hashemite rulers of Iraq and Transjordan, the result of which would be to "greatly strengthen Iraq vis-à-vis Egypt."[6] In order to undermine the Iraqi scheme Egypt proposed as an alternative the creation of a multifunctional confederation of all Arab states, which would not involve any important sacrifices in the sovereignty of member states. Apart from the fact that it would thwart the Iraqi-sponsored federation, Egypt also viewed its own proposed Pan-Arab organization as a useful tool for coordinating Arab resistance to the creation of a Jewish state in Palestine and to a continued British military presence in Egypt after the war.

The views of other Arab states with respect to federation were voiced in secret discussions held in Cairo between Egyptian Prime Minister Nahhas Pasha and other heads of state. Syria alone supported full Arab unification but, unlike Iraq, favored a republican form of government. Transjordan supported a union of itself with Palestine and Syria, to be ruled by King Abdullah, as a counterbalance between Iraq and Egypt. Lebanon leaned toward a looser federation of sovereign states that would allow protection for its religious minorities. Yemen and Saudi Arabia opposed the Hashemite plans but did not present any specific alternatives.* Despite the formidable difficulties involved in reconciling these conflicting positions, Nahhas Pasha was able to announce in July 1944 the formation of a preparatory committee charged with the task of arranging a General Arab Conference to be held in September of the same year.[7]

The results of the conference confirmed the dynastic and nationalistic rivalries impeding unification or federation of the Arab states and testified as well to the growing influence of Egypt in the region. The Alexandria Protocol issued at the close of the conference made vague allusions to the possibility of eventual Arab unity, but basically envisaged a loose grouping of states that would restrict its activities to the economic, cultural, and social spheres.[8] With respect to collective security, it was mentioned that the proposed organization of Arab states should deal with conflicts of an intra-Arab nature, coordinate the Arab states' "political plans," and safeguard their sovereignty. However, it is clear that most of the Arab governments

---

*While Abdullah's proposal was justified as creating a counterbalance between Iraq and Egypt, Abdullah would certainly have cooperated closely with his Hashemite brethren in Iraq. (Robert MacDonald, The League of Arab States: A Study in the Dynamics of Regional Organization [Princeton, N.J.: Princeton University Press, 1965], pp. 35-37; and M. Khalil, ed., The Arab States and the Arab League, vol. 2, International Affairs [Beirut: Khayats, 1962], Document nos. 5 and 6, pp. 12-18.)

viewed the organization as a means to undermine both plans for the unification of the Fertile Crescent states and the proposed Jewish state in Palestine. The creation of a viable intraregional security system was not their first priority. The voting formulas outlined in the Protocol further attested to the ranking of their priorities. The desire to retain maximum independence for the member states was reflected in the fact that all states were to be equally represented on the organization's council. Moreover, all council decisions were to be binding only on those states that accepted them, with the de facto result that unanimous consent was required if the proposed body was to act authoritatively in inter-Arab disputes. The Arab states obviously anticipated serious political differences among themselves, and they did not wish to create a situation where they could be bound by a majority of their compatriots who at any given moment might oppose their interests. The several important political changes that occurred in a number of Arab states during the interregnum between the Alexandria meeting and the March 1945 conference at which the Pact of the League of Arab States was drawn up served to highlight the political uncertainty characterizing the Arab world. Moreover, the political changes brought to power men who were strongly committed to protecting their countries' sovereignty, thus further undermining the possibility of erecting a strong collective security agency.*

The seven independent Arab states—Iraq, Syria, Lebanon, Transjordan, Egypt, Saudi Arabia, and Yemen—formally created the League of Arab States on March 22, 1945. During the next 32 years 14 additional states became members of the League—Libya (1953), Sudan (1956), Morocco, Tunisia (1958), Kuwait (1961), Algeria (1962), South Yemen (1968), Bahrain, Oman, Qatar (1971), the United Arab Emirates (1972), Mauritania (1973), Somalia (1975), and Djibouti (1977). The Pact of the League of Arab States[9] followed the guidelines set by the Alexandria Protocol. It established a Council on which all

---

*Nahhas Pasha was dismissed as prime minister of Egypt, and his counterparts in Syria and Jordan were also relieved of their posts. Also, Christians in Lebanon condemned the proposed League as a potential incursion on Lebanon's sovereignty. (Robert MacDonald, The League of Arab States: A Study in the Dynamics of Regional Organization [Princeton, N.J.: Princeton University Press, 1965], p. 41.) Britain had also come around to support an organization of all Arab states that linked Egypt with the others since it felt that it would best be able to influence political developments in the region through such an organization. (Patrick Seale, The Struggle for Syria: A Study of Post-War Arab Politics [London: Oxford University Press, 1965], p. 23.)

states had equal voting power; it emphasized functional rather than political cooperation; and it stressed the priority of protecting the security and independence of the Arab states. Obeisance was paid to the ideal of Arab unity, but this clearly had little relevance to the immediate future. As for inter-Arab relations, the Pact placed unquestionable primacy on the preservation of the status quo. The declared aim of the signatories was to "support and stabilize" the ties linking League members, and to do so "upon a basis of respect for the independence and sovereignty" of each. [10] They also pledged to "abstain from any action calculated to change established systems of government," [11] and to eschew the use of force in resolving their disputes. [12]

Despite this stress on protecting state sovereignty and preventing intervention, the Pact did not grant the new organization a great deal of power to promote these norms. Although the Council was given the power to initiate mediatory or arbitral missions by a majority vote (excluding the parties to a dispute), its decisions in the case of an actual or threatened armed conflict required the unanimous consent of all League members except the aggressing state. [13] The effect of this stipulation was that a resolution could not be passed against an aggressing state unless it was completely bereft of allies in the Arab world. Moreover, even if a resolution were passed against a state, the Pact cautioned that it would not be binding if it concerned a state's "independence, sovereignty or territorial integrity." Since any conflict involving war or a threat of war could likely be viewed in this light by the parties, the League's decisions in inter-Arab conflicts were not considered to be legally binding. Fayez A. Sayegh pointed to this fundamental weakness in the organization's security provisions when he wrote: "In creating the League, the individual Arab states created an association or an alliance, not a union; they withheld from the organization representing that association both inherent and derivative power; and they bound themselves in advance by no commitment to implement whatever decisions they might approve during the discussions." [14]

In 1949, after the League had been in existence for four years, and its members had suffered a military defeat at the hands of Israel, the Arab states became increasingly concerned with security issues. In the fall of 1949 Iraq proposed a Syrian-Iraqi union to provide security protection to Syria against Israel, and the anti-Hashemite states countered successfully with proposals for strengthening the Arab military defense system. [15] There was also some interest in strengthening the procedures for settling inter-Arab conflicts so that the League would definitely qualify under Article 52 of the UN Charter as a "regional organization" capable of dealing with disputes before any referral to the United Nations. [16] But it is clear that the Arab states were primarily interested in collective defense rather than collective security. Given Arab preoccupation with the Israeli threat, it is not surprising that the Joint Defense and Economic Cooperation Treaty (often referred to as the Arab Collective Security Pact), which was concluded in 1950, [17] failed to improve appreciably the League's means of preserving inter-Arab security. The new treaty did declare that the signatories would regard an act of aggression against one of them as "directed against them all," and the signatories did undertake, "in accordance with the right of self-defense," to aid the victim immediately and to take "all steps available, including the use of armed force, to repel the aggression and restore security and peace."[18] This provision, however, was primarily directed at the aggressions of non-Arab states, and it did not alter the institutions and procedures for managing inter-Arab conflicts. New agencies for collective self-defense—the Joint Defense Council and the Permanent Military Commission—were created, [19] but the Arab Tribunal of Arbitration, mentioned as a possible organ to facilitate inter-Arab security in Article 19 of the League's constitution, still failed to materialize. The Joint Defense Council was able to make binding on all contracting states any plans approved by a two-thirds majority. However, this rejection of the unanimity principle was in fact more apparent than real since the final decision to implement any such plans approved by the new agency remained the prerogative of the League Council, where unanimous approval was, of course, required. The new treaty, in short, was clearly aimed at a non-Arab enemy, albeit from within the Middle East, and contained nothing to facilitate the solution of inter-Arab disputes or to enhance the collective security potentialities of the League. [20]

The last attempt to alter the structures of the Arab League occurred at the Conference of Kings and Heads of State in January 1964. Prompted by Israel's plans to divert the waters of the Jordan River, the Arab states created the Jordan Waters Organization, which was to coordinate Jordanian, Egyptian, Syrian, and Lebanese policies on this matter, and they also set up a joint command under the commander-in-chief of the UAR's military forces. [21] In fact, neither of these organs has been particularly active or successful. The 1964 Conference also modified the decision-making structures of the League in that it made the Conference of Kings and Heads of State the supreme body within the organization (hence making Arab summit conferences official meetings of the League Council). Also created was a Control Committee of personal representatives of all chiefs of state, which was to oversee the implementation of resolutions and to meet officially as the Council every four months. The latter committee has not performed as expected, but the Conference of Kings and Heads of State has been convened approximately once a year and has added vitality, if not always accord, to the diplomatic life of the League.

Another point to note is that although the Arab states were willing in 1964 to create new bodies within the League, they neglected to alter the decision-making rules within League organs to allow the passage of votes by a two-thirds majority, as had been suggested on a number of occasions by the organization's secretaries-general.[22] In recent years the Arab states have begun to collaborate extensively in the economic sphere,[23] but they have eschewed any plans for restructuring the League that might compromise their sovereignty or afford an opportunity for their enemies in the Arab world to intervene against them in intraregional conflicts. While they have often spoken in enthusiastic terms about their loyalty to the Arab "nation" and the necessity for Arab unity, the members of the League have exhibited an extremely protective attitude toward their independence, and have remained deeply distrustful of their Arab brethren.

COALITION CONFIGURATIONS
IN INTER-ARAB RELATIONS, 1946-77

Since the Arab League was created in 1945, serious antagonisms between individual and groups of Arab states have strongly influenced the activities of the League. More than any other region, the Arab world has been characterized by shifting patterns of dissension and competition. These patterns are not always easily discernible, and what will be described below as Arab groupings have not usually been based on formal treaties or alliances, but instead on informal ties and common attitudes toward a variety of international and domestic issues.* Moreover, these alignments have not only been predicted on the issues of ideology and Arab relations with non-Arab states, but have also been influenced by nationalist rivalries and personal ambitions within the Arab world, which often subside as quickly as they arise.[24] While the complex character of inter-Arab relations has made the delineation of the coalitions difficult, and while they are advanced with some reservation, their presentation will hopefully facilitate an understanding of the politics of that region and the role and success of the League in international conflicts.

Before they are described in some detail, the alignment patterns salient to the security of Arab states can be best outlined with

---

*As MacDonald observes, the spate of military arrangements between Egypt and other League members between 1955 and 1957 is an exception to this rule. (Robert MacDonald, The League of Arab States: A Study in the Dynamics of Regional Organization [Princeton, N.J.: Princeton University Press, 1965], p. 78.)

TABLE 7

Inter-Arab Coalition Configurations, 1946–77

Period 1: 1946–Mid–1954

Non-Hashemite	Nonaligned	Hashemite
Saudi Arabia	Lebanon	Iraq
Egypt	Libya (joined 1953)	Transjordan
Yemen		Syria (August–December 1949)
Syria (1946–August 1949, 1950–54)		

Period 2: Mid–1954–56

Positive Neutralists		Nonaligned	Pro-West
Egypt	Saudi Arabia	Lebanon	Iraq
Jordan (1956)	Yemen	Sudan (joined 1956)	Libya
Syria			Jordan (1954–55)

Period 3: 1957–July 1958 (Lebanon Crisis)

Radical Neutralists	Nonaligned	Nonradicals with Western Ties	
Egypt	Sudan	Iraq	Saudi Arabia
Syria (Syria and Egypt formed UAR from February 1958 until September 1961)		Libya	Jordan
Yemen		Lebanon	

Period 4a: August 1958–September 1961

Radical Neutralists		Nonaligned		Nonradicals with Western Ties	
Iraq	Yemen	Lebanon	Morocco (joined 1958)	Jordan	Libya
UAR (Syria and Egypt)		Sudan	Kuwait (joined 1961)	Saudi Arabia	Tunisia (joined 1958)

Period 4b: September 1961–Mid–1966

Radical Neutralists	Nonaligned	Nonradicals with Western Ties
Iraq	Lebanon	Jordan
Syria	Sudan	Saudi Arabia
UAR (Egypt)	Morocco (1961–63)	Tunisia
Yemen (September–December 1961, September–Mid 1966)	Kuwait	Libya
Algeria (joined 1962)		Yemen (December 1961–September 1962)
		Morocco (1964–66)

Period 5: Mid-1966–April 1967

Radical Neutralists

UAR (Egypt)	Algeria
Iraq	Yemen
Syria	Sudan

Nonaligned

Lebanon
Kuwait

Nonradicals with Western Ties

Jordan	Libya
Saudi Arabia	Morocco
Tunisia	

Period 6: August 1967–70

Radical Rejectionists

Syria
Iraq
Algeria
Yemen
South Yemen (joined 1968)
Libya (August–September 1970)

Radical Accommodationists

UAR (Egypt)
Sudan
Libya (September 1969–July 1970)

Nonradical Accommodationists

Jordan	Kuwait
Saudi Arabia	Lebanon
Morocco	Libya (August 1967–
Tunisia	September 1969)

Period 7a: 1971–73

Rejectionists

Iraq
Libya
South Yemen
Algeria
Syria

Accommodationists

Egypt	Lebanon
Sudan	Morocco
Yemen	Bahrain (joined 1971)
Jordan	Oman (joined 1971)
Saudi Arabia	Qatar (joined 1971)
Tunisia	United Arab Emirates (joined 1972)
Kuwait	

Period 7b: 1974–77

Moderate Rejectionists

Syria

Rejectionists

Iraq
Libya
South Yemen
Algeria
Somalia (joined 1975)

Accommodationists

Egypt	Kuwait
Sudan	Bahrain
Yemen	Oman
Jordan	Qatar
Saudi Arabia	United Arab Emirates
Tunisia	Mauritania (joined 1973)
Morocco	Djibouti (joined 1977)
Lebanon	

the assistance of Table 7, which divides the years to be examined
(1946–77) into seven major periods. Period 1, from 1946 until mid-
1954, was, generally speaking, characterized by one key axis of conflict—that between the Hashemite states of Iraq and Jordan and the
non-Hashemite states of Saudi Arabia, Egypt, Yemen, and Syria (except for five months in 1949). A new axis of conflict over security
ties with the West began to develop in this period when Libya in 1953
(the year it joined the League) signed a military treaty with Britain.
At the same time, the relative unimportance of Libya in the Arab
world in the 1950s and the unanimity of the others against the Libyan
move precluded the split from becoming salient to general inter-Arab
relations. By mid-1954, however, this latter axis of conflict did become predominant when Iraq began negotiations with the West for the
formation of a military alliance, which led to its adherence to the
Baghdad Pact with Turkey and Britain. From that date until approximately the end of 1956 (Period 2), the issue of Arab military ties with
the Western states became paramount in inter-Arab politics. Jordan
(at least after February 1956) joined its former non-Hashemite opponents in a coalition of "positive neutralists," spearheaded by Nasser's
Egypt, in opposition to the Iraqi action, thus producing the most asym-
metrical coalition configuration during the 32-year period under study.

During the first half of 1957 this conflict between the "positive
neutralists" and those in favor of military ties with the West was superseded by a new axis of conflict that remained central to inter-Arab
relations (albeit with different alignment configurations and accom-
panying conflicts) until the June 1967 war. This was the conflict between "radical neutralists" who were both opposed to security ties
with the West and interested in bringing about a rapid and generally
socialistic transformation of their societies and "nonradicals" who
favored both Western ties and a more traditional or less revolutionary political system. Some of the lesser members of the respective
groupings did not totally adhere to these viewpoints, but the "leaders"
of each camp held to both the foreign and domestic policies described.
From 1957 through July 1958 (Period 3), there was a distinct bipolar
configuration with Syria, Egypt, and Yemen in the radical neutralist
camp, and Iraq, Jordan, Saudi Arabia, Libya, and Lebanon in the nonradical, pro-Western coalition. From mid-1958 through early 1966
(Period 4) the previously mentioned axis of conflict still divided the
Arab world, but the larger radical neutralist group was also seriously divided into subgroups by intense nationalist rivalries and by
disagreements concerning the types of socialism and neutralism to
be pursued. Iraq, the UAR, Syria, Algeria, and Yemen (except for
a brief period in 1961–62) were always found in the radical neutralist
camp during this period of multipolarity, but, paradoxically, these
states were often more hostile toward each other than toward the pro-
Western, nonradical states.

During the rather brief Period 5 from mid-1966 to April 1967, the radical neutralists buried some of their differences (although some still existed at a low level), and the Arab world returned to a bipolar pattern somewhat similar to that in the 1957-58 period—except that the radical neutralists were considerably stronger in the latter period. Six states now fell into this grouping (namely, the UAR, Iraq, Syria, Algeria, Sudan, and Yemen), whereas five were generally associated with the nonradical coalition (Jordan, Saudi Arabia, Libya, Tunisia, and Morocco). The coming of the Arab-Israeli crisis and war of May and June 1967 brought this period to an end, as all of the Arab states temporarily set aside their political differences for a few months while they confronted the common enemy, Israel. For this brief period, May-August 1967, the alignments of the Arab states have not been classified.

The defeat of the Arab armies in the June 1967 war led to the reemergence of divisions in the Arab world. A new tripolar coalition configuration, based on both the old antagonism between the radicals and nonradicals and on a new issue of whether the Arab states should seek an "accommodation" with Israel, quickly developed in the Arab League system. One polar group consisted of the "radical rejectionists," who supported a revolutionary transformation of Arab societies were basically hostile to the West and, most important, violently opposed any settlement with or recognition of Israel. Included in this coalition were Syria, Algeria, Iraq, Yemen, South Yemen, and Libya (from August 1970). The other polar group was the "nonradical accommodationists," who generally opposed all the positions of the other polar group, and consisted of those states that were labeled as "nonradicals with Western ties" and "nonaligned" in the previous configuration. Their varied motivations for favoring accommodation with Israel will be elucidated below. Between these two polar groupings were a small number of "radical accommodationists" (UAR, Sudan, and Libya during the period September 1969 to July 1970) who supported some of the positions of each polar coalition and, as a result, were seriously cross-pressured.

By 1971 the radical accommodationists had ceased to back the export of Arab socialism to other Arab states and merged with the more conservative grouping to form a large "accommodationist" grouping willing, in varying degrees, to entertain the notion of a settlement with Israel, to cooperate with the Western countries, and to support the political status quo. The key to this trend was the evolution of Egyptian policy under President Sadat. This enlarged coalition was opposed by several radical states that continued to adhere to a "rejectionist" doctrine—Iraq, Syria, Libya, South Yemen, and Algeria. The most important modification in this bipolar pattern during the years 1971-77 (Period 7) was the movement of Syria to a middle position between the two poles in 1974. Syria did not become as willing as Egypt to accept an accommodationist position. However, its views certainly did not accord with the rigidity of the rejectionist outlook and it sought to constrain the Palestinian forces, especially in neighboring Lebanon.

Below the central features and political developments in the Arab world are outlined for each of the seven periods.

Period 1: The Bipolar Hashemite-Non-Hashemite
Configuration, 1946 to Mid-1954

The conflict leading to the division of the Arab world into Hashemite and non-Hashemite groupings has already been briefly alluded to. At its center this conflict, which in its origin antedated the creation of the League, was a dynastic one between the Hashemite family who ruled Jordan and Iraq and the Saud family of Saudi Arabia. The conflict began in 1926 when King Ibn Saud seized Mecca and the kingdom of Arabia from the Hashemites, a turn of events that brought about fundamental hostility between the two dynastic families and, by extension, between the Hashemite states and Saudi Arabia. Their mutual antagonism strongly influenced the discussions concerning Arab unification, since each family strongly opposed any augmentation of the area controlled by its rival. King Saud, for example, was intransigent against any scheme to form a "Greater Syria" or a united Fertile Crescent since the Hashemite domain would be thereby enlarged. And the rulers of Jordan and Iraq balked at accepting any plan that would formally recognize or consolidate Saud's conquest. The issue of Arab unification—especially as it concerned the enlargement of Hashemite control—thus became a central point of conflict among the three states following the formation of the League, as had been the case before the organization's existence. [25]

The salience of this issue, however, was by no means restricted only to Iraq, Jordan, and Saudi Arabia. On the contrary, it assumed much greater importance because of the opposition of other Arab states as well—notably Egypt, Syria, and Yemen—to the enlargement of Hashemite control in the Arab region. Egypt's opposition was the result of a long-standing rivalry between itself and Iraq. Both had been centers of pre-Islamic civilization and, later, of Arab empires, and both had more recently fallen under the control of the Ottomans and the British colonialists. By 1914, however, Egypt had developed fairly modern, Western-oriented social and political institutions and an "indigenous" nationalism "that ran counter to that of the developing Arab nationalism." Iraq, on the other hand, as a "backward province" of the Ottoman Empire, had more traditional social and political institutions and possessed a more doctrinaire Pan-Arabism geared toward the unification of the Fertile Crescent states.[26] Differences stemming from these trends were exacerbated by Egypt's resentment of the harmonious relationship between Baghdad and London.

As has been noted, the enunciation in 1944 of Iraq's plan for Arab unification quickly stimulated Egypt to join forces with Saudi Arabia and exert its strong influence against the plan. The two were also supported by Yemen (generally deferential to Egypt) and by Syria which, while most anxious for Arab unification, steadfastly opposed the unification of the Fertile Crescent or the creation of a "Greater Syria" under the Transjordanian monarch.* Lebanon, while opposing proposals for the unification of the Fertile Crescent, sought to maintain a neutral position in the competition between the two groups since it feared external intervention that might precipitate conflict between its Moslem and Christian factions. By 1946, the Arab world was bipolarized between the Hashemite states—Iraq and Jordan—supporting schemes for Arab unification that would increase their own relative influence, and the non-Hashemite states—Egypt, Saudi Arabia, Syria, and Yemen—intransigent against any change in the status quo that might redound to the benefit of the Hashemite monarchies.[27] The creation of the Arab League as a loose association of states requiring no reduction of national sovereignty and reinforcing the Arab status quo was a victory for the non-Hashemite states at that time—although it did not signal an end to the basic conflict between the two groups.

The Hashemite-non-Hashemite configuration, indeed, remained the fundamental characteristic of inter-Arab politics for most of the League's first decade, and it "colored almost every action of the League."[28] Continually frustrated by the non-Hashemite states, Iraq and Transjordan could only count upon each other to support unification proposals, and were therefore unable to secure any positive results through the organization. The only successful "unification" in the Arab world during this period occurred when Transjordan unilaterally annexed Arab Palestine ("the West Bank") in December 1948 and was threatened with expulsion from the League by Egypt and her allies. It was only because Transjordan agreed to regard her control over the annexed area as a temporary "trusteeship" that the Arab League did not disintegrate over the incident.

---

*Syria swung temporarily to the Iraqi camp from August to December 1949 when Sami Hinnawi was in power, and then under Shishakli from December 1949 to February 1954 Syria generally pursued an anti-Hashemite policy. (Patrick Seale, The Struggle for Syria: A Study of Post-War Arab Politics [London: Oxford University Press, 1965], pp. 13-73.)

While the Hashemite-non-Hashemite conflict was central to inter-Arab relations from 1946 through late 1954, one issue did emerge in 1953 that was to become the central axis of conflict in the Arab world a year and a half later. This concerned the question of Arab military ties with the Western countries. Until 1952 there had been a consensus among the Arab states that they would refrain from joining military alliances with Western powers as a result of the latter's support for Israel and their desire to further their own independence. Libya, having joined the League in 1953, broke with this consensus during July of the same year when it signed a military agreement with Britain providing for the acceptance of bases. The League in September called on its new member to renounce the treaty and offered to compensate it for the loss of Britain's payments. Libya refused and signed the treaty in October.[29] However, its move did not cause a great deal of turmoil in the Arab world because Libya was not only sparsely populated and underdeveloped, but also quite isolated geographically and politically from the traditional centers of inter-Arab politics. When Iraq began negotiations the following year for a military alliance with the West, the reactions of the other states were quite different.

Period 2: The Bipolar Configuration of States
Supporting and Opposing Military Ties with the
West, Mid-1954-56

The axis of conflict centering on the issue of Hashemite expansion began to decrease in importance during the years 1951-54, as the possibility of any unions between Arab states decreased, and in mid-1954 the issue of military ties with outside powers became the major policy question dividing Arab states, although the coalition memberships remained basically the same as before. This trend was greatly hastened by the Egyptian revolution in July 1952 and the eventual installation of Nasser as prime minister in 1954. At first, Nasser was content to retain close relations with the West, even after the Suez agreement of 1954 with Britain.* At the same time, however,

---

*Nasser commented in 1954, for example: "After the Suez agreement there is nothing to stand in the way of our good relations with the West," and he was still anticipating an arms supply mainly from the West. ("United Arab Republic," in Governments and Politics of the Contemporary Middle East, ed. Tareq Y. Ismael [Homewood, Ill.: Dorsey Press, 1970], p. 315.) Despite the opposition of Egypt and many of the Arab states to formal military alliances with the West,

he warned of the alienating effect that any American or Western agitation for military pacts would have on the Arab states.* This warning, as well as the opposition of most of the Arab states to such alliances, went unheeded in Washington and London, and in the spring of 1954 the two powers engaged in talks with Iraq aimed at integrating it and possibly other Arab states into the Western alliance system.[30] These negotiations culminated in Iraq's announcement in January 1955 of its intention to form a military alliance with Turkey, which became known as the Baghdad Pact, and in Britain's announcement in April that it would join the pact.[31] Ostensibly aimed at preventing communist expansion in the Arab region, the pact also seemed to be an attempt to consolidate Western influence in the region and isolate the neutralist forces led by Nasser.[32]

In fact, the effect of John Foster Dulles's "Northern Tier" scheme was to isolate Baghdad and strengthen the neutralists. Nasser quickly made his position clear: in April, he established himself as the Arab spokesman of nonalignment and antiimperialism at the Bandung Conference; in May he established diplomatic ties with Communist China; and in September, he announced an arms deal with Czechoslovakia. These moves found ready acceptance in most Arab states, which associated the West with both the creation of Israel and attempts to curb their independence, resented the failure of the United States and Britain to take action against Israel in its raids into the Gaza Strip in 1955, and opposed any outside aid to their old Hashemite rival.[33]

Opposition to Iraq's move nevertheless was expressed in varying degrees, according to the peculiar national interests of the individual Arab states.[34] The strongest backers of "positive neutralism" (and the strongest opponents of an increase of Hashemite power) were Egypt, Saudi Arabia, and Yemen, which supported a League condemnation of Iraq and the expulsion of that state from the League.† Syria

---

they were still pro-Western in the overall cold war context. (See, Walter Z. Laqueur, The Road to War, 1967: The Origins of the Arab-Israeli Conflict [London: Weidenfeld and Nicolson, 1968], p. 17.)

*Nasser warned: "Agitation for pacts at present would be used by the Communists and ultra-nationalists to stir up hatred and violence against the West." (Tareq Y. Ismael, ed., Governments and Politics of the Contemporary Middle East [Homewood, Ill.: Dorsey Press, 1970], p. 315.)

†Saudi Arabia's opposition was based more on its traditional desire to prevent a growth in Hashemite Iraq's power then its opposition to close links with the West. The royal government of Yemen's support of Egypt in this period and during the subsequent years 1957-61 was based on its anti-British sentiments and its desire to discour-

gave strong verbal support to the basic policy position of this group but was reluctant to go along with sanctions since it was interested in effecting an eventual reconciliation with its Iraqi neighbor.[35] Jordan was sympathetic to the policies of its fellow Hashemite government in Iraq during 1954 and 1955, but following domestic demonstrations against the Baghdad Pact in 1955 and January 1956, Jordan altered its policy to accord with that of the majority of Arab states.[36] Lebanon gave token verbal support to the majority faction, but it basically followed its traditional policy of neutrality and some ties with the West. In the case of the remaining Arab state, Libya, its existing ties with Britain made it an ally of Iraq, but it never spoke out in support of the Baghdad government.

In the wake of the Iraqi move, Cairo attempted to create a new inter-Arab security treaty that would exclude Iraq and supplant the Joint Defense and Economic Cooperation Treaty. This scheme failed because of the conciliatory (or de facto obstructionist) stances of Libya, Jordan, Lebanon, and Syria. However, Nasser's campaign in the Arab world against the Iraqi policy triumphed, albeit in a less spectacular manner than he had wished, when Egypt succeeded in concluding bilateral defense agreements with Syria, Saudi Arabia, and Jordan, with Syria concluding a comparable accord with Jordan.[37] The Egyptian-Jordanian and Syrian-Jordanian pacts of October 1956 would have been unthinkable alliances several years earlier, when the competition between Hashemites and non-Hashemites had dominated inter-Arab relations.

This brief period in inter-Arab relations ended shortly after the Suez crisis, which dominated the attention of the Arab world, and particularly Egypt, for the last half of 1956. During the crisis President Nasser assured Egyptian control over the Suez Canal and secured the withdrawal of Israeli, British, and French forces in what was seen as a major victory for the Arab states. After these successes, Nasser turned his attention to the domestic ramifications of his goal of an Arab revolution.[38] This new focus in Egyptian policy alienated some of its former Arab allies and led to the formation of new coalitions in the Arab League system that were based on different orientations toward both domestic and external politics.

---

age Egyptian intervention. (Manfred W. Wenner, Modern Yemen, 1918-1966 [Baltimore: Johns Hopkins University Press, 1967], pp. 172-88.)

Period 3: The Bipolar Radical-
Nonradical Configuration, 1957–July 1958

During 1955 and 1956 Nasser's Egypt had been successful in
mobilizing a large group of Arab governments behind its leadership
when the central thrust of its foreign policy concerned the contentious
issue of military ties between the West and Arab states. This situation changed in early 1957 as Egypt began to press for socialism,
revolution, and unity and attacked the status quo in the Arab world. [39]
Such nonradical regimes as Saudi Arabia's and Jordan's, which had
been prepared to follow Egypt's leadership on the issue of military
accords with the West, were opposed to Egypt's new agitations for
domestic reform in Arab societies, and even began to seek Western
assistance in resisting the Nasserist forces. Thus, there emerged
two groupings of Arab states, "radical neutralists" and "conservatives
with Western ties," and these groupings exhibited strong differences
with respect to both internal and external policies.

One good indicator of the Arab states' views was their attitude
toward the "Eisenhower Doctrine," proclaimed by the United States
in January 1957. [40] This policy reflected Washington's desire to deter the expansion of communist power in the Middle East and offered
funds and other aid to those states that were prepared to subscribe to
this goal. In fact, of course, this policy was also aimed at preventing the spread of Nasserist influence and radical regimes in the Arab
world. Consequently, Egypt and Syria condemned this doctrine as
"imperialist" and "reactionary," and Yemen, despite its different political orientation, continued to follow the lead of Cairo. On the other
hand, Iraq, Lebanon (which temporarily diverged from its traditional
nonaligned stance in inter-Arab quarrels), Libya, and Saudi Arabia
all accepted the U.S. doctrine during the first half of 1957. Jordan,
in the process of freeing itself from British influence (a trend initiated by Hussein's dismissal of Glubb Pasha in 1956), did not take a
stand on the U.S. pronouncement, but began to accept aid from the
United States in much greater quantities than it had ever accepted from
Britain.* The different stances toward this American initiative exacerbated what was already a conflictual relationship between the

---

*Sands notes that by 1960, Amman was receiving $40 million
per annum in budgetary assistance and $16 million in economic as-
sistance from the United States. (William Sands, "The Hashemite
Kingdom of Jordan," in Governments and Politics of the Contemporary Middle East, ed. Tareq Y. Ismael [Homewood, Ill.: Dorsey
Press, 1970], p. 297.)

Arab groupings, and during 1957 and early 1958 they regularly accused each other of political intrigue and subversive activity.*

The increasing polarization of the two groups during 1957 culminated in February 1958 in the formation of two rival "unions." In early February Syria and Egypt created the United Arab Republic,[41] a centralized union that was to symbolize the unity of the Arab Revolution, and later in the month this move was countered by Iraq and Jordan when they formed a loose association entitled the Arab Federation.[42] The tensions between these Arab groupings were further exacerbated during the Lebanese crisis of May and August 1958 (often referred to as the Middle East crisis of 1958), which pitted the pro-Western government against neutralist and Nasserist forces in Lebanon. The tensions between the rival political groupings during this crisis were acute, but there were signs in early July that the conflict might deescalate as a result of negotiations between the Lebanese factions to form a new government. However, the crisis suddenly escalated on July 14, when the conservative government in Iraq was overthrown by forces under the radical General Qassem. On the following day, the United States and Britain sent forces to Lebanon and Jordan respectively to protect those states against any military challenge originating within or without the two countries. These troops did not engage in any armed combat, but they "effectively counteracted any outside intervention."[43] A new Lebanese government, agreed on in late July, was to be headed by a neutralist, General Fuad Chehab, and its accession to power in September soon returned Lebanon to its traditional nonaligned stance.

The immediate euphoria felt by the radicals as a result of the Iraqi coup, meanwhile, soon began to subside. Baghdad's revolution had at first seemed to strengthen the Egyptian-led camp in inter-Arab relations, as the leading Iraqi nationalist, Abd al-Salam Aref, clearly envisioned close relations with Cairo. But by August, new groups had come to power in the new republic, and Iraqi policy took quite a different turn. No sooner had Iraq severed its former ties to the pro-Western conservative states† than it also restricted pro-Nasserist

---

*In June 1957, Jordan accused the UAR of conspiracy to assassinate some Jordanian government officials, and Jordan banned all Egyptian newspapers. (Middle East Journal 11 [Summer 1957]: 292, 299.) In September 1957, Jordan charged Syria with planning an attack on Jordan and closed their mutual border. (Middle East Journal 11 [Fall 1957]: 422; Middle East Journal 12 [Winter 1958]: 66, 82.) Then, in early 1958, Nasser called Hussein an "imperialist stooge." (Middle East Journal 12 [Spring 1958]: 191.)

† Although Iraq did not abrogate the Baghdad Pact until 1959, it did not participate therein after July 1958. The Arab Federation was

influence within its government, culminating in Aref's fall from office in September. Under the leadership of General Abd al-Karim Qassem, who relied heavily on the support of the Communist party and established very close relations with the Soviet Union (at least until 1960), Iraq now became an independent radical force in the Arab world, and it vigorously challenged the UAR's position as the vanguard of the Arab Revolution. [44] This development ended the short life of the bipolar division between radical and conservative forces in the Middle East, and ushered in a new and more complex regional configuration.

Period 4: The Configuration with a Nonradical
Grouping and Competing Radical Centers,
August 1958-Mid-1966

The fourth period in inter-Arab alignments, which lasted from approximately August 1958 to mid-1966, was characterized by a nonradical grouping, two to three competing radical centers, and a nonaligned grouping. Between the radical states there was often more hostility than occurred between them and the nonradicals, as Egypt, Iraq, and Syria each attempted to establish itself as the only source of ideological leadership for the Arab Revolution.

The entire eight-year period can be subdivided into two subperiods, according to whether there were two or three radical centers. From August 1958 until September 1961, there existed two radical poles—the UAR (supported by Yemen) and Qassem's Iraq, which Nasser accused of being excessively procommunist and undermining Arab neutralism. In order to gain support for his opposition to Iraq, Nasser was himself obliged to mute the UAR's hostility toward the conservative states with Western ties—Jordan, Saudi Arabia, Tunisia, and Libya—and toward the nonaligned states—Lebanon, Sudan, Morocco, and Kuwait (after its independence in June 1961). [45] Within the former grouping, Jordan and Saudi Arabia were the two major pillars, and they took steps to unify their foreign policies in 1958. Libya was a relatively silent ally because it did not want to provoke the radicals' intervention. Tunisia, despite the fact that it did not share the predispositions of its three allies for monarchical political structures, did share its allies' goals to maintain close and friendly relations with the West (although this policy was strained somewhat during the Bi-

---

abandoned in the same month. (M. Khalil, ed., The Arab States and the Arab League, Vol. II, International Affairs [Beirut: Khayats, 1962], Document no. 21, pp. 91-92.)

zerte crisis in the summer of 1961) and to resist the hegemonial aspirations of President Nasser in the Arab world. In fact, Tunisia boycotted the League on many occasions during these years in order to express its opposition to the preeminence of the UAR in the organization.

The neutrals were mainly interested in remaining aloof from inter-Arab quarrels in order to prevent interventions by the two polar groupings, and particularly the radicals, in their internal affairs. Morocco established a progressive image for itself as a result of its membership in the radical Casablanca bloc (the UAR, Guinea, Ghana, and Mali), but this group was oriented primarily toward African, as opposed to Arab, issues and concerns. Moreover, Morocco affiliated with this bloc purely as a strategic move to garner African support for its territorial claim to Mauritania, and it never really exhibited any acceptance of the revolutionary ideology that animated the Casablanca states. Lebanon continued to adhere to its traditional non-aligned stance during this period while Sudan, which joined the League in 1956, did not involve itself extensively in inter-Arab politics. Kuwait was independent only for the last few months of this phase of Period 4.

The first phase of the multipolar system, in which there were two radical factions, ended in September 1961 when Syria seceded from the UAR, which it had entered in February 1958. [46] While the new Syrian government adopted a more conservative stance on domestic political questions, it continued to portray itself as a radical leader of the Arab Revolution, [47] and thus it is classified as a third radical center for the period 1961-66. The memberships of the other groupings were, with some minor exceptions, basically the same as in the first phase. Algeria, after its independence in 1962, generally supported the UAR (as Egypt continued to call itself even after the Syrians defected from the union) in inter-Arab politics, although the two states did differ on some matters. Yemen entered this second phase of Period 4 in September 1961 by continuing to follow its standard policy of deference to Cairo, but this pattern was suddenly terminated in December 1961 when Nasser attacked the royalist government of Yemen as part of his intensified campaign against all conservative Arab regimes. From this point until the ouster of the Imam in September 1962, Yemen was literally forced into the nonradical camp by Cairo's hostility. [48] With the coming to power of the new republican government of Colonel Abdullah Sallal, close ties were reestablished between the UAR and Yemen, and in fact Cairo dispatched large contingents of troops to Yemen to maintain the new regime in power against the Saudi- and Jordanian-backed royalist forces. For Nasser the Yemeni adventure was a means of reclaiming the leadership of the Arab Revolution from the challenges of Syria and Iraq. [49] Turning lastly to Morocco, although it is still classified in the nonaligned grouping, it did definitely move toward greater cooperation with the Western countries in 1964 after its failure to absorb Mauritania and its war with Algeria in October 1963. [50]

The early years of the second stage of this multipolar era (1961–66) were notable for the high level of hostility among almost all groups—especially the three main radical poles. Egypt set about to regain its ideolɔgical purity by reversing its policy of moderation toward the conservatives and entering into bitter verbal debate with Syria and Iraq. In early 1963, following Ba'thist coups in Iraq and Syria, negotiations regarding a tripartite union broke down in an atmosphere of intense recrimination, as did talks between Syria and Iraq, aimed at their association. [51] The hostility between the Ba'thist regime in Syria and Nasserist Egypt remained the most bitter, however, [52] and Iraq largely vacillated between them. Baghdad first made a concerted effort to break its isolation and establish better relations with Cairo, but by September it had swung to Syria, with which it engaged in abortive talks regarding the formation of a federation. This trend in turn was reversed in November when Iraq's President Aref expelled the Ba'thists from his government and modified his hostility to Egypt. [53] Thus, the years 1961–63 were characterized by intense conflict between the radical states.

Beginning in early 1964 there was a definite muting of the hostilities between the radicals and the conservatives and even among the radicals themselves. This was primarily the result of the increasing possibility of an armed confrontation with Israel, which was then completing plans for the diversion of the Jordan River. This relaxation of tensions occurred even while the Yemeni civil war (with Egyptian, Saudi, and Jordanian intervention) was at its height and while the Syrians and Egyptians were describing each other as "traitors" to the Arab Revolution. Egypt's realization that "we cannot today use force" against Israel[54] was shared by Jordan, and necessitated that Syria be restrained, since its Ba'thist leaders had been competing with Nasser in the "familiar Arab game of 'more anti-Israel than thou.'"[55] At the Cairo summit meeting held in January 1964 to discuss the problem of the Jordan River, [56] inter-Arab differences were once again superseded by their anti-Israeli sentiment. Hussein and Nasser met and resumed relations for the first time since 1961; Nasser and King Saud began unsuccessful discussions of a settlement of the Yemeni conflict; Algeria and Morocco discussed their border dispute; and the rivals for Arab leadership, Nasser and the Syrian leader Amin al-Hafiz, at least appeared to be on speaking terms. More important, Syria was made to understand that it was alone in its avowed eagerness to fight Israel at this early date; and the conference finally resolved to cease inter-Arab press and radio vituperation and concentrate on the formation of a united front against Israel.

This trend of muted conflict continued through 1964 and 1965. At the Second Conference of Arab Heads of State at Alexandria in September 1964, there were some signs of a détente between Cairo and Riyadh, and all of the participants were able to agree on the formation of the Palestine Liberation Army. Then in 1965, Faisal and Nasser agreed at Jedda to discuss the Yemeni conflict, and at the Casablanca conference in September (boycotted only by Tunisia) Nasser exhibited some friendliness toward the Syrian and Saudi leaders.

Period 5: The Bipolar Radical-Nonradical
Configuration, Mid-1966-April 1967

It was characteristic of inter-Arab politics that such a low level of hostility could not last for long. By early 1966, indications of an impending bipolarization of Arab alignments into "radical" and "nonradical" camps had again appeared. [57] The Jedda agreement between Egypt and Saudi Arabia ahd apparently only signified a temporary respite in Yemen, and talks between them were broken off in November 1965 when Egypt refused to withdraw its forces. Open fighting broke out again, this time between royalists and two republican factions who were divided by their attitude toward Cairo. [58] In early 1966, a second sign of division appeared. King Faisal of Saudi Arabia embarked in January on a tour of national capitals—including those of Iran, Jordan, Turkey, Sudan, Pakistan, Morocco (which was growing increasingly friendly toward Riyadh), Tunisia, Guinea, and Mali—to garner support for a proposed "Islamic conference."*

While professing interest only in the promotion of Islam, Faisal was immediately accused by Cairo and Damascus of acting as an agent of the West—reactivating the old split between Syria and Egypt, on one side, and Saudi Arabia and Jordan, on the other. Jordan's position was influenced by its growing alienation from the Palestinian Liberation Organization, which was demanding near-governmental status in Jordan and was strongly supported by the extremist Ba'thists in power in Syria. In June 1966, Hussein abruptly refused further collaboration with the guerrilla organization; in July he charged Syria with complicity in a Ba'thist conspiracy against the monarch and ordered the arrest of Ba'thists and Communists in Jordan.

---

*This was originally proposed in August 1965. (Malcolm H. Kerr, The Arab Cold War: Gamal 'Abd al-Nasir and His Rivals, 1958-1970, 3d ed. [London: Oxford University Press, 1971], p. 114.)

As the Saudi-Jordanian axis hardened, so did the Syrian-Egyptian one. The overthrow of Amin al-Hafiz, Nasser's most recent Syrian antagonist in February 1966 paved the way for a Syrian group led by Zu'ayyen and Nur-ul-Din Atassi to make overtures to Cairo.* These overtures were "rewarded" in July when Egypt refused to sit down with "reactionary" Arab leaders and demanded postponement of the approaching summit conference. Syrian-Egyptian relations were resumed soon afterward, and a joint defense treaty was even signed. The long-standing "radio wars" between the radical and conservative groupings were also reinstated, with the activities of the Palestinian Liberation Organization as the main subject of discussion. By the end of 1966, Jordan was reciprocating Syria's call for the overthrow of its government; the head of the Palestinian Liberation Organization, Ahmad Shukairy, was warning that guerrilla forces would enter Jordan when appropriate "whether Jordan agrees or not";[59] and Egypt, accused by Jordan of failing to give sufficient support against Israel, was being increasingly drawn toward the extremism of Syria and the Palestinian Liberation Organization. Iraq, under President Abdal-Salam Aref,† agreed in February with Syria to a mutual cessation of radio attacks as a prelude to their reconciliation, and its relations with Egypt warmed perceptibly despite an instance of possible Egyptian subversion in Iraq in 1965.‡ Similarly, Algeria secured a large loan from Cairo in 1966, while a rapprochement with Syria led to talks aimed at the coordination of the policies of the Ba'th and FLN parties. Additional members of this increasingly cohesive radical grouping were the republican government in Yemen and the left-leaning government of the Sudan. Thus, by mid-1966 two Arab camps had again taken shape, divided by political ideology, external ties, and their professions of loyalty to certain vague Arab ideals and the destruction of Israel.**

---

*This reconciliation of the two radical centers was strongly encouraged by the USSR. (Nadav Safran, From War to War: The Arab Israeli Confrontation, 1948-67 [New York: Pegasus, 1969], p. 130.)

† Aref was killed in a helicopter crash in April 1966 and was succeeded as president by his brother, Abd al-Rahman Aref.

‡ Brigadier Aref Abdul Razzak made an attempt in September 1965 to overthrow President Aref, but was unsuccessful and fled to Cairo. When he made a second attempt in June 1966, Iraq expressly negated the possibility of Egyptian involvement.

**The nature and depth of the divisions were manifest at the September 1966 Arab summit conference. (Walter Z. Laqueur, The Road to War, 1967: The Origins of the Arab-Israeli Conflict [London: Weidenfeld and Nicholson, 1968], pp. 62-63.)

The advent of the Arab-Israeli war in June, however, brought about a temporary hiatus in this bipolarization—even though the outbreak of the war was a mishap of inter-Arab rivalry rather than the product of Arab unity. [60] The presence of Israel had heretofore provided a common enemy for all the Arab states, and the expression of opposition to the Israelis was a common pastime. But as 1967 progressed, the pastime became a competition, and the competition grew more intense. Syria was clearly the leader in this area: as Abba Eban observed later at the United Nations, it alone among the Arab states "lacked the ideology of non-confrontation."[61] Emboldened, rather than restrained, by its alliance with Egypt, it became more and more belligerent toward Israel. If Nasser wished to remain regarded as the leader of the Arab Revolution, he felt he had to do likewise. Saber-rattling by Syria and the Palestinain Liberation Organization thus led to saber-rattling by Cairo. Malcolm H. Kerr has well summarized this process: "Even when the Israelis first appeared on the scene in the weeks before the June war, they were merely there as a football for the Arabs, kicked onto the field by the discontented Syrians, then back again by Nasser. But of course the Israelis took a rather different view of themselves. It became a case of the football kicking the players."[62] Nasser was unable to arrest the events thus set in force, and his request for the withdrawal of the United Nations peacekeeping force and the closing of the Straits of Tiran were the last blundering steps into a war for which he was not prepared. [63]

The militant positions of the radical states, and the Israeli reprisals, also had an effect on the conservative states, which were likewise committed to oppose Israel's presence in the Arab world. The effect was nowhere better illustrated than in Jordan, which on May 30, 1967, made an almost complete about-turn in foreign policy. Amman had already declared a state of emergency, mobilized its army, and accepted Iraqi and Saudi troops on its soil; but now Hussein flew to Cairo and concluded a treaty of mutual defense with the UAR (Iraq joined the pact on June 4). Egyptian-Jordanian radio attacks ceased, and the Arab states temporarily shelved their differences to participate in the war effort. On June 4, at a conference of the Arab oil producers, most states agreed to ban oil supplies to the United Kingdom and the United States, and many severed diplomatic relations with London and Washington as well.* On June 5, with the outbreak of war with Israel, a very brief period of actual cooperation began.

----

*Tunisia, Libya, Saudi Arabia, Kuwait, Jordan, and Morocco did not actually sever their relations with the two Western powers; and Lebanon just withdrew its ambassadors from London and Washington.

The one exception to the general anti-Israel consensus was Habib Bour-
guiba's Tunisia, which had always advocated acceptance of the "Israeli
fact," and now refused to break with its Western allies. Even Bourgui-
ba, however, eventually declared full support for the UAR in its struggle against Israel, and on June 12 offered to lend troops to Cairo. [64]
    The latter part of the hiatus in inter-Arab alignments may per-
haps be better described as a salvage operation by the Arab states to
regain their dignity after the defeat inflicted by Israel. The United
Nations was looked on as the first possible instrument by which they
might reverse that defeat and reclaim their lost territories—Jordan,
the entire West Bank; Egypt, the vast Sinai area; and Syria, the less
significant Golan Heights. But apart from securing a shaky cease-
fire, the United Nations was effectively immobilized by U.S.-Soviet
conflict on the Israeli question. At a special emergency session of
the General Assembly on July 4, four resolutions were considered,
but none achieved the requisite approval. When the issue was referred
back to the Security Council (a move opposed by all 13 Arab states),
the results were little better. In these circumstances, the Arabs,
once entirely opposed to any moderation of the conflict with Israel and
its supporters, began to splinter again. Some dissension was already
perceptible at the end of August 1967, when an Arab summit at Khar-
toum was boycotted by the hard-line governments of Syria and Algeria
and by the more cautious governments of Morocco, Libya, and Tunisia. At the meeting, the remaining nonradical and pro-Western
states—notably Saudi Arabia and Kuwait—agreed with Libya to make
financial contributions to the war costs sustained by Egypt and Jordan,
but at the same time defeated demands that had been voiced by Iraq
and Syria for the continuation of the oil ban. Indeed, it was decided
to resume oil shipments to the West, and many states resumed diplomatic relations with London at the same time. Nasser himself rejected the extension of economic pressure on the West that had been
urged by Syria and the Palestinian Liberation Organization, and also
refused to sanction the revival of Fedayeen activities in Palestine. [65]

Period 6: The Configuration of Radical Rejectionists,
Radical Accommodationists, and Nonradical
Accommodationists, September 1967-70

    By September 1967 there had developed a new pattern of inter-
Arab coalitions that was based not only on the states' ideological orientations but also on their views of what policy the Arabs should
pursue toward Israel. This configuration, which lasted until late
1970, was composed of three groupings. The first included the radical states that were strongly opposed to any "accommodation" with

Israel—namely, Syria, Iraq, Algeria, Yemen, South Yemen, and
Libya (after August 1970).* The other two groupings were both willing to accept some kind of compromise settlement with Israel but
were divided by ideological inclinations. On the one hand, there were
the "radical accommodationists"—Egypt, Sudan, and Libya (at least
from September 1969 until August 1970). These states were cross-
pressured between their desire for a settlement and their wish to remain credible radicals in the eyes of their own people and of other
radicals. On the other hand, there were the "nonradical accommodationists"—Jordan, Saudi Arabia, Morocco, Tunisia, Lebanon, Kuwait,
and Libya (prior to September 1969)—whose anti-Israeli stance was
modified by their disapproval of the radicalism of the Palestinian
guerrillas, a desire to maintain friendly relations with the West, and,
in the case of Jordan, a desire to recover the territory occupied by
Israel.† The conflict between these groups came to center on two
specific issues in this period. First, what response should be made
by the Arabs to the United Nations Security Council Resolution 242 of
November 22, 1967? And second, what support should be given to
the ten guerrilla organizations making up the Palestinian Liberation
Organization,‡ which finally became locked in a bitter civil war with
regular Jordanian forces in 1970?

---

*These antiaccommodationist states, in fact, differed on some
issues. For example, relations between Iraq and Syria were quite
tense after the so-called moderate wing of the Iraqi Ba'thist party
took power in July 1968. (Aryen Yodfat, "The End of Syria's Isolation?," The World Today 27 [August 1971]: 332-33; P. J. Vatikiotis,
"The Politics of the Fertile Crescent," in Political Dynamics in the
Middle East, ed. Paul Y. Hammond and Sidney S. Alexander [New
York: American Elsevier, 1972], pp. 250-51.) On Algeria's policy
and its differences with Syria, (see, Charles F. Gallagher, "The Maghreb and the Middle East," Hammond and Alexander, op. cit., pp.
411-12.)

†Saudi Arabia, Kuwait, and Libya showed some sympathy with
the "no compromise" position and the Palestine guerrillas in the aftermath of the war, but the increasing radicalism of the guerrillas and
their challenge to Hussein tended to alter these positions. (Malcolm
H. Kerr, The Arab Cold War: Gamal 'Abd al-Nasir and His Rivals,
1958-1970, 3d ed. [London: Oxford University Press, 1971], pp. 138-
39; idem, "Regional Arab Politics and the Conflict with Israel," in
Political Dynamics in the Middle East, ed. Paul Y. Hammond and
Sidney S. Alexander [New York: American Elsevier, 1972], pp.
66-67.)

‡The ten organizations represented on a 27-man Central Committee were Saiqa, Fatah, the PFLP, the Popular Democratic Front

Security Council Resolution 242 provided that any settlement of the Arab-Israeli conflict should include the withdrawal of Israeli forces from occupied territory, the termination of all claims of belligerence, the acknowledgment of the sovereignty of all countries concerned, and the adoption of the principle of freedom of navigation through international waterways. It also specified that a mediator should be appointed by the secretary-general to help the parties reach an accord. The most vociferous opponents of both this resolution and all other measures that seemed to accept Israel's presence in the region were Syria, Iraq, Algeria, Yemen, * and South Yemen (which joined the League in November 1967). These states had little to lose —Syria did not place much importance on the Golan Heights—and had much to gain by this policy. Israel not only provided a convenient external enemy to help foster a modicum of domestic unity; it also allowed the radicals to embarrass the UAR among the revolutionary forces and to discredit Nasser's leadership of them. Syria, which was the central member in the group because it had lost territory, denounced the Security Council resolution as a "sellout" of the Arab cause and refused to cooperate with the UN mediator, Gunnar Jarring. Along with Iraq, Syria boycotted a meeting of 25 Islamic states in August 1969 at which the proaccommodation states were seeking legitimacy for their stand. Then, in August 1970, following a cease-fire between Jordanian and guerrilla forces, Syria urged El Fatah and the Popular Front for the Liberation of Palestine to violate the cease-fire. Both Damascus and Baghdad reveled during this period in their ability to paint the Egyptians as traitors to the Arab Revolution as a result of their "soft" policy toward Israel and the conservatives.

The two most important states in favor of moderating the struggle against Israel were the UAR and Jordan, since they were the ones who had lost the most—Jordan, its territory on the west bank of the Jordan River, and the UAR, the Sinai area. President Nasser's policy was at times ambiguous. Opposition in many quarters to his policy led him occasionally to speak of the "seas of blood and horizons of fire"[66] necessary to eradicate Israel, but from the fall of 1967 his policy was basically moderate and conciliatory. In October, he told the press that Egypt was willing to talk with Israel under UN chairmanship—if it withdrew to prewar lines—and the following month he backed the Security Council resolution. Egypt's Foreign Minister

for the Liberation of Palestine, the PFLP (General Command, the Palestine Arab Organization, Action Group for the Liberty of Palestine, the Arab Liberation Front, the Popular Liberation Forces, and the Popular Struggle Front.

*Yemen's loyalty to Egypt disappeared with the overthrow of Sallal after the withdrawal of Egyptian troops in the fall of 1967.

Riad even suggested in July 1968 that the Arab world's "first big mistake was to demand the annihilation of Israel"—a statement later repudiated by the Arab High Command for Palestine.[67] A year later, Hussein, claiming to speak for Nasser as well, proposed a "six-point peace plan" to Washington, which included Israel's withdrawal from Arab territory, but also recognition of the sovereignty of all states in the area. And, after his demands for promises of specific military aid from his Arab brothers were refused at the Rabat Summit in late 1969—a challenge he could expect not to be taken up[68]—Nasser was able to rationalize his acceptance of U.S. Secretary of State William Rogers's peace plan in July 1970. Supporting his Israeli policy and adopting a similar ideological stance were the "progressive" states of Sudan and Libya (from the "coup d'etat" in September 1969 to the beginning of the Jordanian civil war in August 1970).

Jordan was the key member of the nonradical proaccommodation grouping. Concurring most of the time with Jordan's stance were a combination of the traditional conservative and nonaligned states in prewar configurations—Saudi Arabia, Libya (until September 1969), Kuwait, Morocco, Tunisia, and Lebanon. Their economic and security ties to the West and their opposition to the revolutionary policies of most of the guerrilla groups predisposed them toward accommodation. These states were the first Arab states to resume oil shipments to the United States and Britain (two major proponents of a peace settlement) after the June war and to receive U.S. military aid shortly thereafter. The cooperation of the nonradical states with the UAR was facilitated by the "winding down" of the Yemeni war in 1967 and 1968 and by the willingness of the UAR to cease its attacks on them in exchange for economic aid (from Saudi Arabia and Kuwait) and diplomatic support.[69]

The basic division between the nonradical and radical wings of the proaccommodation camp appeared most clearly in their policies toward those Palestine guerrilla groups in Jordan that were members of the Palestine Liberation Organization. As early as 1966, these groups began to pose serious problems for the Jordanian government by organizing the military training of Palestinians, imposing taxes, and supervising the fortification of villages near the Israeli border. Hussein complained about their behavior to the other Arab states that were financing them, but took only stopgap measures to control their activities. Following the June 1967 war, the friction between Amman and the guerrilla groups escalated when the latter disregarded local laws, urged citizens to revolt, and harassed the Israelis—thus threatening reprisals by the latter against Jordan. In September 1970, large-scale fighting finally broke out between the regular Jordanian army and the guerrillas. It was terminated by a cease-fire after the Jordanian army gained the upper hand and had inflicted serious casualties on the guerrillas.

Throughout the confrontation the radical antiaccommodation states gave strong verbal support to the guerrillas. Iraq even threatened to use its 20,000 troops inside Jordan to bolster the Palestinian Liberation Organization, and Syria sent an armored brigade across the border to assist the guerrillas. The radical proaccommodation states, in contrast, particularly the UAR and Sudan, found themselves in a very awkward position, seeing the guerrilla activities as antithetical to their goal of a settlement with Israel, but at the same time feeling pressures at home and throughout the Arab world to support them. For this reason they became very active in the Arab League mediation group (also composed of Libya and Algeria), that sought to achieve a cease-fire in Jordan. During this period many of Jordan's nonradical proaccommodation allies did not lend Amman a great deal of support—although their lack of criticism can perhaps be interpreted as implicit backing. For example, Morocco and Saudi Arabia did not even attend the Arab Heads of State meeting in Cairo in September 1970 to discuss the Jordanian situation, and Kuwait, Lebanon, Tunisia, and Saudi Arabia were absent from the Tripoli Summit following Hussein's final offensive against the guerrillas in July 1971. This policy of relative aloofness was due, on the one hand, to their desire not to incur the antagonism of segments of their own populations and other Arab states who viewed the guerrillas as heroes of the Arab world and, on the other hand, to their desire not to assist the radical guerrilla forces in Jordan or to alienate their Western friends. Like Egypt, these allies of Jordan were cross-pressured by this situation, but for them the pressure was neither as intense nor as balanced.

Period 7: Configuration of Rejectionists, Moderate Rejectionists, and Accommodationists, 1971-77

Beginning in late 1970 certain changes in inter-Arab politics occurred that were to become more clearly manifest in following years. The key transformation was that the middle group of "radical accommodationists" in the previous era dispensed with their advocacy of radicalism or "the export of Arab socialism." This brought forth a bipolarization of the system between a small but vocal group of rejectionists and the much larger grouping of accommodationists.[70] In the aftermath of the October 1973 war a fissure occurred in "the rejectionist front" when Syria and Algeria opened the door to at least some limited type of accommodation with Israel. In discussing this period in inter-Arab relations Gabriel Ben-Dor has noted that it marked the end to "the Arab cold war" and that its alliances were "not on the same ideological level" as previous ones.[71] This is an overstatement in that the hostility on a variety of domestic and foreign policy levels between the hard-core rejectionists and the accommodationists was still very deep. It is just that the rejectionists were now such a small group in the Arab world that the battle seemed less intense at times. (Of course, the one radical rejectionist whose policies were truly moderate at times was the very important state of Syria.)

Particular events that encouraged the changes in the political orientations of Egypt, the Sudan, and Yemen were Nasser's acceptance of the Rogers's peace plan in 1970, the accession to power of Anwar Sadat as president following Nasser's death in 1970, the attempted communist coup to overthrow President Numeiry in 1971, and the tension between the moderate republican government of Yemen and the radical regime in South Yemen. However, there were some deeper forces that brought about these changes. Of great importance was the increasing financial dependence of Israel's Arab neighbors (especially Egypt) on the conservative oil-exporting nations (especially Saudi Arabia). As Fouad Ajami has written: "Saudi Arabia and Kuwait were ready to help, but as their price they demanded that they hear no more of Pan-Arabism."[72] "Yesterday's ideologues were now dependent on the goodwill of the oil states. Indeed, the late King Faisal of Saudi Arabia deployed his oil weapon in October 1973 at the service of Sadat, precisely because Sadat had scaled back Egypt's commitment to pan-Arabist politics."[73] The effect of Saudi financing was felt not only in the front-line states but in others such as Yemen as well. Beginning in 1970, the Saudis were able to persuade the Yemenis to cooperate in encouraging the downfall of the radical South Yemeni regime thanks to the extensive funding that they granted to that poverty-stricken country.[74] Another development encouraging this shift was the judgment of Sadat that recovery of Arab lands from Israel depended on cooperation with the United States. The major sign of this reorientation came with his expulsion of Soviet advisers in mid-1972, but it became even clearer in the aftermath of the October 1973 war, with Egyptian cooperation with Kissinger's efforts to seek Arab-Israeli accords.

Other developments in the 1970s helped to swell the ranks of the accommodationists and increased the commitment of states already in this grouping to seek a political solution to the conflict with Israel and improve cooperative relations with the West. In 1971 and 1972 the oil-rich Gulf states of Bahrain, Qatar, and the United Arab Emirates joined the League, as did Oman in 1971 and Mauritania two years later. Both Mauritania and Morocco became increasingly inclined to collaborate with the Western states and lend support to Western diplomacy in the Middle East following the Madrid Accord of 1975, which divided the Western Sahara between the two states. Both also faced insurgencies mounted by the radical and Algerian-backed Polisario rebels, who advocated independence for the former Spanish colony. To contain Polisario, Morocco and Mauritania sought and received Western—especially French—military aid. The three Gulf states'were characterized by conservative political orientations and also had historical ties to Britain. In addition, of course, they relied on the West as the market for oil, the mainstay of their economies. The predominantly Christian government of Lebanon continued for most of this period to oppose Pan-Arabism and was favorably disposed toward a political solution to the Arab-Israeli conflict since its precarious position could best be safeguarded by the attainment of peace and an absence of violent shocks to the status quo. However, the Lebanese civil war of 1975-76 revealed the extent to which the position of the Beirut government diverged from that of the country's Moslem population. After the Syrian intervention and the 1976 cease-fire the country was in effect partitioned, but the official government continued to represent Lebanon in the Arab League and other international bodies. Djibouti, which joined the League in 1977, has been placed in the accommodationist camp because of both the significant French military presence in the country and the necessity that the government refrain from any actions that might threaten its delicate position between Somalia and Ethiopia on the Horn of Africa. Somalia, which joined the League in 1975, is difficult to classify because of its relative disinterest in many aspects of inter-Arab politics, but with its close relations with the Soviet Union (until mid-1977) it generally aligned itself with the radical states in the Middle East.

During the years 1971-73 Algeria, Iraq, Libya, Syria, and South Yemen were clearly in the rejectionist camp. Not only did they strongly oppose a negotiated settlement with Israel and strongly support the Palestinian Liberation Organization, but they also promoted the export of socialism to other Arab countries, maintained very close military and diplomatic ties with the Soviet Union, and exhibited considerable hostility to most Western states, especially the United States. Libya's close relations with Moscow did not develop until 1974, and once ties with the Soviets were strengthened Libya aided a coup attempt against President Numeiry of Sudan and became embroiled in a limited war with Egypt in 1977. Iraq, Algeria, and South Yemen also became involved in military clashes with conservative neighbors in the 1970s.

The one rejectionist state whose foreign policy did undergo an important change in this most recent period is Syria. That it was able to collaborate with Cairo in the planning of the October 1973 war suggests that its hostility to the accommodationists was less intense than that of its radical compatriots. A much more important sign that Syrian policy was changing came with its acceptance of a cease-fire at the close of the October 1973 war on the basis of Resolution 242.

Moreover, in the aftermath of the war Syria showed at least some willingness to discuss with the United States the possibility of a comprehensive Arab-Israeli settlement; began to receive in considerable quantities aid from conservative Arab governments, notably Saudi Arabia; and kept the Palestinian forces within its territory under tight control. Then, in the Lebanese civil war, Syria intervened to prevent a victory by the Palestinians and their leftist Lebanese allies, its prime concern being to prevent an untimely war with Israel that was widely believed to be inevitable if the radicals emerged triumphant in Lebanon.[75] As a consequence of its activities in Lebanon, Syria incurred the wrath of its fellow radicals in the Arab world. Because of its policies, Syria has been categorized as "a camp" unto itself for the 1974-77 period—namely, that of "the moderate rejectionist." Gabriel Ben-Dor has classified Syria and Algeria together for this period as "the bloc of the undecided."[76] However, in this study Algeria has not been placed into this middle grouping since it maintained a stronger advocacy of the Palestinian cause (as seen by its criticism of Syria's intervention in Lebanon)[77] and also supported radical guerrilla movements such as those active against the governments of Morocco, Mauritania, and Chad. Algeria may have been marginally more receptive to peace talks with the Israelis than were the Iraqis, Libyans, and South Yemenis, but its overall foreign policy stance during this period seems closer to the latter than to Syria.

THE ARAB LEAGUE'S PATTERNS
OF INTERVENTION AND SUCCESS

During the years 1946-77 there were only 17 wars, crises, and military interventions between Arab states. This is a surprisingly small figure since the level of hostility between the different Arab groupings was quite high during almost the entire 32-year period. These 17 conflicts fall into only 3 of the categories of conflicts described in the theory, and most of them, in fact, fall into a single category. Those specific types of inter-Arab conflicts taking place during the 32 years are listed below under the 3 categories of conflicts. Also, the expectations of intervention and success are listed to the right of each category. In examining the Arab League's activities in terms of the hypotheses, some minor changes have had to be made in definitions of types of coalitions as a result of the League's voting formula (namely, the ability of any nonconflicting party to veto a resolution), but these changes have not required any important changes in the following analysis.*

---

*In the analysis of the Arab League it is necessary to alter those definitions relating to the size of coalitions, since the League voting

Type of Conflict	Intervention	Success
Intercoalition (victim a member of a non-dominant coalition)	No	No
Hashemite versus non-Hashemite, 1946-54		
Radical neutralist versus nonradical pro-Western, 1957-67		
Radical rejectionist versus nonradical accommodationist, 1967-70		
Rejectionist versus accommodationist, 1971-77		
Aligned-Nonaligned (victim aligned)	No	No
Nonaligned versus radical neutralist where the latter was the victim, 1958-66		
Moderate rejectionist versus rejectionist or accommodationist where the latter was the victim, 1971-77		
Nonaligned-Aligned (victim nonaligned)— radical neutralist versus nonaligned, where the latter was the victim, 1957-58, 1958-66	Yes	Yes

As is evident in Table 8, there are some divergences between the patterns and the previously stated hypotheses. The two types of conflicts in which organizational intervention was not expected were intercoalition conflicts and conflicts between aligned and nonaligned parties where the aligned was the victim. The League intervened (called for a cease-fire and withdrawal of forces) in only one (8 percent) of the 13 intercoalition conflicts, but it intervened in one of the two conflicts involving an aggression by a nonaligned state against a member of one of the polar groupings. Its intervention in the latter conflict, the Algerian-Moroccan war, was also successful (that is, withdrawal occurred), although the OAU had a more dominant influence

———————————

rules specify that any member except an aggressing state can veto a resolution. (In the other organizations this veto power is held by one-third of the membership.) A "subordinate coalition" (that is, one without the ability to veto a resolution) is thus a grouping that is composed of only a single state, and a "dominant coalition" is one with all member states except one. Only radical neutralist Iraq between 1958 and 1966 and Syria from 1961 to 1966 constituted subordinate groupings. There has never been a dominant grouping.

TABLE 8

Arab League Involvement in Inter-Arab Conflicts, 1946–77

	Hypothesis: No Intervention	Aligned–Nonaligned (victim aligned)	Hypothesis: Intervention and Success, Nonaligned–Aligned (victim nonaligned)
	Intercoalition (victim a member of a nondominant coalition)		
No Arab League action	Syria-Iraq, 1949 (C)(#6) Jordanian civil strife (with Syrian intervention), 1957 (MI)(#22) Jordanian civil strife (with Syrian intervention), 1966 (MI)(#74) Jordanian civil strife (with Syrian intervention and threat of Iraqi intervention), 1970 (W)(#90) Kuwait-Iraq, 1973 (W)(#99) Moroccan civil strife (with Algerian intervention), 1976–77 (W)(#110) Mauritanian civil strife (with Algerian intervention), 1976–77 (W)(#111) Libya-Egypt, 1977 (W)(#115) South Yemeni civil strife (with Saudi and North Yemini intervention), 1969–72 (W)(#89)		Sudan-UAR, 1958 (W)(#25)
Number	9	0	1
Percent	69	0	50
Arab League debate	Lebanese civil strife (with threat of UAR intervention), 1958 (C)(#28) Omani civil strife (with South Yemeni and Jordanian intervention), 1970–76 (W)(#93) North Yemen–South Yemen, 1972 (W)(#97)	Lebanese civil strife (with Syrian intervention), 1975–76 (W)(#109)	
Number	2	1	0
Percent	2	50	0
Arab League recommendation/judgment	Yemeni civil strife (with Egyptian and Saudi intervention), 1962–67 (W)(#49)	Algeria-Morocco, 1963 (W)*(#54)	Kuwait-Iraq, 1961(C)* (#40)
Number	1	1	1
Percent	8	50	50
Number of conflicts	13	2	2

Note: W = war; C = crisis; MI = military intervention; * = success. The number after each conflict identifies the location of the conflict description in the Appendix.

in the management of this conflict than did the League. The type of
conflict in which Arab League intervention and success were hypothesized was that between nonaligned and aligned states where the former
was the victim, and in one (50 percent) of these two conflicts the
League intervened and was instrumental in effecting an end to the crisis. As will be noted below, the divergence between the hypotheses
and Arab League behavior with respect to certain of the conflicts in
the latter two categories is probably attributable to an inaccurate portrayal of one aspect of the coalition configuration within the Arab world
—namely, a failure to identify a strong consensus in favor of preserving the territorial status quo.

Of the 13 intercoalition conflicts, 9 were not even brought to the
Arab League. The first of these occurred in 1949 when the anti-Hashemite state of Syria was threatened by Hashemite-ruled Iraq. Two
others involved attempts by radical neutralist governments in Syria
to assist Jordanian rebels to overthrow the conservative pro-Western
government in Amman in 1957 and 1966. The remaining 6 of these 9
conflicts that failed to elicit even debate by the League were between
radical rejectionist and moderate accommodationist regimes. One of
the most serious was the threatened and actual interventions by Iraq
and Syria respectively in the Jordanian civil war of 1970, which pitted
the government of King Hussein against Palestinian forces. Iraq
threatened to use its 20,000 troops stationed in Jordan against the
Jordanian army if it embarked on military action against the Palestinian guerrillas, but in fact Iraq did not carry out its threat when the
Jordanians did move to crush the Palestinians. Syria, however, did
send a large military contingent into Jordan to assist the Palestinians,
and this Syrian intervention led Jordan to call for Arab League action.
However, given the realization in the Arab world that a consensus was
not possible, the League never convened to discuss the dispute. Following the Jordanian military victory in the civil war an Arab summit
did attempt to resolve the differences between the Hussein government
and the Palestinians, but it did not address itself to the Syrian intervention about which Jordan had complained.

Another intercoalition conflict arose as a result of Saudi Arabia's and North Yemen's provision of base camps and some personnel
to rebel groups seeking to overthrow the radical regime in South Yemen during the period 1969-72. In fact, it was not until 1971 that
North Yemen was persuaded by Saudi Arabia to join it in aiding the
rebels. Despite frequent accusations of external aggression by the
Aden government, it did not seek Arab League involvement, as most
of the organization's members were sympathetic to the rebel cause.
In 1973 rejectionist Iraq attacked and seized a portion of Kuwait, but
individual Arab countries brought sufficient pressure to bear on Baghdad to end the conflict and the League was never involved. Two inter-

coalition conflicts in 1976-77 resulted from the provision of bases to Polisario forces by the radical Algerian government in order to prevent Morocco and Mauritania from partitioning the Western Sahara. The radical Arab regimes supported Polisario's position that the former Spanish territory should become an independent state, while other Arab governments were wary of encouraging the birth of another radical state that would be heavily dependent on Algeria. At the end of the period under study fighting was still taking place—although on a very limited scale in the Moroccan-controlled area—and the Arab League had yet to discuss the dispute. The final intercoalition conflict not brought to the League was the brief war between Egypt and Libya in 1977. Not only were the two governments of the antithetical accommodationist and rejectionist philosophies, but the two leaders, Sadat and Qaddafi, harbored deep animosities for one another. Individual Arab statesmen rather than the Arab League mediated this dispute.

The League discussed but did not take a stand in three intercoalition conflicts, all of which involved external military interventions. The first of these was in 1958 between the UAR and Lebanon. Initially, the former assisted Moslem and leftist elements in subvérting the Christian-dominated government in Lebanon. Lebanon first brought the issue of UAR subversion to the United Nations in May 1958, but was then persuaded by Arab states to endeavor to reach a settlement within the League. At League meetings in early June a consensus could not be reached because of the hostility between the radical neutralist and conservative pro-Western groupings. When the conflict escalated to a crisis stage following the coup in Iraq and the arrival of U. S. troops in Lebanon in mid-July, the Lebanese did not even convene to debate the conflict. At the end of August the Arab states were influential in securing passage of a UN resolution concerning the conflict, but by this time international developments within Lebanon and the Arab world had led to a termination of the crisis. The next conflict involved civil strife in Oman that lasted from 1970 to 1976. The radical rejectionist regime in South Yemen gave strong support to the rebel PFLO movement in Oman's Dhofar province, while the conservative accommodationist government of Oman was given support by its coalition partners, Saudi Arabia and Jordan, as well as by Iran and Britain. The Arab League did not call for a cease-fire and withdrawal of forces in the dispute and only set up a conciliation commission in 1974 after the rebels had suffered serious losses. That commission ultimately failed in its mission in any case, and it was left to the Saudis to bring about a cease-fire in 1976 after the rebel forces had been virtually destroyed.

The third and last intercoalition conflict eliciting debate took place in 1972, and pitted North Yemen against South Yemen. In the course of quelling the Saudi- and North Yemeni-assisted rebels, South Yemeni troops carried out raids into North Yemen, which precipitated a war between the two countries. Again, the Arab League did not issue any resolutions judging the behavior of the parties, although the League Council did call on the secretary-general and a five-nation committee to mediate. The committee and a mediation mission headed by the assistant secretary-general subsequently had a high degree of success, as the two protagonists agreed to a cease-fire and a withdrawal of forces from the border. The success of the mediation mission resulted from the desire of the two parties and their respective allies to bring an end to the limited military encounter following the defeat of the South Yemeni rebels.

The only intercoalition conflict eliciting League intervention was the civil strife in Yemen from 1962 to 1967; this saw a surprisingly large military assistance by the UAR (approximately 60,000 troops) to the republican government and much more modest support by Saudi Arabia to the royalists. During the first year of the conflict, Arab states made several proposals for Arab League intervention, but as the secretary-general observed in a memorandum to the Council, a meeting would be useless since there were two conflicting proposals for discussion on the table: one from the Yemeni republican regime to deal with the alleged aggression of Saudi Arabia and the other one from the royalist supporters to deal with alleged Egyptian aggression.[78] Prior to or at the Arab summit meetings in 1964, 1965, and 1966 Saudi and Egyptian representatives met privately to discuss the conflict and conclude disengagement agreements, but these were never observed. Also, at the League summit meetings themselves no debate of the issue occurred, and President Nasser sarcastically observed at the 1966 Cairo summit meeting that the League "talked about everything except what interests Arabs."[79] Only in August 1967, in the wake of the Arab-Israeli war, did the Arab heads of state address themselves to the conflict. By that time the Egyptian government had decided on its own that it must withdraw its forces from Yemen to defend itself against Israel. The conference issued a formal resolution in support of an Egyptian and Saudi disengagement and created a three-nation (Sudan, Iraq, and Morocco) commission to supervise the withdrawal of forces and assist the Yemeni parties in forming a new government. However, the resolution was really a face-saving device for an Egyptian decision that was taken quite independently of and prior to the Arab League meetings. Thus, the lack of League involvement in the conflict for five years and the circumstances under which it finally did intervene basically support the reasoning regarding such conflicts set forth in the theory. As long as the members of a collective security organization are divided into polar groupings that possess the voting strength to prevent the passage of a resolution, conflicts between the members of these groupings are not ordinarily susceptible to organizational involvement.

There were two aligned-nonaligned conflicts in which the aligned was the victim. The one in which the behavior of the League and its members is supportive of the hypothesis and the reasoning behind it is the Syrian intervention in Lebanon in 1975-76. Syria after 1973 adopted a somewhat middle position between rigid rejectionists such as Iraq and Libya and the moderate accommodationists such as Egypt and Saudi Arabia. During the first stage of Lebanese civil strife in 1975 and early 1976, it dispatched Palestinians under its control and small numbers of its own nationals to assist the leftist Moslems allied with Palestinians in Lebanon against the conservative Christian factions. In doing so, it elicited the backing of the radical rejectionists and some criticism by more conservative forces in the Arab world. However, when in June 1976 it sent in its own army to prevent a victory by the leftist Palestinian forces and to prevent a defeat of the Christians, the reactions of the polar Arab groupings were reversed. (Egypt opposed the Syrians but this was largely a result of previous Syrian criticism of Egypt's disengagement accord with the Israelis.) At neither stage of the conflict was an Arab League condemnation of Syria possible. What the Arab League finally did was to create an Arab League force dominated by the Syrians to keep the peace—thus providing de facto legitimization for Syrian intervention. This accord was basically a product of mediation by Saudi Arabia and had the backing of the very large conservative accommodationist coalition that recognized the benefits of the Syrian presence for the moderate forces in the Arab world. Algeria and South Yemen preferred the exclusion of Syrian troops from the Arab League force and Libya and Iraq bitterly opposed the action. However, since the official Lebanese government approved it, they could not prevent its creation. Syria throughout the crisis always had one polar faction favoring its military policy and thus was protected from a League request for a withdrawal.

The second conflict involving an aggression by a nonaligned party against an aligned one was the attempt by Morocco to seize part of the Algerian Sahara in 1963. And, in this case, the fact that there was Arab League involvement contravenes the hypothesis for this type of conflict. Following the outbreak of war the Arab League Council met and called for a cease-fire and withdrawal to the previous border and created a mediation group to secure compliance with these directives. Morocco refused to cooperate with the League and, in the end, preferred to have the conflict managed within an African (OAU) context. However, the League's unanimous opposition to its action undoubtedly contributed to Morocco's decision to accept a cease-fire and an eventual withdrawal. The key question in this analysis is: Why did all of the Arab states come down so promptly and strongly against Morocco, which was then not associating itself with either the radical neutralist or conservative pro-Western groupings in the Arab world? The reason probably lies in the fact that within the Arab world there existed a consensus on the legitimacy of the boundaries inherited from the colonial powers. In the case of the OAU the consensus is much more obvious than is the case in the Arab League, but nevertheless it appears that a comparable situation does prevail in the Arab world: conflicts involving territorial revisionism evoke a near-unanimous response in favor of the state that is attacked or threatened.

The one type of conflict in which intervention and success by the League was hypothesized was <u>conflicts between aligned and nonaligned states, where the nonaligned state was the victim.</u> Of the two conflicts falling into this category, one, the Iraqi threat to Kuwait in 1961, did elicit a successful League intervention. Following the independence of Kuwait in June 1961, Iraq, which was then an independent radical center in the Arab world, claimed the entire territory of Kuwait. Following a UN debate at which the Soviet Union vetoed a resolution calling for Iraq to respect the sovereignty of Kuwait, the Arab League met and both admitted Kuwait to the League and called for an end to the Iraqi threat. It also decided to establish an Arab League force that would replace the British troops who were then protecting the new state. A force of 3,300 was soon organized, composed of troops from the UAR, Saudi Arabia, Tunisia, Jordan, and the Sudan, and it remained there until 1963 when a change of government in Iraq led to an alteration in its policy. The extent of the Arab states' opposition to the Iraqi policy was significantly attributable to the opposition of both the conservative pro-Western states and Iraq's radical rivals to any increase in Iraqi power and the opposition of the neutral Arab states to any aggressive action against states with their own foreign policy orientation. Concerning the policy of the UAR at the time, Kerr has written: "Iraq was a revolutionary and egalitarian republic, and was the UAR's sworn enemy, and to allow it any encouragement in this venture was unthinkable, especially where the UAR's own forward march had been stalled."[80] Another factor that probably influenced the strong opposition of the Arab states to Iraq was that the conflict, like the Moroccan-Algerian war, concerned a challenge to existing boundaries in the Arab world. In fact, since these two conflicts were the only ones in which the League intervened and also met with significant success during the entire period 1946-77, it does appear that there is a very effective, if rarely articulated, consensus against territorial revisionism in the Arab system.

The other conflict of this type in which the League did not become involved was the UAR's occupation of a small area of Sudanese territory in February 1958. Sudan took the issue to the UN Security Council where Cairo indicated its intention to withdraw during the course of the debate, but there were indications that the conflict could have been managed within the League if the Sudanese government had chosen to do so. Following the Sudanese accusation that Egypt had occupied the area along their border, Secretary-General Mohammed Hassouna of the Arab League (himself an Egyptian citizen) suggested that the conflict be settled within the League. While both the quick retreat of the Egyptian government and the conciliatory stance of Hassouna may have indicated a desire on the part of Egypt not to alienate the small group of nonaligned states in the Arab world, it may also have been a reflection of their perception that the Arab states opposed any attempt to alter existing boundaries—a conclusion that seems quite probable, given later League behavior in the Algeria-Morocco and Iraq-Kuwait conflicts.

The two conclusions that emerge most clearly from the preceding analysis of the Arab League's involvement in inter-Arab conflicts are that thu League can seldom play a constructive role in the management of intercoalition conflicts and that there is probably an effective consensus in favor of existing territorial boundaries that supports League intervention and success in conflicts involving this issue. The two major cases of territorial revisionism, the Iraqi threat to Kuwait in 1961 and the Algerian invasion of Morocco in 1963, were the only real cases of successful League intervention. And in the other two much more minor conflicts of this type involving occupations of very small areas (Sudan-Egypt, 1958; Kuwait-Iraq, 1973) the aggressing states soon withdrew as a result of diplomatic pressure by Arab and other states. The Arab states have not spoken out formally in favor of the maintenance of existing boundaries in the same way that the African states have in the OAU, but there appears to be a strong de facto consensus among them on this issue.*

It is very difficult to draw any firm conclusions about the hypotheses on aligned-nonaligned conflicts. First, there were only two conflicts where the aligned was the victim—and an equal number where the nonaligned was the victim. Second, territorial revisionism was at issue in three of them. In one of those conflicts where the aligned was the victim, Arab states' reaction to the Syrian intervention in the Lebanese civil war supported the reasoning behind our expectation of no successful interventions by the League. But their views on the Moroccan invasion of Algeria seem to have been almost totally dominated by the territorial issue. Both of the conflicts in which the non-

---

*Malcolm Kerr believes that there is such an effective consensus and that the Arab states have probably failed formally to support inherited colonial boundaries because of their anticolonial ideology. (Personal communication.)

aligned was the victim concerned the territorial issue. Whether the speed of the Egyptian withdrawal from the Sudan was influenced by their evaluation that their continued occupation would have an adverse impact on the future policies of the nonaligned states in the inter-Arab system is impossible to discern. However, there is no doubt that Arab governments' reactions to Iraq's threat to Kuwait were affected by the desire of all groupings to limit the expansion of that radical state. In this case both their desire to promote acceptance of existing borders and their opposition to one power's growth in influence predisposed them to oppose Iraq.

A major impediment to Arab League involvement in inter-Arab conflicts has been, and still is, the voting rule that requires unanimity (except for the aggressing state) for resolutions dealing with threats to or breaches of the peace. Such unanimity can only occur where a consensus exists within the membership with respect to a particular issue (such as that on territorial revisionism), or where the threatening or aggressing state is without allies (as was the case with Iraq when it sought to absorb Kuwait in 1961). Since most conflicts in the Arab world have been, and are likely to be, between states with different ideologies and foreign policy orientations, the League is unlikely to be an important agency for managing inter-Arab conflicts. Moreover, there is no indication that the Arab states are willing to alter the voting regulations of their organization in such a way that a simple or two-thirds majority of the members would be able to initiate action in the name of the Arab League. There have been a number of attempts to alter the voting rules, particularly by the League's secretaries-general, but on each occasion the governments have been more worried about preventing action against themselves than about facilitating action against others. [81] As long as this remains the case, the League is likely to remain a relatively inactive and ineffective collective security organization.*

NOTES

1. J. S. Raleigh, "Ten Years of the Arab League," Middle East Affairs 6 (March 1965): 67.

2. Majid Khadduri, "Towards an Arab Union: The League of Arab States," American Political Science Review 40 (February 1946): 90-92.

*There are sometimes agreements at Arab summit conferences to modify general foreign policies that have led to hostile relations between Arab states, but they do not fall within our definition for collective security.

3. George Kirk, The Middle East in the War: Survey of International Affairs, 1939-1946 (London: Oxford University Press, 1953), p. 334.

4. Khadduri, op. cit., p. 92.

5. M. Khalil, ed., The Arab States and the Arab League, Vol. II: International Affairs (Beirut: Khayats, 1962), Document no. 4, p. 9.

6. Robert MacDonald, The League of Arab States: A Study in the Dynamics of Regional Organization (Princeton, N. J.: Princeton University Press, 1965), p. 76. See, also, Nadav Safran, From War to War: The Arab-Israeli Confrontation, 1948-1967 (New York: Pegasus, 1969), pp. 63-66.

7. Khadduri, op. cit., pp. 94-98.

8. Khalil, op. cit., Document no. 28, pp. 53-56.

9. Khalil, op. cit., Document no. 29, pp. 56-61.

10. Prologue.

11. Article 8.

12. Article 5.

13. Article 6.

14. Fayez A. Sayegh, Arab Unity: Hope and Fulfillment (New York: Devin-Adair, 1958), p. 123.

15. P. J. Vatikiotis, "The Politics of the Fertile Crescent," in Political Dynamics in the Middle East, ed. Paul Y. Hammond and Sidney S. Alexander (New York: American Elsevier, 1972), pp. 248-49; Safran, op. cit., pp. 66-67; Patrick Seale, The Struggle for Syria: A Study of Post-War Arab Politics (London: Oxford University Press, 1965), pp. 90-91.

16. MacDonald, op. cit., pp. 224-27 and 244-49.

17. Khalil, op. cit., Document no. 43, pp. 101-6.

18. Article 2.

19. Articles 5 and 6.

20. MacDonald, op. cit., p. 241.

21. MacDonald, op. cit., pp. 237-39; Boutros Boutros-Ghali, "The Arab League—25 Years After," East Africa Journal (June 1970): 8-9.

22. MacDonald, op. cit., pp. 59, 155.

23. "The Arab League—III," An-Hanar Report 5 (August 26, 1974); 1-2.

24. Malcolm H. Kerr, The Arab Cold War: Gamal 'Abd al-Nasir and His Rivals, 1958-1970, 3d ed. (London: Oxford University Press, 1971), p. vi; Abbas Kelidar, "The Struggle for Arab Unity," The World Today 23 (July 1967): 293.

25. T. R. Little, "The Arab League: A Reassessment," Middle East Journal 10 (Spring 1956): 141; Khadduri, op. cit., p. 92.

26. MacDonald, op. cit., pp. 75-76. See, also, Harry Siegman, "Arab Unity and Disunity," Middle East Journal 16 (Winter 1962):

48-52; Anwar G. Chejne, "Egyptian Attitudes Towards Pan-Arabism," Middle East Journal 11 (Summer 1957): 253-68.

27. Little, op. cit., p. 143.

28. Ibid., p. 141.

29. Keesing's Contemporary Archives 9 (October 10-17, 1953): 13183.

30. These talks and the views of the Arab states in 1954 are described in Seale, op. cit., pp. 187-212.

31. Khalil, op. cit., Document no. 196, pp. 368-70.

32. Guy Wint and Peter Calvocoressi, Middle East Crisis (Hammondsworth: Penguin Books, 1957), p. 52; and Tareq Y. Ismael, ed., Governments and Politics of the Contemporary Middle East (Homewood, Ill.: Dorsey Press, 1970), p. 315.

33. Ismael, op. cit., pp. 315-16.

34. A good discussion of their reactions in 1955 is in Seale, op. cit., pp. 213-37.

35. Little, op. cit., p. 147.

36. Willian Sands, "The Hashemite Kingdom of Jordan," in Ismael, op. cit., p. 296; and Safran, op. cit., p. 69.

37. MacDonald, op. cit., p. 234; and Khalil, op. cit., Document nos. 151, 152, p. 252 and Document no. 156, p. 250.

38. Ismael, op. cit., p. 321.

39. Seale, op. cit., pp. 289-90. For policies of radical neutralists, see, Kerr, op. cit., p. 6.

40. For a good discussion of the doctrine and the regional politics surrounding it, see, Seale, op. cit., pp. 281-306.

41. See provisional Constitution in Khalil, op. cit., vol. 1, Document no. 140, pp. 610-17.

42. Ibid., pp. 80-91.

43. Michael W. Suleiman, "Lebanon," in Ismael, op. cit., p. 246.

44. Kelidar, "The Struggle for Arab Unity," The World Today 23 (July 1967): 294-95; Kerr, op. cit., pp. 16-17; Walter Z. Laqueur, The Struggle for the Middle East: The Soviet Union and the Middle East, 1958-1968, rev. ed. (Hammondsworth: Penguin Books, 1972), pp. 25-26, 84-86.

45. Kerr, op. cit., p. 19.

46. Ibid., p. 24. See, also, Amitai Etzioni, Political Unification: A Comparative Study of Leaders and Forces (New York: Holt, Rhinehart and Winston, 1963), pp. 97-137.

47. Kerr, op. cit., pp. 33-35.

48. Manfred W. Wenner, Modern Yemen, 1918-1966 (Baltimore: Johns Hopkins University Press, 1967), pp. 188-89.

49. Kerr, op. cit., p. 107.

50. Charles A. Gallagher, "The Maghreb and the Middle East," in Hammond and Alexander, op. cit., pp. 400 and 410.

51. Ibid., pp. 44-95.

52. Kelidar, "The Struggle for Arab Unity," p. 297; Amos Perlmutter, "Sources of Instability in the Middle East: Two Decades of Nationalism and Revolution," Orbis 12 (Winter 1968): 729.

53. Safran, op. cit., pp. 77-78; Malcolm Kerr, "Regional Arab Politics and the Conflict with Israel," in Hammond and Alexander, op. cit., p. 44.

54. Speech by Nasser in December 1963. Kerr, The Arab Cold War, p. 99.

55. Ibid., p. 98.

56. The summit is described in ibid., pp. 97-102; and Safran, op. cit., p. 87.

57. These developments during the first half of 1966 are summarized in Kerr, The Arab Cold War, pp. 114-22.

58. Ibid., pp. 107-14.

59. Middle East Journal 21 (Spring 1967): 237.

60. The temporary unity is summarized in Abbas Kelidar, "Shifts and Changes in the Arab World," World Today 24 (December 1968): 503-4. The role of inter-Arab conflicts in promoting the war is described in Kerr, The Arab Cold War, pp. 126-28.

61. Kessing's Contemporary Archives 16 (January 14-21, 1967): 21818.

62. Kerr, The Arab Cold War, p. 126.

63. See, Yashpal Tandon, "U.N.E.F., the Secretary-General and International Diplomacy in the Third Arab-Israeli War," International Organization 22 (Spring 1968): 529-56.

64. Gallagher, op. cit., pp. 402-4.

65. D. C. Watt, "The Arab Summit Conference and After," World Today 23 (October 1967): 449. The realignments at the conference are also described in Kelidar, "Shifts and Changes in the Arab World," pp. 505-6.

66. Kerr, The Arab Cold War, p. 131.

67. Middle East Journal 22 (Autumn 1968): 477.

68. Kerr, The Arab Cold War, p. 146.

69. Ibid., p. 139; idem, "Regional Arab Politics and the Conflict with Israel," p. 41; and Safran, op. cit., pp. 356-87.

70. Analyses of inter-Arab politics during this period can be found in Fouad Ajami, "Between Cairo and Damascus," Foreign Affairs 54 (April 1976): 444-61; Fouad Ajami, "Stress in the Arab Triangle," Foreign Policy 23 (Winter 1977/78): 90-108; Gabriel Ben-Dor, "Inter-Arab Relations and the Arab-Israeli Conflict," Jerusalem Journal of International Relations 1 (Summer 1976): 70-96; A. I. Dawisha, Egypt in the Arab World (London: Macmillan, 1976), chap. 10; idem, "Syria and the Sadat Initiative," World Today 34 (May 1978): 192-98; Daniel Dishan, "Inter-Arab Relations," in From June to Octo-

ber: The Middle East Between 1967 and 1973, ed. Itamar Rabinovich and Haim Shakel (New Brunswick, N.J.: Transaction, 1978), pp. 157-69; Yair Evron and Yaacov, "Coalitions in the Arab World," Jerusalem Journal of International Relations 1 (Winter 1975): 71-108; Michal C. Hudson, Arab Politics: Search for Legitimacy (New York: American University Press, 1977): R. D. McLaurin et al., Foreign Policy Making in the Middle East (New York: Praeger, 1977); and Nadav Sairan, "Arab Politics, Peace and War," Orbis 18 (Summer 1974): 377-401.

    71. Ben-Dor, op. cit., p. 82.

    72. Ajami, "Stress in the Arab Triangle," p. 100.

    73. Ibid., p. 101.

    74. Mordechai Abir, Oil, Power and Politics (London: Frank Cass, 1974), pp. 105-13.

    75. Ajami,. "Stress in the Arab Triangle," p. 97; Sam Younger, "The Syrian Stake in Lebanon," World Today 32 (November 1976): 405-6.

    76. Ben-Dor, op. cit., p. 89.

    77. Arab Report and Record, October 16-31, 1976, pp. 643-44.

    78. Middle East Journal 27 (Winter/Spring 1963): 104.

    79. Keesing's Contemporary Archives 15 (October 15, 1966): 21622.

    80. Kerr, The Arab Cold War, p. 20.

    81. MacDonald, op. cit., pp. 59 and 155.

6

Conclusions

"Among the depressing features of international-political studies is the small gain in explanatory power that has come from the large amount of work done in recent decades."[1] So begins a recent article that surveys a number of theories in the field of international relations. This study has made a serious attempt to explain the relationships between coalition configurations and the collective security activities of international organizations, in addition to simply confirming that such relationships are extant. The decision to first articulate a theory and then engage in investigating the "real world" according to the conceptual scheme suggested by the theory is, we believe, the most fruitful method of studying phenomena of interest to students of international relations. As Kenneth N. Waltz has commented: "Theory should guide research by suggesting hypotheses for investigation and, of course, by defining concepts and terms and indicating the connections among them."[2]

The theory of collective security presented in Chapter 1 is predicated on the assumption that the nature of coalition configurations among members of collective security organizations has a crucial and central impact on the activities of these organizations in the sphere of security politics. In particular, it was posited that the likelihood of organizational intervention and success in conflicts is significantly determined by the nature of the coalition configuration prevailing in the system in which a given conflict occurs, and by the affiliations of conflicting parties with the groupings that constitute this configuration. We believe, based on the testing of the hypotheses in Chapters 2-5, that our theory of collective security has proved valuable in that it highlights the role and importance of one very integral factor in the operation of collective security systems. No claim is made that the theory tested here is comprehensive. Needless to say, a host of other factors are relevant to the study of collective security although we would question whether any are as central as the one we have examined. Haas, Butterworth, and Nye, for example, consider seven "world political variables" in their study of international conflict management,[3] and doubtless one could argue for the inclusion of many more. However, given the complex relationships between the single variable—coalition configurations—and collective security, it was not judged to be practical to attempt to incorporate other factors into the theory in a single study. The development of a more refined theory that integrates additional variables is an obvious task for the future. We believe that such a future theory will likely assign a central place to coalition configurations and the affiliation of conflicting parties with particular political-security groupings.

Another strategy adopted in this study was to discuss, in varying degrees of detail, the diplomacy surrounding many of the conflicts. It was felt to be inadequate to restrict our attention to the aggregate numbers of conflicts falling into the various cells, and thus we sought to complement our classifications of conflicts with an element of the case study approach. The purpose of discussing particular conflicts was not simply to substantiate the reasoning behind the hypotheses but also to identify important factors that were not incorporated into the theory. In this way insights relevant to the development of a more comprehensive theory of collective security have been provided. Discussion of many of the individual conflicts helps to illustrate how formidable is the task of delineating both the general coalition configurations and the affiliations of states with the coalitions. As there exists no widely supported approach to establishing states' alignments, the fact that many readers will differ with some of our classifications is hardly surprising and is in any case unavoidable. In seeking to develop and test general theoretical explanations in international relations the researcher necessarily slights the subtleties and complexities that attend states' foreign policies, particular conflicts, or whatever the phenomena under examination. Nonetheless, we have endeavored to provide some measure of balance by embellishing our classifications of states and categorizations of conflicts with considerable supplementary detail, documentation, and discussion. Moreover, we have been prepared to reexamine certain classifications in light of evidence that fails to support our original expectations.

The major foci of this conclusion will be, on the one hand, an examination of past patterns of intervention and success of the four collective security bodies and, on the other, a discussion of the future roles of these organizations. Each section will treat these topics in the light of the adequacy of the theory set forth in Chapter 1 and the possibilities for its revisions and development.

In Table 9 data on the interventions and successes of the four organizations that are relevant to each of the hypotheses in the theory

TABLE 9

Data on Hypotheses concerning Organizational Intervention and Success

	Organization	Conflicts	Interventions		Successes	
			Number	Percent	Number	Percent
A. No Intervention Expected						
Intercoalition (victim a member of a nondominant coalition—that is, allies of victim do not constitute a "voting majority")	UN	18	2		1	
	OAS	3	1		0	
	OAU	14	2		1	
	AL	12	1		0	
Total		47	6	13	2	4
Intracoalition						
Between members of a nonsubordinate coalition— that is, members have voting power to defeat a resolution	UN	23	4		1	
	OAS	0	0		0	
	OAU	1	0		0	
	AL	0	0		0	
Total		24	4	17	1	4
Between members of a subordinate grouping (where the victim is not trying to join another grouping)	UN	1	0		0	
	OAS	0	0		0	
	OAU	0	0		0	
	AL	0	0		0	
Total		1	0	0	0	0
Aligned-nonaligned (victim aligned)	UN	19	2		1	
	OAS	0	0		0	
	OAU	2	0		0	
	AL	1	0		0	
Total		22	2	9	1	5
Nonaligned-nonaligned	UN	11	4		1	
	OAS	0	0		0	
	OAU	0	0		0	
	AL	0	0		0	

Total	11	4	36	1	9
Total for A	105	16	15	5	5
B. Intervention Expected and Success Not Expected					
Intercoalition (victim a member of a dominant coalition—that is, allies of a victim constitute a "voting majority")					
UN	6	2		0	0
OAS	2	2		0	0
OAU	0	0		0	0
AL	0	0		0	0
Total	8	4	50	0	0
Intracoalition (victim trying to join nonaligned grouping)					
UN	1	1		0	0
OAS	0	0		0	0
OAU	0	0		0	0
AL	0	0		0	0
Total	1	1	100	0	0
Total for B	9	5	56	0	0
C. Both Intervention and Success Expected					
Nonaligned (victim nonaligned)					
UN	14	6		4	
OAS	0	0		0	
OAU	0	0		0	
AL	0	0		0	
Total	14	6	43	4	29
Threats to or breaches of the peace contrary to a consensus norm					
UN	0	0		0	
OAS	14	9		7	
OAU	9	4		4	
AL	4	2		2	
Total	27	15	56	13	48
Total for C	41	21	51	17	41
Total for A–C	155	42	27	22	14

Note: The reason that there is a discrepancy between the number of conflicts in this table (155) and the number in the Appendix (116) is that 35 wars and crises appear twice—once as a conflict between UN members and once as a conflict between members of a regional organization—and four wars appear three times as conflicts between members of the United Nations, OAU, and Arab League.

are presented. Section A of the table presents the data on those types of conflicts that were hypothesized as not being susceptible to organizational intervention. Section B deals with those conflicts in which the organizations were expected to intervene—but not succeed. And Section C covers those conflicts in which the organizations were expected to both intervene and succeed. Prior to a discussion of the data in the table two points should be mentioned. First, since it was established that there was a strong consensus in the Arab world against territorial revisionism, the four territorial conflicts between Arab states have been categorized as contraventions of a consensual norm—and hence are included in C(2).* Second, the total number of conflicts (155) in this table is 39 more than the number (116) in the Appendix, since 35 conflicts appear twice—once as a conflict between UN members and once as a conflict between regional organization members—and since four wars appear three times—as conflicts between UN, OAU, and Arab League members.

The general patterns of organizational interventions and successes do provide support for the hypotheses. At the same time the more detailed examinations in Chapters 2-5 offer greater substantiation of the hypotheses as well as of the theoretical explanations. Of the 105 conflicts in which the four bodies were expected neither to intervene nor succeed, they intervened in only 15 percent (16) and succeeded in slightly less than 5 percent (5). Of the nine in which only calls for a cessation of the threats or acts of aggression were expected, the organizations passed such resolutions in 56 percent (5), and in none were they able to bring about short-term compliance. Of the 41 conflicts in which both intervention and success were expected, the organizations backed the termination of the threats or acts of aggression in 51 percent (21), and in 41 percent (17) of these there was compliance.

Turning to the conflicts in which the organizations were not expected to act (Section A), it is clear that all four bodies were unable to manage intercoalition conflicts. The only two successful interventions were the United Nations's involvement in the Middle East war of

---

*The four are Sudan-Egypt, 1958; Kuwait-Iraq, 1961; Algeria-Morocco, 1963; and Kuwait-Iraq, 1973. In the second and third conflicts the League did call for a termination of the threat or act of aggression, and in all four cases the aggressing party withdrew or ceased its threat under pressure from other Arab states. The reason that the conflicts were not classified as breaches of a consensual norm in Table 8 (in Chapter 5) is that the literature on inter-Arab relations, from which the conceptualization of the coalition configurations was derived, did not identify such a consensus.

1967 and the OAU's involvement in the Ghanaian intervention in Niger in 1964-65. The former, as previously mentioned, could very well be categorized as an aggression by an aligned against a nonaligned party, and the success in the latter was due to a unique concatenation of diplomatic events. The two groups of intracoalition conflicts in which intervention was not expected were in almost all cases between UN members, and only in the Cypriot crisis of 1963-64 was the United Nations instrumental in preventing or terminating a war. Likewise, the conflicts between aligned and nonaligned where the aligned was the victim and those between nonaligned states were almost solely between UN members. Not only did only one conflict in each category elicit both a call for a cease-fire and compliance by the parties, but of the six interventions in these two categories, one aligned-nonaligned and three nonaligned-nonaligned conflicts could certainly be reclassified so as to permit a better understanding of them in terms of the theory.*

Of the nine conflicts in which intervention but not success was predicted, the organizations intervened in 56 percent (5) and succeeded in none (Section B). Eight of the nine were intercoalition conflicts where the victim was a member of a dominant grouping. As was mentioned in the UN chapter, there are occasions when dominant coalitions are unsure of what their own policies should be and/or are very concerned that they keep complete control of the conflict's management, and this helps to explain the reluctance of the Western coalition to involve the United Nations in certain conflicts. The single intracoalition conflict where the victim was trying to establish a position of nonalignment (the Soviet invasion of Hungary) was managed as hypothesized. In fact, it indicates only too clearly the proclivity of the other grouping to confine its backing for the victim to diplomatic support for fear of precipitating a major conflagration.

The two types of conflicts in which both intervention and success were hypothesized were those between aligned and nonaligned where

---

*The Arab-Israeli war of 1973 could be divided into two stages so that in the first the nonaligned was the aggressor and in the second the aligned was the aggressor. In a tripolar Asian system, the Indo-Pakistani wars of 1965 and 1971 could be reconceptualized—the former as an aggression by a nonaligned state against a bialigned one (with the third pole—China—not in the United Nations) and the second as an intercoalition conflict. The response to the Rhodesian interventions into Mozambique in 1976 and 1977 actually indicate a consensual element in the global system—opposition to the white-dominated regimes of southern Africa and their attempts to retaliate against nationalist rebels operating from outside their borders.

the nonaligned was the victim, and those involving breaches of consensual norms. The former involved only UN members and the latter were solely between members of the regional organizations.* The frequencies of intervention (51 percent) and success (41 percent) were definitely higher than those in the other categories of conflicts, and as discussed in the UN and OAS chapters, an examination of the character and outcomes of a number of other conflicts lends greater weight to these hypotheses. In the case of challenges to consensual norms, some disputes were resolved in accordance with the norms outside the organizations, and in others the military actions were defeated before the organizations had an opportunity to affect their termination. In the case of aligned-nonaligned conflicts where the victim was nonaligned, the absence of Communist China and North Vietnam from the United Nations definitely impeded its involvement in quite a few cases. Also, there were at least four other disputes in which the Organization intervened and achieved varying degrees of success that could conceivably be reclassified to fall into this category of conflict. †

In reviewing the hypotheses, several analytical problems became evident. First, some conflicts are difficult to classify according to the alignments of the conflicting parties since some states shared particular predispositions of both a major coalition and a nonaligned grouping, and since there were sometimes states with different foreign policy orientations on a particular side. Also, there were often unique political currents relevant to a small set of conflicts that were not portrayed in the conceptualization of the systemic coalition configuration. For instance, the relevance of tripolarity to some Asian conflicts and the general antipathy toward the white-dominated regimes in southern Africa are examples of such currents. The analyst, in examining the relevance of the dominant system structure and the affiliations of conflicting parties with the various coalitions, should always be aware of these problems when classifying individual conflicts. The above problems do not in our judgment argue against the general theoretical approach we have pursued but rather argue in favor of being sensitive to uniqueness and trying to refine the nature of the coalition configurations.

---

*Two conflicts involving threats or acts of aggression by aligned against nonaligned states occurred between Arab states, but they (Sudan-Egypt in 1958 and Kuwait-Iraq in 1961) have been reclassified as challenges to a consensus against territorial revisionism in Table 9. As discussed in Chapter 5, the alignments of the parties probably had some influence on states' policies toward the conflict.

†These are the Arab-Israeli wars of 1967 and 1973, the Cypriot crisis of 1963-64, and the Tunisian-French conflict of 1961.

Another conclusion that emerges from the review of the hypotheses is that regional organizations have been confined largely to managing conflicts in which there was a challenge to a consensual norm. Most other conflicts between their members have tended to fall into the intercoalition category, and they, of course, have not been susceptible to organizational involvement. On the other hand, the United Nations has generally only been able to play constructive roles in conflicts involving threats or acts of aggression by aligned against nonaligned parties or in conflicts that significantly resemble such disputes. Only in these conflicts have all groupings appeared willing to exert strong pressure against the aggressing state to curtail its action.

While this study has focused on particular hypotheses concerning alignment patterns, it is also interesting to ask, on the basis of the previous analyses, what have been the overall roles of collective security organizations in international wars, crises, and military interventions. In fact, data on these matters could facilitate the extension of the theory so as to take into account the magnitude of the conflict. Table 10 provides data on the frequency of organizational intervention and success in the three types of conflicts. Of the 116 conflicts analyzed in this study, the organizations intervened in 35 percent (40) and succeeded in 18 percent (21) (Section A of Table 10). The frequencies of intervention and success of the OAS (63 percent and 37 percent) were considerably greater than those of the other three bodies. The other three organizations exhibited similar patterns although the frequency of success of the OAU and to a lesser extent that of the Arab League were a bit above that of the United Nations.

Wars have definitely elicited interventions more frequently than have crises (39 percent as opposed to 23 percent) (Sections B and C). Interestingly, however, only half of these interventions in wars resulted in short-term compliance by the conflicting parties, whereas all of the interventions in crises proved successful. Obviously the degree of pressure on a state aggressing against another must be greater in getting it to reverse its policy than is the case when it is only threatening to attack. In the case of military interventions the regional organizations intervened in 30 percent and achieved success in almost half of these cases (Section D)—although the lack of success was sometimes due to the defeat of the military intrusions before the organizations became involved. Hence the differences in the overall frequencies of intervention and success in the three types of conflicts are not as striking as one might expect.

When one turns to differences among the organizations in the various types of conflicts, some interesting conclusions emerge. In wars the frequencies of intervention and success by the OAS are con-

TABLE 10

Patterns of Involvement and Success of Collective Security Organizations in Wars, Crises, and Military Interventions

	United Nations		OAS		OAU		Arab League		Totals	
	Number	Percent	Number	Percent	Number	Percent	Number	Percent	Number	Percent
A. All Conflicts										
Conflicts between members	93		19		26		17		116[a]	
Conflicts in which organizations intervened	21	23	12	63	6	23	3	18	40[b]	35
Conflicts in which organizations achieved success	8	9	7	37	5	19	2	12	21[c]	18
B. Wars										
Wars between members	71		7		10		12		71[d]	
Wars in which organizations intervened	19	27	6	86	3	30	2	17	28[e]	39
Wars in which organizations achieved success	6	8	4	57	3	30	1	8	13[f]	18
C. Crises										
Crises between members	22		5		2		3		22[g]	
Crises in which organizations intervened	2	9	2	40	0	0	1	33	5	23
Crises in which organizations achieved success	2	9	2	40	0	0	1	33	5	23
D. Military Interventions										
Military interventions between members	—		7		14		2		23	
Military interventions in which organizations intervened	—	—	4	57	3	21	0	0	7	30
Military interventions in which organizations achieved success	—	—	1	14	2	14	0	0	3	13

[a]This figure of 116 does not represent a summing of the figures to the left of it since there were 35 wars and crises involving members of the United Nations and one of the three regional organizations, and four wars involving members of the United Nations, OAU, and Arab League.

[b]This figure of 40 does not represent a summing of the figures to the left since there were two conflicts (Yemeni civil war and Algerian-Moroccan war) in which two organizations intervened.

[c]This figure of 21 does not represent a summing of the figures to the left since two organizations were judged to have succeeded in one conflict—the Algerian-Moroccan war.

[d]This figure of 71 does not represent a summing of the figures to the left since the wars between members of regional organizations are included in the 71 wars between UN members.

[e]This figure of 28 does not represent a summing of the figures to the left since there were two conflicts (Yemeni civil war and Algerian-Moroccan war) in which two organizations intervened.

[f]This figure of 13 does not represent a summing of the figures to the left since there was one conflict (Algerian-Moroccan war) in which two organizations were judged to have succeeded.

[g]This figure of 22 does not represent a summing of the figures to the left since the crises between members of regional organizations are included in the conflicts between UN members.

siderably greater than those of the other bodies, and the results for the OAU are slightly higher than those for the United Nations and Arab League. With respect to crises, the levels of intervention and success of the OAS are also higher than for the others. However, the number of crises involving regional organization members is quite small. In military interventions, the OAS has been much more active than have been the other two regional bodies, and its low level of success is in these cases attributable to the fact that the aggressors were often defeated before the OAS and its members could affect their activities.

In concluding this summary section on the past roles of collective security organizations in international conflict management, it is appropriate to recall a fundamental assumption of this study—namely, that collective security organizations are basically standing diplomatic conferences whose activities and successes are a reflection of the common, converging, and conflicting interests of member governments. This point is reflected in the judgment of Haas, Butterworth, and Nye who wrote: "These organizations are little more than governments linked in permanent conclave. They have no power and personality beyond the collective will of governments and no capacity to grow apart from the ability of governments to learn."[4] Collective security organizations facilitate states' ability to promote their common and convergent interests, and their interactions within a multilateral context often affect their perceptions of how best to promote their goals. However, as Claude has noted, for states these organizations are "tools" that do not have clear "purposes" that commit them to particular courses of action.[5] Therefore, any judgments that are made of these organizations and their systems of conflict management must ultimately be directed toward the member states and not toward the inanimate institutions that they have created and whose destinies they determine.

One of the most popular—and hazardous—pastimes among students of international relations is speculating about the future. While to do so is necessarily a highly conjectural exercise, we can perhaps risk a few observations concerning the likely future roles of collective security organizations in the global and three regional systems. In particular, we will briefly inquire whether and to what extent changes in the milieus of political and security relations in these systems might influence states' policies and attitudes toward collective security organizations and hence alter the responses of these organizations to international conflicts.

With respect to the OAS, it is clear that the system has evolved to the point where there is both a diminution in Latin American subordination to the United States and an increased tolerance of leftist regimes in the region.[6] At the same time, however, it is highly improbable that either the nonintervention norm or the strong antipathy exhibited by almost all OAS members toward communist influences in the region will soon cease to be central features of the inter-American system. The paucity of conflicts in the hemisphere in the last decade makes it difficult to predict exactly how the organization might operate in the context of existing trends, but so long as the main characteristics of the OAS security system remain essentially intact there is no reason to suppose that the behavior of the organization in conflict situations will undergo any radical changes. It is, in fact, unlikely that competitive coalitions will come to supplant the virtually consensual structure in the near future, although it is possible that a small grouping of states with leftist regimes—for example, Cuba, Jamaica, Guyana (not at present a member of the OAS), and perhaps other states —could oppose a very much larger coalition. However, it may well be that those states that refuse to abide by the norms accepted by the vast majority of OAS members will simply be excluded formally or informally from deliberations on regional collective security, as had in fact occurred with respect to Cuba since the early 1960s. If such a grouping did grow significantly in numbers—an unlikely occurrence in the near future—the OAS system would undoubtedly be stymied in dealing with most conflicts, as has been the case with the other organizations we have studied.

In contrast with the Western Hemisphere organization, the OAU has been faced with many inter-African conflicts in recent years, but on the whole the African organization has failed to play a decisive role in their management or settlement. Political unity exists in African international relations only with respect to the issue of "lingering colonialism" in the form of the white-ruled regimes in southern Africa—and even this consensus is very vague and suffers from some varying orientations among the African states. Ideological and religious divisions among the OAU members have even undermined to some extent the consensus on territorial integrity and the more fragile norm against secession. Although one of the main reasons the OAU was created arose from the desire of many Africans to exclude the cold war and the Great Powers from the continent, it is clear that these extraregional factors remain very important in African international relations and will undercut the OAU's role in conflict management. Some observers view the future of African politics in terms of the intensification of "discontinuities" and inequalities among the African states and the growing strength of certain regional powers within the continent. [7] Such differences in power and a greater focus on problems in particular regions of Africa will unquestionably be permanent features of future African international relations, but there is little indication that divisions on foreign policy orientation at the Pan-African level will disappear. In fact, the need for states to take stands on African issues in the OAU tends to strengthen or reinforce them. Soviet and Cuban interventions in Africa in the last few years may presage an even more direct and extensive Great Power competition in the continent, with France as a very important external actor in addition to the United States and USSR. This could intensify cleavages among African states and make them increasingly reliant on and desirous of external support, both direct and indirect. In short, the Africa of the future could prove to be fertile soil for inter-African disputes and foreign interventions and hence distinctly resistant to the successful operation of the OAU collective security system.

The prospect for political harmony in inter-Arab relations is almost certain to remain as elusive as ever for the foreseeable future. One very important development concerns the possibility that Egypt— and perhaps some other states such as Jordan—might detach themselves from the Arab struggle against Israel, thereby eliminating the only cause around which all the Arab states have been able to unite in some significant way. While such a development may make another Arab-Israeli war less likely, it can only heighten inter-Arab antagonisms. Like Africa, the Arab world seems destined to remain divided into hostile groupings and to continue to be a target for Soviet-U.S. competition. Given the divisions among the Arab states and the intense hostility that characterizes their relations, the future ability of the Arab League to resolve conflicts does not appear promising. Moreover, the near unanimity required before the organization can involve itself substantively in a conflict further emasculates its collective security potential, and there is no sign that the voting rules governing its operation are soon to be altered. It may in the future be regarded as a useful instrument in opposing territorial revisionism or in assisting states in terminating conflicts from which they both want to extract themselves, but its overall ability to manage inter-Arab conflicts is likely to be quite low.

Perhaps the most important possibility to consider in speculating about the future of the world security system on the United Nations concerns the impact that "multipolarity" might have. [8] Some writers think that such a system already exists, and others view its emergence as highly likely. This "new" system has been labeled "multibloc asymmetric" by Haas, [9] and "multihierarchical" by Hoffmann, [10] and Spiegel has coined the term "bimodality" to describe its structure. [11] In general, most scholars seem to agree that a multipolar global system would exhibit the following characteristics: there would be three or more major centers of power or coalitions; the international security coalition configuration would be distinct from configurations based on other issue areas, although there would be extensive linkages between all areas; the major coalitions would have both conflicting and common interests with each other and with other groupings; many states would affiliate with certain states on one issue but with other states on another issue; and the coalitions in the system would be less cohesive than in a bipolar system.[12]

In Chapter 2 the reasons for viewing the entire postwar international security system as basically bipolar were discussed. But if we now concede that with respect to international security politics a multipolar structure might emerge in the future, then the key questions to pose are how the states constituting the international system will respond to international conflicts, and how different state policies toward the UN collective security system will alter the role of the Organization in dealing with these conflicts. It is especially pertinent to inquire how a multipolar system would affect intercoalition conflicts, since these have hitherto been the most resistant to UN interventions. In a bipolar system—whether it is "tight" or "loose"—a successful aggression by a state associated with a major coalition is viewed as an extremely dangerous development. The other major coalition perceives any gain to its rival as a loss to itself, while the nonaligned only tend to oppose aggressions against one of their number. In a multipolar system, however, a successful aggression is unlikely to be viewed by very many states as causing a dangerous change in the distribution of power among the groupings, because power is widely diffused and the existence of cross-cutting interests between groupings of states inhibits any clear alignment with the conflicting parties. Rosecrance has this to say about conflict management in a multipolar system:

> In a multipolar system, it may be difficult to persuade
> nations to engage in regulative action. Even though a
> single disturber may resolve upon actions which are
> inimical to at least one party and which might be the
> cause of violent conflict, other states may not be tempted
> to intervene. In a multipolar order it is not clear whose
> interests are primarily affected by a disruptive act. It
> is therefore possible for a whole series of disruptive
> events to occur without stimulating regulation. In the
> 1930s France, Britain, Italy and Russia were led at
> various times to believe that Hitler's actions were not
> directed against them. Thus there was no need to at-
> tempt a serious regulation on Germany's conduct. In
> a fully multipolar order, many nations could believe
> that while a given state's actions were disruptive, they
> did not require counter-action by any particular nation,
> and a regulated coalition would not be formed.[13]

Another effect of multipolarity would probably be a diminution of the political and security ties of many states with the Great Powers, and this would undermine the willingness of these major powers to defend them. For example, one author has written that with respect to U.S. foreign policy multipolarity will promote a "greater willingness to let events run their course and reluctance to become involved directly in crisis situations. States previously dependent on the United States will be increasingly on their own."[14] The fact that many states in a multipolar security system will share some security and other interests with both conflicting parties and with their allies means that they will be reluctant to back one party or to support the implementation of collective security against the aggressor. There will thus be a much larger group of uncommitted states in a multipolar international security system than is the case in a bipolar system. Using Rosecrance's example of Great Power relations in the 1930s, it is clear that France and Britain were reluctant to apply sanctions against Italy after its invasion of Ethiopia because they both had an interest in cooperating with the aggressing state in the future and sought to avoid driving it into an alliance with Germany. In such a multipolar configuration in which most states share both conflicting and common interests with most other states, there is always a good reason why they should refrain from condemning and alienating an aggressor.

While in an increasingly multipolar system a greater proportion of conflicts would probably be viewed as intercoalition, it is also important to ask what effects such a system would have on the management of conflicts between aligned and nonaligned states—especially those where the victim is nonaligned. The key question here is whether the close allies of an aggressing state would tend to oppose its actions for fear of driving the victim state and possibly other nonaligned states into closer collaboration with a rival coalition. During the postwar era of bipolarity (which is still with us to a significant extent), it was precisely the opposition of many Western states to attempts by their allies to maintain or reassert their influence in nonaligned Asian and African countries that enabled strong UN responses to certain instances of aggression. In a more multipolar world, however, the reaction of coalition members to their allies' aggressive behavior toward the nonaligned could conceivably be quite different. First, if one or more nonaligned states were driven to seek closer relations with a rival coalition, the allies of an aggressing state might not view it as terribly threatening because of the greater diffusion of power in the system and the lower level of hostility between coalitions. Second, because a rival coalition would likely share some important interests with them, the allies of an aggressing state would not be as concerned that the rival grouping would send aid to a nonaligned victim state. In general, the multipolarity of the system could weaken the tendency to view such conflicts in terms of a zero-sum game, thereby diminishing the inclination of rival coalitions to confront each other over any issues in any area.

Thus, it appears that a multipolar international structure is not likely to prove any more hospitable to the successful functioning of the UN collective security system than the bipolar structure whose passing is regarded as either a future certainty or a past fact by some students of international politics. It is no doubt clear to the reader that we regard the scholarly epitaphs on the demise of the bipolar world—which have been enunciated by various authors since at least the early 1960s —as somewhat premature. Partly this view derives from our concentration on international security politics as opposed to, for example, international political economy. Partly, too, it reflects our view that the competition between the Soviet and Western blocs for political influence in the world will remain intense and that the core members will remain relatively cohesive. Increasingly, scholars are rejecting a state-centric approach to the field and are turning their attention to such phenomena as transnational actors and forces as well as to the general issues of political economy. [15] We are not inclined to quarrel with these trends, for they unquestionably reflect a heightened appreciation of the complexities and breadth of the subject matter of international politics. We feel compelled, however, to introduce a cautionary note: security politics and issues remain central to the interests of states, and it is only states that possess the military and political capabilities to make or threaten war. A concern with international violence therefore requires that the analyst turn to the study not only of states but also of the international system as causes and determinants of conflict. To assert the continuing salience of international security issues and the states that are at the center of international politics is not to deny the validity or value of focusing on other issues and aspects of international relations. But, as Waltz has reminded us: "To say that major states maintain their central importance is not to say that other actors of some importance do not exist. The 'state-centric' phase suggests something about the system's structure. Transnational movements are among the processes that go on within it." [16] This study has been concerned with collective security and therefore with the processes of international security politics in general. If we have shed some new insights on these important areas, our effort will have been worthwhile.

NOTES

1. Kenneth N. Waltz, "Theory in International Relations," in Handbook of Political Science, Volume 8, ed. Nelson Polsby and Fred Greenstein (Reading, Mass.: Addison-Wesley, 1975), p. 1.

2. Ibid., p. 5.

3. Ernst B. Haas, Robert L. Butterworth, and Joseph S. Nye, Conflict Management by International Organizations (Morristown, N.J.: General Learning Corp., 1972), pp. 8-9.

4. Ibid., p. 46.

5. Inis L. Claude, Jr., The Changing United Nations (New York: Random House, 1967), p. xvii.

6. See, for example, W. Raymond Duncan, "Caribbean Leftism," Problems of Communism 27 (May–June 1978): 33-57.

7. Timothy Shaw, "Discontinuities and Inequalities in African International Politics," International Journal 30 (Summer 1975): 369-90; I. William Zartman, "Africa," in World Politics, ed. James M. Rosenau, Kenneth W. Thompson, and Garvin Boyd (New York: Free Press, 1976), pp. 569-94.

8. Examples include Ernst B. Haas, Tangle of Hopes (Englewood Cliffs, N.J.: Prentice Hall, 1969), pp. 225-42; Stanley Hoffmann, Gulliver's Troubles, or the Setting of American Foreign Policy (New York: McGraw-Hill, 1968), pp. 33-51 and 243-86; and Richard Rosecrance, International Relations: Peace or War? (New York: McGraw-Hill, 1973), pp. 114-21, 277-94. See, also, Cecil Crabb, Jr., Nations in a Multipolar World (New York: Harper & Row, 1968); Alastair Buchan, "The End of Bipolarity," Adelphi Paper, no. 91 (London: IISS, November 1972); and Ronald J. Yalem, "Tripolarity and the International System," Orbis 15 (Winter 1972): 1051-63.

9. Haas, op. cit., pp. 225-42.

10. Hoffmann, op. cit., p. 356.

11. Steven Spiegel, "Bimodality and the International Order: The Paradox of Parity," Public Policy 18 (Spring 1970): 383-412.

12. Discussion of this point can be found in Louis Rene Beres, The Management of World Power: A Theoretical Analysis (Monograph Series in World Affairs, vol. 10, no. 3, 1972-73), pp. 34-36; idem, "Bipolarity, Multipolarity and the Reliability of Alliance Commitments," The Western Political Quarterly 25 (December 1972): 702-10.

13. Rosecrance, op. cit., p. 116. See, also, pp. 117-18.

14. John Swanson, "The Superpowers and Multipolarity: From Pax Americana to Pax Sovietica?" Orbis 15 (Winter 1972): 1039. A comparable evaluation regarding the impact of multipolarity on American foreign policy is Hoffman, op. cit., p. 359.

15. See, Robert O. Keohane and Joseph S. Nye, eds., "Transnational Relations and World Politics," International Organization 25 (Summer 1971): 329-748; Robert O. Keohane and Joseph S. Nye, Power and Interdependence (Boston: Little, Brown, 1977).

16. Waltz, op. cit., pp. 73-74.

Appendix: List of Wars, Crises, and Military Interventions, 1946-77

This Appendix includes summaries of all the conflicts analyzed in the study, as well as citations of secondary sources that provide more extensive descriptions. Organizational publications and chronologies are not included in the citations.

1. Greek Civil Strife (with Albanian, Bulgarian, and Yugoslav Intervention), 1946-49 (W)

The conflict initially came to the United Nations in January and August 1946, when the Soviet Union claimed that the stationing of British troops in Greece (which did not participate in the fighting) posed a threat to international peace. A majority of Security Council members rejected this accusation. In December 1946 the Greek government charged its three communist neighbors with aggression by providing base camps and material assistance to communist insurgents, and it called for UN action against these states. The Security Council set up a Commission of Investigation and a majority of its members voted for a report endorsing the charges of the Greek government. At a Council meeting the Soviet Union vetoed a resolution criticizing the actions of Greece's three communist neighbors. The Greek government then transferred the issue to the General Assembly in October 1947, and the Assembly passed a resolution that took note of the findings of the Commission of Investigation (an implicit criticism of Albania, Bulgaria, and Yugoslavia), called for an end to external assistance, and set up a UN Special Committee on the Balkans to investigate the dispute and mediate between the parties. The committee visited Greece and substantiated its charges against its neighbors, but was unable to enter the three communist states. The conflict largely disappeared by 1950 as a result of Yugoslavia's defection from the Soviet bloc, U.S. assistance to Greece, and the victories of the Greek government forces. (C. E. Black, "Greece and the United Nations," Political Science Quarterly 63 [December 1948]: 551-68; Edgar O'Ballance, The Greek Civil War, 1944-49 [New York: Frederick A. Praeger, 1966].)

═══════════════════════════

The letters in parentheses after each title indicate the following: W = war; C = crisis; MI = military intervention; and * = success.

2. India-Pakistan, 1947-48 (W)

In October 1948 the Hindu ruler of Kashmir acceded to India.
Soon after accession several thousand Pathan tribesmen from Pakistan entered Kashmir to establish Muslim and Pakistani control of the
area, and they were assisted by the Pakistani government. In January 1948 India called on the United Nations to condemn the Pakistani
aggression. The Security Council asked both parties not to aggravate
the situation and set up the UN Commission for India and Pakistan to
promote a settlement. In April the Council requested the parties take
a number of actions to promote a cease-fire and to facilitate the holding of a plebiscite. The previous resolutions were supported by all
members of the Council except the USSR and the Ukrainian SSR, which
abstained. The UN commission that had been created in January and
reconstituted in April did not arrive in the subcontinent until July.
Between then and December it sought to persuade the parties to end
hostilities. After the parties had fought to a military stalemate, the
commission was successful in arranging a cease-fire in December.
(Michael Brecher, The Struggle for Kashmir [New York: Oxford University Press, 1953]; Josef Korbel, Danger in Kashmir, rev. ed.
[Princeton, N.J.: Princeton University Press, 1966].)

3. Israel-Arab States, 1948 (W)

Prior to the independence of Israel on May 14, 1948, the Arab
states made it very clear that they would fight to prevent its continued
existence. In April the UN Security Council called on both Israelis
and Arabs to cease their military activities, and created a Truce
Commission to promote its directive. Its directive was not complied
with, and on May 15 Egypt, Jordan, Lebanon, Syria, and Iraq invaded
Israel. Between then and January 1949, when stable cease-fires occurred on all fronts, the Security Council called for cease-fires on a
number of occasions, and created a UN mediator and Truce Supervi-
sory Organization to promote its directives. There were a number of
temporary cease-fires, but they did not last long. Israel significantly
expanded its territory during the fighting. The UN mediator assisted
the parties in arranging cease-fires and armistices, but they did not
entail changes in the military outcomes. (Nadav Safran, From War
to War: The Arab-Israeli Confrontation, 1948-67 [New York: Pegasus, 1969]; V. C. Hurewitz, The Struggle for Palestine [New York:
Norton, 1950].)

4. United States, United Kingdom, and
France-USSR (Berlin), 1948 (C)

Beginning in early 1948 the relations between the Western allies and the Soviet Union over the future status of Berlin became very hostile, and from March onward the Soviet Union harassed traffic from the Western zone to Berlin. On June 24, 1948 the Soviet Union established a land blockade of Berlin for the ostensible purpose of persuading the Western allies to compromise on the currency issue. The Western allies soon initiated a large-scale airlift to supply Berlin, and the United States sent 60 B-29s to Europe to indicate its resolve. Throughout the summer of 1948 there were definite indications in the form of statements by the parties as well as their movements of military forces and equipment that an armed clash might occur. By the beginning of September a real threat of a military conflict seemed to have disappeared.

It was not until October, when the talk of a possible armed clash had receded, that the question was brought to the Security Council by the Western powers. Their resolution was vetoed by the Soviet Union. There were some subsequent attempts by UN Secretary-General Trygve Lie and several states to mediate the conflict, but the issue was never considered by a UN body. The final settlement of the conflict in May 1949 resulted from Great Power negotiations. (Jean Edward Smith, The Defense of Berlin [Baltimore: Johns Hopkins University Press, 1963], pp. 235-67; Philip C. Jessup, "The Berlin Blockade and the Use of the United Nations," Foreign Affairs 50 [October 1971], pp. 163-73; and Trygve Lie, In the Cause of Peace [New York: Macmillan, 1964], chap. 12.)

5. Costa Rica-Nicaragua, 1948 (W)

In December 1948 Costa Rica was invaded by approximately 1, 000 Costa Rican exiles from Nicaragua. These exiles were opponents of the new democratic regime of President José Figueres, and were supported by the autocratic Nicaraguan government. Costa Rica was then assisting the organization of the Caribbean Legion, which was dedicated to the overthrow of all autocratic governments in the region. Following the complaint by Costa Rica in December 1948 that it was being invaded, the OAS Council created a five-nation investigation committee. It substantiated Costa Rica's charge that Nicaragua had supported the organization of the invasion, but it also noted Costa Rica's sponsorship of the Caribbean Legion. The Council then criticized Nicaragua's behavior, but also called on Costa Rica to end its support for the Caribbean Legion. It also created a new five-man ob-

servation commission in order to make sure that its requests were
carried out. (Jerome Slater, The OAS and United States Foreign Policy [Columbus: Ohio State University Press, 1967], pp. 67-72; Gordon Connell-Smith, The Inter-American System [London: Oxford University Press, 1966], pp. 225-26; David W. Wainhouse et al., International Peace Observation [Baltimore: Johns Hopkins University .
Press, 1966], pp. 107-13; J. Lloyd Mecham, The United States and
Inter-American Security, 1889-1960 [Austin: University of Texas
Press, 1967], pp. 292-95.)

6. Syria-Iraq, 1949 (C)

In June 1949 the Hashemite state of Iraq tried to pressure the
anti-Hashemite and pre-Egyptian government of President Za'im to
alter its foreign policy. It mobilized approximately 5,000 troops on
the Syrian border, leading Syria to initiate a countermobilization.
While the threat of war was reasonably short-lived, the level of hostility remained very high until Za'im was overthrown in August.
(Middle East Journal 3 [October 1949]: 453; Eliezir Be'eri, Army
Officers in Arab Society and Politics [New York: Praeger, 1970],
pp. 57-59.)

7. Haiti-Dominican Republic, 1949-50 (C)

In December Haiti complained that the Dominican Republic was
supporting a group of Haitian exiles who intended to invade Haiti, and
that it was planning to invade as well during the resulting chaos under
the guise of protecting its own nationals. U.S. ships patrolled off
Haiti at this time in order to remove U.S. nationals if a war did break
out. On January 3, 1950 Haiti formally requested the OAS Council to
consider the Dominican Republic threat, and the latter country soon
requested a comparable meeting to consider the subversion against it
from Haiti, Guatemala, Cuba, and Venezuela. The Council met on
January 6, and created an investigation committee. In March the committee issued a formal report that substantiated the Haitian claims,
and it recommended that a commission be created to oversee relations
among all countries in the Caribbean. In April the Council stated that
the Dominican Republic had acted contrary to the principles of the inter-American system, and it created the Special Committee for the
Caribbean. (Jerome Slater, The OAS and the United States Foreign
Policy, pp. 81-82; Gordon Connell-Smith, The Inter-American System, pp. 227-29; David W. Wainhouse et al., International Peace Observation, pp. 117-24; J. Lloyd Mecham, The United States and Inter-

American Security, 1889-1960, pp. 395-402; Robert Crassweller, Trujillo: The Life and Times of a Caribbean Dictator [New York: Macmillan, 1966], pp. 241-50.)

8. South Korea-North Korea, 1950-53 (W)

On June 25, 1950 the army of North Korea invaded South Korea. The Security Council, which the Soviet Union was then boycotting over the Chinese representation issue, met immediately and called on North Korea to halt its invasion. During the following weeks it also requested all members to provide military assistance to South Korea and to put all of their troops (the largest number being from the United States) under the UN command. Following the entry of Communist Chinese troops on the North Korean side in the fall of 1950, the General Assembly condemned the Chinese military intervention. During the war the General Assembly also established several mediatory committees, but they were not particularly successful. Truce negotiations began in July 1951, but the final armistice did not take place until June 1953. (Leland M. Goodrich, Korea: A Study of U.S. Policy in the United Nations [New York: Council on Foreign Relations, 1956]; and Tae-Ho Yoo, The Korean War and the United Nations [Louvain: Librarie des Barex, 1965].)

9. United Kingdom-Saudi Arabia, 1952 (C)

The crisis developed as a result of a dispute over control of a relatively small area in the southern part of the Arabian peninsula known as the Buraimi Oasis. In early 1952 the area was under the control of the sheikhdom of Abu Dhabi (whose foreign policy at that time was conducted by the United Kingdom), but in August 1952 Saudi Arabia sent a party of about 50 men and some tribal groups friendly to it into the area to assume formal administrative control. By the formal definition of "war" employed in this study, this was not a war, but it certainly did lead to a serious threat of war between Saudi Arabia, on the one hand, and the sheikhdom of Abu Dhabi, the sultanate of Muscat and Oman, and the United Kingdom on the other. The leaders in the former two political entities mobilized their troops and were ready to march on the area when Britain persuaded them to let it try to secure the area through diplomatic means. A "standstill agreement" was negotiated between Britain and Saudi Arabia in October 1952, and this was followed by the establishment of a three-man arbitral body composed of a Saudi Arabian, an Englishman, and a Belgian. (J. B. Kelly, Eastern Arabian Frontiers [London: Faber & Faber, 1964], pp. 142-280.)

10. Peru-Ecuador, 1953-55 (MI)

Ecuador initiated a number of border clashes between the armed forces of the two countries as a result of its claim to a border area that had been ceded to Peru in 1942. Peru never brought the issue to the OAS. Ecuador, however, claimed in 1955 that Peru was planning to invade it and called for OAS action. A committee of the guarantor powers "acting in effect as the Council's Investigating Committee" did not substantiate the charges. (Jerome Slater, The OAS and United States Foreign Policy, pp. 45, 104-05.)

11. Guatemala-Honduras and Nicaragua, 1954 (W)

The invasion of Guatemala by Guatemalan exiles from Honduras and Nicaragua, which had been supplied with arms by the United States, began on June 18, 1954. On the following day, the procommunist Guatemalan government called on the UN Security Council to act against the aggression and to send an observation commission, and it also called on the Inter-American Peace Committee (IAPC) to send an investigatory body to verify the aggressive activities of its neighbors. On June 20 the UN Security Council passed a resolution calling for an end to the bloodshed and asking states not to contribute to it, but it did not back a Soviet proposal demanding a withdrawal of the invading troops or a U.S. proposal calling for a referral of the conflict to the OAS. On June 21 Guatemala asked the IAPC to cancel its request for an investigation since it was placing its trust in the United Nations. As soon as Guatemala had asked the IAPC to withdraw from the conflict, Honduras asked it to continue its involvement. However, without Guatemalan consent it could not conduct an investigation. On June 25 the Soviet Union and Guatemala secured another Security Council meeting, but most members favored OAS involvement. On June 26, Guatemala, realizing that UN assistance was very unlikely, told the IAPC that it should send a committee. On the following day, the IAPC announced that it would do so, but on the very same day the government of President Arbenz fell. The IAPC then chose not to go to Guatemala, and the OAS itself never took up the conflict again. (Ronald M. Schneider, Communism in Guatemala, 1944-1954 [New York: Frederick A. Praeger, 1959]; Jerome Slater, The OAS and United States Foreign Policy, pp. 115-20; Gordon Connell-Smith, The Inter-American System, pp. 229-37; David W. Wainhouse et. al., International Peace Observation, pp. 124-34; and J. Lloyd Mecham, The United States and Inter-American Security, 1889-1960, pp. 445-51.)

12. Costa Rica-Nicaragua, 1954 (C)

The root of this conflict was the deep and long-lasting hostility between the democratic regime of President Figueres of Costa Rica and the authoritarian regime of President Anastacio Somoza of Nicaragua. On July 25 a group of Costa Rican exiles based in Nicaragua carried out a raid into Costa Rica, and while Costa Rican border forces were repelling their raid, they shot at and hit a Nicaraguan plane. The Nicaraguan government then mobilized its army on the border, and Costa Rica responded with a comparable mobilization. In order to deter a Nicaraguan invasion of Costa Rica, the United States sent planes to Costa Rica. [John D. Martz, Central America: The Crisis and the Challenge [Chapel Hill: University of North Carolina Press, 1959], pp. 188-93.)

13. Nationalist China-Communist China, 1954-55 (W)

In October 1954 the Communist regime began to launch attacks against the Tachen Islands that were several miles from the mainland. By February 1955 it succeeded in gaining control of the islands. During the war there was one rather marginal UN consideration of the conflict when in January 1955 the Security Council met to consider a New Zealand proposal to invite representatives from the People's Republic of China to come to the United Nations to discuss the issue. A subsequent meeting never took place since the Peking government indicated that it would only participate if the Nationalist Chinese regime was expelled from the organization, and that it would only discuss the issue of U.S. aggression against China. (China and the U.S. Far East Policy, 1945-1967 [Washington, D.C.: Congressional Quarterly Service, 1967], pp. 71-73, 85-90; J. H. Kalicki, The Pattern of Sino-American Crises: Political-Military Interactions in the 1950s [Cambridge, Mass.: Cambridge University Press, 1975], pp. 120-58.)

14. Costa Rica-Nicaragua, 1955 (W)

On January 11, Costa Rica was invaded by about 500 troops from Nicaragua, most of whom were Costa Rican exiles. Costa Rica called for OAS action against the invasion from Nicaragua, and the Council immediately created an investigation committee. The committee confirmed the attack and Nicaragua's complicity in it, and it stated that it would recommend further collective measures to the Council if the support for the intervention did not cease. The Council then requested that Nicaragua respect its legal obligations—an implicit condemnation of its behavior. The Council also authorized the sale of planes to Costa Rica by the United States. Subsequently the committee threatened to recommend sanctions against Nicaragua if the rebel force did not withdraw to Nicaragua. Following the withdrawal the Council set up two committees to mediate differences between the countries and to create a demilitarized border zone. (Jerome Slater, The OAS and United States Foreign Policy, pp. 72-76; Gordon Connell-Smith, The Inter-American System, pp. 237-38; David W. Wainhouse et al., International Peace Observation, pp. 113-15; and J. Lloyd Mecham, The United States and Inter-American Security, 1889-1960, pp. 402-8.)

15. Pakistan-Afghanistan, 1955 (C)

In March 1955 the government of Afghanistan complained to Pakistan about the further political integration of an area occupied by Pathan tribesmen into the Pakistani state. It claimed that this area was a legitimate part of Afghanistan, and stated that the further integration of the region could lead to grave consequences. A rejection of the note by Pakistan led to an attack on the Pakistani embassy in Kabul. Pakistani citizens then did the very same thing to the embassy of Afghanistan in Islamabad. At the beginning of May Afghanistan apologized for the attack, but it was rejected by Pakistan, which stated that unless adequate amends were made by May 15, Afghanistan would face grave consequences. Afghanistan then mobilized its army along its border with Pakistan, and this was followed by the dispatch of Pakistani troops to the border region. Mediation attempts by Saudi Arabia, the United States, and the United Kingdom failed, but by the end of the summer of 1955 the two countries had reached an agreement with respect to the attacks on their embassies. (James W. Spain, The Pathan Borderland [The Hague: Moutton and Company, 1963], pp. 228-72; S. M. M. Qureshi, "Pakhtunistan: The Frontier Dispute between Afghanistan and Pakistan," Pacific Affairs 39 [Spring-Summer 1966]: 99-114.)

16. Saudi Arabia-United Kingdom, 1955 (W)

The arbitral body that was established to settle the Buraimi Oasis controversy following the 1952 crisis was unable to accomplish a great deal because of a difference of views between the states on its terms of reference. Because of this stalemate Britain in cooperation with the sheikhdom of Abu Dhabi and the sultanate of Muscat and Oman decided to take the area by force. In October 1955, forces from Abu

Dhabi and Muscat and Oman under the command of British officers captured the Buraimi Oasis. Saudi Arabia immediately broke diplomatic relations with Britain (and did not renew them until 1963), but it did not take the matter to the United Nations—despite Soviet support for its position. (Walter Z. Laqueur, The Soviet Union in the Middle East [New York: Praeger, 1959], p. 155; J. B. Kelly, Eastern Arabian Frontiers, pp. 142-280.)

17. Burma-Communist China, 1956 (W)

The Chinese incursion into Burma occurred in mid-1956 when Communist Chinese armed forces occupied a relatively small area of about 1,000 square miles in a very remote and sparsely populated area that the Peking government claimed belonged to it. When Burma announced the border incursion in July 1956, it stated that the conflict was not serious and that negotiations were in progress to settle the territorial dispute. In October 1956 President U Nu of Burma went to Peking to negotiate a settlement, and while the final accord was a compromise, it was probably closer to the original Burmese claim. (Daphne E. Whittam, "The Sino-Burmese Boundary Treaty," Pacific Affairs 34 [Summer 1961]: 174-83; Harold C. Hinton, Communist China in World Politics [Boston: Houghton Mifflin, 1966], pp. 308-16.)

18. Egypt-Israel, France, and United Kingdom, 1956 (W)

During the fall of 1956 Israel was worried about the increasing military strength of Egypt; France was opposed to Egyptian assistance to the Algerian rebels; and both the United Kingdom and France wanted to reassert their control of the Suez Canal following President Nasser's nationalization of it in July. In October the three states planned a coordinated attack against Egypt. On October 29, Israel attacked Egypt. On October 30 the United Kingdom and France stated they would intervene if the fighting did not stop, and they vetoed a Security Council resolution calling on Israel to withdraw. On October 31 they began to bomb Egyptian airfields, and on November 2 their troops landed in Egypt. Following the British and French vetoes of the October 30 Security Council resolution the issue was transferred to the General Assembly, and it passed a resolution calling for a cease-fire and withdrawal by the invading states. By November 5 the three states had accepted the Assembly resolution. The Assembly then created the UN Emergency Force to stand between the parties and to supervise the withdrawal of the three invading armies. (Gabriella Rosner, The United Nations Emergency Force [New York: Columbia University

Press, 1963]; Terence Robertson, Crisis: The Inside Story of the Suez Conspiracy [New York: Atheneum, 1965]; Hugh Thomas, Suez [New York: Harper & Row, 1967].)

19. Hungary-Soviet Union, 1956 (W)

While there was a great deal of international interest in internal developments in Hungary following the accession to power of Premier Imre Nagy on October 24, 1956, it was not until November 1 when Nagy declared that Hungary had severed its ties with the Warsaw Pact and called on the Great Powers to protect Hungary's neutrality that perceptions of a possible war emerged. There were Soviet troops stationed in Hungary, and there was concern that the Soviets would use them to keep Hungary in its alliance system. The crisis was first brought to the UN Security Council on November 2, but no resolution on the crisis was passed. On November 3, the Soviet Union invaded Hungary, and early in the morning of November 4 the Security Council met to consider the war. When the Soviet Union vetoed a resolution calling for its own withdrawal, the issue was transferred to the General Assembly. The General Assembly then called for Soviet withdrawal and established a fact-finding group to go to Hungary and report on the developments there. The Soviet Union refused to comply with the resolution, and the new Hungarian government of Premier Janos Kadar did not permit the entry of UN observers. (Gordon Gaskill, "Time Table of a Failure," The Virginia Quarterly Review 34 [Spring 1958]: 161-91; Samir N. Anabtwawi, "The Afro-Asian States and the Hungarian Question," International Organization 18 [Autumn 1963]: 872-90; Richard Lettis and William Morris, eds., The Hungarian Revolt [New York: Charles Scribner's Sons, 1961].)

20. Algerian (France) Civil Strife (with Moroccan and Tunisian Intervention), 1956-62 (W)

Following the independence of both Tunisia and Morocco in 1956 both countries provided sanctuaries, arms, and other forms of assistance to thousands of Algerian rebels. The French criticized Tunisian assistance when Tunisia brought the question of the French bombing of Sakiet Sidi Youssef to the Security Council in February 1958, but they never called for a UN debate on the matter. (Edgar O'Ballance, The Algerian Insurrection, 1954-62 [London: Faber and Faber, 1967].)

21. Honduras-Nicaragua, 1957 (W)

At the end of April 1957 Nicaragua invaded Honduras in order to secure control of a border area that it claimed. On May 2, the Council of the OAS met to consider the Honduran complaint, and it created an investigation committee to assist the parties in terminating the military clash and to find some way of resolving the substantive conflict. The committee was soon able to arrange for a cease-fire and withdrawal of forces from the disputed area, and it also created a military observation group along the border to prevent future violations. The OAS subsequently secured agreement from the two states to submit their territorial dispute to the International Court of Justice. In November 1960, the International Court of Justice supported the Honduran claim. (Jerome Slater, The OAS and United States Foreign Policy, pp. 64-67; Gordon Connell-Smith, The Inter-American System, pp. 239-40; David W. Wainhouse et al., International Peace Observation, pp. 135-41; and J. Lloyd Mecham, The United States and Inter-American Security, 1889-1960, pp. 408-10.)

22. Jordanian Civil Strife (with Syrian Intervention), 1957 (MI)

In May 1957, Syria sent a military regiment into Jordan to bolster the insurgency of General Ali Abu Nuwar against the conservative government of King Hussein. After the insurgency was defeated, Syria withdrew its forces. (Joseph J. Malone, The Arab Lands of Western Asia [Englewood Cliffs, N.J.: Prentice-Hall, 1973], pp. 121-26.)

23. Syria-Turkey, 1957 (C)

From mid-September through the end of October Syria complained that Turkish troops were massing on their border in order to launch an attack. Syria mobilized a large number of its own troops and Egypt sent troops as well. The Turkish military maneuvers were prompted by the Western states' opposition to Syria's increasingly anti-Western policy and their desire to pressure Syria into altering its policy. Syria submitted the issue to the United Nations in October. It was debated intermittently by the General Assembly during the last ten days of October, and then on November 1 Syria withdrew its complaint as a result of a withdrawal of the Turkish forces along the border. (Nadav Safran, From War to War: The Arab-Israeli Confrontation, 1948-67, pp. 71-72; Patrick Seale, The Struggle for Syria: A

Study of Post-War Arab Politics [London: Oxford University Press, 1965], pp. 296-306.)

24. Spain-Morocco, 1957-58 (W)

This conflict concerned Morocco's claim to Ifni, the Spanish Sahara, and other small Spanish territories. In November 1957, 1,200 troops that were members of a body called the Moroccan Liberation Army invaded the neighboring Spanish colonial territories. The army itself was not a formal government militia, but it certainly had political backing and assistance from the Moroccan government. By February 1958 Spanish troops had killed many of the Moroccan soldiers and had driven the remainder back into Moroccan territory. However, in early 1958 the United States did become involved as a mediator and Spain did cede two small areas, the Tekna protectorate and Tarfaya, in April. (Saadia Touval, The Boundary Politics of Independent Africa [Cambridge, Mass.: Harvard University Press, 1972], pp. 100-02; I. William Zartman, Problems of New Power: Morocco [New York: Atherton, 1964], pp. 64-86.)

25. Sudan-Egypt, 1958 (W)

In February 1958 Egypt claimed some small areas held by the Sudan. It then sent some administrators and armed forces into the areas and mobilized additional troops in the border zones in order to deter Sudanese attacks. The Egyptian action was probably motivated in great part by its resentment over the Sudanese rejection of political union, and by its desire to pressure the Sudanese into modifying their claims for compensation for the flooding of Sudanese territory from the Aswan Dam. Secretary-General Hassouna of the Arab League, himself an Egyptian citizen, suggested that the issue be dealt with by the Arab League. Instead, the Sudan took the question to the United Nations. After a short Security Council debate Egypt declared its intentions to postpone a settlement until the upcoming Sudanese and Egyptian elections had passed and to withdraw pending a final settlement. (Saadia Touval, The Boundary Politics of Independent Africa, pp. 40 and 194-96; Hussein A. Hassouna, The League of Arab States and Regional Disputes [Dobbs Ferry, N.Y.: Oceana Publications, 1975], pp. 47-57.)

26. Tunisia-France, February 1958 (C)

In February 1958 the French bombed the Tunisian town of Sakiet Sidi Youssef in retaliation for Tunisian assistance to the Algerian rebels. Because of this action Tunisia closed all supply lines to French bases inside of Tunisia (which had been granted to France at the time of Tunisian independence in 1956). France indicated its intention to send supplies to these bases; and there were statements by a number of French, Tunisian, and outside parties that a French-Tunisian military conflict could take place if the French tried to supply their troops. Tunisia immediately brought the conflict to the UN Security Council. The United States and Britain soon stepped in as mediators, and were able to persuade France not to unilaterally assist its troops, to convince Tunisia—at least as an interim measure —to allow the provisioning of these troops, and to persuade both conflicting parties to discuss their substantive differences with them. (G. Barraclough, Survey of International Affairs, 1956-58 [London: Oxford University Press, 1962], pp. 432-34 and 440-42.)

27. Tunisia-France, May-June 1958 (C)

During the U. S.-British mediation of the Tunisian-French crisis of February 1958, the Tunisians called for the termination of the French bases in Tunisia apart from the naval base at Bizerte. An accord for the withdrawal of French troops from the bases was then concluded, but the French government failed to ratify it. Therefore, Tunisia began to harass the French troops at a number of the bases inside Tunisia, and in the latter part of May 1958 small-scale fighting broke out between Tunisian and French forces. The Tunisian government cut off supplies to some of the bases, and in early June submitted the conflict, which again brought about a threat of war, to the United Nations. The debate was terminated on June 4 on the request of the French government to allow bilateral talks (in which the United States and Britain again emerged as mediators). On June 18 Tunisia and France announced that French troops would be removed from all bases except for Bizerte. (G. Barraclough, Survey of International Affairs, 1956-58, pp. 432-34 and 440-42.)

28. Lebanese Civil Strife (with the Threat of UAR and U.S. Intervention), 1958 (C)

The civil strife in Lebanon between the pro-Western government of President Camille Chamoun (dominated by the Christian population) and pro-Nasserist rebels (mostly Moslems) began to develop early in 1958. By May it reached serious proportions. At that time the Lebanese government claimed that the insurgents were receiving assistance of arms and men from the UAR and it called for UN action. The

Security Council convened on May 27, but before a lengthy debate could occur, the Lebanese government was prevailed upon to seek a solution within the context of the Arab League. The Arab League failed to resolve the differences between the parties between June 2 and 5, and on June 6 the Security Council began to debate the conflict. On June 10 and 11 Sweden and UN Secretary-General Dag Hammarskjold persuaded the parties and the Security Council to accept the stationing of an observation group in Lebanon that would "ensure that there is no illegal infiltration of personnel or supply of arms or other material across the Lebanese borders." At the same time there was no judgment in the Council resolution that such infiltration was taking place.

Following the creation of the UN observer group there were continued accusations by Lebanon regarding UAR subversion, but by the beginning of July the conflict seemed to be subsiding. This situation changed following the overthrow of the pro-Western government in Iraq on July 14. It prompted the United States and Britain to send troops respectively to Lebanon and Jordan as a result of a fear that antigovernment forces assisted by the UAR might try to overthrow the two governments. The UAR immediately requested a Security Council meeting to consider the U.S. and British interventions, but during the subsequent meetings no consensuses were achieved. What finally brought about an end to the crisis were an agreement among the Lebanese internal groupings on a new neutralist president and a growing hostility between the UAR and Iraqi governments. After the crisis had in fact ended in late July 1958, the General Assembly passed a resolution in August calling on all states in the area to abide by the Arab League's principle of nonintervention. (Fahem Issa Qubain, Crisis in Lebanon [Washington: Middle East Institute, 1961]; Gerald L. Curtis, "The United Nations Observation Group in Lebanon," International Organization 18 [Autumn 1964]: 738-65; Hussein A. Hassouna, The League of Arab States and Regional Disputes, pp. 61-84.)

29. Nationalist China-Communist China, 1958 (C)

During August and September 1958 the Communist government threatened to invade the offshore islands of Quemoy and Matsu. When it began to make threatening statements and to mobilize its forces in the mainland areas close to the islands, the United States sent a large naval fleet to the Formosa Straits. At the end of August the Soviet Union declared that a brink-of-war situation existed, and the Chinese Communists declared that they would soon invade. These statements only prompted a further buildup of U.S. military power. The Peking government informally called an end to the crisis on October 1 when it proposed a truce for the area. (Oran R. Young, The Politics of

Force: Bargaining during International Crises [Princeton, N.J.:
Princeton University Press, 1968]; J. H. Kalicki, The Pattern of
Sino-American Crises: Political-Military Interactions in the 1950s,
pp. 168-208.)

30. India-Communist China, 1958-59 (W)

     In late 1958 and 1959 Chinese armed forces occupied a remote
mountainous region in Ladakh that the government claimed belonged
to China and that was needed to build a road between Tibet and Sink-
iang. India sent military patrols into the area, and they became involved in some armed clashes with the Chinese. India sought diplomatically to secure the withdrawal of the Chinese but was unsuccessful. (Dorothy Woodman, Himalayan Frontiers [New York: Frederick
A. Praeger, 1969], pp. 213-78; M. W. Fisher, L. E. Rose, R. A.
Huttenback, Himalayan Battleground: Sino-Indian Rivalry in Ladakh
[London: Pall Mall Press, 1963].)

31. Dominican Republic-Cuba and Venezuela, 1959 (MI)

     In June 1959 nearly 200 Dominican exiles and other Latin Amer-
ican revolutionaries invaded the Dominican Republic by plane and ship.
The Dominican Republic called for the establishment of an OAS investigatory body to verify its claims that Cuba and Venezuela were behind the armed invasion. Since many OAS members had a strong dis-
like for the Trujillo government and others were hesitant to back its
complaint, the Dominican Republic government soon realized that
OAS support was very unlikely, and it withdrew its request. (Jerome
Slater, The OAS and United States Foreign Policy, pp. 90-92; Gordon Connell-Smith, The Inter-American System, pp. 241-42; J. Lloyd
Mecham, The United States and Inter-American Security, 1889-1960,
pp. 414-15.)

32. Haiti-Cuba, 1959 (MI)

     In August 1959 thirty Haitian exiles and Cuban citizens, who had
come from Cuba, landed in Haiti with the intent of overthrowing the
Haitian government of President Duvalier. Haiti asked the Inter-American Peace Committee to investigate. While Haiti did not actually ac-
cuse Cuba of launching the invasion, it was certainly its intention that
there be some determination of Cuba's complicity. There was probably Cuban government assistance to the invaders since Cuba refused

entry to the IAPC, which was looking into the origins of the attack. Since the attack had been completely defeated, the IAPC dropped the case after it had visited Haiti and had been refused entry into Cuba. (David W. Wainhouse et al., International Peace Observation, pp. 194-95.)

33. Laotian Civil Strife (with North
Vietnamese Intervention), 1959 (W)

This initial stage of the internationalized civil war in Laos involved attacks by both Pathet Lao and North Vietnamese troops against forces of the pro-Western royal Laotian government in the northeast section of the country. The conflict was precipitated by the breakup of the tripartite neutralist government of rightist, neutralist, and communist factions in July 1958 and the accession to power of the rightist faction. These attacks during the summer led the Laotian government to ask the United Nations for a peacekeeping force to patrol the border. The Security Council debated the issue, and then sent a three-man investigatory committee to Laos (despite a Soviet vote against the resolution). While the UN committee was unable to verify the existence of significant North Vietnamese intervention, it did not undertake a thorough investigation. North Vietnamese were almost certainly involved in the fighting. (Paul F. Langer and Joseph J. Zasloff, North Vietnam and the Pathet Lao [Cambridge, Mass.: Harvard University Press, 1970], pp. 60-73; Mark W. Zacher, Dag Hammarskjold's United Nations [New York: Columbia University Press, 1970], pp. 102-6, 167-68.)

34. Paraguay-Argentina, 1959-60 (MI)

Paraguayan exiles living in Argentina frequently entered Paraguay and fought the armed forces of the authoritarian government of President Alfredo Stroessner. Minor clashes occurred between Paraguayan and Argentinian armed forces. Paraguay frequently complained of Argentinian as well as Cuban and Venezuelan support of the exile invasions. [Jerome Slater, The OAS and the United States Foreign Policy, p. 106.)

35. Congo-Belgium, 1960 (W)

On July 6 the Congolese army revolted against its Belgian officers and began to attack Belgian nationals in the country; and on July 8

Belgium sent troops to protect its nationals in the Congo. The Congolese government of Prime Minister Lumumba immediately accused Belgium of aggression, and it soon asked for UN military assistance to remove the Belgian forces. On July 14 the Security Council passed a resolution that called for the withdrawal of Belgian troops and the establishment of a UN force to restore law and order in the country. Belgium withdrew its forces from all parts of the Congo, apart from the province of Katanga, by the end of July, and it withdrew its contingents from the latter province (which had declared its independence from the Congo on July 11) in September. (Ernest W. Lefever, Crisis in the Congo: A U. N. Force in Action [Washington, D. C.: Brookings Institution, 1965]; idem, Uncertain Mandate: Politics of the U. N. Congo Operation [Baltimore: Johns Hopkins University Press, 1967].)

36. Congolese Civil Strife (with the Threat of Intervention by Western, Communist, and Nonaligned States, 1960-63 (C)

Soon after the revolt of the Congolese army, the Belgian intervention, and the Katangese secession, many governments recognized that the most fundamental threat to international peace was not the Belgian action but the possibility that a continued political fragmentation of the Congo would bring about interventions and counterinterventions—thus turning the Congo into an international battlefield. The crisis that lasted from July 1960 to January 1963 can be divided into three periods on the basis of the existence of certain major power centers in the Congo, each of which had important outside backers. From July 1960 to mid-September 1960 the two major political forces were the central government under the direction of Prime Minister Lumumba and the secessionist regime in Katanga under Moise Tshombe. The major supporters of Lumumba were the radical nonaligned states as well as the Soviet Union, and the most important supporters of Tshombe were Belgium, Britain, and France (or at least very important elements within the latter countries). From September 1960 to July 1961 there were three major centers of power: the central government under the control of President Joseph Kasavubu and General Mobutu, the secessionist regime in Katanga, and the radical forces of Prime Minister Lumumba and Antoine Gizenga. The central government under Mobutu and Kasavubu was backed by most of the members of the Western grouping, particularly the United States. At this time Belgium, Britain, and France favored both the retention of power by the Kasavubu-Mobutu forces in the central government and the Tshombe forces in Katanga. From August 1961 to January 1963 the two major political forces in the Congo were the central government under Prime Minister Adoula and the Katangese regime of Moise Tshombe. During this period there was a very tenuous alliance between the central government and the radical forces of Gizenga in Orientale Province.

From July 1960 to mid-September 1960 the majority of the members in the Western coalition supported the creation of the UN peacekeeping force (ONUC) because they felt that its role of preventing violence between Congolese groups would lead to the political integration of the country and thus would prevent external intervention on the side of different groups. By August, when the Lumumba government began to receive military equipment from the Soviet Union, the Western states began to view the central government with increasing alarm, and they therefore did not despair when he was overthrown by Kasavubu and Mobutu in September.

Subsequently, UN members became more vehemently divided in their views as to the course of action ONUC should pursue. The Soviet grouping and some nonaligned states proposed that ONUC restore Lumumba to power and that it reintegrate Katanga into the Congolese state. On the other hand, most Western countries felt that ONUC should confine itself to preventing outbreaks of violence since support for elected authorities or the reintroduction of constitutional rule would mean handing the reins of the central government to Lumumba. It was only after the announcement of Lumumba's death in January 1961 that the Western countries proved willing to see ONUC promote a return to constitutional rule. A Security Council resolution supporting a return to constitutional government in February 1961 was supported by the majority of Western and nonaligned countries and acquiesced in by the Soviet grouping, and it led to the formation of a new central government under Prime Minister Adoula in August 1961. All major groups except for the Katangese accepted the authority of the new government (although the support of the Gizenga forces in Orientale Province was rather tenuous.)

Before the central government was able to exert its authority over Katanga as a result of the UN military operation of December 1962-January 1963, the United Nations engaged in two unsuccessful military operations in Katanga in September 1961 and December 1961. The basic reason why it took from August 1961 to January 1963 to end the domestic and international crisis in the Congo was the reluctance of the Belgian, British, and French governments to see the Katangese secession collapse. However, the United States eventually persuaded them to accede to it. With the unification of the Congo the crisis disappeared although ONUC remained for another year and a half. (Ernest W. Lefever, Crisis in the Congo: A U.N. Force in Action [Washington, D.C.: Brookings Institution, 1965]; idem, Uncertain Mandate: Politics of the U.N. Congo Operation [Baltimore: Johns Hopkins University Press, 1967].)

37. Laotian Civil Strife (with North
Vietnamese Intervention), 1960-61 (W)

This was the second of the four stages of this internationalized
civil war (1959, 1960-61, 1963, 1964-75), and it was precipitated by
the overthrow of the rightist government by the neutralist General
Kong Le in August 1960 and the return to power of Prince Souvanna
Phouma the following month. A civil war then ensued in which the
rightist forces inflicted defeats on the neutralists. The neutralists
then made an alliance with the Communist Pathet Lao in November
1960, and this was followed by a vigorous military struggle between
the Pathet Lao and North Vietnamese forces, on the one hand, and
the rightist forces, on the other. As a result of Soviet and U.S. fears
regarding the conflict's escalation, the superpowers agreed in April
1961 to back a cease-fire, and this was followed by its acceptance by
the conflicting parties. In 1962 the three domestic factions and other
powers concerned with the situation met in Geneva and agreed on a
coalition government and Laotian neutrality. (Arthur J. Dommen,
Conflict in Laos [New York: Frederick A. Praeger, 1971], pp. 94-
200; Usha Mahajani, "U.S. Intervention in Laos and Its Impact on
Laotian Relations with Thailand and Vietnam," in Conflict and Stability
in Southeast Asia, ed. Mark W. Zacher and R. Stephen Milne [Garden
City, N.Y.: Doubleday, 1974], pp. 237-74; Paul F. Langer and
Joseph J. Zasloff, North Vietnam and the Pathet Lao, pp. 70-73.)

38. South Vietnamese Civil Strife (with North
Vietnamese, U.S., and Other Intervention), 1960-75 (W)

The South Vietnamese war, in which over 500,000 U.S. troops
as well as a large segment of the North Vietnamese army were involved, elicited UN debate on only one occasion. At the time of the
Gulf of Tonkin incident in 1964 the United States secured a Security
Council debate of the alleged North Vietnamese attack on U.S. ves-
sels, but as a result of the Soviet veto power was unable to secure
the passage of a resolution. There were many diplomatic discussions
about involving the organization, but they came to naught. Secretary-
General U Thant also initiated a number of private mediatory missions,
but they also were unsuccessful. The NLF and North Vietnamese finally achieved victory in 1975 after the U.S. forces were withdrawn.
(Lincoln P. Bloomfield, The UN and Vietnam [New York: Carnegie
Endowment for International Peace, 1968].)

39. Cuba-United States, 1961 (W)

The U.S.-sponsored invasion of Cuba by approximately 1,000 Cuban exiles occurred on April 17, 1961. The invasion at the Bay of Pigs was defeated within a period of several days. Premier Castro called on the United Nations to condemn the United States for its sponsorship of the armed intervention. While a sufficient number of UN members felt that the Cubans should be allowed to present their charges, the Western states had sufficient voting power in the organization to "bury" the issue in a committee of the General Assembly. It passed a very vague resolution requesting all states to try to remove tension in the area. (Haynes Johnson et al., The Bay of Pigs: The Leaders' Story of Brigade 2056 [New York: Norton, 1964].)

40. Kuwait-Iraq, 1961 (C)

On June 22, 1961, Kuwait became independent, and three days afterward Iraq claimed the entire territory of Kuwait and mobilized troops on the border. Kuwait then requested military protection from Saudi Arabia and Britain, and by July 7, 6,000 British troops had arrived. At a meeting of the UN Security Council the Soviet Union vetoed a U.K. resolution calling on Iraq to respect Kuwait's sovereignty. In August the Arab League met and admitted Kuwait as a member and called for an end to the Iraqi threat. It was also decided to establish an Arab League force to replace the British. A force of 3,300 was soon organized, and it remained there until 1963 when the overthrow of President Qassem ended the Iraqi threat. (Benjamin Schwadran, "The Kuwait Incident," Middle Eastern Affairs 13 [January 1962]: 2-13, and "The Kuwait Incident," Middle Eastern Affairs 13 [February 1962]: 43-53; Robert W. MacDonald, The League of Arab States [Princeton, N.J.: Princeton University Press, 1965], pp. 235-37; Hussein A. Hassouna, The League of Arab States and Regional Disputes, pp. 91-130.)

41. West Germany-East Germany (Berlin), 1961 (C)

In June 1961 serious tensions between the Western and Soviet groupings over the status of Berlin arose following a declaration by Premier Khrushchev that Berlin should be a neutral city, that the Western powers should withdraw, and that the permanent division of Germany should be accepted. During the following two months Western-Communist relations were very tense with respect to the Berlin question, and there were three occasions within a period of about a month when there were some indications of a possible armed clash. At no stage of this 1961 Berlin crisis was there any referral of the question to the United Nations although Secretary of State Dean Rusk did mention in late July that it would be referred if tensions increased. Tensions certainly did increase, but a UN meeting was never requested. (Jean Edward Smith, The Defense of Berlin [Baltimore: Johns Hopkins Press, 1963], pp. 235-67; Hans Speier, Divided Berlin [New York: Frederick A. Praeger, 1961], pp. 125-85; Robert M. Slusser, The Berlin Crisis of 1961: Soviet American Relations and the Struggle of Power in the Kremlin [Baltimore: Johns Hopkins University Press, 1973], pp. 77-178.)

42. Tunisia-France, 1961 (W)

This conflict mainly concerned Tunisia's attempt to secure the withdrawal of the French from the naval base at Bizerte, and to a lesser extent its claim to parts of Algeria. Following the refusal by France to vacate the base in the first half of 1961, Tunisia decided to cut off the water supply for the Bizerte base. French forces then moved out of the base and captured the town of Bizerte. Tunisia called for a meeting of the UN Security Council, and it called for a cease-fire and the withdrawal of troops (with France abstaining). The UN secretary-general and certain Western states then tried to mediate the conflict between the two parties but were unsuccessful. Following their failure Tunisia called for a meeting of the General Assembly in August, and that body requested French withdrawal from the base. Throughout the summer of 1961 France refused to compromise its position. Then, later in 1961, it agreed to complete French withdrawal from the base by 1963. (Werner Klaus Ruf, "The Bizerte Crisis: A Bourguibist Attempt to Resolve Tunisia's Border Problem," The Middle East Journal 25 [Spring 1971]: 201-11; Mark W. Zacher, Dag Hammarskjold's United Nations, pp. 148-50; Hussein A. Hassouna, The League of Arab States and Regional Disputes, pp. 141-62.)

43. Pakistan-Afghanistan, 1961 (W)

In September 1960 Pakistan carried out some repressive measures against Pathan tribesmen who were agitating for the union of their region with Afghanistan. Afghanistan condemned the Pakistani measures, and Pakistan accused Afghanistan of providing men and material to the dissidents. Relations between the two countries remained very tense and then in March 1961 several thousand tribesmen from Afghanistan (many of whom were government soldiers dressed in tribal dress) crossed the border in order to try to expel Pakistani soldiers from the Pathan region. The military conflict between the invaders and Pakistani troops continued until the fall of 1961 by which time the invaders were either defeated or withdrew into Afghanistan. The USSR backed Afghan claims. The United States and Britain were again quite active in seeking a diplomatic settlement. (James W. Spain, The Pathan Borderland, pp. 228-72; S. M. M. Qureshi, "Pakh-tunistan: The Frontier Dispute between Afghanistan and Pakistan," Pacific Affairs 39 [Spring-Summer 1966]: 99-114.)

44. Dominican Republic-United States, 1961 (C)

The OAS was very active in late 1961 in promoting democratic elections in the Dominican Republic, and it secured the cooperation of President Balaguer who had succeeded the autocratic General Tru-jillo after the latter's assassination in the spring of 1961. In mid-November 1961 rightist forces threatened to overthrow the Balaguer government and the United States then threatened to intervene if they attempted a coup d'etat. The U.S. government made verbal threats on November 18, and on November 19 it sent a number of warships off the Dominican Republic coast and some of its planes over Domin-ican Republic territory. On November 20 most of the members of the Trujillo family decided to leave the country. Cuba was the only Latin American government to condemn the U.S. threat, and it called for and obtained brief debates of the conflict by the OAS Council and the UN Security Council. Cuba's complaint was based on a fear of the implications of an international acceptance of U.S. military in-terventions in Latin America—and not on a sympathy with the Trujillo family. (Jerome Slater, "The United States, the Organization of American States, and the Dominican Republic 1961-1963," Interna-tional Organization 18 [Spring 1964]: 278; John Bartlow Martin, Over-taken by Events: The Dominican Crisis from the Fall of Trujillo to the Civil War [New York: Doubleday, 1966], pp. 82-83; Gordon Con-nell-Smith, The Inter-American System, p. 176.)

45. Portugal-India, 1961 (W)

The Indian invasion of the Portuguese enclaves of Goa, Damão, and Diu occurred on December 18, 1961 when an Indian military force of 30,000 troops began their successful attempt to integrate these areas into the Indian state. On the following day the conflict was brought to the UN Security Council by Portugal, and Portugal's Western allies submitted a resolution calling for a cease-fire that was vetoed by the Soviet Union. Following the defeat of this resolution and the Indian military victory there was no further attempt to involve the United Nations. (A. Mezerik, ed., Goa: Indian Takeover [New York: International Review Service, 1962].)

46. Netherlands-Indonesia, 1962 (C)

In January 1962 President Sukarno of Indonesia announced that an Indonesian invasion of the Dutch-held territory of West Irian or West New Guinea might take place. The Dutch were claiming at this time, as they had since the time of Indonesian independence in 1949, that West Irian was not an integral part of Indonesia. In February 1962 Sukarno ordered a military mobilization throughout Indonesia, and in March Indonesia began to send small armed units into West Irian. During the spring and summer of 1962 Ambassador Ellsworth Bunker of the United States acted as the UN secretary-general's personal mediator in negotiations with the two parties. At the same time, his activities were carried out just as much in the interests of the United States, which was concerned that the conflict's continuation could push Indonesia into greater cooperation with the Soviet Union and China. In August 1962 Bunker was able to conclude an agreement between the parties. It provided for the UN's administration of West Irian from October 1962 to October 1963 and its transfer of administration of the territory to Indonesia on the latter date. This agreement was then approved by the UN General Assembly. (Justus M. van der Kroef, "The West New Guinea Settlement: Its Origins and Implications," Orbis 7 [Spring 1963]: 120-49; Paul W. van der Veur, "The United Nations in West Irian: A Critique," International Organization 18 [Winter 1964]: 53-73.)

47. Cuba-United States, 1962 (C)

The crisis officially began on October 22, 1962 when President Kennedy announced that missile sites were being built in Cuba. The president then called for the removal of the missiles, and said that the United States would establish a strict quarantine against the introduction of any offensive military weapons into Cuba. He also called for meetings of the OAS and the UN Security Council. The Security Council was unable to initiate any action as a result of the Soviet-U.S. differences, but Secretary-General U Thant did play a modest role as a mediator. On the other hand, the OAS recommended that all members take action individually and collectively to insure that the government of Cuba did not continue to receive offensive weapons from the Soviet Union and to assure that the weapons already in Cuba did not become an active threat to the Western Hemisphere. The crisis was finally resolved on October 31 when the Soviet Union agreed to dismantle the missile sites and the United States agreed not to launch an invasion of Cuba. (Jerome Slater, The OAS and the United States Foreign Policy, pp. 161–64; M. Margaret Ball, The OAS in Transition [Durham, N. C.: Duke University Press, 1969], pp. 466–68; Gordon Connell-Smith, The Inter-American System, pp. 455–59; David W. Wainhouse et al., International Peace Observation, pp. 156–67; Elie Abel, The Missile Crisis [Philadelphia: J. B. Lippincott, 1966]; and Henry M. Pachter, Collision Course: The Cuban Missile Crisis and Peaceful Coexistence [New York: Praeger, 1966].)

48. India–China, 1962 (W)

In October 1962 Chinese troops invaded India in both the Northeast Frontier Agency and Ladakh. After several weeks of fighting the Chinese on November 8 offered a cease-fire plan. India rejected this, since it would have meant sacrificing territory. China then made further military gains in India, and on November 21 dramatically announced that it would withdraw to the lines it had proposed on November 8. Because of its militarily inferior position, India had to acquiesce in the Chinese occupation. During this war the United States provided strong backing to India, whereas the Soviet Union was outwardly very noncommittal. (Lorne J. Kavic, India's Quest for Security: Defense Policies, 1957–1965 [Berkeley: University of California Press, 1967], pp. 169–91; Alistair Lamb, The India-China Border [New York: Oxford University Press, 1964]; and Neville G. A. Maxwell, India's China War [Garden City, N. Y.: Anchor Books, 1972].)

49. Yemeni Civil Strife (with UAR and
Saudi Arabian Intervention), 1962–67 (W)

The incident that initiated the civil strife in the Yemen was the overthrow of the royalist government of the Imam by republican forces in September 1962. The UAR soon began to send military assistance to the republican government, and by 1965 the number of UAR troops in the Yemen was around 70, 000. During the fighting between 1962 and 1967 several thousand Saudi personnel (mainly technical personnel) entered the Yemen to assist the royalist forces. In early 1963 the United States sent Ambassador Ellsworth Bunker to try to negotiate a settlement. Largely due to Bunker's mediation, a disengagement agreement was signed by the UAR and Saudi Arabia in April 1963 that stipulated that a UN observer force should be created to check on the parties' compliance with the accord. In June 1963 the UN Security Council met to discuss the issue, and both created the observer force and called on the parties to comply with the disengagement agreement. The accord was in fact not complied with, and after a year, the UN observer mission was dissolved.

In early 1963 there was some talk among Arab states about involving the Arab League, but the secretary-general observed that a meeting would not be useful since there were two conflicting proposals for discussion. In 1964, 1965, and 1966 Saudi Arabia and the UAR came to agreements prior to or at the Arab summit meetings that called for disengagement and/or the creation of a coalition government, but these came to naught. The conferences themselves did not debate the issue. In August 1967, the UAR and Saudi Arabia came to a new disengagement agreement since Egypt had to bring its forces home after the Arab-Israeli war in June. An Arab summit conference then passed a resolution supporting the Egyptian-Saudi accord and created a three-nation commission to supervise the withdrawal of forces and assist the Yemeni parties in forming a new government. The civil war ended in 1968 when a reconstituted republican government defeated the royalists. (Dana Adams Schmidt, Yemen: The Unknown War [London: Bodley Head, 1968]; Malcolm Kerr, The Arab Cold War, 3d ed. [London: Oxford University Press, 1971], pp. 107-14, 139; Major General Carl von Horn, Soldiering for Peace [New York: David McKay, 1966], pp. 308-93; David W. Wainhouse et al., International Peace Observation, pp. 421-35; Hussein A. Hassouna, The League of Arab States and Regional Disputes, pp. 179-200.)

50. Upper Volta-Ghana, 1963 (W)

In the spring of 1963 Ghanaian forces occupied a 50-mile strip of land that had been controlled by Upper Volta. Upper Volta publicly objected to the occupation in 1963, but it was not until mid-1964 that it called for OAU action. At the July 1964 Assembly session, which passed a resolution favoring the maintenance of the existing boundaries in Africa, Ghana expressed a willingness to withdraw and to enter immediately into negotiations with Upper Volta to demarcate the border. The OAU Assembly then passed a resolution calling for negotiations between the two states on the basis of this statement. However, the Ghanaian government did not follow such a policy. The matter was again raised in an OAU forum in June 1965 when the OAU Council met to discuss Ghanaian subversion against its neighbors and the threat of many French-speaking West African states boycotting the Assembly meeting scheduled to be held in Accra in the fall of 1965. When Upper Volta raised the territorial issue during the meeting, Ghana reiterated its willingness to withdraw; and on this occasion the government complied with its stated intentions. (Saadia Touval, The Boundary Politics of Independent Africa, pp. 40-41, 86-90, 121, 158, 159.)

51. Haiti-Dominican Republic, April-May 1963 (C)

The crisis started on April 27 when Haitian officials occupied the Dominican Republic embassy in Haiti in which a large number of opponents of the Haitian regime had sought asylum. On the following day the Dominican Republic claimed that Haiti was undermining peaceful relations between the countries by this occupation of its embassy, by provocative statements, and by supporting opponents of the Dominican Republic regime. It then proceeded to mobilize its troops on the border with Haiti. At an OAS Council meeting on April 28, Haiti denied the Dominican Republic charges and claimed that the former country was planning to invade it. The United States at this point sent ships off the Haitian coast in order to evacuate its own nationals in case war broke out. The OAS created an investigative committee to look into the charges. During its short stay the committee was able to alleviate the conflict somewhat by its arrangement of the evacuation of the Dominican Republic diplomats in Haiti and by the transfer of the asylees to other embassies, but it did not look into other sources of friction. The crisis by no means disappeared, since the Dominican Republic was demanding that safe passage out of the country be given to all of the asylees. While Haiti offered safe passage to most of the asylees, it refused to give it to some.

On May 8, the OAS Council met again and created a new committee that had the power to look into all aspects of the conflict and to act as a mediator. At this time the United States as well as the Dominican Republic were supporting military sanctions against Haiti in order to overthrow the Duvalier dictatorship, but most of the Latin Americans were not receptive to collective intervention. Haiti also secured a meeting of the UN Security Council on May 8 to consider the conflict since it felt many OAS members were prejudiced against it, but the majority of Council members preferred OAS management of the crisis. The new OAS five-nation committee arrived in the Dominican Republic on May 13. During the next four days the Dominican Republic demobilized its troops, and Haiti gave safe passage to all but two of the asylees. (Robert D. Tomasek, "The Haitian-Dominican Republic Controversy of 1963 and the Organization of American States," Orbis 12 [Spring 1968]: 294-313; John Bartlow Martin, Overtaken by Events: The Dominican Crisis from Trujillo to the Civil War

[New York: Doubleday, 1966], pp. 416–47; R. St. J. Macdonald, "The Organization of American States in Action," University of Toronto Law Journal 15 [Spring 1964]: 414–23; Jerome Slater, The OAS and the United States Foreign Policy, pp. 217–34.)

52. Haiti–Dominican Republic, August 1963 (MI)

On August 5, 1963 a force of Haitian exiles entered Haiti from the Dominican Republic and occupied a small area. Haiti immediately charged that the invasion had been assisted by Dominican Republic authorities, and it called on the OAS to condemn the Dominican Republic government and to secure the removal of the exile force. The OAS committee that had been created to deal with the May crisis tried unsuccessfully to gain acceptance of a conciliation plan while sitting in Washington. It was only after Haiti claimed that a second invasion had taken place on August 12 that the Council finally requested that the committee leave for Haiti. At this time Haiti was insisting on a condemnation of the Dominican Republic, the acceptance of curbs on Haitian exiles by the Dominican Republic, and an OAS commission to patrol the border. The committee finally arrived in Haiti on August 23, and after several days it stated that it could not substantiate the charges of Dominican Republic complicity. Its judgment on this matter was almost certainly wrong. The presence of the committee did, however, discourage new interventions and it nearly persuaded the two countries to agree on a settlement of exile and asylee problems in mid-September. Its mediation failed when Haiti suddenly retracted its cooperation and took the conflict to the United Nations. The disputes disappeared after September 25 when the democratic Dominican Republic regime was overthrown by the military. (R. St. J. Macdonald, "The Organization of American States in Action," University of Toronto Law Journal 15 [Spring 1964]: 424–26; Juan Bosch, The Unfinished Experiment: Democracy in the Dominican Republic [New York: Praeger, 1965], pp. 188–89.)

53. Laotian Civil Strife (with North Vietnamese Intervention), 1963 (W)

This phase of the internationalized civil war in Laos began in February 1963 when Pathet Lao and North Vietnamese troops attacked the neutralist forces of General Kong Le, which supported the neutralist government of Prime Minister Souvanna Phouma. The fighting was waged intermittently from February 1963 through the summer of the same year, and the neutralist forces were defeated. It was this defeat that prompted the neutralist-rightist rapprochement of 1964. (Arthur J. Dommen, Conflict in Laos, rev. ed. [New York: Praeger, 1971], pp. 224-78; Nine S. Adams, Alfred W. McCoy, eds., Laos: War and Revolution [New York: Harper & Row, 1970], pp. 213-80.)

54. Algeria-Morocco, 1963 (W)

The conflict originated over Moroccan claims to parts of the Algerian Sahara. At the end of September 1963, Morocco sent military contingents into Algeria to occupy several areas, and following Morocco's refusal to withdraw, Algeria counterattacked during the second week of October. By October 14 a full-scale war had developed. Algeria soon called for OAU intervention, but Morocco rejected this suggestion. During the first week of the full-scale war, the Arab League called for a cease-fire and a withdrawal of troops behind the original boundary, and it also set up a mediatory commission. Morocco also rejected its involvement. Morocco soon called for the involvement of the UN Security Council—obviously hoping to secure Western backing for its position; but both France and the United States rejected this suggestion.

During the last week of October, Morocco and Algeria accepted the offer of mediation by Emperor Haile Selassie of Ethiopia and President Modibo Keita of Mali. At this time, Emperor Haile Selassie was able to offer his good offices not only in his own capacity but also on behalf of the OAU since he was then president of the OAU Assembly and since the OAU Provisional Secretariat was at that time entrusted to Ethiopia. At the meeting of the four heads of state in Bamako, Mali, an accord was drawn up that declared a cease-fire, created a military commission of the four states to establish a demilitarized zone, and called for an extraordinary meeting of the OAU Council of Ministers to set up a commission that would determine responsibility for the war and make proposals for the settlement of the dispute.

In mid-November, while Morocco was still objecting to withdrawal from certain occupied areas, the OAU Council approved the Bamako Agreement and set up a Special Committee of Seven to mediate the dispute. It also asked that all OAU members "scrupulously respect all the principles" in the OAU Charter, and this de facto meant that the Council upheld the principle of the integrity of existing boundaries contained in Article III (3). Following the Council meeting the major mediatory efforts to secure compliance with the Bamako Agreement were performed by the cease-fire committee, which, following the OAU resolution, came "under the aegis of the OAU" (Wild, p. 34). In February 1964, Morocco withdrew all its forces. (Patricia

Berko Wild, "The Organization of African Unity and the Algeria-Moroccan Border Conflict," International Organization 20 [Winter 1966]: 18-36; Saadia Touval, The Boundary Politics of Independent Africa, pp. 132-33; Hussein A. Hassouna, The League of Arab States and Regional Disputes, pp. 211-35.)

55. Venezuela-Cuba, 1963 (MI)

During the latter part of the 1963 Venezuela complained that Cuba had landed both guerrillas and arms shipments in its country. In December 1963, the OAS Council met on the matter and established an investigation committee. In February 1964 the committee substantiated the Venezuelan charges. Venezuela wanted further sanctions applied against Cuba, but the OAS did not act on the request as a result of opposition from some Latin American states. It was not until the military coup in Brazil in April 1964, which brought that country into the anti-Cuban camp, that further action against Cuba was feasible. Condemnation of the Cuban subversion in Venezuela and the initiation of additional sanctions were passed at a meeting of foreign ministers in July 1964. (Jerome Slater, The OAS and the United States Foreign Policy, pp. 167-72; David W. Wainhouse et al., International Peace Observation, pp. 175-79; M. Margaret Ball, The OAS in Transition, pp. 468-71.)

56. Dahomey-Niger, 1963-64 (C)

The major cause of the December 1963-January 1964 crisis was an attempt on the part of President Diori of Niger to help his old friend Hubert Maga regain power in Dahomey, and a minor cause was a dispute over an island in the Niger River. When the government of Dahomey discovered the subversive assistance to its internal enemies, it closed the border between the two countries and thus blocked the transit of many goods into and from Niger. Niger then expelled several thousand citizens of Dahomey, and then both sides mobilized forces along the border. They were deterred from initiating military action by the warnings of the French government. During the crisis Dahomey threatened to take the conflict to the UN Security Council, but it was discouraged from doing so by France and a number of other French West African governments that offered their mediatory services. In the immediate aftermath of the crisis and then several times during the following year, other French-speaking West African governments (members of the UAM and "Conseil d'Entente") mediated various aspects of the conflict. (Saadia Touval, The Boundary Politics

of Independent Africa, pp. 41, 121, 198-203; I. William Zartman,
International Relations in the New Africa [Englewood Cliffs, N.J.:
Prentice-Hall, 1966], p. 104.)

57. Cypriot Civil Strife (with Threat of
Turkish and Greek Intervention), 1963-64 (C)

The crisis was prompted by the decision of the Cypriot government of President Makarios to seek a revision of the 1960 constitution
that gave a veto over any constitutional change or major policy questions to both the Greek community (80 percent of the island's population) and the Turkish community (20 percent). The decision of the
Makarios government to alter the constitution led to severe tensions
between the two communal groups, and finally on December 21 serious
fighting broke out. By December 25, the threat of Turkish intervention and the pressure of the Western Great Powers led the two conflicting groups to agree to a cease-fire. The agreement was mediated
by the British, and was then policed by the British force. Immediately
after the establishment of the fragile cease-fire the Greek Cypriot
government requested and secured a meeting of the UN Security Council. Since the threat of war had subsided (although not disappeared)
and since many states (particularly NATO members) did not want to
take sides, no resolution was passed. During January and February
1964 there were sporadic outbreaks of violence between the two groups,
and the threat of renewed large-scale fighting and hence external intervention continued. During this time period there were negotiations
about replacing the British troops with a NATO or UN force. The
Greek Cypriot government as well as the communist and nonaligned
states supported a UN force. On March 4, 1964 a UN force was approved by the Security Council, and a UN mediator was also created
to try to achieve a settlement of the issue. (James A. Stegenga, The
United Nations Force in Cyprus [Columbus: Ohio State University
Press, 1968]; Robert Stevens, Cyprus, A Place of Arms: Power Politics and Ethnic Conflict in the Eastern Mediterranean [New York:
Praeger, 1966].)

58. Rwanda-Burundi, 1963-64 (MI)

The roots of the conflict were the intertribal antagonism between the tribal groups in power in the two countries (the Hutu in
Rwanda and the Tutsi in Burundi) and the existence of a large group
of Tutsi in Burundi who had fled from Rwanda. The Burundi government gave economic and military assistance to the Tutsi exiles from

Rwanda and encouraged their desire to overthrow the Rwandan government. While Burundi had a very traditional monarchical government, it adopted an external policy of nonalignment and support of revolution in order to encourage Chinese assistance. In November and December 1963, the antagonism erupted into military violence when several hundred Tutsi refugees crossed into Rwanda. Rwanda claimed that Burundi had supported the armed intervention, and Burundi countered that Rwanda was inciting the Tutsi by its suppression of their tribal brethren in Rwanda. Burundi complained to the secretaries-general of the OAU and the United Nations about Rwanda's provocative behavior. The OAU secretary-general just declared that the two parties should try to settle their differences, but the UN secretary-general sent a special representative who during 1964 obtained agreement from the two states to take measures to alleviate the situation. (Rene Lemarchand, Rwanda and Burundi [London: Pall Mall Press, 1970], pp. 383-401; Tareq Y. Ismael, "The People's Republic of China and Africa," The Journal of Modern African Studies 9 [December 1971]: 516-17; Berhanykun Andemicael, The OAU and the UN [New York: Africana, 1976], p. 63.)

59. Malaysia-Indonesia, 1963-65 (W)

Indonesia's opposition to the union of the British-controlled North Borneo territories with Malaya was set forth in early 1963, and by August it was sending guerrila contingents into North Borneo in order to discourage the formation of the Federation of Malaysia. After the formation of the federation on September 16, 1963, Indonesia continued to send bands of soldiers into North Borneo and to threaten a much larger invasion, and it was not until the overthrow of the Sukarno government in September 1965 that the fighting ended. During the two-year conflict British and Australian troops assisted the Malaysian army. In September 1963 there was an investigation by a committee created by the UN secretary-general to determine the preferances of the populations of the North Borneo territories on the federation, but the only occasion the issue was debated in the United Nations was in September 1964. At that time a Security Council resolution calling on the Indonesians to halt their activities was vetoed by the USSR. (L. C. Greene, "Indonesia, the U.N. and Malaysia," Journal of Southeast Asian History 6 [September 1975]: 71-86; J. A. C. Mackie, Konfrontasi: The Indonesia-Malaysia Dispute, 1963-1966 [New York: Oxford University Press, 1974].)

60. Ethiopia-Somalia, 1964 (W)

This conflict occurred because of Somalia's claim to that part of eastern Ethiopia occupied by Somali tribesmen. In the latter part of 1963 and January 1964, Somali tribesmen known as shifta conducted intermittent raids into the eastern part of Ethiopia. Then, on February 7, 1964 the military forces of Somalia launched a large attack against Ethiopia. While Somalia requested certain heads of African states to intervene as mediators, it also requested intervention by the UN Security Council. This tack met with failure when both the Soviet Union and the UN secretary-general requested that the parties seek to settle their problem within an intra-African context. On February 9 Ethiopia called for consideration of the conflict by the OAU Council of Ministers, and this was followed by a similar request by Somalia the following day. The Council of Ministers met between February 12 and 14 and called for a cease-fire, requested the parties to enter into negotiations to settle their conflict, and asked all African states with diplomatic or consular missions in the two states to assist the parties in implementing the cease-fire. The Council at a latter meeting in Lagos on February 24 reiterated these requests, but it also asked the two states to settle their conflict in conformity with Article III (3) of the Charter (which supported the territorial integrity of African states). Ethiopia wanted the Council to take an explicit stand on the conflict, but the members, being hesitant to alienate any members and thus weaken the Organization, refused to criticize the Somali claims and actions. During March, President Abboud of the Sudan secured the adherence of the parties to a cease-fire along the original boundary. (Catherine Hoskyns, ed., Case Studies in African Diplomacy: II—The Ethiopia-Somali-Kenya Dispute, 1960-1967 [Dar Es Salaam, Tanzania: Oxford University Press, 1969]; Saadia Touval, The Boundary Politics of Independent Africa, pp. 111-12, 117-18, 133-53, 212-23.)

61. Kenya-Somalia, 1964 (MI)

There developed concurrently with the Somali-Ethiopian conflict, a conflict between Somalia and Kenya over Somali claims to the Northeastern Province of Kenya. Following Kenya's independence in December 1963, large-scale interventions by Somali shifta began. When Ethiopia requested in February 1964 that the OAU Council of Ministers act on the Somali invasion of its territory, Kenya requested that the Council also consider the incursions of Somali tribesmen into its territory. At its first meeting, the Council called on these two states to cease further provocative actions and to settle their dispute peacefully. At the second meeting, the Council reiterated its previous requests, but it also requested that the two states take Article III (3) of the OAU Charter into account in their negotiations. This was an indirect way of supporting the Kenyan position. As occurred in the Somalia-Ethiopia conflict, the armed raids of large groups of shifta ceased after February 1964, but they began again in mid-1965. (Catherine Hoskyns, ed., Case Studies in African Diplomacy: II—The Ethiopia-Somali-Kenya Dispute, 1960-1967; Saadia Touval, The Boundary Politics of Independent Africa, pp. 144-53, 213-22.)

62. Gabon-France, 1964 (W)

On February 17, 1964, President Léon Mba of Gabon was overthrown by a group within the armed forces, and a new government was immediately formed that was headed by Mba's political rival, Jean-Hilaire Aubame. On February 18 and 19, French troops arrived in the capital from Senegal and Congo (Brazzaville) and from a base inside Gabon, and on February 19 they succeeded in overthrowing the new government and reinstating President Mba in power on February 20. As far as can be determined, the political forces that took over the Gabon government following the coup did not have a different orientation to international security politics from that of the government of President Mba. (Brian Weinstein, Gabon: Nation Building on the Ogooue [Cambridge, Mass.: M.I.T. Press, 1966], pp. 147-54, 174-78; Immanuel Wallerstein, Africa: The Politics of Unity [New York: Random House, 1967], pp. 77-78.)

63. Ethiopian Civil Strife (with
Sudanese Intervention), 1964-65 (MI)

The origin of the conflict between the Sudan and Ethiopia lies in the formation of the Eritrean Liberation Front (ELF) in the early 1960s by Moslems (and a few Christians) who favored the secession of Eritrea from Ethiopia. While there was a great deal of sympathy in the Sudan for the ELF from the beginning of the rebellion, large-scale assistance did not begin until the overthrow of President Abboud in October 1964. The policy of the Sudanese government of offering sanctuaries, training facilities, and equipment to the ELF forces led to a number of incursions by Ethiopian troops into Sudanese territory to attack the ELF camps. The conflict at this time was exacerbated by the Ethiopian claim to a small area of Sudanese territory, but this claim was basically an attempt on the part of the Ethiopian government to discourage assistance by the Sudanese government for the

Eritrean rebels. With the formation of a new Sudanese government
in June 1965, the Sudan ended its policy of active assistance. Talks
resulted in an accord at the end of July 1965 whereby the two states
agreed to prohibit the existence on their territory of groups hostile
to the other's government. (Saadia Touval, The Boundary Politics of
Independent Africa, p. 143; Ethiopawi, "The Eritrean-Ethiopian Conflict," in Ethnic Conflict in International Relations, ed. Astri Suhrke
and Lela Garner Noble [New York: Praeger, 1977], p. 138.)

64. Congolese (Leopoldville) Civil Strife (with
Intervention by Burundi and Congo (Brazzaville),
1964-65 (MI)

The rebellion of radical groupings in the Congo began in early
1964 and was under the direction of a coordinating body entitled
"Conseil Nationale de Libération." During the first part of the year
direct assistance to the rebels in the form of training and staging
camps and equipment came largely from Congo (Brazzaville) and
Burundi. With the appointment of Moise Tshombe as prime minister
of the Congo in July and his importation of foreign mercenaries and
U.S. military assistance, some material assistance also began to
flow from the Sudan and Uganda.
In September 1964 the OAU Council called on the Congolese government to terminate the use of mercenaries, requested all parties
to cease hostilities, asked all Congolese political leaders to seek a
national reconciliation, requested all outside parties to abstain from
all action that might aggravate the conflict, and established an ad hoc
commission of ten states to promote national reconciliation and a
normalization of relations between the Congo and its neighbors. In
the next two months the OAU commission failed in its mediatory attempts largely because Tshombe refused to cooperate, owing to his
resentment of the commission's friendly reception of a rebel delega-
tion and its attempts to secure an end to Western assistance to his
government. The situation became worse following the United States's
airlifting of Belgian paratroopers into the Stanleyville area to rescue
Western hostages at the end of November. In December 1964 and
early 1965 both the OAU commission and the Council of Ministers
sought to deal with the situation, but the differences among the African states impeded any common stand. (Berhanykun Andemicael,
The OAU and the UN, pp. 65-73; Yashpal Tandon, "The Organization
of African Unity as an Instrument and Forum of Protest," in Protest
and Power in Black Africa, ed. Robert I. Rotberg and Ali A. Mazrui
[New York: Oxford University Press, 1970], pp. 1155-64, 1173-78;
Catherine Hoskyns, Case Studies in African Diplomacy: I—The Or-

ganization of African Unity and the Congo Crisis, 1964-65 [Dar Es Salaam, Tanzania: Oxford University Press, 1969]; Immanuel Wallerstein, Africa: The Politics of Unity [New York: Random House, 1967], pp. 88-108.)

65. Niger-Ghana, 1964-65 (MI)

In 1964 and 1965 there were complaints by a number of West African countries that Ghana was engaging in subversive activities in their countries, but there only appears to be evidence of fairly large groups being sent into Niger. Several large groups of exiles entered the country in late 1964, and smaller groups entered after that period. Then, on April 13, 1965 there was an attempt on the life of President Diori of Niger by an individual who had been trained in Ghana. At a meeting of OCAM in May, eight French-speaking West African states declared that they would refuse to attend the OAU Assembly meeting in Accra in September if Ghana did not expel the political exiles. Nigeria then called for and secured a special meeting of the OAU Council of Ministers in Lagos in June to discuss the matter. Under considerable diplomatic pressure and fearful that the absence of the French-speaking West African states at the Assembly meeting in Accra would be a considerable political embarrassment, Ghana declared it would expel all political exiles. The OAU Council then passed a resolution in which the promises of the Ghanaian government were noted and all member states were urged to attend the fall meeting of the Assembly. While the subversive activities of Ghana significantly decreased, it did not expel the exiles. This led eight French-speaking West African countries to boycott the Assembly meeting. At the Assembly meeting in October, the issue was implicitly considered when the members passed a resolution against various types of subversion. All subversion terminated with the overthrow of President Nkrumah in February 1966. (W. Scott Thompson, Ghana's Foreign Policy, 1957-1966: Diplomacy, Ideology and the New State [Princeton, N.J.: Princeton University Press, 1969], pp. 365-66, 374-79; Berhanykun Andemicael, The OAU and the UN, pp. 86-87.)

66. Laotian Civil Strife (with North Vietnamese, South Vietnamese, and Thai Intervention), 1964-75 (W)

This last stage of the internationalized civil war in Laos was between Laotian forces aligned with the United States on the one hand and with the Soviet Union and Communist China on the other. The accord between the neutralist and rightist factions in May 1964 stated that the rightist grouping was going to be dissolved, but de facto the neutralists joined the rightists in their dependence on the United States and Thailand. Following this accord the Thai government sent several thousand troops into Laos to assist the government forces against the Pathet Lao, and the United States sent military supplies and advisers to the government forces and carried out considerable bombing raids against the communist troops. South Vietnamese forces also carried out attacks (one large one in 1971) against North Vietnamese forces in Laos. In 1973 a cease-fire accord was signed. In 1974 a coalition government was formed and Thai troops withdrew. By 1975 the Pathet Lao with North Vietnamese assistance controlled the country. (Usha Mahajani, "U.S. Intervention in Laos and Its Impact on Laotian Relations with Thailand and Vietnam," in Conflict and Stability in Southeast Asia, ed. Mark W. Zacher and R. Stephen Milne [Garden City, N.Y.: Doubleday, 1974], pp. 237-74; Fred Branfman, "Presidential War in Laos," in Laos: War and Revolution, ed. Nina S. Adams and Alfred W. McCoy [New York: Harper & Row, 1970], pp. 213-80.)

67. Dominican Republic Civil Strife
(with U.S. Intervention), 1965 (W)

The civil conflict itself began on April 24, 1965 when those Dominicans loyal to former President Juan Bosch ("the Constitutionalists") overthrew the government of President Reid Cabral and tried to restore Bosch to power. The forces supporting the status quo ("the Loyalists"), which were led by the army, immediately counterattacked, and a civil war ensued (largely in the capital region). On April 28, the United States landed 400 marines under the pretext of protecting its nationals on the island, but the real reason was a U.S. fear that the Constitutionalists were strongly influenced by communists. By May 2 there were 14,000 U.S. troops in the country and by the end of the third week in May, 24,000.

On April 30 the United States called for an OAS meeting, and on May 1 it created a five-man committee to seek a cease-fire agreement. While many of the Latin American states were very irritated that they had not been consulted by the United States before its intervention, the majority of them (including some democratic states such as Venezuela and Costa Rica) shared the U.S. concern about communist influence in the rebel movement. On May 5 the parties accepted an initial cease-fire that was negotiated by the papal nuncio, and on the following day the OAS Council approved the creation of an Inter-American Peace Force to replace the U.S. force in the country. This was passed over the opposition of five states. This force finally came into operation during the last week of May with contingents from Honduras, Nicaragua, Costa Rica, Brazil, and El Salvador, but a large majority of troops continued to be from the United States. On May 12, the OAS, faced with periodic breakdowns in the cease-fire and no progress by the parties on a future government, abolished its five-man committee and asked its secretary-general, José Mora, to be its mediator.

During the first several weeks of May the United Nations also became involved in the conflict. The first of the Security Council's 30 meetings during the period May–June was held on May 3 at the request of the USSR. The first several meetings produced no resolutions as a result of Soviet insistence on a condemnation of the U.S. action and U.S. support for a resolution backing OAS activities. Finally, on May 14 the Security Council passed a resolution calling on the parties to accept a cease-fire and asking the secretary-general to establish a UN representative who would report to the Council on developments and would promote a cease-fire. While the UN representative was helpful in securing a cease-fire on a number of occasions and the Security Council reiterated its support for the cease-fire, the United Nations remained tangential to the management of the conflict.

At the beginning of June the OAS replaced José Mora as a mediator with a three-man committee (the most important member being U.S. representative, Ellsworth Bunker). By the last week of June the committee was able to secure agreement on the creation of a provisional government and the eventual holding of elections. During the summer of 1965 and during the period September to June 1966 when elections were finally held, the United States, the OAS membership in general, and the Peace Force on several occasions had to put significant pressure on the Dominican Republic factions, particularly the military, to respect the rule of the provisional government and the organization of democratic elections. In these elections in June 1966, the conservative candidate, Joaquim Balabuer, defeated the progressive forces of Juan Bosch. (Jerome Slater, Intervention and Negotiation: The United States and the Dominican Revolution [New York: Harper & Row, 1970]; Jerome Slater, "The Limits of Legitimization in International Organizations: The Organization of American States and the Dominican Crisis," International Organization 23 [Winter 1969]: 48–72; Dona Baron, "The Dominican Republic Crisis of 1965: A Case Study of the Regional vs the Global Approach to International Peace and Security," in Columbia Essays in International Affairs (III): The Dean's Paper 1967, ed. Andrew W. Cordier [New York: Columbia University Press, 1968], pp. 1–37; Tad Szulc, Dominican Diary [New York: Delacorte Press, 1965]; Yale H. Ferguson, "The Dominican Intervention of 1965: Recent Interpretations," International Organization 27 [Autumn 1973]: pp. 517–48.)

68. Chadian Civil Strife (with Sudanese
Intervention), 1965 (MI)

In early 1965 the new provisional Sudanese government began
to assist the Moslem rebels in the eastern and northern parts of Chad
who were fighting for political control of the country with the pagan
and Christian populations from the southern part. Apart from offering
sanctuaries and equipment to the Chadian rebels, the Sudanese also
allowed the rebels to organize an "Islamic Government of Chad in Exile." In the spring of 1965 President Ngarta Tombalbaye of Chad publicly condemned the Sudanese actions and called for their cessation.
In June 1965 a new government came to power in the Sudan, and in
talks between the two countries from June 29 to July 1 the Sudanese
government committed itself to expel Chadians involved in subversive
activity and to dissolve all Chadian political movements on their territory. (Africa Report 10 [August 1965]: 24; Saadia Touval, The
Boundary Politics of Independent Africa, pp. 42-43, 107-8.)

69. India-Pakistan, April-May 1965 (W)

The first Indo-Pakistani war in 1965 broke out on April 23 when
Pakistan launched an attack involving several thousand troops in the
Rann of Kutch. After several weeks of fighting the British were able
to assist the parties in agreeing to a cease-fire. During the fighting
the United States and the Soviet Union adopted very impartial positions
with respect to the claims of the two sides since they were particularly
worried that any favoritism toward India would drive Pakistan into
closer cooperation with China. (G. W. Choudhury, Pakistan's Relations with India, 1947-60 [New York: Praeger, 1965], pp. 276-78;
S. M. Burke, Pakistan's Foreign Policy: An Historical Analysis
[London: Oxford University Press, 1973], pp. 318-57; Josef Korbel,
Danger in Kashmir, rev. ed. [Princeton, N.J.: Princeton University
Press, 1966], pp. 337-38.)

70. India-Pakistan, August-September 1965 (W)

The second Indo-Pakistani war in 1965 began in early August
when Pakistan began to infiltrate large numbers of men into Kashmir
in order to foment a revolt by the Moslem population against the Indian authorities. The Pakistani infiltrators engaged in numerous
clashes with the Indian army. The war escalated significantly on
August 28 when Indian contingents attacked Pakistani troops who were
said to be preparing an invasion of India to support the activities of

the Pakistani infiltrators. Pakistan soon counterattacked. China
soon threatened to enter the war on the side of Pakistan. On both September 4 and September 6 the UN Security Council called for a cease-
fire and a withdrawal of the armed forces. This was followed by an
abortive attempt by UN Secretary-General U Thant to mediate the conflict. On September 20, the Security Council reiterated its call for a
cease-fire, and on September 22 Pakistan accepted the resolution.
By September 25 the fighting had generally come to an end, and this
was followed by the Security Council's augmentation of the UN military
observer group in Kashmir that was directed to supervise the withdrawal of the parties behind the cease-fire line. The cessation of the
fighting was facilitated by both the failure of the Pakistani army to
achieve a military victory and the diplomatic and economic pressure
applied on both conflicting parties by the Western Great Powers and
the Soviet Union. (G. W. Choudhury, Pakistan's Relations with India,
1947-60, pp. 279-304; S. M. Burke, Pakistan's Foreign Policy: An
Historical Analysis, pp. 318-57; Josef Korbel, Danger in Kashmir,
pp. 338-46.)

71. Ethiopia-Somalia, 1965-67 (MI)

     Between mid-1965 and mid-1967 there were regular raids by
Somali shifta into Ethiopia. There was no formal OAU involvement
in the conflict, but at the September 1967 session of the OAU Assembly the emperor of Ethiopia and the prime minister of Somalia met
and agreed that their governments should enter into negotiations for
the purposes of settling their dispute and normalizing their relations.
While there was no final settlement of the territorial issue, the gov-
ernment-supported raids from Somalia ceased. (Catherine Hoskyns,
ed., Case Studies in African Diplomacy: II—The Ethiopia-Somalia-
Kenya Dispute, 1960-1967; Saadia Touval, The Boundary Politics of
Independent Africa, pp. 226-45.)

72. Kenya-Somalia, 1965-67 (MI)

     Between mid-1965 and mid-1967 there were regular raids of
Somali shifta into Kenya, and President Kenyatta of Kenya stated that
his country was on "a war basis with Somalia." In December 1965,
President Nyerere of Tanzania sought unsuccessfully to mediate the
conflict, and in September 1967 President Kaunda of Zambia initiated
a comparable attempt. This latter initiative succeeded. The parties
promised to cease provocative acts and to restore normal relations,
and their agreement was given the formal blessing of the OAU Assem-

bly at its September 1967 session. (Catherine Hoskyns, ed., Case Studies in African Diplomacy: II—The Ethiopia-Somali-Kenya Dispute, 1960-1967; Saadia Touval, The Boundary Politics of Independent Africa, pp. 223-26.)

73. Chadian Civil Strife (with Sudanese Intervention), 1966 (MI)

On August 7, 1966 President Tombalbaye of Chad accused the Sudanese of providing sanctuaries and assistance to Chadian Moslem rebels who were conducting large-scale raids across the border. He gave the Sudan two weeks in which to expel all the "Moslem bandits" from Sudanese territory. When on August 22 Sudan denied his allegations, he ordered a closing of their border, restricted the movement of Sudanese nationals in Chad, and ordered the army to open fire on any Sudanese aircraft overflying Chad. During the following months there were more rebel attacks on Chad, and there were also incursions of Chadian troops into the Sudan. President Hamani Diori of Niger offered to mediate the conflict, and from October 10 to 14 he met with representatives of the two countries and obtained commitments from them to adhere to previous accords. (Africa Report 11 [October 1966]: 32; Saadia Touval, The Boundary Politics of Independent Africa, pp. 42-43, 107-8.)

74. Jordanian Civil Strife (with Syrian Intervention), 1966 (MI)

In the fall of 1966 Syria was particularly antagonistic toward Jordan since it had given asylum to a Syrian general who had been involved in an attempt to overthrow the Syrian government. In November 1966 Syria sent an armed contingent to assist an antigovernment rebellion in Jordan, but it was withdrawn following the defeat of the antigovernment forces. (Kessing's Contemporary Archives, January 14-21, 1967, p. 21820.)

75. Ghana and Ivory Coast-Guinea, 1966 (C)

In March 1966 Guinea threatened to invade Ghana through the intervening territory of the Ivory Coast. The development that precipitated this crisis was the overthrow of Ghana's President Nkrumah on February 24 while Nkrumah was out of the country. Since President Touré of Guinea and President Nkrumah were ideological allies,

Nkrumah flew to Guinea on March 2 to look into the possibility of mobilizing Guinean support for his return to power. On March 6 President Touré declared that the Guinean army and 50,000 ex-servicemen
would enter Ghana in order to restore Nkrumah to power, and following this declaration the government of the Ivory Coast declared that
Guinean troops were massing on the border. During the following
several weeks the president of the Ivory Coast declared that France
had committed itself to intervene if Guinean troops crossed the border, and officials from the Ivory Coast and Ghana consulted regarding the Guinean threat. After several weeks the Guinean troops were
withdrawn from the border. (Africa Report 11 [April 1966]: 37; and
[May 1966]: 42; W. A. E. Skurnik, "Ghana and Guinea, 1966—A Case
Study in Inter-African Relations," The Journal of Modern African
Studies 5 [November 1967]: 374.)

76. Rwanda-Burundi, 1966 (MI)

The armed incursions of Tutsi tribesmen from Burundi into
Rwanda started in September 1966 and continued on a regular basis
into December. At a meeting of the OAU Council of Ministers in the
first week of November 1966, the foreign minister of Rwanda accused
the government of Burundi of supporting and encouraging the armed
bands of Tutsi exiles, and his counterpart from Burundi claimed that
the actions of the Tutsi were due to the murder of many of their tribal
brethren in Rwanda. The Council of Ministers asked President Mobutu of Congo-Kinshasa to mediate the conflict. Soon after the mediatory mission was formed by the Congo on November 18, the monarchical system in Burundi, which was headed by the mwami, was overthrown by a group under Captain Michel Micombero. This development facilitated the Congolese mediatory mission since Micombero
feared the Tutsi exiles because of the attachment of many of them to
the overthrown mwami. Also, Micombero was worried about the possible invasion of Burundi by Hutu exiles in Rwanda, and did not want
to antagonize the Rwanda government. In March 1967 President Mobutu of the Congo met with his counterparts from Rwanda and Burundi,
and they agreed that all refugees could return to their homes and that
they must give up their arms. During the following months the Congolese army helped to disarm and resettle the refugees. (Berhanykun
Andemicael, Peaceful Settlement among African States: Roles of the
United Nations and the Organization of African Unity [New York: U.N.
Institute for Training and Research, 1972], pp. 64-75.)

77. Venezuela-Cuba, 1967 (MI)

In the first week of May 1967, Venezuela complained about the landing of a boatload of commandos with weapons on its territory, and said that they had been sent from Cuba. During the first week of June 1967, it called for a meeting of the OAS to consider Cuban subversion in Venezuela and in Latin America generally. The OAS Council formed an investigative committee, and in a report issued at the beginning of August it substantiated the charges of Venezuela and other states against Cuba. The Council condemned the Cuban activities and reiterated its support for sanctions. (M. Margaret Ball, The OAS in Transition, pp. 480-82; D. Bruce Jackson, Castro, the Kremlin and Communism in Latin America [Baltimore: Johns Hopkins University Press, 1969], pp. 68-119.)

78. Arab States-Israel, 1967 (W)

On May 16 a threat of war commenced as a result of the UAR's request for the withdrawal of UNEF along the UAR-Israeli border. UN Secretary-General U Thant decided to withdraw all of the UNEF forces from the UAR. The tension in the area increased when on May 22 the UAR stated that it would bar Israeli ships from entering or leaving the Gulf of Aqaba. On May 24 the UN Security Council discussed the crisis, but did not pass a resolution as a result of Soviet backing for the UAR and Western backing for Israel. Following a breakdown of international negotiations Israel attacked its Arab neighbors on June 5. The UN Security Council began a series of meetings on June 6, and between June 6 and 9 passed three resolutions calling for a cease-fire. By the latter date, when a cease-fire was accepted, Israel was occupying most of the Sinai Peninsula in the UAR, the area to the west of the Jordan River in Jordan, and the Golan Heights in Syria. During the latter part of June a special session of the General Assembly considered the conflict but did not reach an accord. Finally, on November 22, 1967 the Security Council passed a resolution that generally called for Israeli withdrawal from Arab territories and the Arab states' recognition of Israel. The resolution also created a UN mediator but he was unable to secure a settlement. (Arthur Lall, The U.N. and Middle East Crisis, 1967 [New York: Columbia University Press, 1968]; Walter Z. Laqueur, The Road to War, 1967 [London: Weidenfeld and Nicolson, 1968]; and Nadav Safran, From War to War: The Arab-Israeli Confrontation, 1948-1967 [New York: Pegasus, 1969].)

79. Cypriot Civil Strife (with Threat of
Turkish Intervention), 1967 (C)

The crisis originated on November 15, 1967 when Greek Cypriots resumed police patrols in a Turkish Cypriot village and were
fired on by Turkish Cypriots. The Greek Cypriots then launched an
attack that killed 27 Turkish Cypriots. The Turkish government immediately obtained authority from its parliament to send troops
abroad, mobilized its troops, and sent ships off the Cypriot coast.
Cyprus called for and obtained a meeting of the UN Security Council
on November 24. While the Council members were unable to formu-
late a substantive resolution, they agreed to support the mediation of
the UN secretary-general. In fact, the most important mediator was
the U.S. envoy, Cyrus Vance, who spent a month in Cyprus and secured agreement on a number of matters exacerbating relations between the local Greek and Turkish Cypriot communities and their respective Greek and Turkish allies. (James A. Stegenga, The United
Nations Force in Cyprus [Columbus: Ohio State University Press,
1968], pp. 191-94; Nancy Crawshaw, "Cyprus after Kophinou,"
World Today 24 [October 1968]: 428-35.)

80. Czechoslovakia-USSR et al., 1968 (W)

The invasion of Czechoslovakia occurred on August 20, 1968
when the troops from the Soviet Union, East Germany, Poland, and
Bulgaria entered the country. They soon forced a change in the government. The conflict was immediately brought to the United Nations
where it was debated in the Security Council between August 21 and
24. At the end of its deliberations a resolution condemning the invasion and calling for the withdrawal of troops was vetoed by the Soviet
Union. (Thomas W. Wolfe, Soviet Power and Europe, 1945-1970
[Baltimore: Johns Hopkins University Press, 1970], pp. 368-427;
Tad Szulc, Czechoslovakia since World War II [New York: Viking
Press, 1971], chaps. XVIII, XIX, and XX.)

81. Chadian Civil Strife (with French
Intervention), 1968-77 (W)

The civil war in Chad was between the government forces of
President Tombalbaye, which represented the Christian and pagan
groups from the south, and the Chad National Liberation Front
(FROLINAT), which was largely composed of Moslems from the north.
While the major goal of FROLINAT was greater autonomy for the

northern region, it also tended to be more socialistic and more predisposed toward nonalignment than the government. Its major external backers were Libya and Algeria (which allowed it to establish
headquarters in their territories). While the military conflict between the forces of the government and FROLINAT began in 1966, it
was not until 1968 that French troops began to fight in support of the
government. By early 1970 the French government had around 3,000
or 4,000 troops in Chad, but under pressure from the French National
Assembly it began to reduce this number in the latter part of that
year. Throughout the 1970s its troop commitments varied but never
fell below 500. (Robert Pledge, "France at War in Africa," Africa
Report 15 [June 1970]: 16-19; Colin Legum, ed., Africa Contemporary Records [New York: Africana, 1977], pp. A94, B486.)

82. Portuguese Guinean Civil Strife (with
Guinean and Senegalese Intervention), 1968-74 (W)

By 1968 guerrillas associated with the Partido Africano da Independencia da Guine e Cabo Verde began to inflict considerable dam-
age on Portuguese troops within the territory. The guerrillas used
base camps located in the contiguous states of Senegal and Guinea,
and this prompted contingents of Portuguese troops on several occasions to make incursions into these territories to attack the guerrillas.
In 1969, 1971, and 1972 the UN Security Council, after complaints by
Senegal and Guinea, condemned Portugal and called for a cessation of
its military attacks. Portugal never sought UN action against the
much larger incursions into Portuguese Guinea (which became Guinea-
Bissau). (Fenner Brockway, The Colonial Revolution [London: Hart-
David, MacGibbon, 1973], pp. 387-419.)

83. Angolan (Portugal) Civil Strife (with
Zairean and Zambian Intervention), 1968-74 (W)

In 1961 Angolan rebels opposed to Portuguese rule began to operate from base camps in Zaire. However, it was not until about
1968 that large numbers began to operate from Zaire and Zambia.
(Neil Bruce, Portugal's African Wars [London: Institute for the Study
of Conflict, March 1973]; Peter Janke, Southern Africa: End of Empire [London: Institute for the Study of Conflict, November 1974],
pp. 6-7, 12.)

84. Mozambican (Portugal) Civil Strife (with
Tanzanian and Zambian Intervention), 1968-74 (W)

Beginning in about 1968 large numbers of Mozambican rebels
opposed to Portuguese colonial control were trained at and operated
from base camps in Tanzania—and to a lesser extent in Zambia. In
the year preceding the 1974 decision by Portugal to grant independence,
thousands were crossing the border every year. (Neil Bruce, Portugal's African Wars [London: Institute for the Study of Conflict, March
1973]; M. Degnan, "The 'Three Wars' of Mozambique," Africa Report
18 [September–October 1973]: pp. 6-13; Peter Janke, Southern Africa:
End of Empire [London: Institute for the Study of Conflict, 1974],
esp. p. 13.)

85. Communist China-USSR, 1969 (W)

On March 15, 1969, approximately 2,000 Chinese and 4,000
Soviet troops fought on Damansky Island (called Chin Pao Island by
the Chinese) in the Ussuri River. The Soviets also shelled Chinese
positions as far as four miles from the river. During the fighting the
Soviets suffered approximately 60 casualties and the Chinese, 800.
The Russians were apparently responsible for the start of the fighting.
They were retaliating for the Chinese ambush of a group of Soviet
soldiers on March 2. At the same time the clash raised Sino-Soviet
hostility to a point where a real threat of large-scale war existed.
(Thomas W. Robinson, "The Sino-Soviet Border Dispute: Background,
Development, and the March 1969 Clashes," American Political Sci-
ence Review 66 [December 1972]: 1175-1202.)

86. Honduras-El Salvador, 1969 (W)

The roots of the conflict between the two countries lay in the
migration of many Salvadorians into Honduras. The Hondurans dis-
criminated against them, and the Salvadorians resented this. The
event that precipitated the war between them was a soccer game between the two countries that was won by El Salvador. The Hondurans
took out their frustration by attacking many of the Salvadorian inhabitants of their country. This led the Salvadorian ambassador to the
OAS to request the Council for an investigation of the Hondurans' behavior on June 24, 1969. On June 27 the Council appointed a three-
man mediation commission, and the secretary-general dispatched the
Human Rights Commission to gather information. Before these groups
were able to perform their functions, a war broke out on July 3 when

El Salvador invaded Honduras. On July 4 the Council met and called for a cease-fire and also created a seven-man peace team to help secure a cease-fire. The war lasted for two weeks and approximately 2,000 individuals were killed. After the cease-fire, El Salvador refused to withdraw until it received certain assurances regarding the future treatment of its nationals in Honduras. On July 23 the Council tried to pressure El Salvador to withdraw by criticizing it and threatening economic sanctions. The OAS secretary-general then became very active as a mediator, and on July 29 announced a settlement that provided for the withdrawal of troops and guaranteed the safety of the nationals of each state living in the other. (Vincent Cable, "The 'Football War' and the Central American Common Market," Interna-tional Affairs 45 [October 1969]: 658-71; Graham H. Stuart and James C. Tigner, Latin America and the United States, 6th ed. [Englewood Cliffs, N.J.: Prentice-Hall, 1975], pp. 80-534.)

87. Congo-Brazzaville/Congo-Kinshasa, 1969 (MI)

The relations between these two states had been poor ever since 1964, and beginning in late 1968 there began a period of intense hostility. Then in November 1969, the president of the radical government in Congo-Brazzaville declared that there had been an armed incursion by commandos from Congo-Kinshasa who had tried to overthrow his government. All travel and economic relations between the two countries were broken off, and the government of Congo-Brazzaville complained to the OAU about the military intervention. An OAU meeting was not called, although the OAU secretary-general did try to mediate the conflict. In December 1970 diplomatic relations and river traffic were finally restored. (Arthur H. House, "Brazzaville: Revolution or Rhetoric?," Africa Report 16 [April 1971]: 18-21.)

88. Ethiopian Civil Strife (with
Sudanese Intervention), 1969-71 (MI)

Following the 1964-65 Sudanese assistance to the secessionist ELF the Sudanese government refrained from providing base camps, with the possible exception of a short period in 1967. Even then the protection probably came independently from local officials. However, with the assumption of power by President Numeiry in 1969 the Sudan again provided military aid and base camps from which the Eritrean rebels conducted raids into Ethiopia. The assistance ended following an Ethiopian-Sudanese accord in 1971. The Sudanese changed their policy in January 1977 and backed the secessionists but, as far as is known, their aid has taken only the form of material assistance for the Eritrean forces in Ethiopia. (Ethiopiawi, "The Eritrean-Ethiopian Conflict," in Ethnic Conflict in International Relations, ed. Astri Suhrke and Lela Garner Noble, pp. 138-39; Africa Report 12 [May 1967]: 24; and 14 [October 1968]: 39.)

89. South Yemeni Civil Strife (with Saudi Arabian and North Yemeni Intervention), 1969-72 (W)

Beginning in 1969 Saudi Arabia provided training and staging camps for South Yemeni exiles, most of whom belonged to the Front for the Liberation of South Yemen (FLOSY). By 1971 North Yemen began to provide comparable assistance. In 1972 the major rebel force was defeated and external intervention declined. (Mordechai Abir, Oil, Power and Politics [London: Frank Cass, 1974], pp. 105-13.)

90. Jordanian Civil Strife (with Threat of Iraqi and Actual Syrian Intervention), 1970 (W)

At the beginning of September 1970 a military campaign by the Jordanian army against the Palestinian guerrillas in the country appeared very likely. Iraq threatened to use its 12,000 troops stationed in Jordan to defend the guerrillas if they were attacked, and Syria made vaguer threats to assist them. When the Jordanian army launched an all-out attack on September 17, Iraq did not employ its troops. But Syria sent in 250 tanks and some supporting infantry to help the guerrillas. The Syrians withdrew after several days, having suffered severe losses. On the day after the Syrian invasion Jordan called for an Arab League Council meeting to consider Syria's "treacherous aggression," but a meeting was not held. (Malcolm H. Kerr, "Hafiz Asad and the Changing Patterns of Syrian Politics," International Journal 28 [Autumn 1973]: 398-400; idem, The Arab Cold War, pp. 148-50.)

91. Guinea-Portugal, 1970 (W)

On November 22, 1970 about 500 armed men led by Portuguese troops invaded Conakry, the Guinean capital, in an attempt to overthrow the regime of President Touré. Guinea appealed immediately to the UN Security Council, which passed a resolution calling on Portugal to cease the attack and withdraw the invading force of Portuguese troops and Guinean exiles. The Council sent a mission to Conakry. Guinea alleged that two further invasions were launched on November 23 and 24. The Council again condemned Portugal on December 8 and called on it to compensate Guinea. Portugal rejected the resolution but no further invasions of Guinea occurred. (Neil Bruce, Portugal's African Wars [London: Institute for the Study of Conflict, 1973].)

92. Cambodian Civil Strife (with North Vietnamese, South Vietnamese, and U.S. Intervention), 1970-75 (W)

The civil war was prompted by the overthrow of the neutralist head of state, Prince Norodem Sihanouk, in March 1970 and the accession to power of a military group under General Lon Nol. It was strongly opposed to the presence of North Vietnamese and Vietcong sanctuaries along its border with South Vietnam, and soon a military conflict ensued between the Cambodian government forces and North Vietnamese and Khmer Rouge troops. In April 1970, U.S. and South Vietnamese troops intervened and sought to inflict serious military losses on the North Vietnamese and Vietcong troops in Cambodia. Although the intervention was not formally approved by the new Cambodian government, de facto support existed. The civil conflict continued until the Khmer Rouge victory in April 1975. But near the end only the North Vietnamese remained and their role had significantly declined. (Sheldon W. Simon, War and Politics in Cambodia [Durham, N.C.: Duke University Press, 1974]; M. Leifer, "International Dimensions of the Cambodian Conflict," International Affairs 51 [October 1975]: 531-44.)

93. Omani Civil Strife (with South Yemeni, Iranian, Jordanian, and British Intervention), 1970-76 (W)

By 1970 the radical regime in South Yemen (PDRY) began to provide military equipment, base camps, and eventually troops to a rebel movement in Oman, the Popular Front for the Liberation of Oman (PFLO). By the early 1970s the PFLO exercised extensive control of the mountainous (jabal) area in the province of Dhofar. In 1973 the rebels lost ground as a result of determined resistance by the government, which was helped by Saudi Arabia, Iran (around 2,000 troops after 1972), Jordan (for a brief time in 1975, about 650 troops), and the United Kingdom (about 300 officers). In 1974 the Arab League set up a conciliation commission to settle the dispute but it failed. By the end of 1975, the insurgents had been driven out of their last strongholds in Dhofar, and they and their South Yemeni allies crossed

back into the PDRY. Saudi Arabia, with its warming relations with
the economically stricken PDRY, facilitated the signing of a cease-
fire on March 11, 1976 and it was generally observed. (D. L. Price,
Oman: Insurgency and Development [Conflict Study no. 53], [London:
The Institute for the Study of Conflict, 1975].)

94. Pakistani Civil Strife
(with Indian Intervention), 1971 (W)

The conflict arose out of the attempt by the Bengali in East
Pakistan to end the domination of West Pakistan. The Awami League
led by Sheikh Mujibur Rahman won the 1970 elections in the east. The
military government of Pakistan tried in March 1971 to suppress it.
A civil war ensued and by December 1971, 10 million refugees had
fled to India. Beginning in mid-November clashes occurred continu-
ously between Pakistani and Indian army units on the eastern frontier.
On December 3 full-scale war broke out on the eastern and western
borders and Indian forces, operating in conjunction with the Bengali,
sought to defeat the Pakistani forces in East Pakistan. On December
4 an emergency session of the Security Council was requested by the
United States and a number of other states. But the Council quickly
became deadlocked with the Soviet Union, vetoing two resolutions calling for a cease-fire and withdrawal of Indian and Pakistani forces
from each other's territory. The problem was transferred to the
General Assembly where on December 7 a resolution similar to those
vetoed was adopted by 104-11-10. It had no effect, though, and on
December 12 the United States returned the issue to the Security
Council, which again became stalemated. On December 16 the Pakistani forces in the east surrendered, and India declared a unilateral
cease-fire, which was accepted by Pakistan, in the west. On December 22 the Council finally passed a compromise resolution calling for
strict observance of the cease-fire and the withdrawal of all armed
forces "as soon as practicable." A peace treaty was concluded at a
summit conference in July, and Bangladesh became an independent
state. (W. Norman Brown, The United States and India, Pakistan,
Bangladesh [Cambridge, Mass.: Harvard University Press, 1972];
William J. Barnds, India, Pakistan and the Great Powers [New York:
Praeger, 1972].)

95. Equatorial Guinea-Gabon, 1972 (MI)

In August 1972 some minor armed clashes occurred between
Equatorial Guinea and Gabon as a result of competing claims over

several uninhabited islands. Their sudden importance derived from the prospect of oil exploitation in offshore areas. In the next two months both states made provocative statements and Gabon threatened to unleash Guinean exiles against Equatorial Guinea. In September both sides sent complaints to the United Nations. Between September and November the presidents of Zaire and the Congo persuaded the parties to neutralize the islands and to allow conciliation by an OAU commission. An accord was reached in 1974. (B. D. Meyers, "Intraregional Conflict Management by the OAU," International Organization 28 [Summer 1974]: 356-57; "Islands Dispute," Africa Digest 19 [December 1972]: 131.)

96. Uganda-Tanzania, 1972 (W)

In January 1971 President Milton Obote of Uganda was overthrown by military forces led by General Idi Amin. Obote and a number of his followers took refuge in neighboring Tanzania. On September 17, 1972 between 1,000 and 1,500 armed followers of the deposed president invaded Uganda from Tanzania. Within days they were routed and in retaliation Uganda bombed Tanzanian border villages. The president of Somalia and the OAU secretary-general secured an agreement for a truce, the withdrawal of troops from both sides of the border, and a promise that neither would support subversive forces. (D. Martin, General Amin [London: Faber & Faber, 1974], pp. 170-97; B. D. Meyers, "Intraregional Conflict Management by the OAU," International Organization 28 [Summer 1974]: 359-60.)

97. North Yemen (YAR)-South Yemen (PDRY), 1972 (W)

In the course of fighting and defeating rebel forces assisted by North Yemen during 1972, South Yemeni troops carried out raids into North Yemen on a number of occasions. In October a large incursion led to a war of several weeks between the two countries. The Arab League Council called on the secretary-general and a five-nation committee to mediate. The committee helped the parties secure a cease-fire and withdrawal. (Mordechai Abir, Oil, Power and Politics, p. 111; Hussein A. Hassouna, The League of Arab States and Regional Disputes, pp. 201-4.)

98. Iraq-Iran, 1972-75 (W)

In 1969 Iran unilaterally abrogated a 1937 treaty giving Iraq sovereignty over the Shatt-al-Arab, a river that marks the southern boundary between the two states. The rest of the frontier was also called into question by Iran. This resulted in a series of armed encounters between 1972 and 1975, which were largely initiated by Iran. The conflict was exacerbated by Iranian assistance for Kurdish rebels in Iraq and Iraq's expulsion of Iranian citizens. In February 1974 Iraq asked the UN Security Council to consider the Iranian incursions. A consensus read by the Council president asked the parties to refrain from the use of armed force and asked the secretary-general to appoint a mediator. The mediator secured an accord to prevent armed conflict and to negotiate the substantive issues. However, border incidents continued during the rest of 1974. In March and June 1975 bilateral accords were secured that backed the Iranian positions on boundaries and that terminated Iranian assistance to the Kurdish rebels in Iraq. (Robert D. Tomasek, "The Resolution of Major Controversies between Iran and Iraq," World Affairs 139 [Winter 1976/77]: 206-27.)

99. Kuwait-Iraq, 1973 (W)

In early 1973 Iraq claimed several small areas of Kuwait—including two islands. On March 20, 1973 Iraq attacked a Kuwaiti border outpost and seized a small area. Several Arab states attempted to mediate in the period March 21-29. The Saudis moved troops to their northern border while Iran, Bahrain, and Jordan offered troops to Kuwait. The Iraqis withdrew in early April. (R. D. McLaurin et al., Foreign Policy Making in the Middle East [New York: Praeger, 1977], p. 144; Anne M. Kelly, "The Soviet Naval Presence during the Iraq-Kuwait Border Dispute," in Soviet Naval Policy, ed. Michael McGuire et al. [New York: Praeger, 1975], pp. 287-89.)

100. Tanzania-Burundi, 1973 (MI)

In 1972 and 1973 several hundred thousand individuals were killed in Burundi in fighting between the Tutsi-dominated government and the majority Hutu population. Thousands of Hutu poured into Tanzania and Rwanda, from which they carried out small armed forays into Burundi. The local governments had little control over them. In 1973 Burundian forces carried out several large assaults into Tanzania, and Tanzania closed the border. In June 1973 President Mobutu of Zaire mediated an accord—including compensation to Tanzania. (T. P. Melady, Burundi: The Tragic Years [Maryknoll, N.Y.: Arbos Books, 1974]; R. Lemarchand and D. Martin, Selective Genocide in Burundi [London: Minority Rights Group, 1974].)

101. Israel-Egypt and Syria, 1973 (W)

On October 6 Egypt and Syria attacked Israel. Military contingents were also provided by Iraq, Morocco, Jordan, and Saudi Arabia. They scored impressive initial gains in the Sinai Peninsula and on the Golan Heights. The Security Council met on October 8 and 9, and a U.S. call for a cease-fire was opposed by the USSR. By October 12 Israel recaptured the lost ground on the Syrian front and in the Sinai a large tank battle developed. On October 16 an Israeli task force slipped through Egyptian lines onto the west bank of the Suez Canal. With the tide of battle favoring Israel the Security Council was convened on October 21 at the request of the United States and USSR. On October 22 it adopted a resolution calling for a cease-fire, the implementation of the November 22, 1967 resolution, and peace negotiations. Israel continued to expand its control and on October 23 the United States and USSR co-sponsored a resolution calling for withdrawal. The fighting stopped and on October 25 the Security Council created UNEF II to promote the cease-fire and withdrawal. (E. Monroe and A. H. Farrar-Hockley, The Arab-Israeli War, October 1973: Background and Events [Adelphi Paper, no. 111] [London: International Institute of Strategic Studies, 1974]; Lawrence Whetten, The Canal War: Four Power Conflict in the Middle East [Cambridge, Mass.: MIT Press, 1974].)

102. Rhodesian Civil Strife (with Zambian and Mozambican Intervention), 1973-77 (W)

In 1973 large numbers of black Rhodesian guerrillas began to enter Rhodesia from Zambia in order to overthrow the white-dominated regime. Beginning in 1975 Mozambique became the main staging area for most of the guerrillas and in 1976 two groups of about 450 each entered Rhodesia. Between 1973 and 1975 South Africa had a paramilitary police force of about 2,000 in Rhodesia but it was not engaged in the civil war. (T. Kirk, "Politics and Violence in Rhodesia," African Affairs 74 [January 1975]: 3-38; A. R. Wilkinson, Insurgency in Rhodesia, 1957-73 [Adelphi Paper, no. 111] [London: International Institute for Strategic Studies, 1973]; Peter Janke, Southern Africa: New Horizons [London: Institute for the Study of Conflict, July 1976], pp. 6-8.)

103. South Vietnam-China, 1974 (W)

Before 1973 both China and South Vietnam claimed the Paracel Islands in the South China Sea. However, they only periodically dispatched personnel and patrols to the islands. In 1973 and January 1974 they stated their claims more forcefully because of the prospect of oil discoveries in the area. South Vietnam then sought to consolidate its claim by sending military missions to several islands and by driving off some Chinese fishermen. The Chinese then occupied the whole group of islands with a force of about 600 troops assisted by 11 warships. On January 20 South Vietnam requested a meeting of the UN Security Council, but its president replied there was not enough support to put the matter on the agenda. The USSR and United States remained neutral in the conflict. ("Like Oil and Water," The Economist 250 [January 26, 1974]: 44; Hungdah Chiu, "South China Sea Islands: Implications for Delimiting the Seabed and Future Shipping Routes," The China Quarterly 18 [December 1977]: 743-65; Hungdah Chiu and Choon-Ho Park, "Legal Status of the Paracel and Spratly Islands," Ocean Development and International Law 3 [1975]: 1-28.)

104. Cypriot Civil Strife (with
Turkish Intervention), 1974 (W)

On July 15 President Makarios was deposed by the Cypriot National Guard, and Nicos Sampson, an advocate of union with Greece, succeeded him. Turkey immediately threatened intervention to protect the rights of the Turkish Cypriots. After requests by Cyprus and the secretary-general, a meeting of the Security Council was called but without any conclusive results. On July 20 another emergency session was held when Turkish forces invaded the island. A unanimously adopted resolution called for a cease-fire, an end to all foreign military intervention, and negotiations. After U.S. mediation, a cease-fire was finally arranged on July 22. Sampson stepped down and was replaced by a moderate, G. Clericles. Peace talks opened in Geneva on July 25 and on July 30 an agreement was concluded on a cease-fire line and a buffer zone. The talks concerning the constitutional future of Cyprus broke down and on August 14 hostilities were renewed with the Turks expanding their area of control. The Security Council called for a cease-fire and on August 16 it was secured, leaving Turkey in possession of one-third of Cyprus. Despite continued calls from the Security Council for a withdrawal of all foreign troops, the situation remains largely unchanged. (C. Foley and W. I. Scobie, The Struggle for Cyprus [Stanford, Calif.: Stanford University Press, 1975]; K. C. Markides, The Rise and Fall of the Cyprus Republic [New Haven, Conn.: Yale University Press, 1977].)

105. Spain-Morocco, 1975 (W)

Spain's announcement in August 1974 that the future of the
Spanish Sahara was to be determined in a referendum marked the beginning of a series of conflicts involving Spain, Morocco, Mauritania,
Algeria, and nationalists within the Spanish Sahara itself. Basically,
the issue at stake was whether the territory should be divided between
Morocco and Mauritania or become an independent country. In 1975,
with the support of Mauritania, King Hassan of Morocco appealed to
the International Court of Justice for a ruling on whether the Sahara
was terra nullius before Spanish occupation or a part of Morocco
as he claimed. Despite the fact that the ICJ ruling of October 16
clearly opposed the claims of Morocco and Mauritania, King Hassan
announced a "Green March" of 350,000 unarmed Moroccans into the
territory. Moroccan troops were also massed near the border. The
UN Security Council asked that states not act to increase tension in
the area and then, following the initiation of the march on November 4,
asked for the withdrawal of the marchers. The march penetrated several miles into the Spanish Sahara only to be halted by a Spanish "dis-
suasion line" and was called off on November 9. During the march
Moroccan troops crossed over the border at several points and engaged the forces of Polisario, which advocated independence for the
territory. The crisis ended on November 14 with the Madrid Agreement: Morocco and Mauritania agreed to share the administration of
the territory with Spain until February 28, 1976, after which the two
African states would divide the territory. (John Mercer, Spanish
Sahara [London: Allen and Unwin, 1976]; and, idem, "Confrontation
in the Western Sahara," World Today 32 [June 1976]: 230-39; "The
Polisario Front: Back Ground to a Conflict," An-Nahar Arab Report
and Memo 2 [January 23, 1978]: 1-6.)

106. United Kingdom-Guatemala, 1975 (C)

In November 1975 the Guatemalan claim to the British colony
of Belize led to a crisis between that nation and the United Kingdom.
After the failure of Guatemalan-British talks, Guatemala mobilized
military forces on the border. Britain's response was to double the
garrison and station naval and air units in the colony. Guatemala
denounced this as an "act of aggression" and threatened to respond
"with force." By the end of the year Guatemala withdrew its extra
military units from the border area. During the course of the crisis
both the UN Trusteeship Council and the General Assembly called for
an urgent resumption of the talks between the United Kingdom and
Guatemala, but it did not call for a termination of the Guatemalan

threat. (Peter Calvert, "Guatemala and Belize," Contemporary Review 228 [1977]: 7-12; "The Belize Conundrum," The Economist 264 [July 16, 1977]: 15.)

107. East Timor Civil Strife (with
Indonesian Intervention), 1975-76 (W)

The Portuguese decided in June 1975 that elections would be held in Eastern Timor in October 1976 for an assembly that would promulgate laws and take over the government after October 1978. However, much tension existed between the three major political parties: the Apodeti—which wanted the land to become an autonomous province of Indonesia; the UDT—which originally wanted a period of continued ties with Portugal followed by independence; and Fretilin, a leftist group—which wanted immediate independence. On August 11 the UDT staged a coup and by August 20 civil war had broken out pitting Fretilin against a pro-Indonesian alliance of the UDT, Apodeti, and other smaller parties. Through September and October border incidents occurred frequently between Indonesian and Fretilin forces. On November 28 Fretilin declared independence and the pro-Indonesian forces, who appeared to be losing, reacted by announcing that East Timor was a part of Indonesia. Indonesia then invaded on December 7. Portugal broke off relations with Indonesia and said it would resort to the United Nations. On December 12 the General Assembly demanded an Indonesian withdrawal by a vote of 72 to 10 with 43 abstentions. Also, in a unanimous Security Council decision on December 22, Indonesia was ordered to withdraw. Indonesia said that only "volunteers" were involved and were there at the request of the East Timorese. By December 28 Indonesia had secured the region. Another Security Council resolution, on April 22, called for an Indonesian withdrawal but the United States and Japan abstained. In July 1976 the territory became the twenty-seventh province of Indonesia. (Michael Leifer, "Indonesia and the Incorporation of East Timor," World Today 32 [September 1976]: 347-54; Robert Lawless, "The Indonesian Takeover of East Timor," Asian Survey 16 [November 1976]: 948-65.)

108. Angolan Civil Strife (with Cuban,
Zairean, and South African Intervention), 1975-77 (W)

Following the Portuguese coup in 1974, the new regime announced that independence would be granted to its African colonies, with November 11, 1975 set as the date for Angola. The three Angolan liberation movements failed to form a united front to negotiate with the Portuguese. The MPLA, a Marxist-oriented group with Soviet and Cuban backing, controlled the capital, Luanda, and the surrounding area. The FNLA, which enjoyed Zairean support, controlled much of northern Angola. UNITA, which had Zambian connections, held most of the south and east of the country. An uneasy alliance prevailed between FNLA and UNITA as both sought to defeat MPLA forces. On July 28, 1975 the OAU passed a resolution calling for a united front and a cessation of hostilities and also created a mediation commission. However, the fighting intensified and foreign intervention ensued. By the end of 1975 there were 15,000 Cuban troops supporting MPLA, 2,000 Zaireans assisting FNLA, and 1,000 South African personnel aiding UNITA, while 5,000 more guarded the Cunene hydroelectric projects 35 miles inside Angola.

In January 1976 an emergency summit of the OAU was held. The members split evenly, one group supporting a Nigerian resolution recognizing MPLA and an equal number backing a Senegalese resolution calling for a coalition government and withdrawal of all foreign forces. South African intervention made it difficult for some African states to support the FNLA-UNITA side. MPLA-Cuban forces soon gained the upper hand and on February 26 the MPLA government was recognized as the forty-seventh member of the OAU. On May 10 Kenya complained, on behalf of the African states, to the UN Security Council about the South African presence. On March 31 the Council condemned South Africa and called for an end to its intervention, and the South Africans withdrew once Angolan guarantees concerning the Cunene hydroelectric projects and border security had been obtained. Throughout the remainder of 1976 and 1977 UNITA and FNLA forces continued to harass and attack MPLA-Cuban positions, and the Angolans accused Zaire in particular of supporting these guerrilla activities. (Thomas Henriksen, "Angola and Mozambique: Intervention and Revolution," Current History 71 [November 1976]: 153-57; Christopher Stevens, "The Soviet Union and Angola," African Affairs 75 [1976]: 137-51.)

109. Lebanese Civil Strife (with Syrian
Intervention), 1975-76 (W)

In April 1975 clashes occurred between right-wing Christians and specific groups of Palestinian guerrillas. There was soon widespread fighting between the predominantly conservative Christian population and leftist sections of the Moslem community. Numerous cease-fires broke down during 1975. Syria first intervened when it dispatched Palestinian groups under its control, the Al Saiqa guerrilla movement and the Palestine Liberation Army (PLA), to protect the Moslems. However, they eventually started playing a peacekeeping role as Syria became concerned to promote a stable settlement. By the end of the year, the PLA was drawn into the fighting on the side of the Lebanese Moslems. In January 1976 Syria sent 50 officers to supervise a new cease-fire. After a period of relative peace, fighting broke out again in March as Moslem sections of the Lebanese army rebelled and demanded the resignation of the Christian president, Sulaiman Franjia. Syria intervened first with Al Saiqa and PLA personnel to save Franjia and finally in June with its own forces. After this latter intervention in June Syria had 15,000 troops in Lebanon, in effect supporting the Lebanese Christians against an alliance of Palestinian and Lebanese leftists. An emergency meeting of the Arab League on June 8-9 decided, with Syria's consent, to set up a "symbolic" Arab peacekeeping force (made up of the Syrian forces and token units of Libyans, Sudanese, and Saudis) and to create a mediation commission. Heavy fighting continued, however, as the commission had no success in establishing a durable cease-fire and the peacekeeping force could not separate the warring factions. Finally, on October 18 a comprehensive peace plan, providing for a 30,000-man "deterrent" force, was signed at a meeting in Riyadh of the Arab heads of state of Egypt, Saudi Arabia, Kuwait, Lebanon, and Syria. At an Arab League summit meeting on October 25-26 the Riyadh plan was endorsed by 19 member countries (Iraq and Libya were opposed). In November the "deterrent" force—still overwhelmingly Syrian—moved to occupt Beirut and other major towns and take up strategic positions throughout the country, bringing about a cessation of hostilities. (Leila Meo, "The War in Lebanon," in Ethnic Conflict in International Relations, ed. Astri Suhrke and Lela G. Noble [New York: Praeger, 1977], pp. 93-126; Sam Younger, "The Syrian Stake in Lebanon," World Today 32 [November 1976]: 399-406; idem, "After the Cairo Summit," World Today 32 [December 1976]: 437-40.)

110. Moroccan Civil Strife (with Algerian Intervention), 1976-77 (W)

This conflict is described in the following paragraph since their roots and development are so similar.

111. Mauritanian Civil Strife (with Algerian and Moroccan Intervention), 1976-77 (W)

Following the Madrid Agreement of November 14, 1975, Spain withdrew its forces and administrators from almost all of the Spanish

Sahara except some coastal areas. Morocco and Mauritania established de facto sovereignty over their respective spheres although
Spain did not transfer de jure control until February 28, 1976. The
armed forces of the two states immediately came into conflict with
the territory's independence movement, Polisario. In late January
and mid-February Algeria sent large contingents into the Moroccan
sphere and major battles ensued. From late February 1976 on, Algeria provided the 5,000-man Polisario force with military assistance
and base camps from which to conduct operations. It also allowed
Polisario to establish headquarters for the Saharan Arab Democratic
Republic in Algiers. Since Mauritania was having considerable difficulty with the rebels in 1977, Morocco sent 6,000 troops and France
provided manned aircraft to Mauritania.

 The UN General Assembly and secretary-general did concern
themselves with the self-determination issue in December 1975 and
early 1976 but UN bodies did not deal with the armed conflicts. The
same was true of the Arab League. The OAU Council of Ministers
split 21-9-17 on the recognition of Polisario in March 1976. In June
1976 it defeated Mauritanian resolutions calling for a cessation of attacks from Algeria. At the same time it approved a resolution supportive of the Algerian position on self-determination, but the Council was not backed by the Assembly meeting in July. The Assembly
called for an emergency summit on the Maghreb issue but it has never
been held. (John Mercer, Spanish Sahara [London: Allen and Unwin,
1976]; idem, "Confrontation in the Western Sahara," World Today 22
[June 1976]: 230-39; "The Polisario Front: Back Ground to a Conflict,"
An-Nahar Arab Report and Memo 2 [January 23, 1978]: 1-6.)

112. Mozambique-Rhodesia, 1976-77 (W)

 In order to prevent and deter guerrilla interventions into Rhodesia, Rhodesian armed forces began to conduct raids into Mozambique in April 1976. In August and October very large raids, in which
hundreds were killed, were carried out. Smaller raids continued
through 1977. In late May Rhodesian forces held a town in Mozambique for three days. The UN Security Council subsequently condemned
the action. (Colin Legum, ed., African Contemporary Record [New
York: Africana, 1977], pp. B910-B911; Keesing's Contemporary Archives, 1976-77.)

113. Ethiopian Civil Strife (with Somalian
and Cuban Intervention), 1976-77 (W)

 The long-standing tensions in Ethiopian-Somali relations, arising from the irredentist claims of the latter, entered a new phase in

late 1976 and 1977 as the Marxist regime that seized power in Addis Ababa in September 1974 soon found itself under attack from the Western Somali Liberation Front (WSLF) and eventually Somali troops. By June 1977 the WSLF controlled 85 percent of the Ogaden region. Somalia denied assisting the WSLF. However, the large amount of Somali military equipment and numerous Somali military personnel captured by Ethiopia indicated heavy Somali involvement.

On August 2, 1977 the Ethiopian government sought unsuccessfully to secure the necessary two-thirds consent to convene an emergency session of the OAU. However, the eight-nation mediation committee created in 1973 to arbitrate the border dispute between the two states did meet. On August 9 the committee issued a statement confirming the inviolability of frontiers inherited from the colonial era— an implicit criticism of Somali claims. The WSLF advance came to a halt in late August as regular Ethiopian troops were reinforced by a "peasant militia." By the end of 1977 the Ethiopians, assisted by some 10,000 Cuban troops and massive amounts of Soviet aid, had recaptured the Ogaden. (Colin Legum, "Realities of the Ethiopian Revolution," The World Today 33 [August 1977]: 305-11; Peter Schwab, "Cold War in the Horn of Africa," African Affairs 77 [January 1978]: 17-20.)

114. Zaire-Angola, 1977 (W)

On March 8, 1977 an invasion of Zaire's Shaba province (formerly called Katanga) was launched from Angola by 2,000 armed men claiming to be Congolese who had fled the country in the wake of the civil war in the early 1960s. The Congolese National Liberation Front, with whom the invaders were associated, announced on March 11 that its goal was the overthrow of the regime of President Mobutu. The government of Zaire alleged that the invaders were "mercenaries in the pay of the Angolan government," and that they were supported by Cuban and Soviet aid and advisers. On March 10 Zaire informed the secretary-general of the United Nations of the attack but no action was taken by the United Nations. By March 16 the poorly trained Zairean forces had been driven back to within 20 miles of the vital coal mining area centered in Kolwezi, and President Mobutu sought and received emergency military aid from Belgium and the United States. President Mobutu made an appeal for African assistance on April 2, and in response Morocco agreed to supply 1,500 troops (who were subsequently airlifted by France). By the end of April the invaders had been driven out of Zaire. (Kenneth L. Adelman, "Zaire's Year of Crisis," African Affairs 77 [January 1978]: 36-44.)

115. Libya-Egypt, 1977 (W)

Relations between Egypt and Libya, which had been strained since Egypt became more Western-oriented after the 1973 Arab-Israeli war, deteriorated further in 1976-77 and finally reached their nadir during an armed confrontation in July 1977. In April 1977, both states complained to the Arab League that the other side was seeking to subvert its government. The League did not consider the dispute; instead, Yasir Arafat of the PLO and President Eyadema of Togo sought to mediate the conflict.

Following a number of border incidents between July 14 and 19, a major military confrontation took place between July 21 and 24, with air attacks and tank battles between the two sides. In general Egyptian forces initiated the attacks. In addition to Arafat and President Eyadema, President Boumédienne of Algeria and the Kuwait foreign minister tried to promote an agreement. On July 24 the mediation efforts succeeded as both states agreed to cease hostilities. Although Libya protested Egyptian "aggression" to the United Nations, OAU, and Arab League, none of these organizations ever formally considered the conflict. ("Not a War, Just a Punitive Action," The Economist [July 30, 1977]: 52; Keesing's Contemporary Archives, August 12, 1977, pp. 28500-502, and December 9, 1977, pp. 28710-711.)

116. Vietnam-Cambodia, 1977 (W)

As early as 1975, there were refugee reports of border clashes between Kampuchea (Cambodia) and Vietnam after communist regimes had taken complete control in those two countries. Fighting did not start in earnest, however, until May 1977 when it was reported that Cambodians and/or Vietnamese operating from bases in Cambodia began harassing Vietnam border areas. By October a full-scale war was in progress as Vietnam began to take retaliatory action with division-size forces. On December 31 Kampuchea broke diplomatic relations with Vietnam. On the surface, the conflict appeared to be over the demarcation of the border—set in French colonial days—in the offshore islands area and the so-called "Parrot's Beak." Permeating the whole dispute, however, is a centuries-old fear that the Kampucheans have of Vietnamese domination. (Marian Kirsch Leighton, "Perspectives on the Vietnam-Cambodia Border Conflict," Asian Survey 18 [May 1978]: 448-57.)

Index

About the Author

MARK W. ZACHER is director of the Institute of International Relations and associate professor of Political Science at the University of British Columbia, Vancouver.

He is the author of Dag Hammarskjold's United Nations (1970), coauthor of Pollution, Politics and International Law: Tankers at Sea (1979), and coeditor of Conflict and Stability in Southeast Asia (1974) and Canadian Foreign Policy and the Law of the Sea (1977). His articles on various subjects in international relations have been published in several journals.

The author holds a Ph. D. in political science from Columbia University.